EMOTIONS DON'T THINK

EMOTIONS DON'T THINK

Emotional Contagion in a Time of Turmoil

Bruce Hutchison, Ph.D.

CROSSFIELD
PUBLISHING

CROSSFIELD
PUBLISHING

www.crossfieldpublishing.com
books@crossfieldpublishing.com
2269 Road 120, R7, St. Marys, Ontario, N4X 1C9, Canada

Copyright the author. All rights reserved. July 2021.
Copyright Crossfield Publishing. All Rights reserved.

ISBN-13: 9781990326004(Crossfield Publishing Inc.)

Published in Canada.

Editing: Emily Bozik, Maura Blain Brown, Glenda MacDonald
Cover image: Omid Armin / Unsplash.com
Cover and interior design: Magdalene Carson RGD, New Leaf Publication Design
Publicist: Nathaniel Moore, moorehype.com

Library and Archives Canada Cataloguing in Publication

Title: Emotions don't think : emotional contagion in a time of turmoil /
Bruce Hutchison, Ph.D.
Names: Hutchison, Bruce, 1944- author.
Description: Includes bibliographical references.
Identifiers: Canadiana 20210289538 | ISBN 9781990326004 (softcover)
Subjects: LCSH: Emotional contagion. | LCSH: Emotions—Social aspects. | LCSH:
    Emotions—Sociological aspects. | LCSH: Emotions—Political aspects. | LCSH:
    Civilization, Modern—21st century—Psychological aspects. | LCSH: Political
    psychology.
Classification: LCC BF578 .H88 2021 | DDC 152.4—dc23

An important note: This book is not intended as a substitute for the psychological recommendations of psychologists, psychiatrists, physicians or any other mental health care provider. Rather, it is intended to offer information to help the reader in a quest for optimum well-being or mental health. The personal case histories and examples are fictional. Any similarity between them and a real person is coincidental. Real peoples' names are used when their names and situations are public knowledge, or when they are well-known public figures, their real names having been reported previously in the media. Names of current or previous presidents or prime ministers are not revealed because their names are in high circulation in public knowledge and they may be prone to trigger various emotions automatically, thereby violating our attempt to remain neutral and objective.

The publisher and the author are not responsible for any goods and/or services offered or referred to in this book and expressly disclaim all liability in connection with the fulfillment of orders for any such goods and/or services and for any damage, loss, or expense to person or property arising out of or relating to them.

Opinions expressed in this book are attributed to the author and are not necessarily those of Crossfield Publishing and its team.

This book is dedicated to
the memory of my late wife, Jo-Anne,
who for decades encouraged me to write
and shared her many fascinating ideas.

Table of Contents

Preface

After having been a clinical psychologist since the late 1960s, I finally retired with more than 50 years of experience. I grew up in Winnipeg, Manitoba, Canada, where, with my parents and many others I survived the Great Winnipeg Flood of 1950. Our street was flooded, and our house and those of our neighbours were flooded halfway up the living room, forcing us to find temporary accommodation. As a child, I didn't realize that this was the first of many interesting adventures I would experience in life.

I eventually received my B.A. at United College, then part of the University of Manitoba, my M.A. in Psychology at the University of Manitoba, and my Ph.D. in Clinical Psychology at the University of Ottawa. My career spanned full-time sojourns as a psychologist at two correctional facilities (one prison and one jail), at a social agency for the disabled, and in rural mental health in Manitoba, totalling about seven years, early in my career. After getting my doctorate, I spent 13 years as a clinical psychologist at a university hospital in Edmonton, Alberta, and also 17 years at a suburban hospital in Winnipeg, where I was Head of Psychology. In both of these settings I worked in the entire hospital, including the psychiatry units, and I also saw patients and provided psychological consultation and therapy in the Burn Unit, ICUs, and general medical units. I also worked with many out-patients.

I was a Clinical Associate in the Department of Psychiatry in the University of Alberta's Faculty of Medicine and an Assistant Professor of Clinical Health Psychology in the Faculty of Medicine at the University of Manitoba. I also spent more than 30 years in part-time and then full-time private practice in three Canadian provinces. Among my experiences, I assessed U.S. veterans for Post-Traumatic Stress Disorder (PTSD) and assessed prospective Canadian border officers and prison officers for their psychological suitability to use firearms. I served on the boards of three provincial psychology associations and was a provincial representative on a national board of psychology in Canada. I was Director of Advocacy for a provincial psychology board and spent many years advocating to governments and public groups about the importance of psychological services in society and how these services need to be increased so more people without financial resources can access them. I write this book from the perspective of all these professional experiences.

I didn't have many academic publications, due to time constraints, but people have always told me that I was a good writer and that I should write. So, after writing a master's thesis and a doctoral dissertation, a few articles in obscure journals, hundreds of professional psychological reports and letters, and many published letters to the editor, I decided that retirement would be a good time to start a second career as an author, using my expertise to comment on the news around us. This book reflects that endeavour. As an avid follower of the news in Canada and the United States, this book offers what I think has been sorely lacking, a psychological perspective on events in contemporary society, with an emphasis on the effect of emotions and how they are contagious and so affect us, and on healthy psychological principles that can be used to help society prevent and cope with emotional contagion.

I wrote this book to reach adults of every age—young, middle-aged, and older—as they cope with the flow of emotions and feelings in life, politics, and society. People today seem to avoid close feelings in interpersonal interactions and withdraw into electronic devices and social media, delegating rewarding social, personal, and emotional connections to a lesser role. Yet, because of their hunger for emotional connection, they may be unwittingly absorbing contagious emotions from others through social media rather than through people in person.

This book recognizes that we are all in life together. As such, it does not intend to exclude any groups of people. Regardless of our social status or wealth, we all have different opinions, emotions, feelings, thoughts, and motivations on how to improve mental, emotional, interpersonal, and general psychological health and well-being throughout society. We need to respect these differences: life would be boring if we all agreed on everything. Thus, I attempt to be neutral in my writing and to respect many points of view. I believe that we can all benefit from this approach, whether or not we have a mental health diagnosis or psychological troubles. Psychology is for everyone.

I share various insights gleaned from my personal, professional, and psychotherapeutic experiences, based on 50 years of observing human nature in the consulting office, and am writing this during my latter years and mostly during retirement when I have more time to do so. What I have learned about life from working in prisons, hospitals, and with many people in many different settings and situations has given me a glimpse into how emotions work in a personal way. I use a blend of intuition, psychological and scientific knowledge, and personal and psychotherapeutic experience. This book is neither pro-scientific nor anti-scientific. I present my ideas based on my insights and clinical intuition, generalized to everyday life. We are all in this together.

The past few years have been difficult for most people in the world. We have had to deal with the COVID-19 pandemic and all the tragic, frustrating, and contentious issues associated with it. There have been many other issues related to conspiracy theories, racism, police brutality, cancel culture, public shaming, and more. Emotional contagion is a large part of what has caused these issues. I talk about how to handle and overcome emotional contagion in the book.

As a Canadian, I get CNN, MSNBC, and Fox News here in Canada and watch them some of the time. I have had American professors and students (here in Canada), have friends in the U.S. and have been there many times. My last visit was just before the pandemic, when my wife and I were in Fort Lauderdale, Florida, where we embarked on a cruise, safely, thank goodness. Living so close to the U.S., an hour away, and pretty much in the same culture, is enough for me to experience similar, but not identical, feelings to those of Americans. We have similar issues in Canada, but experience them to a much lesser degree. At the same time, we live far enough away from the U.S. not to be immersed in their issues. So, as they say, I have "no skin in the game." This allows me to be close enough, but not too close to be blinded by their situation, and a little more objective than if I lived there and were American. It is just the right distance to write this book, close enough but far enough away. But I am affected by Americans' experiences, as we all are, because they touch us all. Canada and the rest of the world are not exempt from these issues.

Emotional and social contagion produce more criminal behaviour in individuals who lack the knowledge and maybe the will about how to regulate their emotions and control their behaviour. Psychological treatment provides emotional regulation for potential offenders. I and many of my colleagues have treated people with these issues, and this prevents them from acting in ways that could send them to jail. But it is not universal in correctional facilities. Because of legal requirements for privacy and confidentiality, the public, the media, and politicians don't hear about this success and look to the police, courts, lawyers, judges, and prisons to treat the problem.

Law is a more glamorous profession than psychology, attracting many students who, as lawyers, deal with PTSD and other mental illnesses in court, after the damage and hurt have been done. This is a more expensive, but ineffective solution for society. Though less glamorous, the fields of clinical, counselling, forensic, health, and rehabilitation psychology would attract students who as professionals could effectively treat and prevent outbursts in a less-expensive and more effective way for society before a crime is committed. This will appear naïve to many cynical people, and obvious to many believers, when there is actually merit on both sides, the cynical and the believers. Many mentally ill people are in prison untreated. Emotional contagion divides us into either-or camps. Instead, let's come together.

Changes in the justice and health systems could facilitate more people being directed to such treatment on a compulsory basis. How many times do we hear a judge send someone to a secure treatment centre run by professionals instead of a "correctional" institution? Or even to receive any form of therapy to learn to manage their emotions? Not nearly enough. A more flexible, enlightened system to enable funds for professionals to provide assessment and treatment, including mental health and/or personal counselling and therapy services including motivational, problem-solving and coping strategies, would make us much safer. Studies have shown that psychotherapy can be successful in prison populations (Johnson, Stout, Miller et al, 2019). Psychotherapy in a prison population is not effective for psychopaths. Updated, effective programs of cognitive-behavioural therapy, dialectical behavioural therapy, interpersonal therapy, acceptance and commitment therapy, motivational interviewing[1], and other newer methods of therapy would be provided for the rest of the prison population, which is in the majority.

As a prison psychologist, I have provided therapy so inmates could be rehabilitated. It was difficult, and only the motivated were successfully rehabilitated. Inmates are a difficult group to treat, especially in a prison setting. The emotional satisfaction that comes from the desire for revenge and punishment among the voting public dictates to the politicians and judges who support punishment and incarceration, with little treatment

---

1   These therapies and many other terms are defined or described more fully in the Glossary

offered. It is emotionally satisfying for voters and politicians to punish someone as a way of getting revenge, so emotion rules. But emotions don't think. Punishment doesn't help offenders; it makes them angrier. I remember watching one of my patients, an inmate convicted of rape, receiving the lash as part of his sentence back in the 1960s when I was in my first professional setting as a prison psychologist. It was very disturbing, and I doubt it contributed to his eventual rehabilitation. This was one of the last times it was used. Some citizens may think they don't deserve to be helped, and while that may be true for a select few, treatment-worthiness is not all-or-nothing. Many deserve to be helped, if only because they will be released someday and live among us, perhaps as neighbours and co-workers. If they were rehabilitated, by learning how to handle their emotions, and make changes in their beliefs, habits and relationships, many would become better citizens and pay taxes rather than live off the government.

Those who weren't rehabilitated wouldn't be released. If you wouldn't release a person from hospital before their disease were successfully treated, why release an inmate whose tendencies were not treated when such a person could kill after their release? I have seen an inmate released before being treated because his time was up and treatment wasn't mandatory. That untreated inmate killed someone out in the community and came back to do a life term. All prisoners deserve a chance to be helped so this won't happen. And so do the victims, who might still be alive. Psychotherapy can save lives. But psychological treatment or counselling isn't mandatory in corrections. It should be, in order to be truly "corrective."

I remember treating a young man who was in prison for break and entry. We had quite a few constructive therapy sessions—but not enough—before he was transferred out to another prison. He ended up being one of Canada's most prolific murderers. Who knows what would have happened if he had stayed under my care for another two or three years and if a proper treatment centre had been available? Lives may have been saved, and his life could have had a better ending. We have the knowledge, and we can develop better methods if given the chance. Why not take it? The victims deserve to live.

Appreciations

I would like to give my thanks and appreciations to the many people in my life who made this book possible. Sam Hiyate, of the Rights Factory as well as So You Want to Write, Michael Pietrzak, Donald Officer, and the many other people at So You Want to Write who encouraged and spurned me on and made various relevant recommendations. Appreciation also goes to my colleagues, friends, associates and many others familiar with my professional work over the years and decades, too many to name, including but not limited to Garrett Kafka, Alicia Ordonez, Bob McIlwraith, Rehman Abdulrehman, Kathryn Ball, Paul Thomas, Peter MacLean and especially David Nozick who have encouraged me to put my ideas into print.

Appreciations also go to Catherine Marjoriebanks for reading my manuscript and making many helpful suggestions, my editor Emily Bozik who had a lot of great ideas and made many helpful changes, as well as a great sense of humor, patience and enthusiasm, my publicist Nathaniel Moore for setting this up and connecting me with Tina Crossfield at Crossfield Publishing. And special thanks go to Tina and her great staff for working with the cover design and many aspects of the book.

And special thanks goes to my wife Catherine Casserly for supporting me and for helping me with backup editing, using her vast knowledge of facts, figures, grammar, psychology, books, history, organizations and people to serve as consultant and coach. Appreciation goes to my adult children Jeff and Robert, for their ideas and input, as well as to my grandchildren Chantel, Leena, Jarek and Alec, and Catherine's grandchildren, especially Alexandra, Sarah and Nicholas, and last but not least to my cat, Spring, who comforted me late at night when others had had enough.

EMOTIONS DON'T THINK

Introduction

Emotions are contagious and infect us all. Contagious emotions can be positive and uplifting or negative and harmful. The turmoil of our time involves behaviour driven by negative emotions. Yet little is written for the general public about the power of contagious emotions. The flow of negative emotional contagion is crucial at this time. Understanding how to handle negative emotional contagion thwarts turmoil. Emotions don't think and yet seem to have somehow kidnapped our minds. I write this book with a goal of overcoming the destructive power of negative emotional contagion, in social media, social life, political life, and everyday life.

In current tumultuous events around the world, it is evident that human behaviour is significantly influenced by psychological factors such as feelings and emotions. Emotions and feelings are an important part of life. We fall in love, we get anxious, we experience joy, we feel happy, we get sad, we worry. We can all relate to this. We experience feelings and emotions every day, and sometimes they are negative. As a long-time clinical psychologist, I regularly helped people deal with their feelings, emotions, and thoughts.

Feelings and emotions spread easily among us. They can infect everyone and make us want to join in. People often feel affected by feelings and emotions from others. When you see someone smile, it can make you smile and then make you happy (Barsade, 2002). Happiness begets happiness. Sadness begets sadness. Emotions can affect you so that you develop the same emotion as the person you are with, the person you are near, the person you are watching, or even the person giving a talk. In a sense, you can "catch" the emotion from that person, so then you have that emotion also. In this way, emotions are contagious.

The phenomenon of emotional contagion is becoming more well known. We have the same characteristics and psychological processes inside us wherever we are. There is no reason why people would be exempt in these social and political situations, since emotions spread from one person to another, from one group to another, no matter what.

As such, it is important to learn about the impact of negative emotions and feelings at this time of turmoil, in a societal and political arena, and how to manage them to lower their impact.

Political parties' positions and decisions, social movements, police actions, extreme left-wing and right-wing positions, racial inequalities, and many other factors play a large part in these troubling events. Police attacking protesters, police killing Black people and Indigenous people in the U.S. and Canada, a mob attacking the U.S. Capitol building, looters and criminals running amok during protests are behaviours driven by emotions.

These factors are better understood if we understand the important role that the spread of feelings and emotions plays in these situations. As a society, when we let emotions take over like this, the people involved—and society along with it—end up losing the battle. Because emotions don't think. Most people get emotional about what they believe, and when their beliefs are criticized, challenged, or attacked, their emotions can get riled up. This is natural. It is human nature to use emotional language, think irrationally, make errors in thinking, and be affected by emotional contagion. Emotions spread, and this happens through emotional contagion. The goal is for us to take responsibility, be aware of the possible unfortunate effects, and work on preventing, reducing, and minimizing these occurrences. This will enable us, to the best of our ability, to prevent negative emotional contagion from affecting us. It is a difficult task to achieve, and there will be times when it will not happen. Emotional contagion is a real and natural occurrence, often a positive one that we value and cherish. When it is negative, we need to understand the spread of feelings and emotions and how it contributes to the outcome of a situation. I talk about this in the book.

It is obvious that emotions do not think. Yet we ignore that fact at our peril. The relatively little-known phenomenon of emotional contagion, where emotions are spread and "caught" by various people, is applicable to situations when people are with other people. This phenomenon happens in events we read about, or see on TV and social media. It makes sense that they are an important factor in the turmoil that is going on. You can't have turmoil without emotions.

Historically, not much has been written about the power of emotions and emotional contagion in a social or political context. There has been little coverage in the media during protests, crises, or revolutions. The article "Bringing Emotions into Understanding Revolutions" (Lašas, 2012) attempted to do this. In 2011, Lašas stated that, "Often overlooked by analysts, and especially by political scientists, factors such as collective humiliation, frustration and anger are the fuel for fundamental transformations in our societies. It only needs a spark to cause an explosion of social activism." Indeed it does. But these factors are still overlooked, to our detriment. Emotions run rampant when we do not talk about them.

In this book, I use my psychological knowledge to explain how to stem the flow of negative emotional contagion in our current social and political environment. It is important to know how to evaluate an emotion in order to decide if it should be acted on as is, tempered, minimized, or stopped.

We can learn how to prevent an emotion, stop it from infecting us, and overcome it if it already has infected us. We can learn to make choices on which emotions we will allow ourselves to catch, feel, experience, and influence us, so as to not absorb them all. Some are infectious or toxic and some are not. Catching emotions allows us to absorb them and let them influence our decisions and our behaviour. But, to do that, we need to decide whether or not we should catch them. Sometimes we shouldn't let that happen, but we do. It depends on the desirability of the emotion and whether it may be harmful, safe, or enriching, before we decide whether to catch and absorb it, just connect with it, or merely let it bounce off and drop. Emotions don't think. Emotions can only carry simple messages. It is important to stop automatically catching emotions and think instead. I talk about this in the book.

We are affected every day by positive and negative emotions and feelings directed at us from many people in our lives. During the COVID-19 pandemic, this has happened less often because we have seen fewer people. Many people in isolation or lockdown became hungrier for direct emotional and social input and may have sought it through social media. This can lead to suspicion, cynicism, anger, aggression, defensiveness, depression, and anxiety, which are contagious. These emotions and other important ones, such as fear and hate, impact us greatly. Some may allow these negative emotions to replace more positive emotions without thinking and then wonder where these negative feelings came from. Many people can feel some confusion and helplessness in dealing with them.

Although I am not an expert on research conducted on emotional contagion (a field of social psychology), as a clinical psychologist I have dealt with emotions and feelings with psychotherapy patients throughout my fifty-year career. One thing to remember is that although emotional contagion has been established in psychology research, its application on a wider scale in society is beyond the scope of research, which, in psychology, is performed in a controlled laboratory setting. I approach the material in this book similarly to how I conducted a psychotherapy session: making observations, giving likely possibilities, sharing insights, and presenting knowledge as I understand it. While I do not knowingly make erroneous claims, I do not claim to be perfect—as I often told my patients—and neither should they. I want to share my ideas in an area that seems to need more attention, the application of psychological knowledge to society, so that people can consider them.

While practising psychotherapy, I became aware that in therapy sessions I was undergoing a type of personal experience apart from observing the verbal, emotional, mental, and behavioural expression of the participant. Sometimes I could feel my patient's emotions and feelings directly, as if they moved across the room to touch me, as opposed to only detecting and observing them in the patient. Psychiatrist Dr. David Goldbloom talks about how his patient's "sadness radiates across the room despite his (the patient's) efforts to contain it, to protect me" as he sits a few feet away during a session (Goldbloom & Bryden, 2016). I have felt similar feelings radiating towards me from my own patients in my sessions as a clinical psychologist. Patients can carry a lot of emotions and feelings and would sometimes emit them subconsciously to a point where I could actually feel them. Perhaps it has happened to you when in close proximity to others who are discussing personal, subjective, meaningful experiences in an emotional way.

It can also happen on a larger, more public scale; we just don't identify it as such. We can feel emotions, especially in crowds: at parties, concerts, sports events, and especially when there are groups who get emotional and protest. In a large, excited crowd, we feel the electricity in the air. Many sports fans are familiar with this. When teams win championships, they celebrate in public. The feelings are "in the air."

We live in an emotional time. During the last few years, political uprisings have occurred, fuelled by emotion related to fear: fear of immigrants, of different ethnic groups, races, or religions. Some people may fear that the core group they identify with is at risk of being dominated or controlled. This perception may develop for some due to instant contact with others around the world through social media.

Settings for emotional contagion abound. In the U.S., emotions have flowed unchecked in recent years: racially driven police brutality, deaths, political divisions, elections, and a very controversial, divisive American president (whom I will refer to as the "former president"[2]) have contributed to political upheaval by inflaming emotions, which caused turmoil. Protests have occurred, Black people have been killed by the police without justification, and conspiracy theories, such as those supported by the QAnon group, have abounded. We need to understand how to handle emotions in order to handle turmoil. Over the past few years, controversial leaders have been elected in some countries, seemingly driven by a motivation to protect their citizens from being overtaken by another group or groups, whether from the inside or outside the country. On top of this, the whole world has been confronted by a pandemic brought on by the outbreak of COVID-19. The virus has magnified our already heightened emotions. Many people live in acute fear of catching the disease.

Dangerous, infectious emotions can spread like a virus and infect others. Pessimism, cynicism, depression, fear, hate, panic, anxiety, disgust, and suspicion are all contagious negative emotions. These emotions seem to spread when society is in turmoil. So do violence, demoralization, and conspiracy worries, which are also contagious. This puts society into turmoil. Some people use emotions to think, but emotions can only feel. Instead, we need to think, by using systematic reasoning and critical thinking.

Our usual focus is on the visible and the tangible, but this is to our detriment. People are becoming more aware of the contagious effects of emotions, as well as the associated phenomenon of conspiracy theories. Because emotions don't think, but rather carry vague messages and information, they seem to have kidnapped the minds of some people, leaving them with less critical thinking and systematic reasoning ability than before, especially at times like this when emotions are so high.

We can choose to listen to messages with our cognitive abilities, rather than choosing to use our emotional reactions in determining how we react. We can use systematic reasoning, critical thinking, and other

---

2   We do not name the current or any president or prime minister in the book because their names on their own seem to be able to trigger off contagious emotional reactions.

methods. We can choose to blend those methods with emotion. Our cognitive abilities can put the necessary proviso on the incoming emotions: figure out what they are trying to say, keep them realistic, add perspective, conditions, and limitations, treat them as only possibilities, and think more about them later. Our cognitive abilities are the executive part of our mind, receiving and considering input, dismissing some, accepting some, and balancing it out. Our emotions are often necessary to provide wisdom, which is the midpoint between cold, hard fact and pure, emotion-based feedback.

This book is designed to provide a psychosocial education, so most readers should adopt the perspective of learning about and working on overcoming the power of negative emotional and social contagion. This perspective will minimize an overly emotional reaction from some readers. We will explore how to overcome negative emotional contagion and how to minimize its impact when it occurs. While it might be impossible to prevent entirely, we can slow it down.

We will explore how to achieve healthy emotional independence and learn how the appeal of emotions, although alluring, can be false. There are ways to block the effects of negative emotional contagion coming from social media, especially the effects of hate and fear. There are strategies to resist absorbing hate and being hateful, practices that use empathy to resist contagion, and examples of how understanding the origin of another person's emotions can prevent emotional contagion.

I attempt to remain objective throughout, take no side in any of the issues discussed, and work to provide a balanced viewpoint to be fair to all, without compromising truth and accuracy. I am a Canadian in Canada. Living in close proximity to, and in a very similar culture to that of the U.S., I can experience similar—but not identical—feelings to people there. I live far enough away to avoid being immersed in American culture. This allows me to not be blinded by being too close to the situation and to be a little more objective. The distance is just right for writing this book: close enough but far enough away.

Sometimes I use the word "we" as if all of us experience or should experience identical feelings. This is not actually the case because we are all separate individuals, and we process feelings and thoughts differently. But we are all in this together, to one degree or another, in our collective, interactive, interdependent society.

Some will read the book with an intuitive, fluid, subjective "go-with-the-flow" approach, and others will read it with a cognitive, discerning, analytical approach. To help the reader get into the flow of a personal, subjective perspective, much of the book is written in the first person, with "we," "us" and "our" referring to all people in society, including myself. This reflects an attempt to be psychotherapeutic and psychoeducational at the personal level, to join these two approaches in an emotional sense, as you may be reading the book out of curiosity about these influences on yourself. If a given situation does not apply to you, even though the word "we" may be used, you could read about that situation from a third-person perspective, as applying to others only. At other times, the book is written in the third person, more objectively and impersonally, with some intellectual discourse. It offers a balance, using phrases such as "they," "people," and "humans" as an attempt to distance from the personal, subjective approach and be objective, intellectual, and reflective. If such a situation does apply to you, you can read it from a first-person perspective. This is an attempt to achieve a balanced approach that appeals to the different needs of readers, and to integrate the two modalities: the affective and the cognitive.

I have not interviewed anyone for this book, know none of the people I write about, and am speaking from my observations as a private citizen but using my psychological acumen. Accordingly, I use words like "seems," and "likely" because of my unwillingness in most cases to make a definitive statement that could be regarded as a conclusion, as it is not grounded in first-hand experience with any individuals mentioned in the book. Accordingly, comments in this book should not be regarded as definitive or conclusive, nor as a psychological evaluation or assessment of any individual or groups of individuals. The book offers my reflections on the emotional contagion in a time of turmoil in the world, and examples are presented from the news as an indication of the likely effect of emotional contagion in real life.

The Nature of Emotional Contagion

We give off feelings, emotions, and energy and transfer them to others, often unknowingly. They touch and affect others nearby, who can absorb them rapidly and automatically. Although they are communicated invisibly, they establish meaningfulness. This can be unhealthy if people don't stop and think about what is happening. People nearby can automatically catch an emotion because of its appeal, and this can trigger action, all without them thinking about it. Contaminated, toxic emotions can produce dangerous behaviour when people don't recognize what is happening or think it through. Emotions carry simple messages. They flare up at times of turmoil in society, as anger, hate, cynicism, fear, and other toxic emotions spread to others. To prevent this happening, we need critical thinking and wisdom, because emotional and social contagion blind us, as we often erroneously believe that "what you see is all there is."

Emotional contagion, a little-known phenomenon, but one that is quickly gaining recognition, occurs when one person's emotions and related behaviours directly trigger similar emotions and behaviours in people nearby, even if this is not recognized at the time. Emotional contagion is responsible for how moods and emotions affect others (Morris, 2017). Emotion spreads to people and becomes one emotion experienced by many people almost simultaneously.

Here is an example of everyday emotional contagion: Jennifer enjoys her job as an administrative assistant at a large company and looks forward to going to work. She is appreciated by her colleagues. She is happily married with two daughters, aged nine and eleven. This morning she has sent her daughters off to school as usual. They are all a bit tired because her older daughter, Addison, performed a solo at her school last night. Jennifer is proud of Addison. Addison enjoyed herself, seemed to love being with the others, and did well. Jennifer got a lot of compliments, and the other parents talked about Addison's performance. Addison feels good and is a little more bouncy than usual, talking about the concert. Jennifer is feeling satisfied and content as she goes to work. She is looking forward to telling her co-workers about Addison's performance. Jennifer is still feeling the spark and joy from it.

She has good friends at work, and she and her co-workers often talk about each others' kids. At lunch, Jennifer tells her friends about the night before. They are interested. She is proud of Addison. Jennifer feels good as she laughs with friends, and they exchange kid stories.

Then she overhears other co-workers nearby talking loudly about something being unfair. The rest of her group hear it as well but ignore it. She can hear some of what the other group are saying and how they are saying it. Someone's child had tried hard at an exam but didn't have enough time to answer all the questions perhaps because the time allowed wasn't long enough. When the child got a low mark, the parent thought it was unfair. This parent sounded bitter and sad, and it was reflected in their voice. Their child may have been affected by an unfair rule. The parent seems to feel depressed and worried. Jennifer feels for the parent and child.

She turns back to her own group, where talk continues about their own children and how they are doing. She starts to recall some of her younger daughter Madison's struggles in school and talks a bit about that. She still feels the other group's bitterness. It stays with her. She starts to feel bitter too. She wonders how Madison is doing today. She starts to feel a tinge of sadness and irritation and wonders why. Her good mood has gone. She forgets about Addison's concert and feels a bit edgy. She worries more about Madison. Is Madison being treated fairly, she asks herself?

Jennifer probably doesn't realize it, but she has been affected by emotional contagion. The bitterness she has heard in the voices from the other table when they were complaining about unfairness has been transferred to her. It was not just their story or the other child's plight—although that is part of it, and it affects her—but the tone of their voices when they expressed their bitterness and sadness that has affected Jennifer. She could feel their emotion. It has been contagious, and she has caught it, absorbed it, and been infected by it. It struck a chord inside her. Her good mood has evaporated. Maybe she is a little cynical now. But others in her group probably heard this too and didn't seem to pick it up. They are talking about something different and don't seem to have been affected much by the nearby conversation.

Her mood stays sad as she continues her day, and she is not sure why. She has caught the others' emotions but doesn't realize it. She finds herself dwelling on her altered mood. She starts to feel pessimistic and depressed. She wonders if she may need an antidepressant, or if she may be bipolar, since she was in such a good mood this morning. Probably neither of these is the case. What she does need is to learn to manage her emotions by working on getting some resolution of any personal emotional issues she may have to help prevent emotional contagion.

Jennifer did not realize that emotion from an overheard conversation could be transferred to her through emotional contagion. This is what happens: the emotion felt from other people can move inside us, especially if we are somehow having those issues ourselves. That makes us susceptible to absorbing it. Instead of being infected by the feeling of unfairness, which probably transferred some contagious feelings of depression and cynicism, Jennifer could have decided not to pay any attention to this overheard conversation and not let this contagious feeling affect her to the extent that it did. It took away her good feelings about Addison's concert.

Jennifer could have constructively refocused her thoughts to prevent herself from catching these contagious emotions as the situation unfolded. Then she could have purposely continued the positive discussion with her own group. To manage her own emotions, these are some thoughts she could have run through in her mind:

- "This overheard conversation does not relate to me."
- "I don't know the full details."
- "I don't know these people."
- "I am going to ignore this conversation."
- "It is not my situation."
- "These things happen, and it is unfortunate."
- "These feelings are not mine."

She could even think silently, "Go away! Not now!" to those intrusive feelings, or tell herself, "I am not going to let my attention stray away from my daughter's success at the concert and my good feelings about it." After telling herself thoughts like these, she can turn her attention back to her own group, wait for an opening, talk more about her daughter's concert, and let the enjoyment take over again. In this way, she overcomes the emotional contagion.

She also could have asked the people in her own group if they over-heard the conversation and what they thought about it. Getting feedback from others who are also hearing it is another important way to tamp down emotional contagion, as the emotion from the other people will interfere, in a positive way, with the emotion that came from the original source.

Emotional contagion converges into one emotion

As Dr. David R. Hamilton (2011) wrote for *HuffPost*, people's emotions can rub off on you. They can then be caught by others, as we saw in Jennifer's example. This happens more than we know: in groups, in families, and within and between organizations and political factions. This effect extends, in a different way, to video, audio, and social media.

Emotional contagion has been defined by Elaine Hatfield, the research psychologist who coined the term, as "the tendency to automatically mimic and synchronize facial expressions, vocalizations, postures, and movements with those of another person, and, consequently, to converge emotionally."(Hatfield et al., 1994). This is the academic definition, which is based on psychological research involving subjects in a laboratory set-ting. In this book, I am using a liberal, non-academic description of emo-tional contagion. Still, findings from emotional contagion as formally researched can be meaningfully generalized to events in society, espe-cially in times of turmoil, when emotions run rampant. The dynamics in contentious social situations might not be identical to those identified in formal research, but neither are they likely to be substantially different.

Emotions are an intrinsic part of what makes a person tick. They are part of the psychological energy that we release, either by expressing them directly or by emanating them—that is, giving off feelings unknowingly.

Other people's emotions can come at us directly, intended specifically for us. They may even find us passively, or implicitly, when we are part of a group, or even on the periphery of an intended audience. We might feel affected by a performer who is expressing emotions intentionally. Or we overhear a conversation in which people are expressing emotions natu-rally. Emotions don't have to be obvious to be expressed. Emotions are often a beautiful, wonderful part of life, one of the most meaningful parts of living (His Holiness the Dalai Lama et al., 2016).

Subjectively, emotions from others can be appealing because they flow easily and touch and affect our own emotions. But there has to be some affinity there; the adjoining party has to be attracted to and connect easily with that flowing emotion in order to catch it. It happens more often in people who are high in ability to show empathy (Dimberg & Thunberg, 2012). This quick jump to the adjoining party happens without any meaningful thought or appraisal on their part; the incoming emotion can be appealing if there is an affinity with it, and if the receiving person has no real inoculation against it. If there is an automatic absorption ability, the emotion can be immediately, automatically absorbed.

Connecting emotionally with another person is not the same as absorbing the other person's emotions. Emotional contagion does not occur just because we make an emotional connection with another person, but it could. An emotional connection is healthy, but automatic emotional contagion that we absorb can be unhealthy if we don't think about it first.

In emotional contagion, you can "catch" the emotions and feelings of others. The emotions come from someone around us and can affect us even though we may not realize it. When they hit you, one of three things may happen.

- you may "catch" them, or
- you may let them merely connect with you, or
- you may let them simply bounce off you

"Catching" something means you hold it, like when you catch a ball, except you feel it inside when you "catch" an emotion, and keep it for a while, perhaps even absorbing it. Absorbing it means you take it in, so that it becomes more durable inside you, probably part of you.[3]

Connecting means the emotion strikes you, and that is okay with you because it feels all right, but you don't keep it for more than a few seconds. You throw it right back, pleasantly, like when you are in a game of catch. Although it touched you, and you had it, none of it stays with you.

Bouncing off you means you don't want the emotion at all. In dodge ball, we are hit with the ball and it bounces right off us right away.

Sometimes when we catch a feeling, we may even bring it inside of us, absorbing it so that it can become part of us, temporarily or maybe even permanently, such as when we are feeling love from a significant other. When we return an emotion that has come inside us, like love, it is more

---

3   As this is written to apply to many people, I use the word "probably" in this and other situations, because I cannot speak for every situation. Think of it as meaning "in most cases."

meaningful because we have it inside us and are returning it because we want to. We have owned it, it is part of us, and still is, and are giving of it from ourselves. This is vastly different from situations when the feeling just bounces off us without really being caught, like dodgeball.

When we connect with a feeling, we like it, and it feels good, but it may quickly be over, leaving residue in us. Often, we return it, or it drops, not because we reject it but because it is received in a weaker, more fleeting state. If you want to catch it, you catch it with a chance to absorb it, and keep it for a while longer, nurturing it and letting it grow.

When it bounces off us, it didn't hurt us, but we reject it, we don't like it, we don't want it. You decide to close yourself off to the incoming feeling, and it will bounce off you.

These choices are significantly, but not entirely, under your control. When we accept the emotion, we catch it, and we may absorb it. We have to be aware of whether or not we want to accept contagious emotions when they hit. We don't have to accept them. Without awareness you may automatically take in infectious, harmful emotions from an external source. This occurs in person, but also extends to all forms of today's media communication. We need to stop automatically catching emotions.

Emotions and feelings: definitions

Let's talk more about emotions and feelings and how they relate to emotional contagion. This will clarify how to distinguish and understand the terms used throughout the book.

Emotional contagion is defined by the American Psychological Association (APA, n.d.) as "the rapid spread of an emotion from one or a few individuals to others. For example, fear of catching a disease can spread rapidly through a community."[4]

An emotion is defined by the APA (n.d.) as a "complex reaction pattern, involving experiential, behavioural, and physiological elements, by which an individual attempts to deal with a personally significant matter or event. The specific quality of the emotion (e.g., fear, shame) is determined by the specific significance of the event. For example, if the significance involves threat, fear is likely to be generated; if the significance

---

4   I cite numerous definitions from the American Psychological Association *Dictionary of Psychology* on the APA's website. The source links for each of these definitions (for example, active listening, affect, cognitive-dissonance, etc.). are provided under an alphabetical listing in the references under "APA (n.d.). " The letters "n.d." included with any reference indicate that no date of publication is available.

involves disapproval from another, shame is likely to be generated. Emotion typically involves feeling but differs from feeling in having an overt or implicit engagement with the world."

A feeling is defined by the APA (n.d.) as a "self-contained phenomenal experience. Feelings are subjective, evaluative, and independent of the sensations, thoughts, or images evoking them. They are inevitably evaluated as pleasant or unpleasant, but they can have more specific intrapsychic qualities, so that, for example, the affective tone of fear is experienced as different from that of anger. [...] Feelings differ from emotions in being purely mental, whereas emotions are designed to engage with the world."

The term affect is a more general term and is defined by the APA (n.d.) as "any experience of feeling or emotion, ranging from suffering to elation, from the simplest to the most complex sensations of feeling, and from the most normal to the most pathological emotional reactions. [It is] often described in terms of positive affect or negative affect."

These formal definitions are objective. Since we are dealing mostly with the personal, subjective side of emotions and feelings, we also need to describe them from an experiential point of view, as we experience and feel them inside of us subjectively. The following paragraphs describe my personal slant on their meanings.

An emotion exists in a person's body because it is visceral—internal but not in a specific place or body part. The emotion is alive and is an important part of the person. It wants something, it needs an experience. It brings energy and represents life, your aliveness inside you. It is zestful; it feels an experience as it lives. An emotion moves, it vibrates, it stirs and has rhythm. It seems to want to say something, although it can't. The emotion does not have an opinion, because that is the mind's job, but it wants to pass on the simple message that it carries. The emotion does move along, not just shaking or vibrating, but moving forward. It is inside you, not necessarily attached, but not detached either. It is a part of the body, it belongs there. The emotion is a source of energy for the person and is semi-dependent on the mind. The mind, the executive, is in charge. The mind thinks. But for some people, it seems the emotion can take control. If it does, then we have emotion mind. But emotions don't think, even though they try, and they are not our executive.

The emotion communicates with the person's body and mind, as it brings meaning and purpose to the person's existence. It also communicates with its parallel in another person. This is emotional contagion. The emotion sends and attracts feelings, needs, experiences, and even simple messages, sharing it all with its parallel in another person. The emotion gives, receives, and connects, when it reaches out to its fellow emotions in nearby people to share and exchange feelings. When that happens, Barbara Fredrickson (2013) says hearts and minds seem to "interweave" in an "intersubjective" process of psychological energy moving between two people. This interweaving appears to be a true movement and interaction of emotional and personal energy. It almost becomes tangible in tears. We cannot see or touch an emotion, but we can certainly feel it.

Feelings are similar to emotions but are usually more subtle. A feeling is an intangible but definite sensation felt within our own body, not ascribed to a specific body part. Feelings come in different forms, are invisible and abstract, but are somehow definite: we experience them inside us as emotional awarenesses, gut reactions, internal vibrations, intuitive senses, internal movement sensations, poignant energy, spontaneous insights, quick urges, sudden hunches, empathic sentiments, and the awarenesses inside us when we have needs, urges, wishes, or yearnings. They are the personal way we sense and experience our own emotions inside ourselves. A feeling affects us personally in a meaningful way, having an impact on our subjective beliefs. In short, it moves us.

Feelings are not thoughts or opinions, as some people regard them, as to what choice to make or who to vote for. Those are not feelings, they are thoughts, assessments of the best course of action. They may have an emotional component that contributes to the opinion, but they are not feelings. Feelings are also not physical sensations like pain or fatigue, although that is closer to the mark. We feel pain and fatigue in our body, but that is really a case of physical sensations in the body, not feelings.

Feelings can seem to have a mind of their own, without our necessarily knowing about them or feeling them. They can have more control when people aren't aware of them, like a flash flood that sneaks up on them. They seem to flow and bubble up inside us, sometimes without our knowing it, and then they can come out suddenly. We may catch ourselves unexpectedly in tears, crying or even yelling when we hadn't intended to. Or we find ourselves doing things we didn't plan on, like a quick reaction, saying something we never meant to. In the extreme, some people may hurt someone when under emotional duress. This is more likely to happen in people who aren't aware of their feelings bubbling up or stirring inside. Emotions are more objective, as seen in observable displays in behaviour, and inferred in situations such as when a person is crying, angry, despondent, and so on.

People can have an automatic effect on our feelings. Some people have more effect, some less. Some people are quiet and reflective, some loud and excitable. Feelings and their emotions arise from inside us, in a quiet trickle or a loud explosion. When we are with people, we often feel their feelings and can be touched by them.

Feelings and emotions are different but can sometimes be used interchangeably. The feelings inside us signal something is meaningful to us. Emotions are a way you express feelings outwardly. Emotions, because they are more open and outward than feelings, are more prone to be contagious than feelings. Emotions are more liable to be shown openly in behaviour, especially where a lot of spontaneous movement occurs, such as at social events or family gatherings, in crowds, or at presentations, parties, sporting events, and concerts. Emotions are the result of fast thinking and automatic thoughts, often in reaction to events involving quick interpersonal movements and occurrences. They are more prone to react to specific events like victories, tragedies, political or social wins and losses, and announced decisions, as well as weddings and funerals.

Feelings, on the other hand, are more personal and private, usually kept inside us. They are more delicate and tender. They are unlikely to be expressed as a way of communicating with others in large public social settings, except by a few extraverts, and are more likely to be expressed in smaller, quieter, more intimate settings, where people are relatively motionless and are nearby. These are often situations when we are with one or more people whom we trust, who are closer to us emotionally. The emotions of these people are less likely to be socially contagious, but emotionally the feelings can be experienced and absorbed. This would constitute a type of emotional contagion; it can be converted into emotional connection by talking about the experience with the others. In this way you can own your own feelings.

The dynamics of emotional contagion

Feelings and emotions flow among people, groups, and crowds. They come from within us. Some people express an emotion and others then feel the same emotion, as if they catch it, or even absorb it. This may be automatic, as some people seem to have an "automatic absorption ability." When we catch positive emotions like happiness, joy, and delight, it is healthy for us. We want to absorb them. They make us feel good and may spur us on to enjoy more things. We can all relate to a situation where a persuasive, positive person (such as a parent or teacher) encourages a child when logic won't work, saying "You can do it." The interaction is based on trust. The emotion in the trusted, caring person is contagious and seeps into the younger person. The trusted person's emotional energy is there and can be felt by the child who allows it to enter, although subconsciously. This is why trust is necessary. But feelings and emotions can also be negative and toxic. They can give us an emotional infection if we don't have a psychological inoculation against them.

When emotions flow between us, we can automatically catch an emotion just because of the strength and appeal of the emotion. Because of its power, the emotion affects us and can result in our taking unthinking action based on it.

When people express or radiate an emotion and others feel the same emotion, and catch it, the feelings and emotions can be contaminated with toxic feelings that are dangerous, especially feelings like anger, hate, cynicism, disgust, depression, panic, and fear. That is why it is better to first connect with emotions instead of catching and absorbing them. It is best to absorb emotions only after your gatekeeper—which is your mind—quickly checks them out to make sure they are safe. Those who are prone to catching toxic emotions need to take time to consider whether it is wise to do so.

People use emotions to think, to hold positions, to make decisions, to decide who to vote for. But emotions don't think. Emotions are only good at feeling. The mind thinks. The mind decides. Emotion is part of a decision. It sets the mood or atmosphere. But if the emotion alone decides, poor choices may result. For example: if a person makes a voting choice based on emotion only, they will possibly make a poor choice. When thinking with the mind, the person weighs the pros and cons, checks candidates' histories, and reviews patterns. Emotional voting cannot do this, so if people vote emotionally, without thinking, they may vote for a candidate who does things they weren't expecting. Emotional voting can lead to a time of turmoil.

Emotions "powerfully, predictably, and pervasively influence decision making"; an emotion "directly influences" how an outcome of a situation is evaluated, changing "how rational inputs are evaluated" according to research by Lerner, Li, Valdesolo, et al. (2015). However, they point out that research on the influence of emotion on decision-making does not clearly elucidate the effects of emotions as a whole, since specific emotions have specific effects different from other specific emotions. They cite sadness, for example, as being able to elicit more systematic thought. Research continues to take place in assessing how emotion affects thought.

Emotion mind, which I mentioned earlier, is a concept developed by clinical psychologist Marsha Linehan and is described as the state of mind when emotions are in control and are not balanced by reason (Linehan, 2015). In this state, emotions control your thinking and behaviour; you are ruled by your moods, feelings, and urges to do or say things. People who are susceptible to the effects of emotional contagion, who immediately and deeply absorb these emotions without first assessing them, are usually in their emotion mind. They place a high value on emotions being their primary guide of action.[5] It is likely that the reason some people put high value on emotions guiding them is because they are very easily stimulated by the direct impact of emotions, without realizing what is happening to them.

For these people, emotions are likely to be at the forefront of their communication style; they like to express emotions because they sense subconsciously that others communicate this way also, as emotions are communicated invisibly between people. Emotion is what establishes meaningfulness, through experiencing joy, happiness, excitement, or even disappointment, loss, and anger. Meaningful topics in the social and political world are susceptible to emotional contagion because of their implicit and sometimes explicit emotion. Many people obtain their identity through their political affiliation.

The concept of emotional contagion refers to effects that occur when people unwittingly take in an emotional flow expressed or emitted by others. The concept of emotional contagion is universal or pervasive, as an emotional impact affecting anyone who experiences it. We conceptualize this as taking in or absorbing some type of emotional experience from others. Such an experience can be stated, or expressed non-verbally, para-verbally, or in emotional behaviour, or it may be indirectly given off by a person when it emanates or is emitted from someone without their awareness. Non-verbal expression is commonly seen in gestures, facial expressions, posture, and the like, whereas para-verbal expression is seen in vocal utterances that are not definitively verbal, such as clearing the throat, small coughs, and mild hesitations, which are timely in the

---

5   Emotion mind as we use it is not identical to emotion mind as used in Linehan's writings, although it seems to be a similar state to the one we read about in situations in a volatile socio-political environment.

conversation and add to the stream of communication. They can be conveyed in pseudo-verbal vocalizations such as *umm* and *uhh.*

We can work on protecting ourselves from these effects that occur from taking in emotions from others. At other times, we need to welcome the positive emotions and feelings coming into our minds and bodies, as they bring health and well-being. We need to be able to tell the difference between the positive and negative, and we need a gatekeeper to direct traffic when emotions affect us, improving the absorption process.

The process of emotional contagion is invisible. The emotion enters the person receiving it from someone else, carrying a quick simple message that tags along with the emotion. It's like the emotion comes along early, triggered likely by the amygdala, the part of the brain that is an early warning system, travelling faster than a thought. The emotion enters the person, enabled to do so by the mirror neuron referenced later, priming them for the quickly following thought. When it does this, we have a version of emotional infection, which is caused by emotional contagion, because the emotion does not carry the essence of the thought. Instead, the emotion carries numerous cognitive distortions in its simple message, often including panic and fear, which then take can over the essence of the thought. Most of the power coming from the initial message comes from the force of the emotion, which is embedded in it, as an implicitly or explicitly expressed emotion. Words carry power, which comes in the emotion connected to the words. Therefore, the emotion can dominate any power of thought for most people, especially if it is done through social media and eye-popping headlines. That is the effect of emotional contagion and social contagion.

If we hear, "Look out!" we feel the force of the alarm about an impending danger. But we also have to check it out, since emotions are not capable of analytical, systematic thought. However, when we are talking about a controversial, complex topic, like climate change, one that carries emotion with it, the emotion is contagious to the thought. The emotion does not have the ability to carry the complex logic involved in the thought. Emotions have simple messages at best, such as fear, hate, or depression. Just a few words. Emotions can't think. The emotion, however, is contagious to the thought when it carries a force that is somehow appealing to the person, who may have previous elements of that emotion retained in themselves as emotional residue they have previously picked up, and it enters and influences the thinking process. So, the thought accepts it, not realizing that the emotion is infectious. The thought gets infected. Fear dominates. The mind mistakenly and almost involuntarily lets go of some or all of its systematic reasoning power, so in effect the emotion overpowers the logic, especially if the individual involved values the emotional message more.

Some people mistakenly believe they just have to listen to the emotion and not figure out what it is trying to say. When the emotion gets more power or influence than reason should allow, it automatically persuades many of us to accept the statement based on the emotion without really examining the logic and content of the thought. This is especially true of the spoken word, when it is not printed out where we would study it with slower, more accurate reasoning. Otherwise, the power of the message can come in the emotion, since emotions are, by definition, powerful and strong, sometimes piercing. This is how cognitive distortions infect the thought. This is not true of every spoken thought, since cognitive ability can accept it via reason or logic, in which case there is no emotional contagion present. We need to use systematic reasoning, wisdom, logic, and critical thinking to assess what is going on. If there is reason for fear, you need a plan to stay safe.

Your gatekeeper is the part of you that decides whether to accept an incoming feeling or emotion as opposed to letting it enter automatically. We need to use logic, facts, and knowledge to make executive decisions on when it is alright to open the gates to allow incoming emotions to be caught and even absorbed, or whether to just connect or let them bounce off you. It is the job of the mind to decide when this is constructive and when it isn't. The mind gives the instructions, and the body responds automatically to the mind's instructions.

Emotional contagion is predominant in society and politics

Emotional contagion can affect society at large. Emotions flare up easily at a time of turmoil, especially around contentious issues. Emotions drive actions. If emotions don't flare up, there is no turmoil. And emotions are contagious. Emotional contagion has contributed to the times of turmoil of the 21st century. Anyone can be infected by toxic emotions like hate, fear, or suspicion, regardless of their political leanings. We need to be aware of this, so we don't automatically absorb it. Think about it first. With emotional contagion hitting the public on a regular basis, we feel the effects of the emotional residue, the lingering feeling or memory of the toxic emotion, such as suspicion.

Emotional contagion runs rampant at a time of turmoil in politics. Emotions are not good at thinking. They are good at feeling. Emotions don't think. Negative emotions like fear, hate, and suspicion carry simple messages, and many people like simple messages. If you catch and absorb the wrong emotion, you can be infected by it without thinking. Emotions like hate and fear can grab you, almost automatically, so that you don't have time to think and you simply react. But you don't have to absorb it; you may not want it to be part of you.

Turmoil is caused by negative emotions. When negative emotions such as anger, hate, cynicism, disgust, depression, panic, and fear get stronger, and out of control, turmoil usually results. Negative emotions like these attract each other through emotional contagion and easily and quickly move from one person to another, or from one group to another. Emotions work and move fast. Before you know it, the feeling has been absorbed. When people get emotional, they can act quickly. They can do dumb things without real thought.

You can't have turmoil without having emotions, dangerous and infectious emotions that spread like a virus and infect others. It is time to curtail the spread of negative emotional contagion. Once we begin to absorb emotions from society, we get accustomed to it and do it more easily. The residue builds up over the years. It gets to be too much. Many people become demoralized. What we need instead is critical thinking, systematic reasoning, and wisdom. Wisdom is an amalgamated balance of thoughts and feelings with various perspectives.

Mirror neurons: the physiological explanation

Scientifically, interest in emotional contagion was initially stimulated, according to Daniel Rempala (2013), in part by the discovery of "mirror neurons." (referred to earlier). In humans, brain activity consistent with that of mirror neurons has been found in four different areas of the brain. A mirror neuron system is a group of specialized neurons that "mirrors" the actions and behaviour of others (Rajmohan & Mohandas, 2007). Bob Avenson (n.d.) says: "The mirror neurons activate the areas of the brain associated with the emotion of the speaker, thus conjuring up the emotion as if the receiver were experiencing it naturally." Humans utilize the mirror neuron system to understand and predict others' actions. (Myowa-Yamakoshi, 2014) Emotional contagion may occur through mirror neurons in that we easily pick up and absorb emotions portrayed by other people, and then feel them ourselves.

This is the physiological or medical explanation. It gives us a physiological basis for emotional contagion. We feel emotions through the effects on our own facial movements, vocal tones, and body postures. Facial mimicry is an important mechanism for emotional contagion to occur (Dimberg & Thunberg, 2012). The effects come via automatic mimicry of subtle synchronization of movements of an adjoining person's body (Avenson, n.d.), occurring at a microscopic level in the muscle fibres of the face and body. Different movements of parts of the eyebrows or the lips correspond to various emotions. They are activated in milliseconds as you interact with another person.

As Sigal Barsade (2020a) says, the term "infectious" comes when "through a variety of physiological and neurological processes, we actually feel the emotions we mimicked—and then act on them. "They become ours and we feel them, even if we do so subconsciously. You can let it connect momentarily, catch and absorb it, or drop it almost right away if you are aware of it. That is your goal.

A seatmate on public transport is weeping

Let's look at an example of how emotional contagion can affect us. Imagine that you are in a good mood and are flying home after a lovely vacation with family. You take your assigned seat next to someone already there, a stranger who you notice is weeping. You look at them. They don't look at you, don't say hello. You say hello and try to talk with them, but you can see that they aren't in the mood for a conversation. It seems from their mumbled comments that they may have experienced a real loss or setback. You look at your phone and scroll through pictures of your family but can't avoid noticing your seatmate. You're not sure what has affected them, but you see that they are sad. They continue weeping. You offer a few words of support and comfort. They are still not talking to you. Your good mood evaporates, and you start to feel sad inside for no real reason. You start to recall losses and setbacks you have experienced. You become emotional, feeling sorrow rising inside yourself. You still don't know why your seatmate is sad. You start to feel a little overwhelmed. You forget about your vacation. You are catching their emotions.

Now let's say you are a different person but in the same scenario, in a good mood as you fly home after a lovely vacation with family. You sit in your assigned seat next to this same person, who is behaving in exactly the same way. Only this time, you don't say anything, you don't notice this person, and you don't realize what is going on with them. You look at your phone, those pictures of your family, and become absorbed in them. You enjoy the pictures. You sense someone else is next to you, but do not realize that the other person is feeling distressed, weeping and muttering a few words. But you pick it up subconsciously, or subliminally, their feelings not identified by your conscious mind, but still having a small influence. You may start to feel a little sad and ignore it. You had a good time with your family. You are still not consciously noticing the person next to you. You look at your pictures some more but aren't really enjoying them as much. You still feel a little sad but hardly realize this. The airplane takes off. You can't wait to get home. You just don't quite feel as chipper as when you first got on board. We can absorb feelings subconsciously like this without our conscious awareness. This happens. It is not supernatural.

In these two examples, you caught the sad feelings from your seatmate in different ways and to different degrees. When you feel the same feelings as the other person, we say you have caught their emotions, in the same manner of speaking as if someone caught a cold from another person with a cold. Their emotion was contagious to others who would then have the same feeling, in the same manner as if someone caught their cold from their germs. They were contagious. If someone were immune to catching another's cold, they would not catch it. In a similar way, someone could learn how to become immune to catching emotions from someone else.

These examples are at two extremes. It is better to be more aware than in the second example but less susceptible than in the first. In the second example, you didn't pick up on what was happening. In the first, you did, even without really talking much to the sad person. With emotional contagion it is important to notice such things. What if the seatmate were muttering angry, cynical words? What would happen to your good mood? You probably wouldn't want to feel angry. But you want to be able to make that decision yourself so that you don't just pick up the feeling automatically.

Do you want to feel sad now? Probably not. We need to build up psychological immunity to automatically catching emotions from others so that they don't overtake you. It is natural to feel some sad feelings, but not to let them overtake you. Just offering a little empathy may help the other person. Some people seem to catch another's emotions without being aware that they are doing this. What we need to do is to learn to judge whether or not it is, in fact, a good thing to catch and absorb this particular emotion from this particular person at this particular time. Handling it in an active way, like showing empathy, would usually minimize the impact of the emotional contagion, because it lessens your introspective, ruminative reactions (such as opening your own sad memories), making it more difficult for the incoming feeling to take over. In the first example, responding with empathy (something like, "I know that sometimes the holiday season doesn't go well.") could have stopped the emotional contagion, because now it is out in the open.

Emotional contagion spreads

Emotional contagion flows more easily in an active, animated, interpersonal setting, where sources of emotions are many and hard to specify. We are more prone to take in emotions that others express or emanate when a larger number of people are interacting spontaneously, with heightened sound and increased proximity. A large number of people in agreement seems to add a quality of credibility and legitimacy, raising the contagious effect. This is especially true when participants seek social approval and there is some interconnectivity of emotion. This happens in some political and business meetings, where various people are susceptible to emotional contagion. We often take in other people's feelings when there is emotional noise, communicating an emotional tone as noted in the tones of voices, any music, as well as quality and rhythm of the others' expressions. Most people often respond automatically, replying to the emotion with an opposite emotion. It is ideal to reply with firmness and empathy, not simply a gut reaction. As the contagious effect heightens, tension may build. This could happen more easily in informal gatherings.

Emotions often motivate us and give us the energy to take action. We may quickly and easily be stimulated if we experience an emotional situation, perhaps where someone is openly emotional, or if a story or event that has affected someone strongly touches us deeply. We have to be careful about how we handle it. We know that we need to think first, but we may momentarily forget that because of the power of the emotion. We may say "yes" instead of "no," or "no" instead of "yes," to a business decision, speak illogically when arguing a point, or forget to think critically when choosing a mate, making a big purchase, or supporting a candidate because of the emotions we suddenly feel. But as the game show host smartly asked, "Is that your final answer?" A verbal or behavioural reaction to the emotion should not be automatic. Think rationally first and then respond. Be objective, step outside yourself, and ask, "How would my friend, someone I trust, think about this?" We need to screen the emotion and approve or disapprove the resulting decision.[6]

Most people don't catch every feeling coming at them from other people. It might connect, or it may just bounce off. There has to be something going on inside us that invites it in, something emotionally intertwined into our attitude, for the feeling to be felt inside. When we find our feelings strongly affected by the other person, we really allow it to happen, although it is quick and subconscious. Some people like feeling others' emotions. It may fit with their values. When the other person shows it, expresses it, exudes it, or sends it off in various directions, it hits the receiving person, who recognizes it and knows if they want to let it in. They may like it. Letting it in helps them feel it and experience it. We have to recognize this and be aware of it, as some incoming feelings might be harmful.

Emotions can cause a lot of negative energy, through jealousy, hate, anger, and other infectious feelings. Emotions provide the energy for action. People living with depressed roommates may develop some depressed feelings. Being around someone who is suspicious may make you suspicious. If you have felt anxious then you can pick anxious feelings up from someone else who is anxious. Depressed, anxious, and suspicious moods produce similar actions, and so can affect our choices or votes. Political leaders may be cynical, spreading and strengthening cynicism among others in their political party and the public who may also be leaning that way. There has to be an emotional process occurring within you subconsciously that is similar to the incoming feeling to make it appealing to you. Sometimes that emotional process may consist of emotional residue from previous occurrences. It should be similar enough that you would catch and absorb it instead of just connecting.

People with different personalities, characteristics, tolerances, and yearnings for emotional experiences, as well as different levels of denial, repression, sensitivity, and acceptance will handle the flow of feelings coming towards them uniquely. Music, a deep voice, a catch phrase, a parade, or spontaneous laughter are among many things which stimulate and augment feelings and their expression on us. Our feelings are

---

6 Comments like this on how to prevent, block, or overcome negative emotional contagion will appear throughout the book. The last few chapters of the book are devoted to overcoming the contagion. Readers wanting recommendations on overcoming negative contagion are advised to read the entire book, since there is no guarantee that such comments in the opening chapters are also covered in the latter chapters on overcoming negative contagion, and vice versa.

influenced by what is popular, by what feels good, by the physical environment. Some people will resist, others will accept. The flow of emotions can be resisted, deflected, or repelled, like a dodge ball. Sometimes they should be. Or the flow can be automatically caught, accepted, or absorbed, which is what happens with emotional contagion. We can go with an infectious positive flow and let it take us with it, but we do not have to let a flow overtake us or overwhelm us automatically. Letting it connect but not catching it is a better idea. We need to be inoculated against the automatic contagion. Your gatekeeper will help you get control over this.

"If somebody else is feeling a feeling, then I should feel it too." This seems to be what emotional contagion is saying on a subliminal level. The answer as to how to combat it? *We don't really have to feel what someone else is feeling.* It is not required. This is obvious when we think about it. There are many wisdoms along this line: we have a right to our own feelings; to each their own; no one can tell me what to feel; my feelings are my own; I don't have to feel that way; that's their feeling, it's not mine; and so on. Then why would it be that if someone else is feeling a feeling that I must automatically feel it too? And even act on it? Because that is what is going on when emotions are contagious, despite going against these various wisdoms. Actually, these are good sayings to tell yourself in order to resist emotional contagion and change from automatic to manual. You just have to remind yourself.

Intangible quality is transmitted

Emotions flow. There is a perception or feeling of the movement of emotional energy between people, or even within a person.[7] It is a process that is a crucial component of emotional contagion. It is an intangible but definite quality which seems to be transmitted by people at a barely perceptible level, independent of the content of a message. It is the expression of an emotion's energy from inside an individual, a movement coming towards you from others. It requires clarity, depth, and authenticity, and is related to the person's inner emotion or state of internal psychological energy. It consists of feelings, emotions, affect, mood, and consciousness that radiate from the person. Emotional contagion refers to the contagious or infectious influences that this emanation of energy has on others, as if it seeps into another person and affects their emotions.

---

7   Our use of the term "flow" in this context does not refer to the type of flow described by the psychologist Csikszentmihalyi: an internal flow state, inside the person, in which the person is completely immersed in an activity with intense focus and creative engagement, deep concentration.

Two systems of the mind

Daniel Kahneman, a Nobel prize winning psychologist, talked about two systems of the mind, System 1 and System 2, in his best-selling book, *Thinking, Fast and Slow* (Kahneman, 2011). System 1 is thought to operate automatically and quickly, with little or no effort in thinking and no sense of voluntary control. It is the fast system, where quick, emotionally laden thinking dominates. System 2, the slow system, allocates attention to effortful mental activity, including complex computations, agency, choice, and concentration. It takes longer to make computations and comparisons, thinking reasonably and purposefully, than it does to think automatically and involuntarily. Kahneman states that mood affects the operation of System 1. It would make sense, then, that emotional contagion is more common in System 1. When the person enters Stage 2, it makes sense that the level of emotional contagion is decreased, if not absent, and the ability to reason is recovered.

In situations involving emotional contagion, there may be a rush to judgment, likely caused by automatic processes in System 1. Emotional contagion tends to be plentiful as people make judgments based on emotion rather than reasoning or logical analysis. It would be helpful to realize the emotion is there and treat it as something to be considered when engaging in reasoning. One way to do this is to consider how important the emotion is, from a cost-benefit, or cause-and-effect, analysis, instead of letting the emotion itself pull one into a decision.

Remember, when you read examples in this book, that you may be prone to agree immediately with reasonable thoughts that are presented if you are mentally in System 2, where you can be objective and logical. Readers often approach books such as these in System 2, from an analytical, intellectual perspective, because they are in cognitive mode to understand the points being made. But if you put yourself in the midst of the same example and treat it as if it were happening to you, at that moment, in an emotionally based situation, you are likely to be sent into System 1 and be affected by the contagious emotion that triggers the quick, distorted, automatic thought, forgetting about the analysis momentarily. Many of us get into System 1 thoughts every now and then, so it is better to be aware of this discrepancy and prepare for it by seeing yourself in System 1. This is one of the ways to learn not to allow emotional contagion to come in, because it likely occurs when you are in System 1. Put yourself into System 2 by seeing things objectively, analytically, as if you were an outsider.

There is a reason why most people sit down in chairs for discussions. In a sense, they are putting themselves into System 2, aiming to have a purpose, to sit down, to think carefully and critically, to use slow thinking to reason things out, to recall knowledge, to take time to be philosophical, to consider other perspectives—all ways to prevent emotional contagion from taking over one's mind. We know that standing and moving among other people, as happens in riots and protests, is not conducive to clear thinking, and is more prone to keep people, especially those susceptible to emotional contagion, in System 1.

A lot of the mistakes humans make are caused by System 1 thinking tied to the effects of emotional contagion infecting our mind. Many books and articles refer to human mistakes. "Do not make the mistake of believing that these problems [in using social media] are not tied to who we are and how we conduct ourselves," says Guy Harrison (2017). How we conduct ourselves usually becomes a problem when we are infected by emotions doing the job reserved for our mind. Emotional mind becomes the main problem we have, because if we think rationally the problems with conduct wouldn't occur. Emotion brings a lot of joy and meaning but the negative part of emotion can dominate our thinking, producing mistakes.

Social contagion

Emotional contagion differs from social contagion. Social contagion refers to emotional effects that happen in a social environment, heightening emotional reactions. It involves "the spread of behaviours, attitudes, and affect through crowds and other types of social aggregates from one member to another. [...][It is] sustained by relatively mundane interpersonal processes, such as imitation, conformity, universality, and mimicry."(APA, n.d.) It also occurs in electronic media, on social media, and through gossip and rumours. It is more impersonal, and the social realm can be the medium. Even though interpersonal contact sustains it, those are the more superficial types of interpersonal contact in predominantly social environments such as crowds, parties, and malls where more intimate communication is less likely to occur.

Face-to-face contact and communication with others is lessened by use of social media, when communication occurs through social platforms like Skype, Zoom, and FaceTime. In these impersonal situations, the determining factor is that the physical presence of the other person in the here-and-now is void. Instead, the other person is there-and-now, at a physical distance, their image, voice, and movements portrayed electronically, so that the flow of feelings and energy between people is reduced. This distanced aspect is likely why negative social media posts have been found in research to spread faster and further than positive ones. Empathy is lessened in the impersonal, shallow interactions, writes Helen Reiss in her book *The Empathy Effect*. (Reiss & Neporent, 2018) "Words on a screen lead to a growing sense of detachment and indifference" she says, adding that internet agitators don't tend to view their victims as real people (Green, 2019).

In one study, conducted on Weibo (A Chinese version of Twitter) in China, researchers Fan, Zhao, Chen et al (2014) examined more than 70 million tweets and found that anger spreads faster than other emotions. They found that the correlation of anger among users is significantly higher than that of joy (on social media) which indicates that angry emotion could spread more quickly and broadly in the network. In general, it is easier to be angry when the other person is not in front of you. When the other person is present, perhaps expressing fear, making eye contact and triggering your guilt, which you then pick up through emotional contagion, your moral compass easily gets involved. This guilt tells you not to hurt the other person, especially if they are presenting fear. You may not realize this when you are on social media and no one else is present to trigger your moral compass.

When on social media, the distorted phrase "What you see is all there is" affects you, and you believe it, your quick, easy thoughts of System 1 don't take details into account. It is easy to express anger when you don't think of the consequences of the other person being real. But they are real. You are unlikely to experience an immediate interaction face-to-face where you would feel, through mirror neurons, that the other person is real and has feelings of fear. So your moral compass is not triggered. Social media robs you of that experience, as does the anonymity. Social contagion then may be more dangerous than emotional contagion, where empathy for others is more likely to be experienced.

It is clear then that we need to pay more attention to the contagious effect, since it is powerful. And the contagion from social media, although seeming innocuous, can be more dangerous than we may have thought at first glance. Emotional contagion has a powerful effect on our daily lives, in many modalities.

2

The Flow of Emotions

Emotions, including negative contagious emotions, spread and "flow" among people. When they hit us, they can automatically inflame our emotions, automatically taking charge of their action. If we resist this effect, many positive things can be accomplished. We need to appraise the emotions hitting us and be aware of our own desires and motivations. Negative contagious emotions can blind people; they often drive negative social events like riots. Some of us need warnings about these dangerous contagious emotions. Our mind, as our gatekeeper, with good ideas and priorities, needs to think, interrupt our emotions and take action. Otherwise, we are affected automatically by emotions that we absorb. In political turmoil we are more susceptible to catch contagious emotions that contribute to more turmoil in society.

Emotions move from one person to another. We feel what someone else feels but not all the time, and not with everyone. We don't feel exactly what they feel, not to the same degree or depth. But emotions can rub off on us, affecting us, sometimes without our realizing it. There is a process involved here, one that we need to know more about.

People talk from the brain or from the heart. If they express an idea and use impersonal, factual words, it is usually a cognition, a mental type of statement, made with the mind with some deliberation. If they express an emotion or feeling, like a wish, a hate, or a fear, and use personal types of words, laden with emotion, it is usually straight from the heart or the gut. They speak from the heart when expressing romantic or tender feelings and from the gut when anxious, scared, or angry. These are statements that are expressing affect, with little or no reasoning. It is this feeling that can be caught through emotional contagion. When a person's words are slow and calculated, they are often speaking from the mind. When they talk quickly with some rhythm and variation of tempo, they are likely talking from their heart or gut.

Think of how a difficult situation in life involves emotions. The emotion the person is expressing or emitting affects you, especially if you allow it. Often, we need to decide whether to initiate an action as a result. That requires your mind thinking about how certain comments or actions on your part could affect another person. You don't really know exactly what the other person is feeling, or whether they are okay with you taking action. If you act, be prepared for a response. Be gentle and tentative. They may not want you to intervene, but if you are gentle and sensitive, they may respond positively. If they don't, patiently let it come on its own.

There are many words and phrases in our vocabulary to reflect both internal and interpersonal flow of emotions. There is emphasis on movement when we describe emotions, or flow, in our daily speech. We get enthusiastic, and there can be a "flood of emotions." Words express the sense that real movement is happening internally: "She does something to me," and, "He says he's fine, but I can just feel his sadness." The emotions and the feelings are contagious. We feel them. We catch them. We absorb them. But remember—we should not catch them immediately.

Automatic absorption ability

Some people seem to have an automatic absorption ability when it comes to taking in others' feelings and emotions. We see it in romantic relationships, in families, in friendships, in crowds. And we see it in politics, the media, and business situations. Many people can become automatically inflamed, especially if they feel challenged and sense a threat to their self-esteem, security, or reputation. Then the emotions tend to take over, taking charge of the decision-making. Instead, pause and hold that reaction and put the mind to work. There is probably a smarter way to do it.

Sometimes major life choices will be made in a flash. Maybe someone said or did something that was mean, unfair, cruel, or even crooked. The person on the receiving end catches the emotion. It's contagious, as anger often is. This person throws it back angrily in an emotional counter-contagion, a quick reaction to the contagious effect. Feeling angry, he retaliates, perhaps in a passive-aggressive manner. Maybe he makes a major decision in a flash. People in these situations could end a relationship, quit a job, or drop out of college. These big decisions often happen after a confrontation with someone that brings up tough emotions. Negative emotions produce spiteful actions, and potentially bad choices.

Sometimes we may feel someone else's anger about a cause and not like it. We may feel fear instead. Hatfield calls this counter-contagion: becoming scared of someone else's anger (Hatfield et al., 1994, as quoted in Flora, 2019). She says that anger is indeed "caught" in these cases, but is quickly swamped by fear, caused by a sense of self-protection. Alternatively, it can prompt us to feel more anger. Counter-contagion usually has the effect of keeping us in an emotional state, but it switches the emotion over to either fear or more anger in retaliation. This can happen when a person has issues with topics of controversy in society or politics.

Instead of reacting right away, take a break. It's not how fast you act, it's how smart you act. Change your immediate environment. Go somewhere else and work it through in your mind. If you were sitting, go for a long walk or jog. If you were walking, go and sit somewhere. Listen to some music. Take some deep breaths. Talk it over with someone who is supportive or understanding.

When you are ready, write down what happened, what your thoughts were, and then work at it constructively. Identify any "hot thoughts," such as "what a sonofabitch!" Change them to cooler thoughts, like: "I am angry, but maybe he was just having a tough day." Work it through with a psychological cost-benefit analysis (Grant, 2018).

When someone lashes out in anger, we may feel hurt because we have momentarily picked up the other person's angry reaction to us. We take it personally, forgetting that the other person is being emotional and isn't thinking calmly or clearly. We are now both in emotion mind. We may react to that hurt impulsively and aggressively but remember that this person wouldn't usually have reacted this way. Wait for them to cool down, and don't take it personally. Let them vent. In this way, we decide not to automatically catch all the incoming emotions and let them affect us so immediately.

Interrupting the flow: the emotional ping-pong game

When real life situations happen, more people need to handle their emotions by using slow, reasoned thinking, not the quick reactions common to a ping-pong game. Keep ping-pong balls for the real ping-pong game.

Contagious emotions often flow from contentious issues or controversies, and people who react quickly do so because emotions don't think, they just get into the emotional ping-pong game. Back and forth. *Ping,* with an angry comment, and then *pong*, right back with an angrier comment, so *ping*, even angrier, and so on. But that doesn't work. Interrupt the flow. *Stop!* Otherwise, feelings get hurt, friendships end, and the damage is done as you try to one-up someone. Emotions don't think, but your mind does, so use it. Take a break. Distract yourself. Take a deep breath to stop the back-and-forth emotional ping-pong game and think instead about whether one-upping is important. Emotional contagion is an automatic process. Purposely interrupting this flow will interrupt the automaticity of it.

Take this example. A close friend angrily tells you that someone spread graffiti all over his house. His voice is raised and has an edge to it, and a few expletives come out. You will probably feel angry too. You didn't tell yourself to feel angry, you just feel anger. It has just swelled inside you, automatically. And if your friend wants to take action—maybe take revenge for the graffiti—then no matter how unusual or risky this might be, you may be inclined to join him. You don't know exactly what revenge he has in mind, but right now you don't care. This is the effect of emotional contagion. But rather than reacting automatically, you need to stop and consider this revenge, and maybe decline to join in. This contagion effect can be strong or weak: you might decide right away to join, or perhaps you only imagine yourself seeking revenge, but don't act. If there is no emotional contagion, then you don't feel any of this and do nothing; it is just a story to you. That's what we want. Revenge is not helpful. The graffiti vandal is looking for this emotional reaction because it means he has upset the person who owns the house and that may be gratifying to him, because his motivation may be to upset them. The emotional contagion spread depends on your friend's manner of expression as well as your tendency to absorb emotions. Both factors are usually necessary for emotional contagion to occur. Without a tendency to absorb the emotions, the automatic pattern stops. Using some wisdom in a case like this could result in you as a friend showing empathy, sharing emotion, and helping him paint over the graffiti, without taking revengeful action.

Emotions transfer from person to person. According to research (Barsade, 2014a) we are used to automatically, subconsciously taking on the moods and feelings of others around us, especially when we work together in small groups. Experiments show that when positive emotion is spread, groups who catch that positivity work more cooperatively, unaware that it was caused by the spread of positive emotions. If you talk to a friend who is sad because her parent died, you will likely feel sad too, even if you didn't know the parent. Emotional contagion also flows through society, not just with close connections like friends. When we hear a distressing or frustrating story, we can pick up anger or cynicism automatically. Empathy for someone else's emotional pain can cause those infectious feelings to spread. If we are impulsive and quick to judge, we may be particularly susceptible to catching these infectious feelings without hearing the whole story or thinking rationally about both sides of the argument. We need to consider whether we should indeed feel angry or cynical, and whether we really do agree with the point being made. Finally, we need to consider whether to keep those feelings with us or let them go. We can have a degree of emotion about the story without completely agreeing with its conclusion, and it is our brain that does the agreeing, not our emotions. If there is little or no empathy on the part of the observer, emotional contagion often becomes more influential and potentially more problematic, as the emotion likely becomes too strong. Empathy, which involves both the mind and emotion, provides a boundary to regulate and modulate the flow of contagion.

This phenomenon is not just a theory. Research shows that emotion can be transferred through subconscious or unconscious induction of emotion states (Schoenewolf, 1990). People can track moment-by-moment subtle facial changes in people they observe (Hatfield et al., 1993). Hatfield says that emotional contagion appears to be a basic building block of human interaction—assisting in "mind-reading" (allowing people to understand and share the thoughts and feelings of others) and facilitating the coordination and synchronization of those interactions. She adds that such contagion is also an important component of empathy (Hatfield et al., 2014). She says that emotional contagion comprises "social, psychophysiological, and behavioural phenomena," and is "comprised of many components—including conscious awareness, facial, vocal, and postural expression, neurophysiological and autonomic nervous system activity, and instrumental behaviors." (Hatfield et al., 2009)

Hatfield says emotional contagion in its primitive form is "relatively automatic, unintentional, uncontrollable and largely inaccessible to conversant (conscious, verbal) awareness." This comment refers only to primitive contagion, which we can all feel. This may be the case in situations like crowds at a sports event or emotional political rallies or protests.

Emotional contagion in more mature situations, like individual meetings, seems to indeed be able to be controlled, slowed, guided, regulated, and even stopped by individuals who receive its impact—if those individuals were aware of methods to do so. Your mind permits or disallows it.

Hatfield states that more mature appraisal processes and an awareness of one's own desires and motivations may enter the picture after a primitive outburst and reverse primitive contagion (Hatfield et al., 2014). The awareness and appraisal would likely develop into mature contagion, when our mind can act as gatekeeper for incoming emotional processes. Then the emotions wouldn't automatically control our behaviour. This would be likely to work with training, using methods and techniques similar to those used by clinical, health, and counselling psychologists, if these methods were adapted to the daily life where emotional contagion is likely to occur.

After all, many professionals remain calm in spite of the emotionally laden input inherent in their work. In my career as a psychologist I have had people come into group therapy in prisons and psychiatric wards expressing anger and demands to me. I did not argue back. (This doesn't mean I gave in to their demands.) By resisting the aggressive emotion individuals were conveying, as well as the temptation to reply angrily, many positive things were accomplished. We teach respect and trust. We acknowledge some truth in their position (as there usually is a modicum of truth), and by validating and addressing it, we make progress. I did not raise my voice and used respectful words, even when refusing their requests, knowing emotions communicate in ways we don't realize. People communicate subconsciously with emotions.

When the angry feelings of someone are validated, they lessen their anger. The listener can validate the feelings but not absorb them. If it triggers primitive tendencies to be angry and argue, ignore and block that feeling because that will not be helpful. It would inflame things, give the person what they want, and put them in control. Predicting this result gives you permission to ignore that feeling inside yourself.

Therapists are inoculated from being significantly infected by emotional contagion so that it does not infect them. It does not take over their behaviour and make it negative. There is no reason why you cannot learn to do this too. Learning how to interact constructively can prevent turmoil from happening.

Emotions magnify situations

When someone expresses emotion quickly and unexpectedly, you don't usually pause and think, "Now let's see, what could that have been about? Why are they doing that?" Instead, you also tend to react quickly. It is our brain's amygdala reacting. You catch the contagious emotion, reacting quickly with sudden emotion, an impulsive reaction to the contagion in the unexpected emotion that was just expressed. If we are not prepared, an emotion will automatically pull for another emotion to be expressed, as if they speak the same language: short, simple phrases, somewhat like children. This reaction is often angry and defensive, making tempers flare, like in the ping-pong game I discussed earlier. Or you may react by avoiding or withdrawing from the other person.

Try to think of a time in your life when you felt unexpected, surprising emotion, or perhaps a lot of emotion being expressed: what went on, what was said? Was it simple, a few words or short phrases? Probably. People don't think about using correct grammar in this state; that takes precious seconds to figure out, and by then the emotion is gone. People are more concerned with getting the words out quickly to express the emotion (or doing the reverse and impulsively avoiding the situation). But you can take ten seconds to assess the situation, think it through, and decide if you could and how you should respond. Or you could have a ready-made, short, empathic or helpful phrase to use, like "What's going on?" or, "Are you okay?" This can buy you more time to assess the situation and come up with a more meaningful phrase or action.

Having ready-made phrases like these to use in our own self-talk will help in these situations. Telling yourself that this is emotion in an emotional situation, that it could be emotionally contagious, and that you need to think before you act will help. Telling yourself, "Watch it," or, "Think first" can work. "Take it slow at first, make sure this is right." These short, pointed phrases you tell yourself will allow you to avoid impulsive behaviour. You could also include some positive phrases, if they fit, such as, "This is nice (the emotional situation) and if I go along with it, I'll make sure I am okay with what it represents and that it's not against my principles." And a few moments later, you'll make those judgments.

Sometimes self-talk isn't enough. The emotionality that flows in interpersonal discussion can overrule a more reasonable answer. A powerful, interpersonal flow from a dynamic person can produce automatic, impulsive thinking—especially when considerable movement is occurring. The contagion is more powerful when transmitted with little or no effort, with little sense of voluntary control. Crowds creating significant movement are situations which, by their nature, reward spontaneity and fast, intuitive, emotional thinking. Emotions become strong when people are physically close and catching feelings from each other. Crowds and parties are often places of emotional contagion, as psychological energy flows easily among people and most of us are not inoculated against it. This is why it is often best to avoid being around potentially inflammable situations that magnify emotions.

Problem situations involving tempers can easily develop, especially as that energy strikes people who have no awareness of the dynamics. Emotions spread like wildfire. Knowing this should be a caution not to catch other's emotions automatically as that could make such people more likely to behave impulsively. Thinking about what could happen in problem situations beforehand could help people either avoid them or resist the temptation to behave impulsively, since impulsive behaviours are usually driven by emotions that lead to poor decisions. Many people catch an emotion from someone else and react automatically, getting themselves into trouble, like when challenged to a fight, where some men foolishly think their masculinity is at stake.

It is best to defuse tense situations. A few words of empathy and concern would be a good start, reflecting on the words you hear and feelings you feel. It also defuses your tendency to be counter-contagious by reacting impulsively and defensively, an instinct seemingly designed to protect oneself if we are feeling challenged.

Taking perspective in order to handle emotional contagion

To illustrate how emotional contagion can sometimes oversaturate us, leaving us with more emotion than may be bearable, let's look at different perspectives by discussing how some people feel when living creatures die.

Extreme sadness or crying can be hard to bear and needs to fit the situation. Each person has a right to their own feelings, but you need to appraise the emotion first, before you absorb it into yourself, making sure it fits for you. For example, you probably don't want or need to cry about a dead bird, but if your friend finds one they might.[8] Crying doesn't usually fit that situation; most of us don't cry about a bird's death. It is a little sad, sure, and there is no right or wrong about it, but crying in this

---

8   If this example doesn't relate to your concerns, it is important to substitute other minor causes that can come up and apply these methods to the new situation.

case is not common for teens or adults. If your friend does cry a lot about it, that is their right, but it could be overdone and be hard to bear for either of you. If you find yourself crying just from feeling your friend's sadness about it, you are being infected by emotional contagion coming from your friend. In some instances this can be okay, but in this case it is probably not healthy. A few tears are understandable, because the bird is a creature of nature and has died. It is sad. Does it make sense to catch and imitate your friend's exceptionally sad feelings about the dead bird? Consider this carefully. If you feel yourself becoming sad or tearful, question whether this reaction fits you. Was the bird very special? Or very beautiful? If so, maybe it fits. There is no easy answer. As for the contagion, you can decide whether to allow it to affect your mood and how much. You could think about other things or simply change the subject. But don't rely on the other person to stop, because that won't work. This is for you. If you choose to do so, tell yourself not to absorb these feelings. They are not yours. They are the other person's feelings. There is no need to tell the person that; just tell yourself and then try to redirect your friend onto other topics. If it is hard for the friend to do that, you can think about other topics yourself, or look around for different things to see and think or talk about.

What if your friend's pet died? Many of us may feel very sad automatically. Your friend will probably be very sad for a while. Pets usually mean a lot to us, but the bird probably didn't. You may pick up your friend's feelings through contagion and feel them yourself. This is okay. You may feel this way if you are emotionally close to the friend, or maybe you can relate to it if you have (or had) a pet yourself. This is natural, healthy emotional contagion. Perhaps you have had previous positive contact with the deceased pet yourself and are sad; in that case, you share the feeling and may also absorb it through contagion. You probably had a relationship with the animal, and the animal had a name, unlike the bird.

Sharing is not the same as contagion. Sharing means you each have your own feelings directly from the source—in this case, the pet's death, if you knew the animal. Contagion means you take on your friend's feelings yourself. It is possible to do both: you can have your own feelings from the source while also absorbing some of your friend's feelings. If you didn't know the pet, you may just absorb some of your friend's sadness through contagion.

Negative emotional contagion in arguments

Feelings will flow during contentious public situations such as protests, riots, shootings, or volatile election campaigns. They often drive these events and provide the motivation for them to occur. We may feel angry, empathetic, or have other emotions when we observe a protest or riot on TV. These events may also be quiet and peaceful, but emotions can stir in quietness as well.

There are usually good points on both sides of an argument, but one side may be stronger because of well-thought-out reasons. You may fight for one side before assessing the other side fully. You may think—or even say—that the people on the opposing side, such as your political opposites, are "idiots" with "nothing good" about them. Then we get into the "us versus them" dilemma. These "hot thoughts" produce the angry feelings you may feel inside you. They produce the internal emotional language that can blind you to seeing something positive about the other side. This is another form of emotional infection. If you don't feel angry feelings, but are inclined to think those angry thoughts, it would be good to work at getting in touch with those angry feelings. You are probably not aware of them and need to tone them down to help defuse the angry thoughts or to get another perspective, such as "People have a right to a different opinion from mine, and I don't need to take it the wrong way. I have a good opinion also." This doesn't mean you have to change your view or give in; it just means you are trying to calm the anger and possible disrespect inside yourself to make your approach more manageable and more presentable. Then you can agree to disagree, remaining cordial instead of getting into an argument.

We need warnings about dangerous contagious emotions. They can be like lethal emotional viruses. They can spawn homicide, suicide, and other toxic actions. We have heard about that happening! But we can't wait for warnings or actions from government to stop toxic actions. We have to begin the process ourselves. We have to develop our gatekeeper to be able to close the gate to prevent toxic emotions from entering us. This keeps us safe and healthy.

Quite a few people can get easily worked up or upset, and as a result of contagious emotions that come forth, in the extremes they can lose their jobs or relationships. When we hear opinions on controversial topics, we also feel others' feelings. The emotions don't have to be obvious. They can be implicit. Feelings spread and are unwittingly caught by others who are affected by them.

Reacting to the emotions with a rational response to deflate the emotion could work. It could help change the course of action by introducing reasonable discussion. A wise step would be to realize that winning or losing is not at stake here. Winning the battle is not the same as winning the issue. With systematic reasoning and critical thinking, we realize that we can disagree. It does not mean that someone wins and someone loses. That is immature thinking; mature thinking means recognizing that we are different people and we see things differently. There is always more than one perspective to a situation, so it is better to agree to disagree. This way we respect each other's right to an opinion, even if we disagree with it. Why is it so important to have others think you are right? People can work on learning how to make mature individual choices. Nothing is learned in an argument or fight. When people are treated with respect, they don't need to fight back.

Emotional contagion is at play when the toxicity in the emotion feels threatening to the person who receives it, and they instinctively fight back with an emotional response. Emotions don't think. Emotions just feel. When you react with a feeling, the reaction back is immediate and impulsive. But the mind can think, and it needs to step in, interrupt the emotions, stop the back-and-forth game of emotional ping-pong and make a decision. This can be done by taking a deep breath and resisting the temptation to react. Making a comment from a neutral stance can help. Moving your body in a different way changes the pace and puts the rational mind back in control. Tell yourself that no, emotions are not in charge here, the mind is, and this is not a loss. The mind allows you to agree to disagree. Disagreeing is fine; people are different. You don't lose, you just disagree. You aren't humiliated, if someone else thinks you are, they are just showing immature thinking. You don't need to absorb the other person's simple emotional messages. Even if you did get the facts wrong, you are entitled to make a mistake. Nobody is perfect.

Our gatekeeper, the mind, decides when to allow incoming feelings to enter

You can develop your gatekeeper with effective thinking. Ask yourself if you want to feel these incoming emotions, taking them inside to be with your own emotions. Maybe you do, and maybe you should. Maybe you could let them in a little, or maybe not at all. You have to judge. Ask yourself, "What could go wrong if I were to act on this feeling?" Would the feeling add to the quality of your emotional well-being? You could regard what's happening in front of you to be just a story, one that has little impact on you. To do that, pretend you are watching a movie of what is happening. Does a deep voice mean you should believe the words spoken? Does a parade (that you might be watching) mean you should feel good? Is there anything the parade or the deep voice seems to be persuading you about? Are they celebrating a good cause? How do they persuade you? Are they correct? Do they just feel correct because of the deep voice or the loud music in the parade, or does their logic convince you? You need to ask yourself these questions, and they are really tough ones. Don't be an automatic skeptic or pessimist though. You don't want to block off good, healthy feelings. Just be aware. Your answers to your questions can be partial; they may not necessarily be one or the other. For example, you could allow yourself to enjoy the music in the parade but decide not to support the cause if you do not believe it is worthy.

Remember that positive emotions can be healthy for us, as long as our gatekeeper assesses them to be positive. A positive emotion would result in something generally legal, prosocial (contributing to social cohesion), and benefit and enhance well-being. Our gatekeeper, our mind, can allow positive feelings from positive triggers to blend with our feelings before the new positive feeling fully develops, so that when they start to overtake our mind, we trust them and allow it. When we love someone, or admire a teacher or politician, or are happy about an accomplishment that is positive, after our mind assesses objectively (not just with feelings) that these people are desirable for us, we absorb them fully.

We can be infected when we are around someone who feels happy. We can feel it as they show their happy feelings in their expressions. We sense it as they move around eagerly, spontaneously, trusting their movements, laughing, smiling, being optimistic and enthusiastic. They are probably making hopeful plans and anticipating a positive outcome. Our gatekeeper feels it and will likely allow us to start feeling happy ourselves, as long as the plans are along the lines of our personal ethics. It rubs off on us. The happiness is contagious.

Many may balk at the idea of stopping the automatic absorption of emotion because they may feel that catching and taking in another's emotions is a positive and wise choice, especially in our personal lives. That is true: taking in and absorbing a person's emotions and feelings can be a wonderful, joyous experience. That's not always the case. We have to ensure that there is a truly positive, appropriate activity that is associated with the positive feeling, and in order to do that the response should not be automatic. That's why we need a good gatekeeper to decide when to open and when to close the gates to incoming emotions. If you accept the positive feeling, sometimes the activity associated with it is also automatically accepted, when in fact it could be risky and this positive person may be a reckless thrill-seeker. Acting as gatekeeper is the job of the mind; it is the executive in charge of our behaviour, so we run the details of the plan through our mind and make sure it fits our principles, our style, and decide whether it is practical and safe for us now.

Emotions don't think, they just carry simple messages. Emotions feel, they react quickly; if they feel threatened, they get protective or aggressive, and we know that under acute stress, people fight, flee or freeze. This is the Triple F. Emotional contagion affects us all in society, but some more than others. Some are more susceptible to it perhaps because they are suggestible, or because they are heavily dependent on others for respect, self-esteem, or satisfaction, or maybe they have a greater need for emotional stimulation or affection. Research is not comprehensive in identifying the distinctions between various characteristics of susceptibility but indicates that people who are more susceptible to emotional contagion are more sensitive to others, have a higher self-esteem, and are more empathic compared to people who are less affected by others' emotions (Doherty, 1997). This is probably because their gatekeeper works well, increasing the benefits of emotional contagion. As well, emotional contagion for positive emotions and for negative emotions are partially distinct from each other (Manera et al., 2013).

Given what we know from research about the communication of emotions, emotional contagion in small groups, the importance of mirror neurons, and the voice's ability to carry and convey emotions, it is expected that emotional contagion would be present in contentious issues in society and make a critical contribution to turmoil. Accordingly, it is important for all of us as citizens, voters, neighbours, activists, politicians, managers, elected officials, governors, mayors, prime ministers, and presidents to learn how to manage our emotions in a responsible manner to reduce the infections of negative emotional contagion, thereby lowering the emotional temperature in society.

Negative or toxic feelings spread easily and contaminate rational thought

Studies show that emotional contagion most often occurs at a significantly less conscious level based on automatic processes and physiological responses (Barsade, 2002). Emotions have no logic, no rationality, no brains. Emotions at a subconscious level can carry their force right into the rational mind, sometimes overtaking it like a strong wind that you can't fight against, or a torrent of water that drags you down. Then the emotional interpretation dominates the rational thinking and makes it emotional. That's one effect of emotional contagion, and it happens without our realizing it. That's why it is important to learn to identify emotional contagion in daily life, assess the situation first, and develop our gatekeeper. You learn to recognize it this way, so that emotion doesn't automatically dominate and infect rational thinking. One of the ways to do that is to be more aware of your interpersonal environment, what the people around you are doing and feeling, what feelings they are expressing and exuding, and how those feelings strike you.

The problem with emotional contagion comes when the incoming emotions are negative and potentially harmful. That is why we call it contagion. Other than the spreading of disease, contagion is also defined as "the spreading of a harmful idea or practice"(Lexico, n.d.). An emotion or feeling can infect a person, taking over their rational, logical thought. This occurs because of the power of the emotion. A contagious negative emotion can seep into rational thought, contaminating and infecting it with the negativity of the emotion. For example, if we are hit with a feeling of hate or fear, that feeling is strong and so could infect us and affect our actions and decisions. We can learn to ignore the feeling: we don't have to act on it or even believe it is true. Just because it feels strong doesn't mean it is correct, because emotions don't think.

Emotional contagion can be harmful when we absorb hate, anger, distrust, cynicism, disgust, fear, depression, anxiety, and other painful emotions. These are infectious emotions that energize dormant beliefs and activate behaviour. We can spread the infection to hurt others. Emotional infection, like the dangerous viruses that spread germs, spread toxic and harmful feelings through emotional contagion.

Emotional contagion is not unhealthy if we let go of it right away, instead of absorbing it if it does not fit us. You catch the ball and realize that it is hot and you drop it. It is a split-second choice, depending on your judgment. A connection is not a catch. You make a choice to keep or reject the emotion. You probably want to reject these negative emotions; they do not fit. They bounce back, like the dodge ball. It may feel like they fit, but that's just because you've grown accustomed to the emotions and they are familiar. Familiarity is not a fit. Let it bounce back.

Emotional contagion infects rationality, rendering the mind incapable, for that moment, of being rational. Emotion, by definition, is irrational. It does, however, have a message, a simple one. When rationality integrates with that emotional message, resulting in wisdom, we can have some good judgment. Otherwise, there can be a torrent of negativity that completely overwhelms reason. We see this in the toxicity of depression with its distorted thinking, such that a person feels they are a failure, although failing (a verb) does not make you a failure (a noun). Everyone fails at something, but no one fails at everything. Alternately, the emotional infection can consist of a wave of happiness and optimism that also overwhelms reason, so that we think everything is good and that we should always be happy, when that is not logical.

Quick thinking instead of reasoned-out thoughts can be emotionally contagious

In Kahneman's System 1, discussed earlier, quick, emotional thinking dominates. System 2 allocates attention to slower, effortful mental activity. We have both systems. In System 1, quick automatic thoughts occur and result in emotional judgments, which haven't been thought through. There are many occasions in regular life, as well as in political life, where situations of emotional contagion occur when people engage in System 1 automatic thinking. Automatic thinking means there is no sensitivity to "the quality and quantity of the information that gives rise to impressions and intuitions" (Kahneman, 2011). It jumps to conclusions without evidence.

Jumping to conclusions means for many people, as Kahneman says, "what you see is all there is." Of course, this isn't so, but these people don't have a whole perspective. They have blinders on and fail to look around for evidence, or into the distance, literally and figuratively, possibly because of the emotion they feel about what they are looking at. Emotion can have that influence on someone. It can take over and appeal to the person so much that they don't look around for supportive information, and so probably don't think things through. If we can remember that there are different perspectives to consider in any given situation, even though the first one looks good, we can think more effectively. We are familiar with this when we go shopping. We see an item that appeals to us and we want to buy it. If we don't look around, we don't see the other item that is even better and is on sale that day. We need to look around some more. Many of us do this in a store or online but tend to forget when we don't have tangible items or pictures in view. For example, when you don't look around to see another candidate in an election to weigh the advantages and disadvantages of voting a certain way, and weigh them accordingly, as in a cost-benefit analysis, you are just reacting to all that is in your visual field: the one candidate you see and the emotion you may feel about him or her. Instead, you need to take off your blinders and consider the attributes of more than one candidate. You may be surprised at what you see.

When you are affected by emotional contagion, you can quickly get excited at what you see, and this involves emotion and blinders. When there are popular stances on either side of the political or social spectrum, people often ally quickly with one of those sides. This is done with quick thinking, which tends to rely on emotional input. Some people see something, get excited by it emotionally, and make their decision. Emotional contagion does that to us. The emotion infects the reasoning ability. This is important in voting. Reasoning can correct the feelings, which are often based on distorted thoughts. If there is an any alternative, consider it as well. This is systematic reasoning in its elemental stage.

Quick thinking seems to have the effect of making poorly thought-out statements that are delivered with stronger underlying, implicit emotion than well-thought-out statements. This is noted in subconscious emphasis on syllables and words when articulating the thought. Implicit emotion may have the strongest input. Statements can be emotionally contagious because of the emotion involved not only in a controversial issue, like abortion, but in the embedded, implicit emotion expressed when the position is taken and the corresponding statement made. The emotion embedded in the quick thoughts can affect us in ways of which we are often unaware because they may be subconscious. We are not just picking up the words or the opinions in the message, we are also picking up and even absorbing the anger, the anxiety, the blame, or the cynicism that goes with the negative message. These feelings can spread to others through emotional contagion. These feelings can become an urge due to the contagious emotions involved. False assumptions, fake news, rumours, and conspiracy theories fall into this category and are appealing to some people due to subconscious emotional contagion.

We see this in a lot in the drama that has unfolded in many of the controversial issues in 2020, and in previous years and decades. The recipient feels an emotion which speaks to them, and this emotion will often sway them to adopt a position, especially if they are leaning that way in the first place. Or they may vehemently disagree and enter the game of emotional ping-pong, arguing emotionally. Either way, the adoption of the position is affected by emotional contagion; people are then more likely to catch the emotion in the thought, probably because it feels good, or reject it immediately. Immediate rejection is caused by a phenomenon called counter-contagion, where the emotion is thought of as disgusting and is immediately repelled. This would be less likely to happen in a reasoned-out thought. Upon first hearing about a social or political stance, people who quickly ally themselves with one side or the other without any reflection may do so because it feels good to feel affiliated with a group of like-minded people. This is done instead of having a deliberate thought which would not be influenced unduly by potential emotion, and the feeling of acceptance and belonging involved in affiliation.

Having a philosophy of life with prepared positions on contentious issues will help as it can help you choose how to react when challenging situations crop up. When blended with having a respectful attitude towards others who may have different opinions, you can react in a reasonable, empathic way when you disagree. Put it this way: have a heart when you disagree. As Eleanor Roosevelt said, "Many people will walk in and out of your life, but only true friends will leave footprints in your heart" (AZ Quotes, n.d.).

To value life, you need to value both your life and the life of the other person in the discussion or argument, and value comes from respect. A reasoned-out thought has less emotion involved in it and so is less likely to have an emotional meaning to the person receiving it. A logical, reasonable, empathic thought that is meaningful and has good perspective would have a good blend of reason and emotion. It would be satisfying.

If a thought feels really good, it may have an emotional meaning. The emotion can automatically trump reason, so the suggested opinion needs to be verified or endorsed to ensure its reasoning is intact. And when the thought is based on emotion, most people do not reflect on it to see if it is logical, emotional, or halfway in between. A halfway thought is a wise thought, with some reason and some feeling, or maybe a little less emotion than reason. That is the safest kind.

In order to arrive at a reasoned-out thought, a person must spend more time choosing the words to form the thought, and in so doing block out the spontaneous input of the emotion. This is a good way to limit or minimize the production of contagious emotions, including contagious implicit emotions. It is important to remember the following if you want to reduce emotional contagion:

- Think and choose words carefully.
- Use fewer emotional words.
- De-emphasize drama in language.
- Minimize emphasis on certain emotional words when articulating the thought.
- Portray situations as accurately as possible with a focus on facts and details.

With thought, deliberation, and contemplation, people are more likely to independently come up with reasonably accurate thoughts based on their cognitive thinking process rather than their emotional process. This will involve a different part of the brain.

Any emotion should follow the cognitive aspect used, not contribute to it. In other words, well-thought-out concepts are less likely to be dominated by emotion and less likely to produce emotional contagion when spoken. People are more likely to catch the emotional thought, perhaps because it feels good, than if it were simply a reasoned-out thought. With a reasoned-out thought there is less emotion involved, and so is less likely to produce emotional contagion and have an emotional meaning to the person receiving it. The emotion has to be injected with some non-verbal enthusiasm by the speaker.

It is different when emotion takes over our thinking. We will then have many automatic thoughts that suddenly pop into our mind, and they are usually inaccurate and emotional, leading to distorted or inaccurate thinking. We need to be careful about the quick, automatic thoughts we have inside ourselves regarding the situation in front of us as they can be distorted by emotion, leading to dysfunction. When we are affected by emotional contagion in our personal lives, we are prone to react impulsively, triggered by an emotional challenge from the other person when they express strong feelings, especially in a rude, challenging way. We are then likely to be subjective, establishing our own point of view, and this is usually because it means something to us personally and emotionally. That's also what happens politically when people suddenly become defensive.

It is better to be objective in that moment to defuse tension from the emotional contagion and to slow down quick thinking. When you are objective you are blocking off your own personal reaction to the topic. You are also not commenting to yourself on the topic—or if you are, you can use empathy to tell yourself and the other person, "Yes, I can see why you are upset; you may have been wronged." The other person will often calm their emotional reaction if they sense you are agreeing or showing empathy. This would be true even if you haven't actually agreed, because you haven't actually concluded that the person has been wronged, or vice versa. You are just raising the possibility. This way you are buying some time, which allows you to switch from emotional arguments to cognitive-based evidence.

This prevents the emotional arguments that tend to set off our personal reactions. Emotional arguments and reactions give us internal sensations which can blind us to the reality of another perspective, so we may be lacking constructive, realistic thoughts in that moment. It is when we are caught up in emotionally based situations that the emotional contagion pushes these reasonable thoughts out of our mind. Many times, when we assess situations objectively, not in the midst of a situation, we will and do have reasonable, objective, accurate thoughts.

Toxic emotionality in politics and public discourse

When there are arguments or heated discussions, in order to maintain reason we always have to assess whether the opposing side's positives actually do fall short of the appeal of your side. They might, or they might not, but if you don't assess them objectively you are blinded to anything good about the other side. This is difficult emotionally and can be difficult politically.

Look at the facts objectively. Consider possible outcomes of the opposition's argument. Assessing things objectively takes you out of emotional thinking. You could then calmly say to yourself, "Although my opponent has a vastly different opinion from me, and doesn't see the likely impact of his plan, he has a good approach." Be specific about that. You could think, "He has people who take his position vigorously." You may know that already, but thinking it to yourself in the moment enables you to think clearly and not emotionally. It doesn't mean you are changing your mind. And you can take steps to tone down your own anger. Own your anger; tell yourself, "I really don't like his opinion." Do not tell yourself something like: "What an idiot!" Then you are letting your anger dictate your thoughts. That is internal emotional contagion, producing toxic emotionality. If you find yourself saying this internally, you can still challenge it ("I am letting my anger dictate my thoughts") and change it to a more constructive internal thought.

Toxic emotionality is really an emotional thought from emotion mind. It is difficult to measure, but we need to recognize it. We need to recognize the influence of emotional contagion dominating the political dialogue, both among the public and in the media— especially in areas where the dialogue gets emotional, dramatic. People can then get divisive. If we don't recognize it, we can't control it or regulate it. Otherwise, although we pride ourselves on being rational, we are in fact affected by the emotions that we pick up and absorb more than by the actual point being made. Then we could find that our viewpoint is changing, perhaps gradually, a little at a time, because it is affected by the feeling or implicit emotion that went along with the comments made. The changes can be gradual or sudden, but they are significant. We have a social and moral responsibility to understand and correct this.

These emotions are contagious because they are appealing to those people who absorb them into their own psyche. The emotions are strong and leave the person no room to think critically about what they are feeling. One's own emotions and feelings can change when people think seriously and analytically about them, but this doesn't happen with these overpowering emotions in these susceptible people, likely because they are so appealing and alluring. When this happens, those emotions take over and communicate with similar emotions found in other people. They feed off the emotional contagion of each other, pulling more in like magnets. The emotions come together in commiseration.

When emotions come together like this in people who have felt powerless and suspicious, they create an environment for conspiracy theories to start. Suspicion and cynicism are contagious feelings. Many people are cynical because there is a lot of corruption around us. People who have felt victimized look for an enemy, and powerful people are identified as having dominated them, robbing them of opportunity. Conspiracy theories will grow and grow, reinforced by the satisfying feeling that accompanies it and takes over the mind. Concrete, simplistic thinking develops, leaving any reasoning far behind. When emotion dominates, it is difficult to discern between corruption and power, wealth and authority. Not all people in authority are corrupt. Not all wealthy people are dishonest. But people who believe in conspiracy theories have a hard time differentiating this and instead lump them all together. These are people who group together and feel power that is very satisfying to them. They feel like they have an answer and have identified an enemy for their problem. Often the perceived enemy, when thinking simplistically, is someone in authority—cue the mob storming the U.S. Capitol building in January 2021. These are the results of the theatrics and drama in our current political environment.

Emotions only have simple messages, and they can be appealing to people with a shortage of emotional fulfillment. The messages seem absolute, but they are incorrect. By being absolute and appealing to people who do not practise critical thinking or systematic reasoning, these simple, emotional messages are easy to accept.

So don't play emotional ping-pong. Use rational thinking to realize that no one wins in these situations. Reason things out and think wisely instead. This is more important than winning a ping-pong game.

3

Coronavirus and Emotional Contagion

Emotional contagion has been front and centre during the COVID-19 pandemic. Peoples' emotions naturally have been hitting new heights. Fear has become contagious: it spreads and grows, as do anxiety and depression. Peoples' emotions are close to the surface; when this happens, emotions are contagious—they affect us and each other when we really do not want them to. We are irritable, have short fuses, and get impatient more easily. Isolation produces more family problems. We absorb many traumatic emotions from the pandemic via emotional contagion, subconsciously and consciously. It has a strong emotional impact on most people, and this affects their judgment. Fear and suspicion are rampant. When that happens, people may react emotionally when they wouldn't usually do so. Changing perspectives helps.

Emotional contagion has been front and centre during the COVID-19 pandemic. This is an unparalleled tragedy because millions of people have died. It is traumatic, and it is normal to feel traumatized. Emotional contagion affects us very significantly in situations like this. The rising death toll is announced every day. That gives us even more emotional impact. There are many who didn't believe it, dismissing it as false news. The disbelievers and the anti-vaxxers have also been affected by a strong emotional impact, and they contribute to the emotional climate (although they are using counter-contagion to deal with it).

Throughout the coronavirus pandemic, peoples' emotions have been hitting new heights and lows. Fear flows, people worry, and panic sets in. We are terrified as a society in many ways. Fear has become contagious, and it spreads and grows, as does anxiety and depression. Peoples' emotions are close to the surface; we are irritable, have short fuses, and get impatient more easily. Isolation produces more family problems. We absorb many traumatic emotions from the pandemic via emotional contagion, subconsciously and consciously. The pandemic has a very strong emotional impact on most people; they can get very emotional, and this affects their judgment. When that happens, people may react emotionally when they wouldn't usually do so. Emotions are contagious—they affect us when we really do not want them to. It is important to realize this about ourselves and those around us in order to understand what is happening. The fear, the dread, the depression, even the fatalism and pessimism can be more prominent because of the coronavirus.

The heightened emotions that result build on the strong emotions that are already present in the divided political world, and spread further. Emotions from one person or group can combine with emotions from another person or group as they come together. Emotions may tangle and create conflict in counter-contagion because they are very quick to get into that ping-pong game. They begin to one-up each other, which is how fights and conflicts start. People may argue about things they wouldn't usually argue about, due to the heightened emotion. Emotions don't think. They just react. When this happens, damage and destruction often result.

Although the pandemic and politics are different, they are related; the former president shut down the pandemic task force already set in place by his predecessor, who had foreseen the possibility of a pandemic. The feelings from the pandemic then collided with the feelings about the political divide, setting each other off. Some people thought the reaction to the pandemic was a political focus, and others thought it was a health focus. In a high-level game of emotional ping-pong, they came together in a dangerous mix of emotions, producing conspiracy theories, heightened suspicion, and heightened vulnerability, resulting in a need to protest perceived destruction. The threshold for emotional explosion (the level of tolerance for internal suppression of emotion) would be lower in some individuals at a time when emotional turmoil is high.

Perspective, context, and the role of emotion

But let's slow down, stop, and think. An important way to overcome the effects of emotional contagion is to look at the data, facts, and figures. It is important they be accurate, focused, and relevant. Data can help us keep focused and calm and look at the facts in an unbiased way. Study the data then let yourself react emotionally.

Worldwide, millions have died from COVID-19 (Statista, n.d.). We might think as a result that getting COVID-19 is an automatic death sentence. People who hear of the large death toll while thinking with their emotions may irrationally interpret it as doomsday. However, far more millions have recovered from COVID-19—about 95 percent. That figure should make us breathe easier than we would by looking only at the high death toll. Data can also have the effect of making us believe what we want because of confirmation bias. That might make us interpret a recovery rate of over 95 percent to mean we can disregard the danger of the disease, because the interpretation's positive emotion could convince us to drop our guard. We can't. COVID-19 is a lethal disease. If there were a 5 percent chance that a glass of water contained toxins that would kill you, would you drink it? No? Good choice.

Recognizing the number of people who have recovered from COVID-19 puts these figures into balance. Although caution is still important, we know that the disease is not an automatic death sentence. It could, however, still result in death, and that is where the panic sets in. The virus is real. It has affected our lives in a tragic way. We can't comprehend the large number of deaths conceptually, especially since each death by itself is a significant loss. It is a very large number. The individuals who died blend into each other and there are so many we can't appreciate them as individuals. We can't process this well. It is very sad and makes us fearful. Those emotions are contagious. This emotional contagion affects some people significantly, rendering them housebound and fearful of going outdoors at all, even with a mask, because of fear of infection. This is severe anxiety infecting our judgment. While we need to be cautious, we don't need to be housebound. To do so suggests we are almost sure to be exposed just by going outside when the reality is nowhere near that bad, unless we are immunocompromised, in which case it is a rational choice.

Other fatal illnesses

It is important to change our perspectives to get us out of the narrow thinking that causes emotional contagion and coronavirus panic. Think of it this way: In the U.S., there were about 80,000 deaths from influenza in the winter of 2017–18 (Stat. CDC, 2018). That's just a few years ago. Those deaths were not broadcast daily on CNN, Fox News, or MSNBC. There was very little fear. Let's give this more context. The number of deaths from nephritis, nephrotic syndrome, and nephrosis in the U.S. in 2017 was 50,633 (Centers for Disease Control and Prevention, n.d.). That is a large number, but that figure was not broadcast daily on the news either. Many people do not even know what nephritis is, let alone that it was one of the leading causes of death in the U.S. that year. (It is a kidney disease.) Should there be a strong emotional impact from this? Probably. We could get a kidney disease. The possibility could be scary—but it wasn't. We didn't know about it, and the news media didn't keep track of the number of daily deaths. If it had, we might have been scared.

In the U.S., heart disease and cancer, the two leading causes of death, together account for 1,258,682 deaths per year (Centers for Disease Control and Prevention, n.d.). These totals are not on the news either. That is a lot more deaths than those caused by COVID-19. But we know how to treat those two, whereas COVID-19 is a new disease.

Let's examine this in the context of emotional contagion. This provides a perspective for discussing the impact of the pandemic's deaths so far. We could think that that the number of deaths from COVID-19 seem exaggerated when compared with deaths from other diseases. It seems that the coronavirus pandemic is somehow being highlighted. But these are real figures. Even so, some people do not believe the numbers are real. This is cognitive dissonance, "an unpleasant psychological state resulting from inconsistency between two or more elements in a person's cognitive system. It is presumed to involve a state of heightened arousal and to have characteristics similar to physiological drives. [...] [It] creates a motivational drive in an individual to reduce the dissonance" (APA, n.d.). For these people who believe the pandemic is fake or exaggerated, seeing a huge number of people sick in the hospital from a rampant, lethal virus is against their beliefs about what could happen. Rather than being flexible and altering their thinking to include this new information, they let the statistics trigger suspicious and cynical thoughts in order to maintain their position that this couldn't happen. This lets them keep their own perspective of the situation. Their cognitive dissonance and its unpleasant state are reduced. Any belief in data exaggeration comes from a person's unconscious bias, which they superimpose on the data to interpret it the way they want. That will produce emotional contagion or counter-contagion, as people keep old beliefs and undertake risky behaviours, like refusing to wear a mask. Because of emotional contagion, many people are tense and quick to condemn those whom they perceive as wrong. If they are condemned for this behaviour, then division occurs, and people are split into two camps. To prevent this, we need to be sensitive and empathic when dealing with such people, withholding our anger while pointing out the serious risks to them.

For conspiracy theorists who believe that COVID-19 doesn't exist, the situation seems so large that it is incomprehensible. It is understandable how that happens when other data is minimized in the news, confirming that there is always an ounce of truth in a person's perception. This is an emotional effect, short-circuiting the brain's logical, critical thinking. To deal with this overwhelming environment, they then decide it is fake. This is massive denial, which calms them down and gives them a feeling of control over their fear. But it is not fake; these are real figures. The confirmed recovery rate is over 95 percent. That ounce of truth is only an ounce. It is truly sad that their perception that it is fake is not correct.

Majority and minority opinions

In precautions against COVID-19, most people are either "for" or "against" masks, and it has become a political issue. This is typical of emotional contagion, when people go into one camp or another and fail to see any merits in the other side. When emotions run high in society, people tend to forget to look for strengths and weaknesses on both sides. They don't choose a more logical approach based on merit. Finding merit and evaluating pros and cons will help tone down the emotion. There is nothing political about this: that perception of politicization comes from the reactions of people with panicked emotions.

Logic succumbs to the effects of emotion as the emotional stakes are raised. Many people are suspicious of being told what to do, especially by the government. This is emotion-based, likely reflecting trust or fear issues. As a result, there are many people who are against wearing masks, physically distancing, and washing hands regularly, despite being warned frequently about the risks. Emotion will trump common sense if people don't think about it. There are people, including some world leaders, who thought originally that COVID-19 was a hoax. *USA Today* reported near the onset of the pandemic that they received letters from people "who truly believe the virus is 'no worse than a cold' or 'another strain of the flu' unduly panicking 'knee-jerk sheeple.'"(Carroll, 2020). This denial of fear and resulting irrational labelling are effects of emotional thinking.

It may feel risky emotionally to take a minority position in society. Most informed people do not equate COVID-19 with a cold since there have been so many deaths from the virus while colds are not lethal. With contagious emotions running rampant, it feels like it would take some courage to side with the minority, or even see some positives in their viewpoint, when that position is not consistent with the facts.

However, one of the effects of emotional contagion is that we are swept to one side or the other by contagious emotions. People who judge with their emotions want to be in the majority, to be accepted; alternately, they are willing to fight for a minority position, because they are fighters. These are decisions that can be influenced by internal emotions, making them prone to emotional contagion. We need to overrule this and ensure that our decisions are primarily influenced by objective fact.

Since emotional situations occur when people take opposing sides, let's do an exercise seeing the positives on the other side of the coin instead of immediately, angrily pre-judging, which often happens when emotions run high. For this exercise, let's try to side with the minority in an argument, in order to work on overcoming the effects of emotional contagion. We don't have to agree with anything we don't think we should agree with but it will help us learn to do this process. In order to do so, we have to discuss this while at the same time agree not to let our emotions take over while it is being discussed. We have to use rational thinking and not be emotional. This way we learn to lower the emotional reaction; it also allows us to catch what distorted thoughts we may have that are causing that reaction. We all have distorted thoughts. The goal is to reduce them, not eliminate them.

To start with, it is important to realize that there is usually some merit on both sides of an argument or position, even if it is only a small amount. It is rarely a case of one side being totally right and the other side being totally wrong. For example, perhaps someone told the story that their grandparent, who had a cold, but died of pneumonia, died of a cold. They misconstrued the cause of death as a cold because they were emotional about the death. When someone close to you dies, you may not attend to the details. So, in a way, they were right, although not factually, and so they should be treated with sensitivity and respect, not scorn. Misunderstandings like this are often the cause of misconstrued cause-and-effect that come up during emotional times. Right or wrong is technically decided by facts and data, but at a time of loss, facts take less importance for the bereaved. A better way of saying it could be *correct* or *incorrect*, since using terms like *right* or *wrong* could provoke emotional reactions. Even deeming something correct or incorrect has to be determined by someone, and emotional contagion can cause people to argue with those in authority, and sometimes even with the facts. Some people find fault with authority figures.

It is important to respect people on both sides of an argument, regardless of their position on a topic. They have feelings, and if we disagree it is important to withhold any contempt about their opinion. Valuing the freedom in our countries means we have to respect the rights of all people to have their opinions without being angry, defensive, and emotional about it, as long as people are responsible and civil. When we approach the discussion, people on both sides need to be willing to be rational, not emotional, and consider the possibility that the other side could have some valid points to make. There is usually some merit to either side of a discussion, and people just want recognition for that.

Some people want to be right and win their case so badly that they put their ego out front. There is a lot of competition for value and credit. Many people feel that there is not enough credit given to the "average" person these days, and when contentious issues come up, "average" people want some credit. When they don't feel like they get credit, some may fight for it, sometimes by taking a controversial position that gets them attention. There is so much suspicion and cynicism. Many people don't trust experts, so they go to other ideas of where the merit is, often in the minority viewpoint. They will often do this just to get attention, hoping for some credit.

It is the idea of winning or losing that stirs up emotions when someone takes it as a personal reflection on themselves. The facts and details may favour one side over another, but that doesn't mean the person is a winner or loser, because we all win at some things and lose at other things. The emotion attached to a topic may provide emotional fuel for an argument to attack their sense of self-worth, even when there is no accuracy, truth, or merit to either argument. Everyone has ideas, some more than others, but so what? That doesn't make the person with more ideas a better person, or more worthy. There is always merit on each side, even if one side is favored by the facts. We don't need to allow a loss to dictate our sense of self-worth because then we are the victim of emotional infection, likely started with the effects of emotional contagion. We can discuss and debate many topics over a lifetime without being a winner or loser. That is emotional thinking. We can all make mistakes and have mistaken opinions and still be worthwhile.

The fact remains, however, that individuals have perspectives on situations, and this causes emotions. This is natural. But the emotions, although genuine, should not colour one's perspective on the whole topic unless wisdom is used to tone down the emotion. We want to be sensitive, tender, and caring for people who are hurting, because it could be us and we would want to be treated that way. We want to show compassion for people who are on both sides of an argument. That works. Arguing and fighting don't. We know that. No more ping-pong, back and forth trying to one-up someone or proving who is right. It doesn't matter. Our status as a human being is not at stake here. We are all right and wrong some of the time. If people are judgmental about a mistake, ignore them. We all make mistakes. We usually try to correct them. If you have to pass judgment, do it in a sensitive, respectful way.

Does it feel strange to give emotional support, in a sense, to people on both sides of an argument? People commonly feel resentment when an opposing argument is made, as if the person making the point were favouring the other side. This isn't the case. We are respecting people on both sides of an argument, or a situation, since there is respect and merit on both sides. Remember, winning or losing does not really matter, although many people think it does.

Grieving as a society has to be postponed

The world needs to grieve. We need to allow ourselves to feel the feelings after the fact, when we are no longer in the middle of handling the trauma. This means allowing ourselves to feel emotional pain, to be sad, angry, worried, depressed, and then put it behind us and move on. But there has been no time to grieve as the pandemic continues. We are still scared, sad, and worried. Grieving as a society will happen towards the end of the pandemic when we can look back. During it, grieving is left to individuals or small groups. Later, people will be angry about this and look for a villain. Then emotional contagion will take over again. To help with grieving and adjusting to a new, post-pandemic world, changes to prevent this from happening again will need to be real and trustworthy in order to lower people's sense of fear and build trust.

Grieving needs to be done with others, through memorials, services, and tributes held in public venues. Otherwise they are feelings more than emotions because they sit inside all of us who grieve, worry, and fret privately, not always expressing them. A feeling is usually private, and certainly personal. In some people, especially the introverts, a feeling will sit inside of us without being expressed directly. It contributes to the psychological underground, as it often holds a simple message, like despair or disillusionment. It would be healthier to discuss and express them openly. Those same repressed feelings can ooze out anyway, emitted unknowingly through behaviour or comments, contributing to the emotional atmosphere. It affects all of us in one way or another, coming from many sources.

A one-to-one relationship exists between each person and the source of their grief, be it death, or suffering, or feeling empathy for those who have been affected. Apologies and condolences to those who have been affected; my heart goes out to you. Many of us pick up the sadness and worry circulating throughout the emotional atmosphere. We talk about it and share our feelings with each other. When feelings and emotions are shared, it can lessen the effects of emotional contagion.

Many are grieving tangible losses. We are sad. Let's face it: this pandemic is a terrible thing. We grieve for the many who have died and grieve in empathy with those who have lost loved ones. We need to grieve, but cannot grieve fully until it is over, and even then not right away. It will come gradually. We are also worried. Grief is contagious but we don't always let ourselves feel it. We need to. It values life and addresses the emotional effects of the loss of life. And many young people died during the pandemic, adding a real shock to the sadness. When we expect death, say if the person is quite elderly, we have already started to grieve a little. Not so when a young person dies, that is often very shocking.

Part of grieving is dealing with angry feelings towards something—in this case, towards the virus. People are frustrated, irritable, and angry. That is natural. They carry suppressed anger. Being angry at something does not necessarily mean you have strong outbursts of anger, rage, or hate. In fact, anger is a normal emotion. What is involved here is carrying around strong dissatisfaction and unhappiness at something, which may cause the grouchiness.

Even though the virus is not a person, it is still possible to feel angry at it. This anger is contagious as we can both relate to it and share that feeling with others. But remember that it is easy to feel angry at other things when you are already angry at one thing. Guard against that internal emotional contagion.

You might think that you can't be angry at an intangible thing. But you can. You probably have a lot of angry feelings at the virus for disrupting your life, putting you at danger, and killing many, many people. It may show up not as outward anger, but as irritation, annoyance, or a short temper. That is a natural offshoot of carrying this suppressed anger.

To handle this anger, write an emotional letter. "Dear virus, you have made me angry because..." Write down your feelings about why you're angry at the virus. Give examples and situations. Don't worry about whether it makes sense or not. Don't hold anything back; don't worry about logic—you are purposely using emotion in your letter. You could, for example, write that you are angry because the virus has murdered over a million people in the world. You could make it more personal, writing how it has disrupted your life. There are many different reasons you might be angry at this virus. You're getting your feelings out, and that's healthy. Use emotional, irrational language at this time. See what comes up and how you feel after doing it. You could discard the letter after you have written it, or you could keep it for awhile to honour those feelings.

When you get your feelings out in this way, you are releasing suppressed, pent-up emotions. It can help make contagious emotions less appealing to you because when you deal with your emotional baggage, you are less likely to attract emotionally contagious feelings that would combine with your underlying unresolved feelings.

The media, the news, and contagious emotions

The emotional reaction to the news can be instant. We have seen this often in the last few years, and it has been worsening. We are not protected from the news. We are told it is our responsibility in a democracy to get the news. But news is not presented as just facts. It has an emotional tone. It is often presented in a dramatic way, which spreads contagious emotions. Then the news about the pandemic and the political divide and many other contentious issues catches the contagious emotions and spreads them to susceptible people, and so creates an even higher emotional tone among the public. It is up to us to lower this by carefully considering how we consume the news and how much we take it in.

An article in *Health Psychology* (Garfin et al., 2020) about media coverage of COVID-19 warns that information to the public should "be conveyed without sensationalism or disturbing images" to avoid "increased anxiety [and] heightened stress responses that can lead to downstream effects on health, and misplaced health-protective and help-seeking behaviors that can overburden health care facilities." They give examples of previous public crises, like acts of terrorism or other epidemics, "where media coverage of events had unintended consequences for those at relatively low risk for direct exposure, leading to potentially severe public health repercussions." Emotional contagion produces panic through media and social media, and many people catch it. Instead, the authors recommend that the public "should be advised to avoid speculative stories and limit repetitious exposure to media stories." Many people tend to believe what they read, as if that's all there is to it, instead of wondering if there may be more to the story. This can induce serious emotional contagion. Having healthy skepticism about the news or thinking critically about different aspects to any given situation the media covers can prevent emotional contagion.

Repeated media exposure to the outbreak can cause psychological distress. This has serious implications for immediate suffering but also for continued negative effects on physical and mental health over time. The article states that: "heightened stress responses during and in the immediate aftermath of a threatening event are associated with adverse physical and mental health outcomes over time." (Garfin et al., 2020) Emotional contagion would seem to spread these mental health outcomes. Suggestibility and emotional outbursts are more likely in stressful times when we are more susceptible to the influences of emotional contagion. Remember when you are watching the news that good things are always happening, but they don't usually make the news.

With suggestibility we get conspiracy theories. We have to ensure we don't continuously take in too much of the bad news about COVID-19. It is too stressful, and that stress spreads. We may not realize that we are in emotional denial about the vast numbers of deaths from the coronavirus; it is difficult to comprehend the impact, so we overlook it.

The media uses "headline news," as when the Olympics were cancelled, or when all major league sports in North America were cancelled, or when all soccer games in Europe were played mostly without spectators. The media does its best to sensationalize events like these, which inflames and spreads the emotional contagion. *Politico* even referred to a need to stem panic gripping huge swaths of the nation in the early days of the virus (Rayasam & Reddy, 2020). The term *huge* is defined as great size, scale, or scope, while *swath* is defined as a long broad strip or belt (Merriam-Webster, n.d.) So "huge swaths" refer to extremely large areas of land. It would seem, then, that extremely large areas of land are gripped by panic. Even if we know consciously that this is not true, images of chaos can produce subliminal anxiety and panic. They then contribute to the development of anxiety disorders in those who think with an emotional mind. When people become anxious, they can spread the feeling. But we don't have to absorb that emotionally contagious anxiety.

Consider this: in one of the most obvious cases of emotional contagion spread by the media, *Politico*, in the same article as mentioned above, wrote: "The world is drowning itself in hand sanitizer and suffocating itself with fear." This is hyperbole. Even though most people are aware this is a metaphor, the wording itself— and the image it evokes—insensitively uses *drowning* and *suffocating* as descriptors. This spreads a lot of subconscious fear by referring to horrendous ways of dying, at a time when people are especially afraid of death. It even manages to ridicule people who are taking necessary safety precautions. Applying critical thinking to a headline takes cognitive effort, which is not what headlines are designed to allow.

Much of this is irresponsible journalism. People in the media can catch emotions also. This is how emotions are heightened and spread, because they affect us subconsciously through System 1. People who are prone to emotion mind are likely to have their mental processing occur in images and come to quick judgments, as emotions don't think. They feel. So, we get a greater degree of emotion, in many people, through emotional contagion. So-called hysteria occurs among people, that emotion spreads, and news media and social media contribute to it. We need to ask if the headline writers are affected by emotional contagion themselves because they certainly contribute to it and pass it on in a heightened manner. Or maybe they just know readers want it, so they provide it.

As you take in information from the media, you may have angry reactions and other strong emotions. You have a right to feel angry at various politicians, leaders, governments, countries, hospitals, and a myriad of other entities. But you have to manage your anger first so you can take responsible action, the type that will likely have more positive impact. Destructive anger proves nothing and only gets people into trouble, and certainly does not get your point across. If you channel the anger into appropriate methods, it is more likely to be effective. Use the anger to be assertive but not aggressive. Don't give up: you can write letters, make phone calls, and join political parties and action groups and work on making changes. But first you need to deal with your anger. A good way of dealing with your anger is to make healthy changes, which would come, in part, from your own positive actions.

Another aspect we need to remember during the coronavirus pandemic (and during other stressful times) is that stress weakens our immune system and actually increases our risk of infection (The Conversation, 2020). You need a strong immune system to fight the virus.

Disgust, cynicism, and fear regarding coronavirus and the influential psychological underground

In the early stages of the pandemic, panic affected people so much that they became "panic buyers" of toilet paper. It now seems that there are two different personality types: those who felt the need to buy many rolls of toilet paper in case the supply ran out, and those who didn't understand why the others needed to buy so much. This is a classic example of emotional thinking because people are not using facts. They want control and security, and accumulating toilet paper somehow gives it to them. They may not believe the news media or the government because they are cynical. Cynical people do not trust the experts to empathize with them; in this case they assumed that stores would close, leaving them unable to buy toilet paper. This is the effect of fear and depression overtaking our ability to reason, think, and apply knowledge at a time of great crisis. We easily catch other's emotions.

The "Psychology Works" Fact Sheets produced by the Canadian Psychological Association (2020) says that fear is contagious, so when you see people buying too much toilet paper, you start to believe that toilet paper may run out, leading you to rush out and stock up needlessly. People feel inclined to assume that there is a good reason for the desperation they see around them, and worry they have missed some important development. They think, erroneously, that they had better follow suit just to be safe. This is emotional contagion in action. If you ask a person why she is buying so much toilet paper, you will probably sense the desperation and panic in her voice when she says, "I need to get it now before it runs out, because you never know." This isn't a rational reason, but you could pick up her desperation and think there is something else going on. In reality, however, the bad news about coronavirus spreads the feelings of disgust, fear, cynicism, depression, and panic. These feelings are contagious and spread, producing the toilet paper rush.

Unfortunately, this has serious consequences when it affects the economy. Fear hit the stock market, and it reportedly initially experienced its greatest crash since 1987. The BBC (2020) reported that "stock markets dived as investors worried that the world's biggest central banks may now have very little ammunition left to deal with the effects of the coronavirus if the global economic climate continues to worsen." Some people thought the virus would affect the stock market. But viruses cannot infect abstract entities. It is common for experts who are less familiar with psychology to leave people, with their many characteristics and differences, out of this equation, giving an incomplete picture. The virus has a very strong impact on people, making them emotional, and these contagious emotions affect their judgment. It is emotional contagion that is having a very profound impact on the market. People were worried that their pension values will drop and think that investment performance will influence their savings. People do panic, and panic begets more panic. The same emotions that people experienced with their toilet paper rush transferred to fear that the market would crash. It transfers so easily if we don't stop and think about it.

We know that when the unknown is involved, people will default to imagining the worst possible scenario. This will affect how they handle their investments. Panic selling occurs. This creates a self-fulfilling prophecy, when one predicts something so strongly based on their own fears and prejudices that it comes true through desperate actions. Then it multiplies when people see it happening and do the same thing. One cannot help but suspect that our actions driven by contagious fear, and not the virus, is the real culprit causing the stock market to crash.

People in general tend to think of the worst-case scenario when they think the unknown is going to happen. Fear is there in the emotional atmosphere in a time of turmoil and is contagious. It is natural for fear to infect us so that we tend to stay away from things due to fear of the virus. This could, at times, be irrational. This thinking is likely to continue to infect us beyond the pandemic, as fear will influence our thinking and beliefs about safety and health heading forward. We fear the unknown, but the term *unknown* is misleading. We don't know what will happen. But we do know that some things are known and hence predictable in life. It is natural to be afraid. We tend to exaggerate when we are anxious. Panic could make some of us exaggerate and create fictional doomsday scenarios that we think are real. But we know about a lot of things.

We know the sky remains above us and gravity keeps us on the ground. We know how to handle many stresses. That doesn't mean we know it all. In many ways we are in uncharted territory, but it is not completely uncharted. We have overcome health scares many times; this is a bad one, but, whether short-term or long-term, it is temporary.

Even after social distancing and mask-wearing ends, fear is likely to continue, at least for awhile. People are likely to be socially phobic and agoraphobic, thinking that they have to avoid circulating in public for a few months to ensure that the pandemic is really over. Fear prevents them from doing normal things, like going outdoors. There are those who deny the possibility of illness, and then proceed to fall ill, and even die of COVID-19, demonstrating how strong fear is in controlling our minds, even through denial. If we deny that we are fearful, it lingers in our subconscious and can cause physical health issues through psychosomatic means, or by allowing the stress to suppress our immune system. It is usually better to face the fear and overcome it.

As the pandemic drags on, most people seem to become more pessimistic that recovery will be soon. But change does happen. It is inevitable, just not always immediate. When it is over, you will want to appreciate that you survived, and you played it smart, even if the recovery process takes years. You have the rest of your life to live. Don't expect it to be over and back to normal soon because then you will become depressed. This doesn't mean it will continue forever in a tough way. We can hope for the best—just don't expect it. We have to anticipate that some changes will be permanent, and that's okay. We have adjusted to many changes over the years.

We know that when people feel good (which we will again), they will buy and spend, and the market will recover. Use that knowledge to continue to make wise decisions. Short-term pain brings long-term gain. It is worth the wait. The short-term pain may last longer than you thought, and hopefully it's not horrible for you. Enjoy the positives about socially isolating if you can. Take up a hobby. Make your life more enjoyable and meaningful.

Fear of death

What's behind the virus panic is the possibility that you may die waiting for a cure. This is a real fear for people. The focus on the coronavirus (and the drama and anxiety it brings) attracts a lot of viewers for the news networks, but it also reminds us to make our lives more worthwhile and meaningful while we are still alive, and to take the opportunity to stay healthy and continue to grow and develop while we still can.

Many people have anxiety about dying, and that may be why they are anxious about the virus. Emotions like anxiety can bring simple but false messages, like "Be careful," "Bad things are happening," and "It is scary." Ironically, it is tempting to accept the anxiety without knowing if we should. Fear is contagious, so check out the facts. What bad things are happening? People are dying from COVID-19. That is scary. But how prevalent is it? Were the people who died taking precautions? Do you? How many have died in your region? Did they have underlying conditions? How likely is it that if you physically distance, wear a mask, and wash your hands that you will be safe? Do you follow public health guidelines? Have you independently checked the science to see if the rules are reasonable? There are a lot of questions to ask. Collecting data helps you make an informed decision about the likelihood that you will die. That's what you need to do: make an informed decision.

Psychologically, two things seem to lie behind the fear of death. First, what will happen to us when we die, and second, what are we leaving behind on Earth? Most cultures and traditions accept that when we die either we will cease to exist in any form, or we will exist in some form of an afterlife. If the former is true and there is no continuation of existence at any level, we will not have a consciousness to know about this, and so it doesn't really matter. If the latter is true, then we deal with it in whatever exists in the afterlife, predicting without certainty that a better-lived life will have a better afterlife. So if we live a better life on earth, and the first option is true, then we will be more fulfilled and productive when alive. If the latter is true, it will continue into an afterlife. We can't know for sure, so we may get anxious because we may think the worst will happen. That is just anxiety speaking.

Regarding the second factor: this is the worrisome part, because we will no longer be alive for others to benefit from our existence, and we think we will miss the experience of being alive and seeing our loved ones. So we need to improve our relationships with others, making sure there are no regrets, that all guilt is resolved, and that we have told our loved ones that we love them. Let's live a good life, and that is up to you to define it. What constitutes a good life, and how could you change your life for the better right now?

We see emotional contagion flourish in the anxiety in the coronavirus pandemic. We need to be aware of the anxiety, as it is largely justified, without letting it get the best of us. Being aware of it allows us to contain it. There are many methods to deal with anxiety. Because otherwise, when crises hit, the anxiety that comes takes over and produces outcomes likely worse than the actual crisis.

Conspiracy Theories

Conspiracy theories flourish in a crisis like a pandemic. Suspicion is contagious. Rumours spread. We get cynical. Some people rebel. In an atmosphere of danger, conspiracy theories blossom and become contagious in the "collective subconscious." Collective emotions accrue. People seek meaning by thinking emotionally when things are uncertain, in an attempt to gain control. So they may believe false details to be true facts. Vaccine hesitancy reflects trust issues and disgust issues. For large issues like COVID-19 people seek large causes, like 5G cell phone towers, to match the extent of the issue.

Conspiracy theories flourish in times of crisis, when massive distrust is spread through emotional contagion. People need control and predictability, and they can get it by making up ideas and events.

Emotional contagion has been rampant throughout the coronavirus pandemic. Conspiracy theories have been around for decades, but recently they have become more plentiful. Suspicion of legitimacy is high and easily spreads to susceptible people through emotional contagion. It becomes contagious as trust falters. If a person is already suspicious of the government's motivations, it is easy to catch more suspicion from others. This happens if a person hears suspicious comments, and the distrustful emotion in someone else's tone. They are likely to feel then validated and accepted by their like-minded peers. As a result, many people may believe their suspicion is legitimate, and that feeling builds a little more, creating "proof" that they must be right. This is the effect of emotional contagion: the positive feelings from having others validate a suspicion leads to emotional infection, which infects our reasoning processes. It may then spread to a greater number of people who are susceptible to catching it.

A few people being suspicious of the same thing can indicate some weak justification. Corruption among the powerful exists and justifies some suspicion. The effect of contagious emotion, however, makes the suspicion much stronger than it should be. Then it spreads to produce suspicion among people in ways that can become dangerous and lead to conspiracy theories. Confirmation bias tells us that many people will fit the facts to their beliefs, rather than the other way around. This can be emotionally satisfying, especially to those who feel relatively power-less. Confirmation bias is "the tendency to gather evidence that confirms pre-existing expectations, typically by emphasizing or pursuing support-ing evidence while dismissing or failing to seek contradictory evidence" (APA, n.d.). Confirming pre-existing expectations is so satisfying to many people that they would let it overrule their logical mind to the point of dis-missing contradictory evidence. This may be because the emotional need to be suspicious is especially meaningful to those people who like to take control and cannot tolerate anxiety from ambiguity.

If there are greater numbers of people who feel suspicious about some-thing, it is not proof. There is no proof in numbers. It is the impact of the buildup of emotional and social contagion among suggestible people, often over the internet, that ends up in a conspiracy theory. People can share those cynical feelings together socially, commiserate together, and even organize plans of action, even if ineffective. It is easy to take concrete action and blame something tangible and visible, like a 5G cell phone tower. Among people who think this way, it is almost as if someone is not cynical then something is wrong with them. For example, some people believe that it should be obvious to everyone that all governments and cor-porations are corrupt, and that we shouldn't listen to them. This is a very toxic, infectious belief, resulting in the public defying recommendations, distrusting their government, and gathering in public places without masks and without keeping social distance. A few months into the pan-demic, many people reportedly thought the coronavirus was being used as a cover to install tracking devices inside their bodies. Later, rumors spread online that a tracking microchip planted by the government to sur-veil the movements of Americans was an ingredient in Pfizer's corona-virus vaccine (Wu, 2020). Coronavirus denial was still rampant in some spots late in 2020.

This seems to be caused by a need to rebel against authority and might be true for those people who have felt a loss of control of their lives. They are having difficulty understanding how this happened, so they find a reason in fantasy. There may be a cynical, anti-social assumption that all governments and politicians are corrupt, so it is smart to realize this and rebel. They see the coronavirus pandemic as a hoax, and proof that the government is corrupt and has caused this pandemic for their own selfish interests at the expense of the people.

It is hard, though, to dispute that the government and companies might be corrupt these days (Abramson, 2020; Stedman, 2019). It is easy to see how these theories can be calming for people who correctly feel much distress about the loss of control occurring in society. It can be tempting to believe them when they bring relief, since relief brings positive affect which is reinforcing. That positive affect is scarce these days, as we don't get a lot of good news. This is so even in the medical area. Jodi Vittori, writing for the Carnegie Endowment for International Peace (2020), discussed a study that had been published in the *Journal of the American Medical Association*, "[estimating] that $98 billion were lost to fraud and abuse in Medicare and Medicaid in 2011 alone." So it is natural, reading these stories of corruption, to develop the idea that we have lost control and people cannot be trusted. Jan-Willem van Prooijen, an expert on conspiracy theories, says that "the tendency to perceive conspiracies is universal." He adds that "not all conspiracy theories are irrational. Sometimes corruption does happen. It's natural for people to be on their guard for that." (Resnick, 2017).

During a tough time, that attitude seems to harden. Conspiracy theories seem to blossom when danger is perceived. They give us a feeling of control to quell our anxiety by feeling that we can predict when something will happen. When people talk about it in unison, over social media, it feels good, and that good feeling spreads and bonds tighten. That is important for some people, especially when they are anxious, distrustful, and looking for a solution and control. Unfortunately, it is false control.

The anxiety and uncertainty that people feel seem to be contagious and spread like wildfire at a time of turmoil. Even without the pandemic there is a myriad of issues, like racism, unstable leadership, police brutality, and economic uncertainty that produce anxieties. Then the anxiety felt by individuals seems to be contagious and connects with anxiety in other individuals, again reinforcing and magnifying it. Emotions beget other emotions in new people. For those individuals who do not tolerate feeling anxious, they pick up the feelings of anxiety from others and convert it into other emotions such as insecurity, suspicion, and mistrust, or treat it with various types of substances.

The conspiracy theorists seem to take this and run with it, exaggerating the problem to the point that they see it as rampant throughout the system, a classic case of vast overgeneralization. They may think that if some people are corrupt, then everyone must be corrupt.[9] If there is anxiety, some people may think, "I will solve this issue. I will tell them who is really causing this anxiety so they will not have to squirm anymore." Subconsciously they may want to become a hero. They are thinking with emotion mind. They may think if they state that someone like Bill Gates is causing the pandemic, or that the Chinese wanted to create it, they will be a hero. It is really a feeling, not a thought, as the emotion has likely affected their thought processes. Other emotions such as hurt, anger, and cynicism will also enter the fray, as individuals have different emotional makeups, but have enough in common for there to be a significant overlap. These feelings can dominate any ability to think rationally.

These feelings probably come from a previous time in someone's life when they have been abused, hurt, or wronged, losing their trust. Emotions, including suppressed and implicit emotion, seem to have overpowered the rational mind. They may think that if they don't view the government as having caused this pandemic, they are part of the problem. Their motivation is admirable, since they seem to have a "save the country" complex, pointing out what seems obvious to them.

Douglas, Sutton, and Cichocka (2017) quote research that suggests that belief in conspiracy theories is "stronger among people who habitually seek meaning and patterns in the environment, [...] [or] when events are especially large in scale or significant and leave people dissatisfied with what they perceive to be mundane, small-scale explanations." They may believe that scientific work in laboratories is small-scale or unimportant in comparison to, for example, large cellphone towers, when it is in fact the opposite. These people focus on large, obvious, visible things they can see, like cellphone towers, police cars, or paper money to come to their conclusions. They may not know much about laboratories and so disregard them as invisible or meaningless. That is emotional thinking through contagious suspicion. The authors write that "research suggests that conspiracy belief is stronger when people experience distress as a result of feeling uncertain," likely as a result of their difficulty tolerating uncertainty and ambiguity. Fear of catching the coronavirus, or the anguish of knowing people who have caught it and died, could be sources of anxiety, although they may deny them. Denial pushes the knowledge

---

9   I have experienced this personally when I made comments on social media advocating for increased psychological services. Others responded with the suggestion that psychologists only wanted to enrich themself, when that was certainly not the case.

into the subconscious. Their theories give them certainty and control that they believe in because they want to believe them. They do not trust science or academic research because they do not trust authority. Distrust is emotional, promoting emotional contagion which others catch.

These same authors state that "conspiracy theories may promise to make people feel safer as a form of cheater detection, in which dangerous and untrustworthy individuals are recognized and the threat they posed is reduced or neutralized." This would obviously be the case, except that they do not prove that the individuals are, in fact, dangerous and untrustworthy. They likely believe it is true because it fits their preconceived idea, a case of confirmation bias. They may even appoint themselves as police, like the shooter in Nova Scotia who in the spring of 2020 committed mass murder while wearing a police uniform and driving a replica police cruiser.[10]

The same article says that "studies have shown that people are likely to turn to conspiracy theories when they are anxious and feel powerless [...] [and] feel unable to control outcomes." They conclude that "conspiracy belief appears to stem to a large extent from epistemic, existential, and social motives." There is also the possibility of a delusion, a false belief, maintained with firm conviction, in spite of evidence to the contrary, likely derived from emotional material. The need to believe is so strong that they truly believe false details to be facts. They give themselves power and control over outcomes, the way they think it should be. Indeed, in March 2020, a poll by YouGov (*The Economist*, 2020) found that 13 percent of Americans believed the COVID-19 crisis was a hoax. Many people were desperate to believe the pandemic is not real. A short film called "Plandemic," about a global plan to take control with a fake pandemic (referring to the coronavirus pandemic), went viral after a well-known women's health physician shared it with her nearly half a million Facebook followers. Soon after, a thousand of those followers also shared it in a classic case of social contagion (Frenkel et al., 2020).

"Conspiracy theories, misinformation, and disinformation are more often found on social media, anonymous message boards and fringe websites that deceptively disseminate false or misleading content under the guise of legitimate news" says Dastagir (2021). People who trust only these sites have a cynical attitude about mainstream media providing the

---

10　This description of his motivation is psychological conjecture on my part.

truth, and so are ready to take in disinformation. They probably feel more comfortable being cynical and look for information consistent with their cynicism. Then it builds as they read more information from different sites, and emotionally feel more and more gratified, as if someone finally believes them.

Conspiracy theories will abound when we feel emotional and fearful about likely causes of human-made tragedies. This situation provides cognitive dissonance, a consequence of a person's performing an action that contradicts their personal beliefs, ideals, and values; it also occurs when a person is confronted with new information that contradicts those beliefs, ideals, and values. Some people resolve the dissonance with a story that there was more than one person involved, or a famous person, as if this justifies the power involved in the event and the extent and scope of the losses and deaths involved. It happens because of social and emotional contagion. When some people pick up fear from someone else, they often then feel the same fear and so it multiplies through emotional contagion and passes to many people, just like flames from a burning building can jump a gap and engulf an adjoining building. When emotion spreads through a crowd of people, it multiplies and becomes very strong. It turns into not merely a rumour but an accepted belief, buoyed by the weight of a crowd and the power of the emotion, even though it has not been proven. When powerful contagious emotion and an abstract concept are involved, the crowd will often accept the message as fact, regardless of its truth.

Cynicism is contagious and when it develops and strengthens, we get conspiracy theories which strengthen, and become contagious themselves in this time of turmoil. It can be appealing for some people to think that organizations are against them, because in their minds, organizations are powerful, and people are helpless. They then identify a suspected villain, whether or not the facts support it, because of the relief that identification brings. We feel helpless and when we do, we subconsciously strive for power, which we can feel in numbers. We identify villains and vote for people we see as powerful to overtake them. We then ally ourselves with that powerful person.

Vaccine conspiracies

A study by Hornsey, Harris and Fielding (2018) found that "anti-vaccination attitudes were highest among those who were high in conspiratorial thinking, reactance (skeptical of consensus views and intolerant of being told what to think), disgust toward blood and needles, and held individualistic/hierarchical worldviews (opposed to big government control). The authors suggest persuasive arguments might alter their positions by aligning with their personalities in suggesting that the anti-vaccination movement is also a big pressure movement with highly conformist views against vaccinations, and where individual freedom is also not valued.

There is a fear of getting a vaccine not just because it is a trust issue but also because of disgust issues, and in giving control to someone else to put something foreign into our body. This is an issue for those prone to distrusting authorities, and for having difficulty in accepting ambiguous, unknown (to them) entities. People who have lived their lives without experiencing trusting parents or relatives being kind and helpful are very likely to be on guard, especially when the sanctity of our bodies are involved. When some people don't know clearly what is in the vaccine, if they also have serious trust issues and feelings of insecurity, they are likely to doubt that there is a helpful ingredient in the vaccine. They may be used to being tricked, being taken advantage of, being neglected, even when injured or sick. So their attitude is that people are not to be trusted. They may default to thinking that the vaccine is a negative thing. Some people even think COVID-19 is fake, and that the vaccine will inject them with microchips (Hruska, 2020).

Discussion is not always helpful when many people think the coronavirus, or the vaccine, are fake. It may be helpful to show pictures of truly sick people who have COVID-19, along with their relatives to validate it so the cynical do not think they are actors. Give them some respect, rather than being angry, because they have personal reasons for distrusting that we do not know about. You can do that in a sensitive, tender, caring way, saying that you know that sometimes it is hard to trust, and that's understandable. It can be hard to be tender and caring. It is not helpful to be angry. You have to approach them this way in order to get their trust because trusting is hard for them. They expect you to fight or be uncaring or even destructive and so they will be suspicious of your kindness. If you are aggressive, it will just widen the divide. A technique called motivational interviewing could help them change. In this technique, therapists become a helper in the change process and express acceptance of the person, while using therapeutic techniques and persuasive arguments activating the capability for change that the person has (University of Massachusetts Amherst, n.d.). This technique may help people accept the vaccine. Health care professionals such as psychologists familiar with this approach are crucial in developing the trust necessary for hesitant patients to accept the vaccine.

Gender and conspiracy theories

A study sponsored by Cambridge University found that the willingness to actually endorse a conspiracy theory as being real is primarily a male phenomenon (Cassese et al., 2020). Learned helplessness and belief in conspiratorial thinking in males was found to be influential on their tendency to develop conspiracy theories. In other words, if you feel helpless and powerless in explaining the cause, you may conjure up ideas that seem plausible, stemming from a tendency towards suspicion and mistrust. Most men usually have difficulty dealing with their own emotions and are prone to act on them without addressing them. Many men like to be in charge, solve problems, and fix things. They are stereotypically expected to be able to explain things, and it can be a boost for the male ego to be lauded for this ability. Some are prone to feeling inadequate when they are unable to do so. Some have difficulty tolerating the feeling of helplessness when they are unable to explain a situation or develop a solution. They may get angry and frustrated, feeling inadequate. Some men do not have good emotional intelligence. They may be more likely to come up with an explanation, even bordering on a conspiracy theory, as to why something is happening to save face and prevent embarrassment.

Conspiracy theories are thought to be contagious (Friedman, 2020). People reject rationality if they suspect hidden reasons. Many men may feel better about themselves if they can figure out what is behind a problem when others can't, so they deceive themselves into believing there is more to it than meets the eye (when there really isn't). A big reason for this rejection of rationality is that some events are just so monumental, like the Kennedy assassination, or 9/11, and now the coronavirus pandemic, that it is hard to accept that they had simple causes (Horsey, 2020). People find enormous reasons, such as a media hoax, to match its magnitude. It must be a satisfying feeling for a developing conspiracy theory to be expressed and accepted among a crowd of supporters. This satisfaction seems to underly the contagious effect of the conspiracy theory. It has allure and is appealing to many men who may feel disempowered, and other alienated groups (Douglas et al., 2017).

Men, who as a group are usually less comfortable with handling emotions and feelings than women, are likely to project their own feelings of helplessness and powerlessness onto external sources so they don't have to accept them, likely for fear they would somehow be less masculine. For some men to bond without admitting they are actually bonding (since that might be seen by them as weak), they find an imagined enemy, the supposed perpetrator of this hoax, to expose. This is a similar dynamic to other conspiracy theories. The allure and appeal appears to enable the contagion of many emotions to move across individuals and groups, from one to another. It is very reinforcing emotionally to feel supportive emotions for one's cause from another person, and when one is in particular need for such emotional gratification—such as those who are insecure, feel helpless, or need to belong to a group—they will easily take in the emotion without carefully scrutinizing it for objective truth. In this way the implicit emotions are the unrecognized connecting rod between these people and do the thinking for them—although very ineffectively, because emotions don't think.

Cynicism and conspiracy theories

A normal feeling of helplessness can develop into a strong characteristic through emotional contagion. Reasons for suspicion abound such as dishonest politicians, events not being real, businesses lying to their clients, and CEO's stealing money. Once you develop feelings of suspicion, those feelings can become cynicism, which is more resistant to change than suspicion. Such people become hardened. They hurt, and interpersonal trust is affected. They look for a solution. If they don't find one, they need an outlet. It hurts to feel this way and it shouldn't have to happen. Some people might not experience much in the way of truth in their daily lives. What do they do then? There is no outlet. Cynicism is a natural result.

People are likely to keep this cynicism secret. It is perhaps even subconscious so that they may not even be aware of it. It is not socially desirable to be cynical, except among the cynics. It is even less socially desirable to believe in conspiracy theories. Some people may share it tentatively with a few others, but it doesn't become a firm theory when it is at the cynical level, likely because of the social unattractiveness of having an unpopular opinion. When there is no other outlet, and cynicism and depression result, we may hear of a situation that has occurred that attracts and reinforces our suspicious attitude. We may subconsciously let ourselves believe that corruption is so widespread in society that it supports the conspiracy belief. For example: Jeffrey Skilling, the former chief executive of ENRON, was sentenced to twenty-four years and released after twelve (Stevens & Haag, 2019). This may reinforce the perception of favoritism.

When we feel others being supportive, eventually the conspiracy theory becomes socially desirable and attractive, as cynicism becomes more contagious. One will often disregard systematic reasoning or critical thinking which would otherwise put this into a more reasoned perspective. The feeling that being cynical or accepting conspiracy theories as probable is now emotionally attractive, since it gives us some explanation, even if unproven, that confirms our bias and is satisfying.

Emotions gradually seem to push suspicious ideas into a more complicated "plot," as cynicism and the accompanied emotions of suspicion and pessimism reinforce each other. One person's suspicion strengthens another person's pessimism, that person's pessimism strengthens another person's cynicism, and that person's cynicism reinforces the next person's conspiracy. There is no critical thinking, only incomplete or lazy thinking, perhaps replaced by emotion.

Willis tells us that "the executive function control of the brain centers develops in the prefrontal cortex, which gives us the potential to consider and voluntarily control our thinking, emotional responses, and behaviour. It is the reflective 'higher brain' compared to the reactive 'lower brain' where emotional responses are triggered" (Willis, n.d.). She says that students need reason, logic, creative problem solving, concept development, media literacy, and communication skills, all part of critical thinking and systematic reasoning, to be ready for the daily complexities of life. To combat emotional contagion and prevent its associates, conspiracy theories and runaway thinking, we have to use the executive control function of the brain to use crucial thinking skills, such as critical analysis, induction, deduction, relational thinking with prior knowledge activation, and prediction. Learning "how to think" along these lines is a critical part of overcoming emotional infection on our thinking skills.

Situations that attract suspicion are events that are abstract, uncertain, and complicated. Many people cannot sort it out and do not have the training, resources, or even the time to do so. Some need to find a "culprit." When others are also suspicious and cynical, and find a culprit, they automatically catch those emotions and it becomes firmer as a belief, sometimes becoming a conspiracy, being reinforced by supporters. That reinforcement of the initial suspicion brings feelings or emotions that become such a powerful force that they cannot be resisted.

Underlying, unresolved emotional issues determine attraction to conspiracies

One of the things that we want most is for our underlying grudges and resentments to be accepted and validated. Perhaps the initial tormenter from our childhood or adolescence who was abusive, or caused these resentments, is, in our minds, symbolically denigrated and belittled as a result of other meaningful people accepting and validating them as villains—regardless of whether the initial abuse relates to the topic of the conspiracy. It helps us move on in life, aids in our maturity and psychological development. That is one of the basics in psychotherapy.

When it is done symbolically, rather than directly, it loses its psychotherapeutic effect.

The person is likely to continue striving to denigrate the initial tormentor, even symbolically. By substituting another person or entity for the initial tormentor, such as the people who are making a hoax of the virus, the person involved in thinking this thought is unconsciously targeting their initial tormentor. They keep it up as a substitute for the initial tormentor, who is long gone. Symbolically, it may mean that the hidden abuser is discovered and captured because of their hidden roles in causing these evil events, even though this is not true. To the person abused as a child, the residual agony of the abuse is so strong that it parallels the report of death in a major news item. The childhood fantasy gets mixed up with present-day adult news, and the adult is left with a false, fantasy version of adult tragedies. Their fantasy is reinforced through emotional contagion because emotion and fantasy override rationality to produce a false belief.

In a sense, the people behind the problem they are now targeting (for example, those who developed the 5G network), may psychologically, remind them somehow of their original abuser, perhaps an insensitive, abusive father, uncle, teacher, or other authority figure. If they can't damage the original abuser, they can destroy the current person's commodities as a revenge, hoping to destroy in some fashion the person they are targeting as part of the conspiracy. It becomes real to them because they have a delusional belief. If they carried this off and the targeted person were then sentenced to jail or prison, the assumption would be that such punishment would "teach them a lesson," and the victimized person would change.

Because of years of feeling insecure and inferior, and probably being called names like *loser* by many peers, people who believe in conspiracies are deeply insecure and alienated from mainstream society and have many unresolved issues. This is not an attack on them. It is an appeal for their needs to be recognized, accepted, and met by society in an effective way. Their self-esteem has taken a beating and they are devastated; they are not equipped to handle it. People who call them *losers* are unaware of or indifferent to the negative psychological effect this would have. It would seem to be another form of psychological abuse in an ultra-competitive society. Emotional contagion may cause this because of the feeling of power that comes in a competitive society. This feeling of power provides an implicit emotion that overrides rational judgment, resulting in the associated need some people have to put down others. They are engaging in the labelling cognitive distortion by assigning this name. These people want to have power, want to be a winner, and who can blame them with a "winner or loser" mentality that affects many in a dysfunctional society. The need to feel powerful is a strong social need for many people.

No one is actually a loser. They are just assigned that label by society. Terms like *loser* or *winner* are only accepted because of the power of social contagion, not because of any logic. We don't need to apply those terms to people; they are just labels to put oneself artificially higher in the standings of social power, or to put others lower in the standings. It is as if we want to see ourselves atop the social hierarchy. It is best to not take part in that setup. Some so-called losers may have ineffective life skills, or perhaps a psychological difficulty, like cognitive issues or a lower intelligence level, and that is not their fault. Or maybe they don't; we can all be ineffective or "stupid" at times. Putting people down by calling them losers means more about the person speaking than it does the recipient of the put-down. It may mean that they are succumbing to the feeling of gratification they get. We need to have compassion and empathy for these people while at the same time disapproving of their beliefs and actions.

Videos show people protesting and rebelling, gathering in crowds despite the pandemic rules. It has been contagious. Crowds promote emotional contagion; they prompt susceptible people to protest also, because they begin to feel similar feelings to the protesters. People are displaying signs demanding freedom. They are forgetting that freedom is relative, because we all stop for red lights, pay for meals at restaurants, and respect rules, regulations and laws. We abide by the rules when we realize they are there for a purpose; many people tend to forget the "order" part of the "law and order." Rules and regulations regarding the pandemic are part of "order," implemented for safety, just as speed limits are.

The collective subconscious spreads in the psychological underground

Psychology Today quotes Daniel Jolley, a psychologist and conspiracy theory researcher, who says: "Conspiracy theories bloom in periods of uncertainty and threat, where we seek to make sense of a chaotic world. They often provide a simple answer to a complex problem [...] which can make them very appealing. The 'official' answer does not always meet this need, is usually more complex, and is often provided by the government, a group that some people do not find trustworthy. People would prefer to focus on explanations provided by the underdog." (Muller, 2020). The article goes on to say: "that research shows that conspiracy theories satisfy unmet psychological needs and provide security of knowledge in a time of uncertainty."

The only part missing in this description would be the crucial role that emotional contagion plays. Conspiracy theories are contagious. They seem to spread through social media by tapping into the collective subconscious, or what Jung called the collective unconscious (Jung, 1971). As the *Psychology Today* article insightfully says, many people feel like they are the underdog, without power. They prefer explanations provided by the underdog, instead of the people in power, the regular news providers, who they do not trust because they are owned by powerful corporations. This feeling seems rampant in society to the point that we can say it exists in what we will call, with apologies to Jung, the "collective subconscious." The subconscious is closer to the conscious mind than the unconscious, so this description seems more apropos for our times.

Conspiracy theories are reinforced and strengthened through emotional and social contagion by the ubiquitous presence of anonymous social media where people can theorize safely about conspiracy theories and get reinforced by others who think the same way. The rewarding emotion some people may experience comes in the feeling of satisfaction and power they get by rejecting the mainstream and developing their own collection of trusted sources, partly through social media. These contribute to and enlarge the collective subconscious phenomenon and brings it into consciousness. These people have likely been isolated and lonely in the past but now have a social support network and arrange meet ups so that the theories abound and multiply. This also constitutes important emotional and social support for these people since it provides a feeling of invincibility for these individuals' vulnerabilities. This is crucial from a psychological viewpoint. Social contagion only occurs if emotional contagion reinforces it. This does not, however, give them more objective credibility about the truth of the theories.

The collective subconscious contains a type of collective emotion, a similar emotion that spreads through people who have this issue, such as feelings of hurt and resentment about being the underdog. Barsade (2018) states that emotional contagion may be a key explanatory mechanism of how collective emotion forms through both conscious and unconscious emotional social influence. It also would form through the subconscious, where ideas and feelings are suppressed but still available to some conscious awareness, as well as possibly the unconscious where ideas and memories are repressed and not available to conscious awareness. Many people can relate to feeling like they are the underdog, as shown by the number of people who root for underdog sports teams (Stromberg, 2015), and likely underdog performers and companies. Only one team comes out on top, so the vast majority of teams are not winners, and we can identify with them, as they appear to be more similar to us, as the so-called average person, and yet they are competitive. They have less to lose and yet remain viable. Do you remember Avis' successful commercials saying, "We're number two"? (Stevenson, 2013) These feelings of identifying with the underdog are usually subconscious, but may be conscious, as many people agree with it and attract each other through emotional contagion.

Since the individuals seem to have ongoing psychological problems, it would be healthier to acknowledge that and work on it. There is the tendency for people who have been ostracized to believe more strongly in the conspiracies than others. Some people are devout believers. People need to ask themselves if it is possible that they are attracted to these conspiracy theories for an underlying reason. They may have some points to discuss and listen to, but we have to ask them, therapeutically and in a curious way, if it is not possible that the coronavirus is real, and not fake news. Yes, it is real. But we recommend this approach because we don't want to alienate them. Otherwise, you are being beset with contagious emotion from their anger, and may resort to a knee-jerk angry reaction, setting off the ping-pong game common in people who fight back. This should be done by trained therapists, perhaps trained in motivational interviewing, a collaborative therapy technique. This approach may be able to be modified to treat conspiracy theorists. Therapists are trained not to catch the patient's emotions or react to them in an angry, defensive way. As well, we need to show the disbelievers that the hospitals really are full, and that people are dying, so that they can believe us and realize they are wrong. To do that, they need people who are doctors, nurses, or, better still, real coronavirus patients who are everyday folks and not media stars. TV shows have begun featuring real hospital scenes and we see some hints of real coronavirus patients, although they can't be fully shown because of privacy concerns.

Careful therapeutic alliances with both parties (the conspiracy theorists and the coronavirus patients and families) would be important. The theorists may see the patients as not believable because of their insecurities and their tendency to project their suspicions outward. Remember, suspicion and anger can easily be contagious. Those patients should be willing to describe their symptoms, their pain, their fears, and their treatment to the theorists. Perhaps this could be done by video, to make it easier. They would all have to be chosen carefully, with the only partially believing theorists chosen first, and similarly appropriate coronavirus patients who are not too badly affected and prepared to have a reasonable discussion.

Conspiracy theories have hit the big time because those people who distrust the authorities in the tough times of the COVID-19 have taken a sense of control unto themselves by developing their own reasons as to what is going on in society the past year or two. The have tapped into pervasive distrust of politicians and think COVID-19 is a hoax and developed their own explanations for what is going on. Conspiracies are contagious for those many suspicious people who are impelled to think this way, and it is magnified multifold during times of insecurity in society when we feel lack of control.

Implicit Emotion

Emotional contagion can be implicit, beyond immediate awareness. It can occur via auditory channels such as voice tone. Emotion is invisible yet has a large impact. Only words and actions naturally get press coverage. Politicians pass on their messages through contagious implicit emotion; followers "catch" the message through catching the emotion. We accept beliefs partly because of the implicit emotion embedded in them; negative emotions can be conveyed subconsciously. Strong emotions pull ordinary positions to extremes; emotional people take extreme political positions, but emotions can be regulated and in turn settled down by cognitive reappraisal.

When we talk about emotion, we are also talking about implicit emotion: that emotion which is present under the conscious level, not immediately obvious or noticeable. Emotional contagion is not limited to open expressive displays of emotion, but also includes the effect of implicit, hidden emotion, which can happen during interpersonal encounters even if people are reserved or not demonstrative.

When we hear others' comments and opinions about personal, social, and political topics, we also hear their feelings. Feelings are not opinions but are internal types of emotions. We feel these internal emotions when people give their opinions on various topics. The emotions can be implicit; we not only hear their comments but also infer and sense their emotions. Although emotion is expressed under-the-surface and is not readily noticeable, people can be affected by this implicit emotion. A smile, glance, gesture, utterance, rhythm in the voice, an emphasis on syllables, or a subtle body movement from another person are enough to emit an impactful emotion from that person. These are not necessarily obvious to the eye or ear, or conscious to the mind of the listener, but they have a significant effect on them. Emotional contagion can be implicit, beyond immediate awareness. We just can't go on the words spoken because the implicit emotion expressed along with the words may make us believe the statement more than we should. If we recognize this, we can limit our intake of negative feelings and implicit emotion by telling ourselves that this is happening, and that we don't want to absorb those negative feelings.

Try reading a comment made by someone in printed form; compare that to the same comment in spoken form and you can pick up the difference quite easily. Emoticons don't do it. Implicit emotion is involved in the voice style, quality, and tone and has a strong role in conveying the message. When people express opinions, their voice raises, ebbs and flows, usually accompanied by gestures, all revealing the inner emotion. We pick it up subconsciously. Feelings exude from others and can have unexpected emotional effects on us internally: suspicion, anger, defensiveness, pride, confidence, enthusiasm, being overwhelmed, feeling anxious or worried. We may feel defensive if we feel challenged by their emotion, overwhelmed if we are bombarded by their affect, proud if someone close to us beams out pride.

Emotion is carried by the voice

Recent research shows that the voice is an "extraordinarily rich" and pervasive medium that conveys emotion. Emotional contagion seems to come more through auditory channels. The spoken word is more immediate, and sound carries emotion in vocalizations. Cowen, Elfenbein, Laukka et al (2019) found that vocal bursts were found to convey complex blends of at least 24 distinct emotions, revealing an extremely rich catalog of various types of emotional expression. They say that human beings communicate emotion through prosody—the non-verbal "patterns of tune, rhythm and timbre in speech." It interacts with words to convey feelings and attitudes, including ideas described in speech. Feelings and ideas are integrated so that feelings and emotions are incorporated into ideas, meaning that expression of an idea would also mean expression or conveyance of a feeling. They also say that "hearers can judge five different emotions in the prosody that accompanies speech: anger, fear, happiness, sadness and tenderness." These authors also say that people also communicate emotion in the voice with vocal bursts, brief non-verbal sounds in the midst of speech, such as cries, sighs, laughs, shrieks, growls, hollers, roars, and the classic *oohs* and *ahhs*. Vocal bursts predate language and as such would be what constitutes Hatfield's primitive contagion. Vocal bursts also structure our social interactions and regulate relationships. It would make sense that emotional contagion occurs in all these instances, including the five that are included as emotion that is conveyed by speech. Since vocal bursts convey 24 dimensions of emotion, voices not only convey emotion but also regulate relationships. They evoke specific brain responses which can activate specific areas of the cortex of the brain. For example, screams activate the amygdala, that part of our brain that is alert to danger.

Voice is produced through a contraction of muscles and is transformed into sound through vibrations of the vocal folds—a crucial aspect which is involved in mimicry or imitation of behaviour which, in turn, is critical for emotional contagion to occur. It makes sense that emotional contagion is transmitted primarily through the voice, rather than through the actual words spoken, thereby delivering the implicit emotion, a critical role in transmitting emotional contagion. Hence the voice of the individuals, especially those with deep, loud, confident voices, are powerful in conveying the implicit emotion embedded in interpersonal communication. Emotional contagion can be transmitted to others through the voice, as well as through mimicry and similarity of actions involved in the turmoil, and is a primary component of the emotional turmoil that was conveyed throughout society in 2020, as many people protested with their voice while parading through the streets. People naturally radiate emotions and feelings and pass them on to others, who either absorb them in agreement or reject them in counter-contagion, impulsively and quickly, like a dodge ball, while in System 1.

Research says that implicit emotional contagion is usually more subtle and automatic than normal explicit contagion (Morris, 2017). It includes embedded communication done through non-verbal cues which convey the importance or meaningfulness of the comments. Subconscious synchrony in heart rate, breathing rhythms and hormonal levels can be involved (Prochazkova & Kret, 2017) as can different non-verbal channels involving body, face and touch (App et al., 2011). The unintentional manner in which the emotion is given likely boosts the contagion, from a subjective viewpoint, because it is the emotion that is contagious.

Implicit emotion is often strongly involved in political statements or dialogue. Emotions such as anger, fear, and sadness, identified by the researchers as being conveyed by voice, are expressed repeatedly in the voices we hear in protests and riots. Yet it is only the actual words that get press coverage, although the invisible emotion seems to have the strong and contagious impact. You can't print invisibility. As long as the verbal content does not state an obvious falsehood, and the verbal statement somehow connects with the listener internally, the emotional emphasis subtly given by the speaker often carries the force of the statement. That is the implicit emotion conveyed by the voice which is uttered with the words of protest. So we may end up accepting something that we are ambivalent or uncertain about if only considering it on an intellectual basis, because of the effects of the implicit emotion that go along with the words spoken.

That force can dominate and even overwhelm the listener. This includes the fear and sadness of the protesters, and the anger of the rioters. The importance of implicit emotion in political dialogue cannot be replicated in reports by journalists in the media. As politicians state their positions on important issues, implicit emotion, not exclusively the words, passes on the message, which, being contagious, is likely to spread to others. We need to learn how to deal with these implicit emotions and the importance they have, how to handle them as we hear them, and how to decide whether to inoculate ourselves from their effects, and if so, how to do that.

The effect of negative emotions such as cynicism and suspicion, hate and fear, expressed in the voice's tone, can become embedded in a mental attitude towards a topic, especially at a time of turmoil. When activated, it can propel action by expressing these emotions through the voice in a heated environment, such as a social occasion or political event where people gather to discuss or debate issues. When a politician speaks loudly, their emotion is expressed through the voice, often beyond the immediate awareness of the participants. People hear and identify loudness but not necessarily emotion, although they pick it up. The effect of emotions spread through a voice can be much stronger than the actual words spoken. We can see the negative effect of implicit emotional contagion in influencing others.

Emotional involvement may include implicit emotion as an emotional basis for positions, even if the individual may not appear emotional in their overt expression. This is because people can catch implicit emotions. The former president of the U.S. seemed to have a way to influence people other than through his actual words, almost like others caught and absorbed his emotions without thinking. His supporters absorbed the emotional parts of his messages very clearly. Emotions don't think but they convey simple messages, usually through the deep, loud voice of the speaker.

The effect of emotional information

Experiments consistently show that positive emotional information promotes the cognitive responses by a recipient while negative emotional information inhibits it (Clore & Huntsinger, 2007). This involves implicit, internal emotions experienced, but not expressed. For example: feeling happy will likely empower an individual to feel certain and entitled to claim something, if they are already inclined that way. Positive emotion strengthens the effect of reason and increases the strength of belief in the thought.

Physiological involvements help explain how implicit emotion occurs. Experiencing a stimulus such as a politician's speech triggers a spread of activations in various brain structures. These are likely to bring out implicit emotional responses from listeners. Such reactions reveal the expression of unconscious material involving implicit ways of regulating emotions (Almohammad, 2016). This researcher points out that a complex network of neural pathways often results in the amygdala's active nodes stimulating the networks of neurons in the brain's cortex in regions involved in cognitive functions. The anterior cingulate cortex in the limbic system of the brain then manages and controls uncomfortable emotions and connects to the frontal lobe, where the executive part of the brain is located (Bush et al., 2000). In this way, there is a physiological component controlling emotions and connecting to the executive part of the brain. It can be regulated and controlled by the individuals in the way they talk to themselves, interacting with their own subconscious by having conscious talks with their own underlying thoughts, and directing their own actions.

The speaker often does not realize how much or how little anger, sadness, or despair he is expressing, because it involves implicit emotion associated with the words he is speaking. This would also be true for the listener, who might not be aware they are absorbing emotion from the speaker. Nevertheless, emotional contagion can occur implicitly, subconsciously, and thereby have an effect. We might end up accepting the beliefs because of the effect of the emotion involved implicitly in the comment, although we didn't realize it at the time. The emotion may be vague, ambiguous, or even irrelevant to the conscious mind, which is looking for the word being used, while at the same time the implicit, embedded, or buried emotion possibly has a powerful impact on the receiver, maybe even more powerful than the actual word. This impact may be positive or negative, but as a result of the emotional impact our opinion may be influenced, affected, or even changed. This impact hits us on a daily basis in many different areas of life, including hearing words spoken while viewing a speaker on TV.

The voice's volume, rhythm, sharpness, tone, or pitch carries the emotion. The voice is the prime expresser of the implicit emotion. It rarely gives false emotional messages (Ekman, 2003). Implicit emotion also emphasizes the importance or relevance of the statement as the speaker intends it. They will emphasize, perhaps subconsciously, which actual words in their statement are important by the inflection they give those words. This reflects their opinion of what they are saying. In this way, it is the implicit emotion that pushes the envelope. It has the advantage of being right there out in front, although few recognize consciously that it is. People hear the words but feel the impact of the feelings that are being expressed. Most people may think that they are responding to the words, and they are, but they are primarily responding to the feelings and emotions being expressed implicitly in the statements. That's why words and phrases and even syllables are emphasized by the speaker. The implicit emotion is invisible personal power.

Implicit emotion, when embedded subtly but habitually, in controversial topics with non-verbal emphasis, can be responsible for attitudes swinging from one extreme to the other. This is emotional contagion in action: the rebound effect. When emotion is implicit and embedded, it will cause attitudes to swing quickly and impulsively. We know that emotion quickly rebounds and reacts impulsively because emotions don't think. The mind does and can block the emotion's reaction if the mind is aware of it.

Implicit emotion is strong if delivered with authenticity, confidence, variable rhythm, pitch and tone of voice and emphasis on the right words. Implicit emotion in the voice and facial qualities will contribute to the meaningfulness someone receives in any given conversation. The implicit but definite emotion, especially communicated by someone with a deep voice and said in a calm, strong, stern way, delivers the real point of the message, even if not expressed as such in actual words. It would make sense for the speaker to attempt to regulate the voice's volume, rhythm, sharpness, tone, or pitch when speaking or uttering vocal bursts in order to modulate the contagious emotions being expressed, as much as possible. Regulating the expressing or emission of emotions involves regulating one's voice and manner of speaking.

Implicit emotion in contentious political and social issues

It is important to be aware. The impact of implicit emotional contagion may also come from input from the media on political topics, or on speeches made by politicians and broadcast on the news. It is noted by a subtle emphasis on an idea said in a personal way, as if it were not meant to be actually taught but comes through a very powerful method of suggestion. Sometimes a speaker can have a "magnetic," spell-binding type of impact, one that verges on the hypnotic. It comes from affective input or even from the type of expression in their eyes, their voice, and other facial and postural features. In this way the listener could be absorbing an emotion from them that carries some appeal over which the listener has no awareness. As a result, their internal judgment might be suspended without realizing that it is happening. It is a powerful way to transmit something to someone, especially if you are adept at non-verbal communication. You can prevent this from happening by being aware, and silently rebutting the message, asking yourself if it makes sense, or if you even really agree.

The speaker may deny advocating for a position because there was never an actual statement made that could be quoted. For example, a politician could say something about a group of people, like, "When our people work hard, the immigrants, well, they..." and there is a pause and a glance, and the rest of the comment goes unsaid, and then the speaker resumes with the sentence, "When our people work hard, they apply themselves, and our economy really grows." The implication left hanging by the use of the word *our* in combination with the words *immigrants*, and *apply themselves*, if that word and its syllables were emphasized, could be that the speaker really believes that immigrants do not contribute much to the economy, and instead are lazy, do not work hard, and only take from the economy. Yet there is no real quote or actual statement, and the spoken word appeals to the inner emotion of the receiver, who may have had this bias beforehand. That way it strikes the receiver subconsciously because they hear what they want to hear: that immigrants are lazy, whether it is true or not. It strengthens the recipient's belief. Yet the media have no such word to quote.

There have probably been previous incidents where terms like *immigrants* and *race* have been emphasized in a similar manner. Subconsciously the attitudes that coexist with these terms are infiltrated with implicit emotion. People easily pick up the hidden message about immigrants if they already lean this way. When people speak about race, citizenship, or countries of origin, and discuss which one is best, they will often accentuate certain aspects and features involved by emphasizing the words and syllables to express the depth of feeling that they have about the topic.

Many insecure people have the need to think they are surpassing people who they feel are challenging them for status and money. They fear being seen as insecure; this can be disastrous in a competitive society. The unspoken implicit emotion strikes the receiver at a subconscious level and can strengthen their belief about themselves being superior, which leads to a confidence boost. Its impact seems to be stronger than people realize, especially during a time of turmoil, where people can be divided. It is the implicit effect.

The effect of negative emotions, such as cynicism and suspicion, in a social context can become embedded in a mental attitude towards a topic. When activated, they can propel action in a heated environment, such as at a socio-political event where people gather to discuss or confront political issues. Here we can see the negative effect of emotional contagion. Negative emotions are perceived to be stronger and quicker than positive emotions. The effects of painful experiences last longer than the effects of positive experiences. The emotional energy in implicit, negative emotional acts creates stronger and quicker responses than emotional energy in implicit positive emotional acts. The more negative the emotions are and the higher the energy, the stronger our reactions might be. Morris says that this is what results in our changes in mood and contributes to emotional contagion (Morris, 2017).

Implicit emotional contagion is an important type of toxic energy, where the emotion that is contagious is embedded into a negative type of expression, such as skepticism or cynicism, and accompanied by negative, painful emotions such as depression, insecurity, fear, anxiety, suspicion, anger, distrust, and hurt. This emotion is likely to be perceived as stronger and more long-lasting. These emotions are embedded in the non-verbal (stares, smiles) or para-verbal (grunts, moans) behaviour of the person expressing the opinion—for example, in their voice's quality, intonations, rhythm, and pitch, as well as by the person's facial expression.

That subtle, implicit emotion is what prompts the impact and the spread of the opinion because it is the emotion that is more readily caught by the observer and not the words themselves. The emotions drive the words home so that they make the point. Emotions are fluid; they flow and move easily, but emotionless words do not. It is the emotion that is contagious, not the actual opinion, even though the emotion is subtle and embedded in the words. Emotions such as insecurity, fear, suspicion, skepticism and cynicism obtain some reinforcement by being shared with like-minded cynical people. They are easily transferred this way, being contagious and reinforced by commiseration, strengthening the feeling. Becoming emotionally independent comes from not automatically absorbing these contagious emotions, which you can do by noticing them when they are there, and by telling yourself not to absorb them: they're not yours.

Reinforcement, or the anticipation of it, activates the brain's dopamine system, which works in anticipation of the reinforcement, or reward. "Activation of that system puts you down a pathway toward what is important socially and for survival," says Gary Slutkin, as quoted in the article by Flora (2019).

Affective, emotional reactions influence the impact of information in judgments and decisions. Wyer, Clore, and Isbell (1999) state that the role of affect, encompassing implicit emotion, is important in the development of liking between people. It would also, then, be important in liking politicians. Reinforcement, or the anticipation of it, comes with interpersonal attraction and appeal, which, in some cases, is rewarding. As we begin to like someone, we develop an internal feeling towards them, and it can overtake our ability to use reasoning or logic effectively. In this way the emotions often overtake the mind's ability to use logic or reasoning in deference to the power of the contagious internal emotion or implicit affect. This occurs especially in times of turmoil when we are looking for social support in a group we can identify with.

The more important an issue is to an individual personally, the higher the degree of emotion they feel. They will focus more on that issue because the impact of the high degree of emotion will direct focus in that direction. Their perceptions are likely to narrow, and confirmation bias is more likely to occur under this impact. Many people who feel strongly about a subject are prone to have narrow perspectives, and so they are more likely to be subject to various cognitive distortions that support their position. It also makes sense that the more emotion the individual carries in relation to their position, the more influence the person allots internally to the emotional processing that defines their position on a particular belief.

The effect of emotional contagion on people who have experienced trauma

Emotionally alienated people, who are relatively unrecognized in a competitive society, will have a greater impact of emotion on their thought process, in comparison to those without that disturbance. Emotion strongly affects cognitive processing. If we speculate about the likelihood of some individuals being susceptible to emotional contagion, we can see that extreme social stances or political perspectives will appeal to people with significant, unresolved emotional issues much more strongly than those without. These positions can then be likely to precipitate emotionally based behaviour, such as what we saw during the January 6, 2021 storming of the U.S. Capitol building.

It is also likely that they will be susceptible to developing cynicism and believing in conspiracy theories which provide them with a feeling of power. A few people in a time of turmoil are likely to take sides and attack. To attack is to give in to emotional contagion through a counter-contagion type of response, which is unhelpful and divisive. Instead, we need to understand that this reflects the powerlessness that people with unresolved emotional issues seem to feel in a competitive society. This does not condone destructive actions in the riots. People with unmet emotional and social needs are likely to be vulnerable to acting out their suppressed hostility especially when reinforced by an authoritative personality who takes their side.

As well, those people who have experienced trauma or abuse have a hyper reactivity of the limbic system and amygdala in the lower part of the brain. According to Slutkin, this causes them to be less in control, so that they are more likely to get angry and quick to react. They develop hostile attributions so that "small things are perceived as large affronts." (Flora, 2019) Misunderstandings occur until eventually someone can get injured. This is characteristic of those with attraction to conspiracy theories. This is an example of how the effects of emotional contagion easily occur to some people because of the strong emotional effects of trauma or abuse. People with a history of trauma or abuse are likely to externalize or project blame onto outside forces and are likely to develop and strengthen these trends as small offences are perceived as large affronts. They are very sensitive to this but like to deny sensitivity and instead develop an internal strength through force. The final result can often be an aggressive, impulsive, and sometimes violent action. When the amygdala is a little larger and hyperactive, as it probably is in many of these situations, amygdala arousal occurs, and the emotional reaction will be greater. It is difficult—if not impossible—for most individuals who are easily aroused to restrain themselves.

Social and political extremes

"Feelings of distress prompt a desire for clarity, and extremist belief systems provide meaning to a complex social environment through a set of straightforward assumptions that make the world more comprehensible." (van Prooijen & Krouwel, 2019). To achieve this comprehension, some people think they need to take things to the extreme. Emotions take attitudes to the extreme, as we try and become the "most" or the "greatest" something. People are attracted emotionally to drama through emotional contagion and feed off it.

Some people feel that taking their position to an extreme is the way to be strong and resolute about it. This isn't the way to be strong. It is wiser not to argue aggressively and instead be assertive with your point while moving a little towards a more moderate position. To do that, however, the person has to forgo the feeling of power that they get from going to the extreme. That is a temporary and false feeling; you won't win by going extreme yourself; you just create divisiveness and more enemies. You are likely to be rejected. Stepping back isn't losing. The person with the other viewpoint is just another person: there is nothing to fear from them. When there is permission for the rational mind to be involved, we can use empathy and wise thinking, since wisdom comes from of a blend of rational and emotional input.

Wise thinking is more likely to produce positive emotional contagion. It is wise to state facts and details in milder emotional language, such as by stating simply: when we do x (a trigger that causes something undesirable), then we get y (the sad undesirable result). For example, in making a protest sign with someone who has very strong feelings, you could say: "It's a neat sign, but when you add a swear word on a protest sign, you lose people. People are more likely to agree with you if you don't use the swear word." Let the facts speak for mostly for themselves and add mild but meaningful emotional language when you speak.

Language is important when politicians talk about their opponents because when they use extreme language, they rouse up emotions against them. But extreme talk may not sound like extreme talk at face value. If they are not swearing, some may not realize it is extreme. It is a way of using implicit emotion as a weapon against the opposition. Some people fail to use systematic reasoning and critical thinking, which would say only the very extreme people in the party are like that. Radical means departure from tradition, an extreme position of a political party. For example, they might think the politician would do extreme things, like give money to everyone because they are "socialist" (which in the U.S. is an extreme term, and an example of a radical position), which a major party is not likely to do. Saying they are radical does not make it true, even though there is implicit emotion in these statements that makes it sound true. Emotions don't think. If you just catch the emotion without thinking you might believe its message is true.

Instead, we need a co-operative environment. It is important to leave that competitive mindset behind and enter a mindset of cooperation and respect, where a change of focus does not mean you are a loser, weak, or being tricked. You have your own choice as to your belief. It means you are joining a respectful group where you work at accepting each other, regardless of race, IQ, gender, education, religion, nationality, size, birthplace, dress, hairstyle, spoken language, sexual orientation, or age. There is one condition that should be required in order to join a respectful, cooperative group: psychopaths cannot take part (Babiak & Hare, 2006).

Belonging and affiliation

People identify with many different types of organizations and gain personal meaning from them. Introverts look for belonging and get it from affiliation with groups, such as social movements or special interest groups, although they might stay in the background. Groups such as churches, organizations, companies, schools, neighbourhoods, cities, political parties, sports teams, regions, and countries mean a lot to all of us. When we affiliate with a group, we get attached to it. We develop this meaning, and meaning is always involved with emotion, because it involves belonging or fitting in, and brings some form of affinity or happiness that is important to us. This is the inner emotion, an important component of implicit emotion. It is not immediately apparent to outside observers, unless we are wearing a cap with a logo, or a team's jersey, but this affiliation is one of the strongest feelings we can have.

The internal emotional feeling involved in taking a position on a personally meaningful topic is very strong. It can be reinforced by speaking about the topic and associating with others who hold the same opinion, experiencing emotional contagion, and thereby heightening the internal emotional experience, which often trumps reason if we need to defend our beloved organization. The emotion is strong because attachments are strong and mean a lot to us. This is an example of inner, implicit emotion that we carry inside us and which can dictate our emotions.

If we have a very close emotional bond and are closely attached to a status or a place, we can develop a fear of it ending. Somehow implicit emotion can be subconsciously associated with fears of rejection, eradication, or even annihilation (Azarian, 2020). We easily feel threatened if our group is criticized or judged as weak. It can feel as if we ourselves are being attacked and our survival is at stake. If we think this way, it probably means we are insecure ourselves. When we identify with a group, it brings a feeling of security which trumps reason. Then emotions become contagious because the feeling of survival tends to spread as a form of group bonding, or collective subconscious, because we can all relate with it. When we feel threatened, we group together for solidarity, security, and mutual support. This is a universal feeling. It is easy to see how emotions spread throughout society when we think survival is at stake. We have to find a way for wisdom to spread also. If we didn't feel so insecure and threatened, we wouldn't have to cling so hard to these organizations to feel secure. We have to ask ourselves if there is really a serious threat. Is it as bad as it seems? Maybe, but through emotional contagion it seems widespread and irrational.

People often get drawn to an extreme side of an argument by the private internal emotion which is involved in disputes. This is the emotion that comes with identifying a certain position as part of oneself which causes implicit emotion. The emotion pulls an opinion to the extreme, which produces behaviour which can become destructive. Emotions don't think. They have no reason to so do; they flourish and seem strong when they take extreme opposite positions, like left wing and right wing. Extreme positions cause stress and conflict and can result in destruction.

Most people likely take positions which fall somewhere in the middle, even if somewhat to the left or right of centre. We often have to compromise to achieve that. That takes reasoning and consideration. Implicit emotion comes in the personal meaning we give to positions we take in debates. It can stop our thinking from moving to the middle if we get worked up about the point and take it to extremes. We may see a move or yield as losing but it's not losing, it's compromising. It's giving to someone else. Sometimes we take; we deserve it too. Just not all the time. Others have to win sometimes, and that's okay. Empathy tells us that.

If we fear losing, we take things to extremes. It feels like we don't trust the opposition because we think they are dangerous. That is a major cognitive distortion. Often fear of annihilation or domination is involved in these situations. Sometimes we are concerned about this, possibly subconsciously. We have to question the idea that our survival, our existence, is threatened. It may not be. But don't be lulled into a false sense of security. The survival of anything is never guaranteed. There is always a risk to survival because life is uncertain. On the other hand, there is no risk to the survival of human beings. People will continue to enjoy people, emotional and caring, feeling their love for each other as individuals no matter what. Each of us has to do our best to stay alive to be sure we continue to be part of this. Each of us will die one day, but giving and receiving love, and being caring and compassionate is immune to extinction. It is a basic human instinct and will never disappear. If we think of ourselves as belonging to only one group, the human race, we would all come together and unite. We can't be annihilated.

Emotional regulation

It is important to regulate emotions so they don't become extreme. Implicit processes are vital in the self-regulation of emotion. There are two components of self-regulation: behavioural self-regulation and emotional self-regulation (Ackerman, n.d.). Manage and regulate your behaviour and manage and regulate your emotions. Both are important for managing emotional contagion. Arlin Cuncic (n.d.) writes that "self-regulation involves taking a pause between a feeling and an action," thinking things through, implicitly, in a way that "allows you to act in accordance with your deeply held values or social conscience and to express yourself appropriately." Pauses in one's own thoughts are examples of implicit processes.

Koole and Rothermund (2011) write that "implicit emotion regulation can be broadly defined as any process that operates without the need for conscious supervision or explicit intentions, and aims at modifying the quality, intensity, or duration of an emotional response." It is an automatic unconscious or subconscious process regulating emotions to keep them balanced. Implicit emotion regulation is vital in offsetting the impact of impulsive emotional responses that are triggered automatically by events. Since environmental events often bring on some degree of emotional contagion that needs to be offset, implicit emotional regulation will do so. Your deeper beliefs, values, and philosophies of life and beliefs about expressing emotion in various settings are involved when you are regulating your emotion implicitly. These beliefs exist under the surface, usually privately. It would appear to be crucial in managing a response so that emotional contagion could be lessened when environmental events impact on us. There would be a small automatic gap between the event and your feeling as you take the event in, so that you can quickly assess whether the feeling is in accordance with the event, and a larger intentional gap of a few moments as you make time to decide what is the best action to take. This is the job of your gatekeeper.

Research recognizes the important role that subconscious and unconscious beliefs play in emotion regulation (Hopp et al., 2011). Individuals who implicitly valued managing and regulating their emotions exhibited greater levels of psychological health, but only when they were high in cognitive reappraisal use. Cognitive reappraisal means they identify their cognitive distortions and reappraise, or reconsider more reasonable, accurate ways of describing their inner thoughts through constructive self-talk, talking to yourself from your logical mind. The unconscious and subconscious emotional regulation processes will interplay with conscious emotion regulation processes this way, related to cognitive reappraisal. Identifiable conscious thoughts in self-talk help in this process of emotional regulation. Make sure your self-talk coincides with what you believe deeply to be your core values. This strengthens cognitive reappraisal's effectiveness when people are infected by emotional contagion, so that it doesn't get too deep or strong.

Koole, Webb, and Sheeran (2015) say that people rely on implicit processes when choosing their emotional regulation strategies, since they live busy lives. When stressed and/or active, we can rely on more habitual emotional regulation strategies when dealing with less desirable emotions. This is where problems can occur. When situations are unpredictable, people use implicit processes to select emotional regulation strategies of a more familiar context. The authors state that implementation intention strategies will help people increase the likelihood of enacting their chosen strategy for emotion regulation. This means that if we mentally prepare ahead of time that, if x happens, it is best to do y instead of z, and have carefully considered the effect and results of both outcomes y or z, occurring, before choosing one, it is much easier to implement the emotion regulation strategies when an event happens and end up with effective emotion regulation. Some rehearsal of how to do the chosen outcome could help. This is what should happen when people prepare for potential emotional contagion situations.

Emotional regulation strategies encompass both positive and negative feelings, along with how we can strengthen them, use them, and control them. Chowdhury (n.d.) says it involves three components:

- initiating actions triggered by emotions
- inhibiting actions triggered by emotions
- modulating responses triggered by emotions

Chowdhury's article quotes Kris Lee (2018) who says that "with emotional regulation, we can allow the initial upsurge of emotions to settle down and zoom out of the situation before reacting to it." The field of psychology teaches that the time between a stimulus (the trigger to the person's response) and a person's response to it is crucial. "Increasing that time gap between stimulus and response restores the mental faculties that involve rational thinking and reasoning," says Chowdhury (n.d.). It allows us to regulate our emotional reactions. "As a result, we can save ourselves from sudden emotional breakdowns or burnout." says Chowdhury. We could also prevent or minimize emotional contagion in difficult situations that way, by increasing the gap. In short, it gives us time, even 30 seconds, to think or reason things out.

We may be familiar with sports teams practicing, to prepare for games, and actors rehearsing for performances. Like them, it makes sense to practise management of our emotions, thoughts, and behaviour ahead of time for real-life situations affecting relationships, opinions, and even political choices, so as not to be unduly affected by the emotional contagion that is likely to occur in moments like contentious conversations. This would involve practising by visualizing yourself in a realistic, stressful situation. Let's say you were having dinner with some friends and were discussing controversial political topics. Sometimes these people are difficult, and let's assume you have seen it before. Practice would prepare you ahead of time for potential controversial comments being expressed with contagious emotions, and help you decide how you could handle them: whether you want to absorb the emotion and how you could react effectively. Let's say you anticipate someone making a controversial political statement during dinner which makes you upset. Someone says something that you do not agree with, something that may stir you up and infuriate you. Visualize how you should handle those emotions being expressed towards you in case it happens.

When we rehearse it, we don't actually have to respond right away. We can take a few minutes to think it through and react slowly, with hums and haws, to prepare for the eventual real thing. If someone says something you really dislike, and in a sarcastic tone, and you react by swearing, you can predict there will be a major argument that might affect your relationship with that person. But if you acknowledge what the person says, reply by saying there might be something to their opinion, (that is a purposely vague statement which is usually true) and then change the subject, you might predict the mood would stay calm. Avoid controversial arguments. Visualize this person saying something you dislike, and practise handling it this new calm way.

You want to keep things calm, so when you practise, hear the controversial, upsetting comment in your mind that the other person may say, and tell yourself to stay cool. You do that by taking a deep breath. You may also want to think something helpful like, "She always says sarcastic, controversial things to stir up talk; I'm not going to give her that satisfaction." People may not recognize that the emotions they spread are contagious, but may recognize the behavioural pattern of others reacting to their controversial comments emotionally. You could reply and say, "that's interesting," or, "there might be something to it." If you want to disagree, keep your voice calm and neutral and mention your opposing comment, keeping it objective and not personal. Whatever your choice, don't bite, and don't get upset: the other person probably likes to stir things up, and you may surprise them by not biting. In that way, you don't get drawn into her emotional stance, which is your goal. Stay neutral, with more neutral vague positive comments. You are not really agreeing; you are defusing the anger. It is likely to prevent unfortunate, destructive emotional outbursts, either outward (swearing or storming out) or inward (becoming depressed, or anxious to the point of overindulging later in alcohol). Remember it is not just the words you are picking up from their initial statement, but the feelings and emotions that are expressed, often implicitly, in the tone of their voice that could trigger your automatic response. In this example it could be the sarcasm. That is how emotional contagion happens. So you resist it.

Some people are needy or self-focused and have no empathy or sensitivity for the person who is receiving their emotional flow. They may be outgoing, attractive, and appealing. However, they are likely focused on their own needs, and hope that their own needs can somehow be met by the person receiving the emotion. Any care or consideration for the receiver of their emotional flow is likely minor or missing. Their need could be the validation of their position on some controversial topic.

People generally pick up, consciously or subconsciously, a subtle feeling or implicit emotion expressed by the other person who is speaking. This is a tough situation. We would not expect ourselves to be aware of this on a moment-by-moment basis. People need general awareness of others and their manner of expression and possible effect on us. It is best to keep this to a personal, private thought about any emotion being expressed or emanated during conversation. Then we may be able to develop some awareness of the subtle feeling or implicit emotion being expressed, and possibly the contagious effects, so that we can be conscious of it happening. This can be called a filter: we have to process conversations or emotions. By being conscious of its occurrence, we develop some immunity to the contagion. We have control over whether or not we accept the emotional contagion, depending on if we want to feel the emotion or not. You can't block it if you aren't aware of it. With general awareness of this phenomenon, our internal gatekeeper takes the job and looks to see if it is happening. The gatekeeper can thereby discern if we want to accept the contagious effect. This comes from listening to the cognitive aspect of the expression and using reasoning to determine if we want to accept it cognitively; that is, whether we agree with it factually. The agreement should be based only on the words, the statement, the logic. The emotion should feel like it follows in spirit from the words spoken. That is not emotional contagion, since it follows from the words and doesn't infect the meaning—unless there are a lot of emotional words in the statement with a lot of rhythm and cadence in the voice emphasizing those words that infect their meaning.

It is desirable to use the cognitive part of thought, logic, and facts to decide if we agree. Using emotion as the criteria for acceptance allows the emotion to influence the acceptability of the thought, rather than the rational part. The cognitive or rational part is the fact found in the words, the logic connected with it, and the knowledge you have about it already and whether they fit cognitively. The emotion and thought can blend together, and you can come up with wisdom when you add some perspective.

Let's take an example. If someone says that abortion after six months is acceptable, you have to determine for yourself if a six-month period for an abortion is acceptable before allowing yourself to have emotions about it. The emotion you have should be your own, not absorbed or transferred from the person making the statement. It needs to be congruent with the six-month comment. You would accept the emotion if you accepted its association with the six-month period as valid when examined logically. If the received emotion is a little stronger when emitted by the other person than we feel, then we could allow ourselves to heighten our internal emotion if it is our style to do so, and if we evaluate the heightened emotion as congruent with the statement. If the heightened emotion is significantly stronger than it should be based on the statement, then the emotion itself is adding commentary and may be infecting the thought, overriding its logical and verbal essence.

We have our own style for the emotion. We have to ask ourselves if the emotion and the content of the statement fit both our cognitive belief and our emotional style. We have to own our feelings. We don't need to have as strong an emotion as the other, but we may allow ourselves to feel or express the emotion a little more if it is congruent with our belief and adds to it.

Marsha Linehan (2015) presents important information in developing emotional regulation skills, a necessary component of dialectical behaviour therapy (DBT), which she developed. A quick internet search will provide a list of her books, DVDs and her website. She says emotional regulation requires application of mindfulness skills, the nonjudgmental observation and description of one's current emotional responses. She teaches skills such as understanding and naming emotions, changing unwanted emotions, reducing vulnerability to emotion mind, and managing extreme emotions.

Intrinsic emotion then is a critical part of the emotion that we have to be aware of in resisting and blocking the effects of emotional contagion, as it is often expressed by people when expressing their opinions verbally. Recognizing this and tuning primarily to the verbal content of an expression is an important way to handle this.

The Power of Emotional Contagion

Emotional contagion is the greatest emotional process humans can experience. If there were no emotional contagion, then love would not move between people. However, toxic interactions overshadow positive ones. Distrust, cynicism, demoralization, and pessimism spread. The role of toxic contagion is often minimized in politics. In larger-scale political events, effects of toxic interactions with a leader linger and produce contagious negative emotions, which then spread to others, sometimes with debilitating effects. Moods can influence judgment and abstract situations and influence votes. Emotions are vastly under-rated in their importance although they have produced wars and the turmoil of our recent times. They also show the power of dignity, respect, and wisdom.

Emotional contagion is crucial in human relations and in society. It is evolutionary, relating to the way living things develop over millions of years. According to CogniFit, a company that writes about cognitive tests, emotional and mental processes, and brain training, we are born "equipped with the evolutionary capacity of emotional contagion to help synchronize our emotions and express our wants and needs." (Morris, 2017). They give the example of a newborn baby crying to be fed because it's the only way the baby knows how to get food from its mother. The baby is, in effect, using emotional contagion to communicate with its mother. It is evolutionary, pre-linguistic, and instinctual. The power of emotional contagion is that strong. Without it, human beings might not exist, as many babies would not survive. The mother-child bond is one of the strongest bonds humans have. Love does not have to be spoken; it is felt through contagion. It seeps through borders between people, finding its own way, especially through sound and touch.

When a baby is born, the power of emotional contagion comes forth naturally and almost immediately. It is contagious; we can feel it and sense it. The first communication comes from the helpless baby's cries, the only way the baby can reach out. The baby's very first cries may be its way of drawing breath, but the first instinctual communication conveys emotion. The only way the communication of love occurs is through this contagion, this evolutionary force that enables communication where words are not yet possible. A cry itself is noticeable because of the sound, but it is the emotion that is contagious: the desperation, neediness, urgency, and helplessness that are conveyed in the crying. When the mother hears the baby's cry, she feels the natural maternal instinct to hold her baby. The cry speaks to the mother—the baby cries to be fed. Its voice conveys need combined with emotion. It comes through nature, and when the force comes from nature, you know it is a very powerful force.

There is no doubt that emotional contagion is the greatest emotional process humans can experience, with love being communicated through its power. This is the positive part of emotional contagion. If there were no emotional contagion, then love would not move between people. Emotional contagion gives love its magic.

The role of emotion in life, although one of the most powerful forces, is often minimized. We don't often identify its importance. Sometimes emotion automatically leads us do the things that they say we should do, without thinking. Just like that. Strong emotion simply moves us: to cry, to run, to protest, to fight, to jump, to shout, to sing. It has such great power—it is the most powerful, invisible, intangible force that emanates from a human being, and it is contagious and infectious!

The power of emotion in everyday life

We often don't seem to realize the power of emotion in social, interpersonal situations. The power of emotion is shown in research (Barsade, 2014a), where a research confederate in a work situation spread positive emotion among others, who then experienced an increase in positive mood. There was also more cooperation and less interpersonal conflict, and groups in which people felt positive emotions actually worked better. The people did not recognize, however, that their decisions, and their group's decisions, had been directed by the displayed emotion of the confederate in the research. Positive emotional contagion creates a workplace culture of "companionate love" (Barsade, 2014b), which has been shown to boost employee satisfaction and teamwork, as well as reduce absenteeism and emotional burnout. Most people do not consciously tend to notice the strong power of emotion as it affects us positively in this way.

In these cases, the same research shows that the mood of the team was directly impacted by the mood of the leader. A Linked-In article by Elizabeth Solomon says that "the more upbeat the leader, the more productive the team. The more down the leader, the worse the team performed. This is [...] emotional contagion—when people in power dictate the mood of everyone around them." It is very powerful. It increases productivity in the workplace. Think of what it could do for world politics.

Solomon (2020) goes on to say that "when it comes to work, memories of toxic interactions with a leader are stronger than memories of what has gone well. When a leader loses emotional self-control, those events stand out and one toxic interaction overshadows a disproportionate amount of good." Painful memories can dominate pleasant ones. It makes sense, then, that in larger-scale political events, a similar emotional phenomenon occurs. This produces the distrust, cynicism, demoralization, and pessimism that becomes contagious as negative emotions spread.

Information conveyed by affect or emotion is crucial

Both positive and negative emotions have important impacts on our thoughts. Research about emotions and judgment indicates that information "conveyed by affect" or emotion is crucial, especially if the source of the affect is vague or uncertain (Clore & Huntsinger, 2007). When something is conveyed, it has to be received or caught by another party. Emotion carries information, although it is simple and straightforward. It is crucial for good judgment. Emotion influences how people process information and make decisions. We may know this as a fact, but we often don't recognize it as it happens. It makes sense then that the opposite could be true: that the power and even the existence of mild to moderate negative emotional contagion is unrecognized as it happens in the moment.

It is important to manage the emotion so that it can do this job properly, because emotions influence the process. Positive emotional information promotes, and negative emotional information inhibits the cognitive responses accessible to a person in a normal, neutral situation. A thought that is in the mind will come forth as the dominant thought when the emotion is positive and will stay in the back of the mind when the emotion is negative. But stronger negative emotions that are more forceful provoke a more contagious reaction when there are negative emotions prominent in the person's subconscious. This would relate to a thought regarding a discussion being heard, coming from a speech by a politician, or anything that one was listening to when the position the person was leaning towards was brought out by the feelings given off by the presenter. This would occur especially if the listener were uncertain and uncommitted to their own position but was already leaning in the direction of the speaker. The positive emotions expressed by a politician bring the positive thoughts in your mind into the open, pushing negative thoughts further into the background. However, the definition of what constitutes "positive" information or emotion is in the mind of the beholder, the person listening. A citizen who suspects racism or white supremacy may have merit, while listening to a politician's comments favouring a white person, would have dormant white supremacist thoughts brought forward into consciousness.

When an agreement is reached between two parties, there is usually a sense of satisfaction felt by both. These feelings of pleasure or happiness about an agreement shows the power of the positive emotion and affect that both parties feel. It lends credence to the idea that an incoming emotion embedded in a presenter's statement will contribute to the likelihood that mirror neurons will be triggered in the recipient already leaning that way. This would produce an automatic emotional contagion effect which may result in more global changes in attitude. If the recipient weren't leaning that way, it would not produce the automatic shift, only limited, smaller changes. The researchers indicate that if there is no obvious cause, affect will attach itself to whatever is available, which is why moods can influence even irrelevant judgments (Clore & Huntsinger, 2007). This is evidence that emotions don't think. If there is an obvious cause for an emotion, then that emotion would be limited and determined by a factual thought.

When thoughts are vague, or situations are abstract and open to judgment, emotions take over and attach themselves to something that seems good to them, even based on rhyming, alliteration. and other poetic effects, putting words together because of how they sound instead of what they mean. In this way emotions can spread and easily become contagious. This can happen in political campaigns with complex situations, such as reproductive issues, and results in emotion unduly influencing votes, since the message in an emotion is simple. A situation many people think is negative, like building a wall, may feel good to others who think the wall will protect them. That is why situations with differences of opinion get so emotional. With complicated situations, emotions can drive people to simple messages, like "walls protect us," due to cognitive ease and incomplete thinking, and that alone may determine their votes. Decision leaders need to make issues easier to understand, since simplicity drives emotion and makes a message more popular. For example, do walls really protect us? It may not really do that, but many people feel good if they believe they are protected by a strong leader who builds a wall.

Empathy requires clear boundaries between people

Rempala (2013) pointed out that usually the ability to feel and catch what others feel is thought of as valuable because it can facilitate empathy and be helpful to social interaction. However, empathy does not necessarily lead directly from emotional contagion, because empathy requires enough self-awareness on the part of the observer to avoid confusing his or her own subjective experience with that of the target person or group being considered. If we were to think that the comfortable middle-class people in North America have a similar experience with frustration and pain as that of impoverished refugees from the war-torn parts of the world, because we think that all people are the same and have the same experiences, then this would be false and does not lead to true empathy. Some people do not separate their own experiences from those of the target group. They may, then, judge refugees negatively, not fully appreciating the turmoil they have gone through. This is especially true if they don't have an understanding of world affairs and cultural differences and have not travelled much outside their comfort zone. They have a subjective bias that influences their judgment.

Emotional contagion does not have to lead to empathy. Empathy is a separate quality that can block the emotional contagion as we realize we do not want to absorb all of another's emotion, because we are not them. We need to set the personal boundary clearly. Empathy requires enough cognitive ability on the part of the observer to take on the perspective of the target, the person being observed, while still being ourselves (Decety & Jackson, 2004). Empathy requires us to separate ourselves and see the other person as if we are them, while realizing that we are not them. In emotional contagion, that "as if" quality is weaker. That allows the emotions to flow in a contagious way, crossing the boundary of the other person, infecting them.

In true empathy, there is some distance and definite emotional boundary between oneself and the person one feels empathy for. The person takes poetic license and imagines themselves in the same situation as the person they are empathizing with; they visualize themselves "as if" they were that person, put themselves metaphorically into the person's shoes to get a sense of how it might feel, while remembering they are not actually in the same situation. With emotional contagion, the emotional boundary between the two people is blurred, since knowing which one of them owns the emotion cannot be determined. Emotion can flow so easily between people that sometimes we need to be able to use effective thinking to know who owns the emotion.

Emotional contagion makes one vulnerable to the negative emotions of others. A study indicated that people living with mildly depressed roommates were more likely to become depressed themselves over time (Howes et al., 1985). Emotional contagion of negative emotions can lead to personal distress when the recipient is infected with emotional pain. It could be debilitating, especially if one picks up sadness, anger, and, even hatred, cynicism, and pessimism, and is unable to add the "as if" quality. People can react to personal distress caused by a cognitively dissonant source, where information doesn't jibe with the person's beliefs, with extreme denial and an opposite emotion. Rather than feeling sad, they may feel hateful and cynical because to feel sad would be somehow approving of the issue facing them—of which they disapprove. For example, perhaps they feel sad for an individual from a race they despise who is experiencing a loss. To combat the cognitive dissonance, they may turn that sorrow into hatred in their own mind. Instead of doing this, they need to acknowledge their own psychological issues. We all have issues.

You can't have turmoil without emotion

Emotions seem to be poorly understood by society and the media, possibly because they are invisible. They are potentially thought of by analysts as a "soft" factor, when compared to social and political developments. But turmoil does not come without emotions. They are, in reality, crucial, primary "hard" factors because they affect people and cause the turmoil of our times. You can't have turmoil without emotion, which drives violent, destructive actions. Psychologists call it "acting out" emotions; for example, a person expressing their anger through destructive behaviour.

The power of emotional contagion affects us daily: in our everyday life, in our social sphere, and also in the news of the world around us. That is why differences of opinion get so emotional. Emotions don't think.

In the time of the coronavirus and a divisive American president, fear abounds. Protests and riots and killings have occurred. People catch divisive, controversial emotions automatically and some react to them impulsively. Anger and anxiety increase. Cynicism and conspiracy theories flourish. Erratic behaviour runs rampant. Families are disrupted. Relationships are damaged. People march and protest. People are divided. And, sadly, people are injured and killed. These are the results of fear, hate, and other negative contagious emotions. Emotions drive behaviour. We have to learn how to get it under control, to bring emotions back to dominating positively by being in the loving, caring column where they belong. It starts with each of us.

In 2020, we saw the great effects of positive emotional contagion in massive protest marches across the U.S. We saw the effects of emotional infection in the widespread murder of Black and Indigenous people. But, as with emotion, it also brings positive emotional contagion, like in the power of the people. We see the power of emotional contagion spreading the love, brotherhood and sisterhood, cooperation, and in the long overdue and tentative arrival of the power of wisdom in society. The power comes in the ability to feel the love in a tangible way. We see the commitment to peace, the commitment to love for each other, regardless of colour, the commitment to kindness. In peace marches we see a few wise commentators, a few wise politicians, but mostly we see wisdom in the patience, the endurance, and the signs of the protesters. The power of positive emotional contagion turns potential into action as the protest marches spread across the world. Emotional contagion, as it spread between and among people, motivated them to come together. It was a very powerful force, more powerful than words alone. It was the emotions of love, dignity, and respect. This action was the antidote to negative emotional contagion. When love is spread through positive emotional contagion, it is the greatest force known to human beings.

Emotion at a height: popularity and charisma

We can see how, in the midst of the coronavirus fear, when talk is focused either positively or negatively on it, that anyone who denies sharing that heightened emotion risks being ostracized. This is an effect of contagion.

Talking about whatever topic it is that elicits a strong emotion is a way of feeling included. There is a social risk of not doing so, but that is alright as it is important to express your true feelings. Taking that risk means being able to withstand the negative feeling that often comes with being excluded. To do that, one needn't take the exclusion personally as meaning anything negative about oneself.

The height of the emotion is so strong that it defines the nature of the mood circulating in society, sweeping through and taking over the prevailing opinion, whether it is reasonable or not. A person takes some social risk when disagreeing with the prevailing opinion simply because of the strength of the shared emotion associated with that opinion. People think that because the emotion is so strong, it must be the correct stance to take, as if the emotion is an independent agency that speaks for itself. It is not. In that way, the emotion is contagious, being so appealing, alluring, and powerful that some people are just drawn in by the emotion itself.

Similarly, it would appear that emotional and social contagion are the mechanisms that produce the heightened emotions necessary for the phenomenon of popularity. Since popularity involves the presence of strong likeability and other positive emotions related to the person, group, or thing which is popular, it makes sense that emotional contagion is involved in producing the movement of emotions necessary for popularity to exist. This movement probably accounts for the occurrence of popularity itself as a phenomenon which spreads from person to person in society, because it requires a great number of people to like someone or something for it to be popular. But it is really more than that. This assumes that if something is popular, that somehow there was a direct one-to-one connection between the popular person and each individual citizen. No, it mostly comes from emotional and social contagion amongst people.

Oxford's dictionary *Lexico* defines *popularity* as "the state or condition of being liked, admired, or supported by many people." This definition neglects the bond between the people, which is likely to have caused the popularity through emotional and social contagion, where feelings are exchanged and absorbed based on mutual like. Liking can be due to reciprocal liking, interpersonal attraction, and similar factors.

Now with social media so prominent, especially with streaming videos, it is much easier for a singer to become popular, as long as they have the talent. Concerts demonstrate the height of emotional and social contagion. That establishes, reinforces, and strengthens the popularity of an individual as emotions spread among people. People even raise their hands and sway and move in rhythm together to the music at a concert, sharing the excitement and togetherness, as contagion establishes the phenomenon. So by that token, the same dynamic also influences the popularity of any person, trend, or group. Popularity becomes common and widespread among individuals as people pick up the contagious feeling of excitement from each other. Many social and interpersonal dynamics are involved as the contagion produces popularity.

Popularity is not just something that affects people who idolize popular stars like Billie Eilish, Taylor Swift, Ed Sheeran, or Ariana Grande. Adults in responsible, decision-making roles can make an important decision based on the popularity of a trend or fad. It might make no logical sense, but we are all prone to wavering in the face of popularity, fueled subconsciously by emotional and social contagion. That is the thing about emotional contagion: it comes in and affects our decision making when we wouldn't expect it to, in effect determining the course of society, contrary to wise decisions based on data and knowledge.

For example, in the year 2019, thoughts of a pandemic were not top of mind. COVID-19 hadn't happened yet, so it wasn't in the present moment where emotional and social contagion exist. The possibility of a global pandemic ranked very low on the list of relevant factors to consider when making decisions because it wasn't current. It wasn't a popular topic, nor part of public awareness, so warnings were ignored. In the U.S., decisions were made to disassemble pandemic review boards. In Canada, the Global Public Health Intelligence Network (GPHIN) warning system was abandoned, so that doctors and epidemiologists were not allowed to warn of potentially deadly outbreaks. This is related to popularity because it was not in the forefront of people's minds; it was not in the zeitgeist at that time. Popularity reflects the status of an issue in the public mind as it occurred through emotional and social contagion, as it is contagion that pushes a topic to the forefront. That's why experts are needed who use data and facts and who are not prone to emotional contagion.

Greater than popularity is the flow of charisma. It involves positive, appealing emotional energy moving towards others. We wonder why people with charisma have so much influence. It can be magnetic. The person exudes some emotional energy, often conveying the meaning of the verbal message that it is carried in. This emotion is contagious, as if it just catches you and grabs you, and you find yourself getting caught up in the words and the emotion in message simultaneously. It may seem like you have no choice. It may feel like someone has cast a spell over you, since it just pulls you in. It is not really a spell, and is not the same as hypnosis, but it may be similar. Political and social movements can be like this, so that reason and logic can be lost, or vague as you get swept up in the flow. Charisma has this impact. Don't let it do that if you don't want it to. It is important to be aware that you do have a choice: you are able to choose whether to resist it or to go with it. It can be very difficult to resist it when you are physically around other people who are absorbing it and then emanating it themselves.

Popularity and charisma are not good reasons to absorb emotion. A million people with commitment and charisma may not be right, and what happens is that the emotion builds to a crescendo from those million and it prompts others to absorb it because of the force behind the emotion. It is hard to resist, especially if a "hot topic" is involved. This is not a good reason, however, because emotions don't think. They just carry a simple message. Keep in mind a silly example: if a million people think two plus two is five, it is still four. But if a million people think two plus two is four, it is still four. People are essentially irrelevant to this solution. The answer is yours, but it must be based on fact and thought. Remember that fads and emotions are temporary and fickle: people quickly turn to the next one.

Disfavour or humiliation in society is also caused by negative emotional and social contagion. We pick up a negative vibe and it can quickly turn us against someone or something, becoming disfavour. Emotion is involved. This spreads very quickly and very easily as people have less tolerance for error. People can quickly—and sometimes unfairly—fall out of favour. This occurs as people grow intolerant of something unpleasant, especially when it involves disgust, so rapid emotional judgments are made that become contagious. This often produces humiliation, "when someone deliberately does something that makes you feel inferior or look bad in the eyes of others" (Fokkinga, 2021).

To understand this, consider the act of humiliation as a display of power between the "humiliator" and the humiliated person. The humiliator shows that he has a superior status to the humiliated person by putting him down, often in the public eye. This involves the act of rejection when someone stimulates shame in a type of power play to position oneself higher up the social ladder. Humiliation, however, is an emotion which stems from what an individual thinks people thought of them. It is a combination of mind-reading and feelings of shame and humiliation coming towards someone in a contagious effect. Only when a person absorbs this does it constitute actual contagion, otherwise it is better to let the emotion bounce off oneself rather than giving the humiliator the feeling of power and satisfaction. If the humiliated person feels this feeling is deserved, then they will often absorb it. However, a person should not let humiliation lower their self-esteem: There is no sense in letting the humiliator have control over your self-esteem when it is up to you. If you are humiliated by what a group or person does or thinks, you are probably letting it bother you because you value their opinion. Don't. The group is not giving you a good reason to value them. Just because they are popular doesn't mean they have a healthy interpersonal philosophy. That's how infection occurs: you allow an infected emotion to enter inside you because of the group's popularity. You may need to find another group which handles contagion better, as the act of humiliation comes via group contagion; ridicule is often promoted in the hopes of getting the leader's approval. Any leader who values humiliating someone is not a healthy leader.

Feelings and emotions seem to move across a therapy room in a quiet, personal, trusting setting to touch the therapist. It is likely then that this also occurs in many life situations where others interact in close proximity, including in large, public venues where excitement and turmoil flows. It probably goes unreported and unrecognized, or, at best, minimized. This is something for which proof is admittedly wanting or impossible to establish, although the phenomenon of mirror neurons in these situations substantiates it. It is real, and emotional contagion is the start of the awareness of the phenomenon. Emotions are very powerful and contribute very significantly to the mood and atmosphere of public events as they spread. They are invisible but not absent. They are not seen or heard, but they are real and can be felt.

We feel feelings especially in crowds, at parades, parties, churches, concerts, sports events, and especially when there are groups who get emotional and who protest. We feel the electricity in the air in a large, excited crowd. It feels like something is happening. Feelings and emotions have a real impact. When we are impacted by moving, flowing emotion, it just takes over. It is like a kind of intuitive harmony, when we are being swayed by the emotional impact of a band in a large audience. It flows towards us and around us. People can certainly feel the flow of excitement and adoration during concerts and sports events. It just flows. Usually it is positive. Sometimes it isn't. We usually just accept it, but sometimes we shouldn't. We may not realize that. We need to step back and appraise it. It is important to be able to discern if a situation may be risky.

Hearing someone speak in an emotional, heated, urgent manner to deliver a message may be risky and difficult when you are the receiver. It is not usually done purposefully or consciously, but it is a method of strong persuasion nevertheless, because the person uses contagious emotions to have a strong impact that may dominate and overwhelm the receiver. It is best to "disarm the anger" by responding calmly, rationally, and with a small degree of emotion. To do that the receiver needs to manage their emotions purposely at the time. They don't have to respond with an equally strong emotion.

These methods trigger a sensitive area for a receiver who may have self-doubts and who gets automatically defensive or aggressive when others talk this way. It is better to stand aside, in a sense, and see what the speaker is trying to do, what impact they are trying to have on us by speaking this way. Do they want to make us vulnerable, insecure, doubtful, or weakened in some way? When we feel emotional like this, we are not likely to respond with reason or logic. We would be likely to respond emotionally, beginning a game of emotional ping-pong and contributing to the contagion by infecting someone else with this emotion. That could happen if the third person is not immune to being infected by emotional input, doesn't resist the infection, and also becomes emotional. The emotional effect spreads and eventually dominates logic, so that we come to an illogical or incomplete conclusion. This is the effect of emotional and social contagion. It divides us and creates conflict so that a strong, divisive power can intervene.

Emotion has a powerful force that can actually be felt, especially when politicking. People can use it so that we don't realize what is happening. With actual voices given power in auditory delivery there is no time to concentrate on complex ideas, but the effect of the emotion gets through in the voice. We hear it in a politician's voice, even on TV; this, however, may not be the best way to develop an opinion, as reasoning ability is likely nullified. This is why we end up with emotional voting. This is likely a major contribution to the turmoil in recent times when we realize that emotion contributed in a major way to recent American presidential elections and votes for Brexit.

Certainly, to the trained individual, words carry more power than emotion, but to the vast majority of the population the power comes in the emotion connected to the words. It multiplies when in crowds, or when more than one person speaks emotionally. That's why you can say, "one person at a time, please." Not only is there too much sound, but there can also be too much emotion. Too many people responding all at once magnifies the force of emotion. Emotional contagion integrates with social contagion and as a result they often take over our cognitive abilities.

As the emotional effect strengthens, it can multiply. Before long, many people may be speaking only from their emotion, not using reason, knowledge, or memory, not recalling facts or details, and instead giving an impulsive System 1 reaction. The general population, when listening to a politician who has contagious effects, may find themselves using implicit emotional referents to judge their comments. People will then speak in generalities or in emotional language, and they may think emotionally; the emotion, although implicit, is the major motivator for their thoughts on a topic. In political discourse they may then tend to use implicit emotion as a guide to their response.

There are many explicit emotions also, especially at a time of turmoil when the implicit ones break through into consciousness. Sometimes in life feelings overwhelm us, and we may cry, scream, yell, or curse. Emotions drive actions, so we may break something, punch someone, run away, or drive too fast. Bad things can happen. Sometimes people absorb feelings which they cannot tolerate, like jealousy or envy. Sometimes we can have a reaction to this inability to tolerate the internal emotion, in ourselves or in someone else, a reaction which often produces counter emotions such as anger, hate, or depression. In a heightened emotional state people can act impulsively and irrationally on these feelings. Instead, we need a gatekeeper. We really need to know what's going on with our feelings so that we are not overwhelmed. We need to know how to maintain the right balance, how to let ourselves have plenty of positive feelings, how to keep them as our own, how to stop taking on others' feelings, or to not let ourselves be affected by other's feelings in ways that we really don't want to be. If this happens and we are overwhelmed, we really can't function very well anymore. We may be in a weaker position or even in some danger, so that in the worst case we could find ourselves doing things we regret later.

It may be acceptable for feelings to take over as long as our thoughts guide us. It is like a car, the driver, and the gas. The thoughts make the decision about where to go like the driver does, and the feelings give us the energy and power to go there, like the gas does. But we can become overwhelmed by feelings and then we get paralyzed. The car stalls. This is anxiety.

The feelings can propel us to good things, like discoveries, when propelled by wisdom, hunches, plans and goals. Or they can propel us to horrible things, like war and violence, driven by emotional energy, related to hate, fear and demoralization, and under focused thoughts to undertake destructive actions. Emotional contagion and infection are very powerful, but we don't often recognize their tremendous power. Emotions cause war, although strategies win them. Often, strategies prevent wars. This involves thinking. The mind thinks. Emotions don't think.

Racism, Justice, and Emotional Contagion

Deaths, protests, and riots spread around the world in 2020, caused largely by a pandemic of heightened emotions. Extremists caught contagious emotions, which were spread and magnified, spreading false theories. Leaders caught contagious emotions, which infected their reasoning. In these situations, some people then lost their judgment. Emotional thinking dominates in "hot topics." Racism is pervasive and produces strong feelings of hate; people, including police, act on their contagious emotions, producing actions such as police brutality. Fear and anxiety produce counter-contagious emotions of anger and power. Violence is a contagious disease and serious health problem, yet anti-violence programs are minimized. We need awareness, systematic reasoning, cognitive restructuring, and wisdom to handle negative emotional contagion.

People's emotions have been raw during the pandemic of 2020–2021 because they have been restricted from normal socializing, thanks to physical distancing and self-isolation. They are missing their usual outlets to express feelings and emotions, like live sports, shopping, concerts, and movies. There are few opportunities for eating and drinking together, talking, telling stories, and laughing. These are all ways of expressing emotions. Many people can't do that now, due to the pandemic, so their emotions, good and bad, are closer to the surface.

True, raw emotions

During the pandemic, many people have been more irritable, anxious, suspicious, and depressed. Tempers flared and relationships soured. These are true, raw emotions, but during ordinary times they are generally kept in check. Experiencing a catastrophe like the pandemic highlights the need for people to learn how to handle their emotions more effectively when they are frustrated. When emotions are heightened, everyone is affected. Suppressed feelings about tensions and issues in society are expressed. Police, being human, may also be on edge as others show little ability to suppress their emotions when they are out in public. This all occurs because emotions are not given the required priority. This is a pandemic of emotions.

During the pandemic, there was an erratic man as president of the United States, who, for most of his time in office, had to be held in check because of his impulses. For example, before the pandemic, he tried to unilaterally strip a well-respected CIA director's security clearance, and threatened to do the same to nine other very high-ranking security people. He called the CIA director a "loudmouth," and a "hack" (Frum, 2019) phrases designed, probably subconsciously, to elicit a defensive emotional response. These are also phrases suggestive of an impulsive, erratic approach. This elicited a non-emotional reply defending the director from 60 former CIA officials, according to Frum.

The combination of causes for heightened emotion, both the pandemic and this president's behaviour while in power, has been deadly as emotional contagion has flared, showing its great power. It has been terrifying. Deaths, injuries, protests, riots, and looting all occurred in 2020, and early 2021, on top of the many deaths from COVID-19. Emotion provides the energy for much of this. And emotions don't think.

The rioting and insurrection in Washington, D.C. on January 6, 2021 was a clear example of how emotions don't think. A mob of extremists stormed the U.S. Capitol building, pure emotions driving their behaviour—based on their false, entitled beliefs that they were taking over the government and fighting what they believed was a rigged election. The rioting reflected extreme emotional contagion in action, triggered by the former president in his last days in power. The emotions spread and were magnified among the members of the mob as they came together. They accepted false theories not through the power of logical reasoning or shared responsible behaviour (although they may say it was), but because of the power of emotional contagion and conspiracy theories infecting their reasoning ability. Their perspective was narrow, simplistic, and driven purely by emotional thinking. When strong negative emotions flow through like-minded individuals moving around in a crowd, they mimic each other, mirror neurons are very active, voices express strong emotions, and powerful irrational actions and erratic, irresponsible, dangerous behaviour results. Emotions don't think. We rarely remember to think logically when we feel strong emotions, or even attempt to keep them in check. We give our emotions permission to take over when we are in a socially sanctioned emotional situation, like when our favourite sports team wins a championship, and we celebrate—although even then we have to continue to be responsible and obey the laws.

The mob at the Capitol Building said things like: "It is time for war," and, "We're not backing down [...] this is our country." They declared it as if they were protecting their country from an enemy when they were, in fact, domestic terrorists attacking their own country's seat of power. This illustrates the power of emotion related to beliefs with aspects of mass delusion. It was complete emotional infection, a feeling of invincibility so strong that they felt they alone had the ability to overtake the U.S. government with support from the outgoing and defeated president, technically still in power. The emotion drove their behaviour to the point where there was no sense of actual political reality; they thought they were defining reality to the point of re-creating a new political system. This is the power of mass delusion.

The necessary components of emotional contagion were there as many in the mob crowded together, subconsciously synchronizing facial expressions, vocalizations, postures, and movements with those of the others, and, consequently, converging emotionally. Many were dressed similarly as they moved together in unison. With the crowding together, planning together, all while under the "magnetic" influence of an emotional authoritarian leader with a strong impact on his followers' emotions, the emotional contagion was powerful.

The power of strong emotional contagion often blinds people to reality and other perspectives of a situation. They take the what-they-see-is-all-there-is approach to the immediate situation. The *New York Times* reported that a sixty-seven-year-old retired landscaper, who was a protester but not really a rebel, ascended the Capitol steps as the crowd surged forward but said he did not go inside and disapproved of those who did. Even so, he said he would never forget the sense of empowerment as he looked down over thousands of protesters. "It felt so good, he said, to show people: 'We are here. See us! Notice us! Pay attention!'" (Barry et al., 2021) This was the verbal report of his feelings that drove him to do this; the subjective report of a participant who was, in effect, saying that the sense of empowerment and recognition was such a grand feeling for him that it was worth the risks. It likely replaced a sense of inferiority, inadequacy, and lack of recognition that has perhaps been lifelong for him, so that joining with others who likely felt similarly was emotionally satisfying.[11] He may have had mild depressive feelings and chronic demoralization leading up to this behaviour that day. But good for him for using reason and judgment to refrain from entering the Capitol building. His demoralization likely lessened when he had important second thoughts which resisted the emotional contagion's appeal to enter the building. He seemed to overcome the power of that emotional feeling. Several days after the storming of the Capitol, he appeared to feel guilty and wondered if he went too far. This is the long-term guilt that comes after short-term emotional satisfaction; short term gain brings long-term pain. "Should I get down on my knees and ask for forgiveness?" he said in an interview. "I am asking myself that question." (Barry et al., 2021). The emotional contagion had passed, and he appeared to be in his rational mind again when asking that question.

Five people died. There could have been many more. This demonstrates why emotional contagion is perhaps the greatest power in society. The power of emotion when it overrules reason, and drives action, as it did here, is immense.

We should ask whether we should have been giving rioters like this man, in the months and years prior to this event, the recognition he needed and craved, or the counselling, psychotherapy, or psychoeducation that could have helped him put things into proper perspective. Of course, we don't know if he previously received it or not. He may have, or perhaps he also achieved recognition. But sometimes it takes an actual event to demonstrate to some people, such as this man, the real meaning and emotion behind the words and the lessons learned in counselling to provide the perspective of the situation. Many people do not receive the necessary psychoeducation. This does not imply that anyone who protests needs counselling and psychotherapy, or is mentally ill, but many of those who riot at an event such as this probably would have benefitted proactively. Many people benefit from psychotherapeutic techniques although they are not mentally ill. Because this particular event was destructive and violent, appearing to involve individuals who lost their judgment,

---

11 These comments about this man are psychological speculation on my part, since I have never met him, and did not talk to him. The comments are not meant and should not be regarded as a psychological evaluation or assessment of the man, but as an example of the effect of emotional contagion in real life.

and blindly followed their perceptions and emotions, this may be true for them. The severe emotional pull probably drew in the rioters, making them delusional about the situation.

We can prevent the negative effects of emotional contagion if we do not expose ourselves to potentially problematic emotional situations. The problem is that there was a strong appeal to do so because the perpetrator was the president of the United States, an authoritarian, emotional leader who appealed to the needs of those who had been victimized in life. He was a type of rescuer who seemed to satisfy people's fantasies of being rescued by a white knight, a hero figure. To prevent the associated emotional contagion, it would have been important to check one's assumptions about whether things truly were as they appeared to be. Otherwise, one is relying on emotional reasoning, but emotions don't think, they just give simple messages. This was likely the case here. The mind thinks, and the mind can verify assumptions by thinking critically. Some people will reject this possibility, likely because of the allure of emotions. This again leads to the idea that these people are attempting to overcome the effects of years of feeling inferior through rebelling, allying themselves with an authoritarian leader who has no true loyalty to his followers. They probably didn't want to relinquish this ideal in case they were perceived to be weak and inferior. Instead they need humility.

This illustrates the need for societies, involving its citizens, and governments, to recognize the prevailing collective subconscious and take steps to address the message it contains. This would build the trust immensely and help overcome the potential for more turmoil and violence. We can be sure that the legal system will not do this and should not. The health system doesn't usually address it either, but this involves social health, or the lack of same. We ignore it to our peril.

The appeal of power; the danger of power

Power feels so good when you have it, that for some people who join the police it seems difficult to resist and too tempting to let go of. Some police officers seem to like to have complete power and control, possibly as psychological compensation for earlier years in their life of feeling insecure, violated, or relatively powerless. A police officer, later incarcerated for an incident eight years ago when he pointed a gun at an innocent man's head, said in an earlier incident that "I can do whatever I want." (McMahon & Morrow, 2020). This raises the possibility that the police departments may attract people who like power more than the average person does. This is what happens when the need for power in the police force goes unexamined; it spills over and becomes dangerous.

In the U.S. in 2020, the military was sent to Black Lives Matter (BLM) protests. Authorities talked about martial law becoming a possibility, as if peaceful protesters were dangerous. Government leaders, who distrusted them, became so fearful they referred to the protesters as rioters, which they were not. This is emotional contagion in action, as emotion infects their reasoning abilities, as the mind catches the contagion of the emotion. Fear takes over judgment, or, worse, perhaps those in authority saw it as a way to appeal to the fear among the public. While there were a few looters and some rioters, the vast majority were peaceful protesters simply exercising their democratic rights. Some unperceptive leaders may become fearful of the peaceful protesters to the point that they become anxious that they are taking over, as if they fear—in a moment of severe irrationality—that their country and their citizens will be severely overwhelmed by the protesters. The fear becomes so strong (even when based on limited evidence) that emotional contagion infects the thinking and trust of those in the public who feel vulnerable.

One of the things that happens through emotional contagion is a vast overgeneralization into all-or-nothing thinking. Police officers who have abused their social power by being violent have inadvertently spread feelings of anger and revenge. Some people begin to think that all police are guilty, and none are innocent. They may have been controlled by police for decades, so it is likely that the power of emotional contagion stemming from the emotional reaction to this control is strong. The feelings of anger and revenge spread in a contagious way, affecting society's judgment of anyone wearing a police uniform as if every single police officer were violent, brutal, and murderous. We know that many police officers are caring, decent, good people, not involved in these brutal actions. Their stories are not usually covered in the media. Consumers of the news have to realize that stories being broadcast are of unusual things happening, and not typical of an entire group.

It is tough to resist emotional contagion in a "hot topic" area such as this. Police brutality is real, and people do die from it. Thousands of people around the world protested police brutality. The massive power coming from the 2020 BLM protests was so strong that it was hard to disagree with the protesters. It is a hot topic emotion. Alternatively, some might feel that they absorbed the strong energy of the protest through emotional contagion and so later come to feel that they were wrong to agree with their message initially. We can disagree with some things without disagreeing with everything, without standing against the BLM protesters or thinking they are a bad group. The peaceful protesters we see on TV are mostly good people. Emotional contagion can make us think that we are taking sides when we think emotionally, in an "either-or" scenario. We may feel guilty in disagreeing. But that is the power of free speech. Emotional contagion fires up each side to take extremes. Try and think in the middle. You can disagree with some things protesters say or do but agree with many. Some looters don't make the whole group bad; they are the outliers.

Police and security are habitually on guard, looking for and thinking in terms of criminals and potential danger. They fail to perceive the overall context, which is a feeling of peace among the protesters, seeing instead only mayhem or death. When this happens repeatedly, we see a miasma, an influence or atmosphere that tends to deplete, corrupt, or obscure, causing narrow thinking and tunnel vision, in the police. We may be so immersed in it that we are catching negative emotions from the people in our lives, preventing us from seeing the contagion or its cause, Flora (2019) says. Instead of seeing the contagion for what it is, we sense we are in an unhealthy environment. In worst-case scenarios, emotional contagion leads to harmful actions. Instead, seeing it as emotional contagion allows us to step back and see our reactions as a result of emotional infection from contagion. Identifying it as such allows us to resist it, thereby preventing the harmful reactions. Otherwise, an oppressive or unpleasant atmosphere occurs, as emotions of suspicion, fear, and anger dominate, in spite of the reality that could easily be perceived with a wider perspective. When we are overwhelmed with the emotional contagion of these negative emotions, we take a narrow perspective which blinds us, and we feel impelled to act on them.

The power of emotion blinds us to details. All protests seem to be against a large group of people, so that we perceive everyone to be guilty. And some of the police perceive all protesters as rioters. Then the police can abuse their power, sometimes mistakenly perceiving individual citizens as potential criminals or rioters. They may then be in a state akin to emotion mind, as emotions flow easily in a state of quick thinking and moving about when there is tension in the air. But the police officers who do not think this way do not garner media attention: they do not act irrationally and so do not make the news. Because of emotionally infected thinking, people generalize from news reports of police abuse and think that the whole police force is the same. So some call to abolish the police instead of calling for true reform of the police.

Similarly, among people who are racist, the anger towards the target race overflows. All members of a group are identified only by the group they belong to. The people with unconscious bias towards other races, those who are infected by emotional thinking, may start to think that all Black people deserve to be targeted. Racism produces strong feelings of hate which can take over the judgment of many people. This causes them to take out their anger on innocent Black men or women. Then Black people naturally start to fight back. This is all emotion, and emotions don't think. Emotion, when it gets very strong and when it is negative and contagious, is the most dangerous power on earth. We need to learn to moderate it, to manage it, and to regulate it across society, from police to Black people to white people to Indigenous people to Asians to politicians, almost to everyone.[12]

When racism rears its ugly head, it is like a river flooding its banks; the river of emotion spills over and takes over our behaviour. We are influenced by emotional contagion also, or counter-contagion. The power spills over for a few and they lose their judgment and act with their emotions. Then tragic mistakes can happen. Emotions don't think. When actions are caused by emotions, under acute, severe stress, distorted and unprofessional thoughts may occur in some individuals in the police, security, military, or others, thoughts that come mere seconds before shots are fired. These thoughts are primitive and are prone to come out at times of acute tension, when more mature and recently learned thoughts are forgotten, due to emotional infection. So thoughts like, "I'm going to teach him a lesson," or, "There's only one way to stop him," or, "I'll show him who's boss," can come into consciousness and dictate the behaviour of some people in power.[13] These are dysfunctional thoughts of power common to adolescents and immature adults—usually men. These thoughts can occur in spite of simple training. More professional, sophisticated

---

12 Everyone except babies, young children, and people with severe brain damage or severe dementia.

13 These types of thoughts likely only occur to a few police officers involved in these apparent mistakes of judgment.

ways of handling it are available, with further relevant screening of psychological suitability and more intensive psychological training for those found suitable.

Unfortunately, the many situations where police security or military officers handle difficult situations very well may be overlooked because of the power of emotional contagion in the media and the public. The contagion spreads the emotions of fear and anxiety, and counter-contagion spreads anger and power so that we judge many police unfairly. As a result of emotion's overwhelming impact on our reasoning powers, people on either side can erroneously generalize the incidents involving individual police to apply to the entire entity. Many people who are wary of protesters may think they want to abolish the police, and so, naturally, become afraid that society will be overrun by criminals. That is fear talking. Emotions don't think. If we take time to think, we realize that all police would never be abolished. Many who are wary of the police may actually want to eliminate the police in order to eliminate police brutality; they can get emotional about it. They may fight, scream, and lose emotional control. This is the case where emotional contagion takes both sides to opposite extremes where they can get very emotional and target their perceived opponent. Then, typically, emotional contagion wins as serious conflict can occur.

This results in the call to "defund the police," which, as a slogan, attracts attention because it rolls more easily off the tongue than a more reasonable approach, such as "re-direct some of the police funding," which would address social needs like housing, education, vocational training, mental health services, psychological treatment, and counselling programs that would prevent crime. Otherwise, police services require funding. Perhaps standards will be raised, and applicants will require more education to become police officers, with more professional training as we said in preceding paragraphs.

Psychological screening is necessary because the possession of guns in the police force creates a sense of power which can create an emotion which overrides more reasonable thinking, especially for insecure people who need powerful feelings to suppress their feelings of insecurity. Some insecure people likely enter the police force to attain a feeling of security, which is impossible because security is an inner characteristic which does not rely on external assets like a gun and uniform. So they are still insecure, although it doesn't show. Or an officer may exist in an environment of toxic masculinity, where brutal strength, domination, and guns satisfy an insecurity. Feelings of insecurity and vulnerability can easily occur and trigger automatic, primitive ways of getting power. Some individuals with more than a few feelings of insecurity can become police officers if they are not screened properly psychologically.

It is crucial to stop automatically catching and absorbing destructive emotions from others. It is wiser to just perceive the anger and keep it at a surface level. That is constructive. A constructive, objective System 2 thought would be: "There is a mid-twenties tall male with dark hair firing a shotgun at people. I need to disarm him now, while keeping things as safe as I can." A destructive, emotional System 1 thought would be: "I'm going to teach that sonofabitch a lesson." Actions come from thoughts and feelings, so we can decide which of these two thoughts is likely to result in a bad ending.

If the extreme right and left each move a little closer to the centre (but not right to the centre), neither has to give up so much and they have a better chance of getting their cherished points listened to, and perhaps accepted. That is compromise; it produces togetherness, and this begets safety, respect, and unity. True, it may mean modifying or relinquishing some extreme perspectives, but unfortunately extreme points are not immediately—if ever— accepted in an integrated society. It takes time, a lot of time, and a little change may be better than none because it puts you closer to the long-term goal.

Psychological problems but no psychological treatment in the justice system

We see the effects of emotional and social contagion through media reports of unfortunate incidents involving individuals from cultures we are not familiar with. Someone suffering from post-traumatic stress disorder (PTSD) may be vulnerable to emotional contagion since the memories of their initial trauma and the related emotions of fear and suspicion are likely near the top of their ongoing awareness, according to research by Durand, Isaac, and Januel (2019). They found that PTSD patients seem to have more emotional memorization of negative information. Such information is likely to consist of images of events that elicit emotional memories. PTSD includes the development of a stronger and a more emotional memory of the traumatic event by the victim. As a result, they would likely have limited immunity to emotional contagion. They have probably felt various troubling emotions that were similar to those they were exposed to in the initial trauma that caused their PTSD. This does not imply that similar emotions are, in fact, present and caused directly by the new situation. In PTSD it is the memory of the initial event that re-triggers any emotions. They may be re-triggered because they are near the surface of the individual's emotional memory. Without treatment, they may just accept their new feelings and related thoughts as fact.

There was an incident involving an Iraqi family running a restaurant in the U.S. A man walked in and threw a chair at a waiter's head (Phillips, 2017). The perpetrator was a decorated Marine sergeant major apparently suffering from PTSD due to years of combat. He was reportedly unable to obtain treatment for his chronic disorder. This is sad because there are many psychologists who treat PTSD effectively. The prosecutor charged him with felony-level hate crime and assault charges that carry a mandatory prison sentence. Lack of treatment for PTSD ends up in a prison sentence where many with mental illness languish, costing society more money than treatment would, and more suffering because of the possibility of re-offending—producing more contagious cynicism and demoralization. Emotional and social contagion can produce criminal behaviour in susceptible individuals with a lack of knowledge (or lack of ability when there is cognitive impairment) about how to regulate their emotions and control their behaviour.

Psychological therapy provides this treatment for potential and actual offenders, but we need more. Prisoners are generally not required to obtain psychological or psychiatric treatment for their issues. Because of privacy and confidentiality policies, the public doesn't hear about such success when it does happen. We continue to support the distorted idea that police forces, courts, lawyers, judges, and prisons will treat the problem. A psychologist, or other helping professionals, can assist some of these individuals. Changes in the justice and health systems could facilitate more people being provided with treatment, saving lives in the future, lessening demoralization.

How many times do we hear a judge sentence someone to a secure treatment centre for inmates run by professionals? There is no such centre. If we took some money designated for police services and our criminal justice system, and instead redirect some of these funds to specialized psychological treatment, including mental health assessment and personal counselling and therapy, we would be much safer. We might think that, based on a few studies, psychotherapy doesn't work in a prison population, but that is only for true psychopaths, who usually comprise less than half of the prison population. We are not referring to classical Freudian psychotherapy but to updated, effective programs including cognitive behavioural therapy, dialectical behavioural therapy, acceptance and commitment therapy, motivational interviewing, and other newer methods of therapy, as well as some updated psychoanalytical psychotherapies. This would also encourage the development of other innovative and effective methods of treatment. As well, other needs such as housing, education, and vocational training are necessary. It seems cruel to withhold it. Even though it's costly, it beats having dangerous people running around homeless, costing even more money for legal services and corrections in the future. There is no true justice in cruelty.

We need to redirect some funds intended for the justice system, or direct new money to such a program so police can maintain their funding. When people are in danger, they call the police. That is appropriate, and police should appear on the scene, but the police then become the default method to defuse danger when there are other methods as well, such as Non-Violent Crisis Intervention (NVCI), developed with mental health professionals. A mental health or therapy team also needs to be involved in these situations.

The rehabilitation of inmates is difficult, especially in a prison setting, and only the motivated are successfully rehabilitated. But the public's emotional satisfaction with punishment dictates this approach to the conservative politicians and judges who support punishment and incarceration. It is emotionally satisfying to punish someone, and both the voter and the politician, who may like the powerful emotion rendering punishment brings, allow the emotion to rule again. But that doesn't help the offender.

Some may think offenders don't deserve to be helped, and it may be true for a select few, but it is not all-or-nothing. That sounds like anger and revenge dominating reasoning abilities. Many deserve to be helped, if only because they will be released some day and live among us. Let's assume that we want them to be rehabilitated so they become better people and learn how to handle their impulses. If you wouldn't release a person from hospital before their disease was successfully treated, why release an inmate whose criminal, violent or even murderous tendencies were not at all treated? Everyone deserves a chance to be helped. It would save lives. Rehabilitation through psychological or psychiatric treatment or counselling isn't mandatory. It should be. We have the knowledge, and we can develop better methods. As a civilized society we need to take that chance.

Indeed, it would be preferable to send offenders to a hospital-like facility—not a hospital, not a prison, not an asylum, not a correctional institution—but to a type of treatment centre for inmates that currently doesn't exist, with proper custody and security. Here there would be primarily professionals, and treatment would be mandatory, and treatment protocols would be developed. This would allow the development and implementation of proper psychological, social, vocational, educational, and psychiatric assessment and treatment modalities. These would improve with time, just as all treatment methods are improved with time. The inmates would be released not after a set time, but after the problem was corrected, whether that took days, weeks, months, or many years.

In my experience, about 20 to 30 percent of convicts in Canadian federal prisons are incorrigible because of habitual, criminal characteristics and related psychopathy and sociopathy in their personality, but the other 70 to 80 percent could be helped, making progress in rehabilitation. But emotional contagion infects the public's thinking. Democracy rules but doesn't account for people using System 1 thinking to develop their opinions. Many in jail are labelled a "convict," "rapist," "murderer," or something even worse, like "scum"—and yet when released are the same people. These "rapists" and "scum" may live long, healthy, successful lives after treatment and release, without re-offending. I have seen it happen. This person is no longer a rapist after decades, although they were once convicted and sentenced to prison for rape. How long does it take for someone to not be scum or a rapist anymore? It is a hard question to answer. That's partly because the emotional trauma associated with rape has a contagious effect on our thoughts about the person. Start to overcome this by separating the person from the act. Not everything they do is criminal.

Racism, protests, and violence

Gary Slutkin, an epidemiologist, has correctly recommended that we treat violence as a contagious disease (in Flora, 2019). He has an anti-violence program for interrupting contagion called Cure Violence. The major news networks often inflame the problem by reporting the lethality and extent of violence without emphasizing possible cures, such as a program like this. This program claims a 63 percent reduction in shootings in New York City. Yet the media minimizes this, despite the presence of violence and repeated mass shootings and killings in our society. It is clear that individuals who are perpetrators of mass shootings are by and large emotionally disturbed men, and although the shootings are criminal by definition, this is an ongoing very serious health problem that should be treated as such.

History has been close to repeating itself. On May 4, 1970, during protests on college campuses across the U.S. against the Vietnam War, the National Guard shot and killed four students who were protesting at Ohio's Kent State University. A civil suit was later filed by injured Kent State students and the bereaved families of the deceased, and a settlement was reached in which the Ohio National Guard agreed to pay those injured in the events of May 4 a total of $675,000 (History.com editors, 2021). The National Guard issued a statement that said, "In retrospect, the tragedy [...] should not have occurred. The students may have believed that they were right in continuing their mass protest [...]. Some of the Guardsmen [...], fearful and anxious from prior events, may have believed in their own minds that their lives were in danger. Hindsight suggests that another method would have resolved the confrontation. Better ways must be found to deal with such a confrontation"(Kent State University, n.d.). Indeed. This is slow, rational, system 2 thinking, not present at the time of the event. Have today's enforcement people studied and learned from this?

Emotions are especially high when death, a virus, race, police, and an ineffective, unpopular leader are involved at the same time. We had a simmering pot that became a boiling pot for emotions because of the effects of emotional contagion. One emotion pulled for another automatically and they all magnified and came together as one, and it culminated in nationwide protests. Recent incidents in the U.S., like the 2020 murder of George Floyd, have revealed that the pot is boiling over. It has been a triple jeopardy: hate, power, and fear. Emotions have been increasingly boiling over, especially in the face of widespread police brutality causing harm to civilians. For the police, especially in crowds, it is a case of us against them—hatred for Black people by some police, hatred of the police by many citizens, power felt by irresponsible police officers who have strong authoritarian personalities, and fear felt by Black people for their very survival. This is the effect of emotional contagion.

Multi-racial support of the BLM movement seemed to come together at once, after too many years of Black suppression. Multiplied by the emotion society felt because of the frustration, worry, and fear from the coronavirus, the tension of three years under the former president, and the pandemic death toll rising above 100,000 in the U.S.—these all likely contributed to the emotional contagion that developed and worsened. These factors all were part of the outburst which brought about many nights of protesting where crowds mingled, and emotions were kindled. It is through such kindling that emotions flow when emotional contagion is strong and high. It is probably what happened during some of the American BLM protests. (This in no way dismisses or minimizes the importance or relevance of any non-violent protest in inducing social change. Emotions were often channelled appropriately, and emotional contagion minimized in spite of its presence in some pockets).

When strong emotions strike a chord within us, they inflame emotions, as if our "inner chords" all get together and share feelings of commiseration, multiplying them and their power. It is a concept causing an emotional feeling like flames coming up inside ourselves and spreading to adjoining combustible material, like in kindling, so people next to us also feel these feelings through emotional contagion, catching them as they feel compatible, as opposed to a process like spontaneous combustion. This is a way emotional contagion can occur, looking at it subjectively. We can get inflamed by adjoining contagious emotions entering us from others if they strike our own similar, inner combustible feelings, if our gatekeeper allows them in. With strong appeal and power, the contagious emotions can force themselves past a weaker gatekeeper who is unaware of the power of emotional contagion. Systematic reasoning, such as logical thinking, critical thinking, recall of factors, looking at a wider perspective, and considering competing evidence would challenge our perception and make the gatekeeper stronger. If we focus on systematic reasoning and other cognitive therapy methods and use them forcefully in our self-talk, their impact will be minimal. Behaviourally, when interacting with others, they take a little more time and sensitivity of thinking, so as to put us into System 2 and not challenge or confront others in ways that are off-putting. Comments and suggestions about wider perspectives, perception-checking, and thinking wisely can trigger people to keep the systemic reasoning in mind, to keep the emotional contagion at a minimum, and to contribute to the development of a group wise mind.

This systematic thinking is necessary because when others' feelings like resentment flow together and join in with similar feelings in the crowd, they can also be caught by us if we are in sympathy. They are then likely to be experienced by us also. They develop power and become contagious when others feel similar feelings and have similar thinking processes. Of course, the degree to which we catch it depends on a number of factors, such as our personality, our openness to experiencing emotions, and our degree of sympathy and agreement with the issue at hand. That is the point. If we don't agree with the issue, or don't generally experience and express emotions openly in public, a strong gatekeeper won't allow us to absorb the feelings. They may just connect momentarily and then bounce off.

When power strikes a crowd, if it feels rewarding to have blending emotions in a crowd, it spreads. With wisdom attached, it is positive power, and is constructive, but without wisdom it can be raw emotion and often becomes destructive. You can feel the wisdom there when the movements are a little slower and purposeful.

This gives an illustration of how the power of a meditative peacefulness can convey some non-verbal wisdom in a public setting. A nineties documentary series by Bill Moyers, *Healing and the Mind* (BillMoyers.com, n.d.), offers a video of a peaceful man on a rough street corner in China who was not attacked because he took the approach that it takes two to fight. He was not willing to fight and he stood there peacefully, meditating, so he wasn't attacked by hoodlums. This teaches us that people subconsciously, or sometimes consciously, look for a fight, argument, or dispute to meet their aggressive and angry emotional needs. If we do not reciprocate, and do not get aggressive, or even try and defend ourselves, there will be no fight. Mindful peacefulness is a good defence.

Crowds, however, do affect us. Strong emotion runs amok in some crowds and strikes a chord within us. This is so even from something seen on TV, like the protests following extreme police brutality in the spring of 2020. The collective subconscious becomes conscious as we read the protesters' positions in the signs they carry. The signs likely illustrate thoughts many people have carried subconsciously, or in the psychological underground, which is conscious among certain people. If many have similar subconscious thoughts, it is the collective subconscious. They come out in times of conflict and mutual perceptions, especially when like-minded people gather in crowds and protests. They need some spokespeople. They need to be interviewed in an organized way by the media, since those in power seem unaware of the benefits of conversation, active listening, dialogue, collegiality, problem-solving, and other methods which are standard types of exercise in the underrated therapeutic psychology fields. Or perhaps they are unwilling to use them in this context. Leaders will meet with other world leaders in an organized manner, like at the G7 summit, but not with their own citizens when an issue like this occurs. We need this in order to work towards a resolution. It seems so basic. The government probably fears giving power to their own citizens, when, in fact, listening to their citizens in a concerned way is the antidote that is needed. Citizens are, after all, voters. The power of fear is too great here. Fear begets emotional contagion. When unaddressed, it spreads, and infects the systematic reasoning that would be available were there conversations and dialogue occurring in an organized, peaceful setting about the issues the citizens are raising. Failure to identify the factors at play, as discussed here, blinds people from seeing the way out.

A powerful interpersonal flow is especially predominant under automatic, impulsive thinking, where others are around and when movement is present, such as in crowds. Crowds are places of action and excitement, so there is a lot of emotion, implicit and explicit. Movement, groups, and crowds are situations that by their nature require little thought and reward spontaneity. This is the place for fast, intuitive, emotional reactions, as people mix and merge and something exciting or entertaining is going on. Emotions become strong as people are in close proximity, catching feelings from each other. If there is an empathy with each other, and mutual agreements, we have a mutual collective subconscious. The emotions are then magnified as emotional contagion occurs. Impulsive behaviours occur, usually driven by emotions. It seems natural but it isn't. You may act without thinking because you are not in thought mode. Inoculation comes from independent thinking, taking in feelings from others but being careful to keep your own. For example, not letting yourself get so spontaneous that you could touch someone inappropriately, but still feeling spontaneous anyway. You act spontaneously but still have a gatekeeper to ensure your thought mode is still active and can override the spontaneity when necessary. This will prevent you from automatically catching others' emotions and then doing something without thinking. Thinking about what could happen in these situations before you get into them helps you to handle them when they happen.

The power of positive emotional contagion in the protest marches has spread across the world and has set the stage as people march together. This is the beginning of an antidote to emotional contagion, and it is seen rarely, only in ideal situations, in the wisdom of crowds (Halton, 2021). This antidote refers to the idea that large groups of people are collectively smarter than individual experts. First popularized by the writer James Surowiecki (2004), this theory states that for crowds to be wise, they must be characterized by a diversity of opinion, and each person's opinion should be independent of those around him or her. That independence is impossible to obtain in a large crowd and does not account for group dynamics or emotional contagion (which is a given in large crowds). Instead, one can only look for snippets of this in small groupings and closely cohesive enclaves and hope that it spreads via the collective subconscious between small groups and continues to be promoted to the greater consciousness by interdependent intelligent comments with a smart and positive perspective.

When emotional contagion is managed properly in a group, it can end up merging and becoming wisdom when its emotion is integrated with intelligence and takes a problem-solving direction. There are signs of it happening in the wisdom of protesting crowds in 2020, but not in the mob that attacked the U.S. Capitol in early 2021. It is important, of course, for the emotion to be present and integrated with the intelligence and knowledge and for the resulting wisdom to direct an effective problem-solving approach to the problematic situation. Integration means neither the emotion nor the intelligence is ignored and each is considered in a meaningful way.

Crowds and protests have become wiser over the decades. They have goals. It seems like the feeling moves from one person to the other. In fact, moving around together seems to be a universal way of celebrating in a crowd, no matter what culture. It seems to be a way of signalling to others, a way to join, connect, and share with those around us, contributing to the energy flow. At times it may be a subconscious way of connecting with and sharing the collective subconscious, making it conscious, as sign after sign passes our view.

The internal emotional flow is being facilitated, magnified, and expanded by the external emotional flow impacting on it. Think about what flow does coming from a human being with voice, gestures, and emotion emitted, when it is interpersonal rather than intrapersonal, when it is between people who co-operate. This comes much more easily than the internal flow within a single person. The interpersonal flow impacts that part of us which wants to put out less cognitive effort to understand. In human interactions, the most meaning seems to be imparted when there is easy comfortable flow, a comfortable blend of thought and feeling attaining wisdom. It's not just reason and rationale, but a pleasant flow that feels right. Thought and feeling. This flow is very powerful. We see this clearly in co-operative crowds. Wisdom and intelligence flow when brought along by the emotional and social contagion spreading throughout co-operative crowds working together in a united harmony.

Racism is pervasive

In Canada, and the U.S., there is discrimination against Indigenous and Black people caused by emotional infection; the emotions infect the mind, blocking reasonable thinking and producing racism. In many cities, people who appear to be under the influence of a substance, living in a seedy part of town, panhandle and accost some people, in an irresponsible way. In emotional thinking, it can be that something different about the person is determined to be the problem, the person's race, becoming a trigger when it shouldn't. In reality, it is severe psychological and social maladjustment and addiction problems in some people that relates to their irresponsible state or judgment. They may have been the victim of racism in the past, but some people behave this way although they are not racialized.

These people are psychologically and perhaps psychiatrically disturbed, and probably socially disadvantaged, as any person of any race can be. That is why we need to tone this fear down and instead think rationally and calmly. We desperately seek a simple cause, because simpler causes are easier to ascribe to when one is thinking emotionally. We easily go into "us against them" thinking, as if we represent a group (a race, a nationality, a gender) that we think is all the same, and are in a fight against another, opposing group—a different race, nationality, or gender that we think is all the same. Seeing the individual and realizing they have feelings, a family, pain, and distinct uniqueness will overcome the generalization and stop the all-or-nothing thinking characteristic of tunnel vision.

Racism has been a pandemic around the world. It produces emotional contagion as some people unnecessarily panic at the sight of a person whose skin happens to be a different colour. It flies in the face of knowledge and reality. The next time you cut your lawn with a lawn mower, consider that a Black person, John Albert Burr, invented the lawn mower in 1899 (Bellis, 2019). The next time you sharpen a pencil, consider that a Black person, John Lee Love, invented the pencil sharpener two years earlier (Bellis, 2020). There are many other examples of Black people who were great inventors[14]. The Black women mathematicians who worked for NASA during the space race in the 1950s and 1960s, inspired the movie Hidden Figures in 2017, which made a profit of $95.5 million (Fleming, 2017), indicating the popularity of the topic of black women who fought against the contagious emotions of hate and power associated with misogyny and racism. And when you search for information on the Internet, consider that a Black person from Barbados named Alan Emtage invented the world's first search engine when he was at McGill University in Canada (Internet Hall of Fame, n.d.). Ask yourself why it took until 2008 for a Black man to be elected president of the U.S, and why no woman has yet become the U.S. president.

Adam Rutherford, the British geneticist, says that "race doesn't exist but racism does. He says in the *Guardian* article "There is no genetic basis that corresponds with any particular group of people, no essentialist DNA for black people or white people or anyone" (Rutherford, 2015). In other words, we are all the same except for our skin. This is a pure example of the power of emotional contagion, which produces the phenomenon of racism, over genetic fact, which says that race doesn't exist based on science. If this disturbs the reader, this may be because of cognitive dissonance, "an unpleasant psychological state resulting from inconsistency between two or more elements [beliefs] in a person's cognitive system. It is presumed to involve a state of heightened arousal and to have characteristics similar to physiological drives. [...] [It] creates a motivational drive in an individual to reduce the dissonance"(APA, n.d.)

Consider that in Canada, Indigenous people comprise 30 percent of the population of federal inmates while comprising only 5 percent of the country's population. How many of those are descendants of residential school survivors? It is not just the Indigenous people who are racialized in Canada. Lysandra Marshall established that there are substantial racial

---

14 Thanks to Rev. Dr. Anthony Bailey, Pastor and Diversity and Racial Justice Trainer, Parkdale United Church, Ottawa, Ontario, Canada, for this information about Black inventors.

differences in the traffic stop rates in Kingston, Ontario: "The odds of a Black person being stopped were 2.5 higher than for whites."(Marshall, 2017)

In Canada, there is social instability that is related in part to the archaic, primitive, and now-defunct residential school system that took Indigenous children away from their homes, parents, and culture. Alcoholism, drug abuse, homelessness, and rootlessness, as well as many other psychosocial problems, resulted from this cultural genocide and now further contribute to instability. These former students may have been taken away from their parents as children by the government for no other reason than their race and did not develop psychologically as a result. As well as losing their culture, this is what caused the myriad of psychosocial problems. No one in the white, nationalistic culture that dominated Canada for decades taught these people how to cope after the government tried to erase their culture.

The systemic abuse that occurred in residential schools trickled down to the descendants of these students who were left with few coping skills. Many Métis (mixed Indigenous and Euro-American ancestry) feel that they don't belong anywhere and they receive no respect from either white people or the Indigenous people on reserves who carry treaty cards. In the 1960s, many Indigenous children were taken away from their families and adopted by white families. Many of these now adults feel that they have no viable identity and are sadly unable to connect either with their white family's traditions, or to their own Indigenous culture.

This is the result of emotional contagion: the emotions that constitute hate and prejudice skewed the judgment of people who let feelings of power and a simplistic, wildly inaccurate opinion based on skin colour demolish and destroy generations of culture and tradition, reaching cultural genocide. This is one of the reasons why negative emotional contagion is the most powerful destructive force known to human beings.

Impact on Society

A repetitive spiral of social and emotional contagion creates and increases turmoil in society. Many episodes of uncertainty and chaos leave a residue of emotional turmoil. Trauma experienced by strangers affects us emotionally, leaving some of us in tears which are often emotionally contagious. Opinions on controversial topics are exchanged with emotion that affects you. Let the emotion bounce off you, so it doesn't trigger you. Our gatekeeper, our mind, can stop us from being overcome by the emotion in negative ways. Otherwise, emotions become primary and carry the flow of a dialogue, attracting each other. In this way negative emotional and social contagion produce cancel culture and public shaming, which move the cycle into depression, ostracism, and social anxiety. "Hot topics" infect us if we don't question their premise, as our thinking becomes "lazy."

The situation can look much worse when we consider the political turmoil in many parts of the world and how the electronic and visual media communicate it. Facebook, Twitter, Instagram, and other social media platforms easily transmit emotions. With horse-race elections during which many people focus more on headlines than on in-depth news, emotional and social contagion make a strong impact on voters. They influence us in many ways, from the intimate to the personal, from the social to the political, and at all levels in between. They seem to be strengthening the turmoil in a cyclical way. This turmoil in society puts emotional and social contagion into a repetitive spiral of increasing influence, in turn increasing the turmoil even more. Although we continue living and functioning, there is more and more anxiety out there, likely due to the cyclical effects of emotional contagion in a time of uncertainty. The coronavirus pandemic, the protests, instances of police brutality, mass shootings, conspiracy theories, insurrection attempts, and political instability all contribute to it. It all adds up as there is a residue of emotional turmoil left after each episode, especially with live TV updates streaming constantly into our homes. The long-term presence of the coronavirus and its hundreds of thousands of deaths contribute to a lot of it. Many people are virtually frozen in fright; some are housebound out of fear that they might contract COVID-19. Although we can't avoid it, we do not have to catch all these emotions automatically. If we did, we would all be behaving like mirrors to each other, feeling extremely anxious. There would be no such thing as emotional independence.

We know that people in public life affect us deeply and can raise or lower the level of turmoil. Think of it. People can be affected by the death of someone they have never met, like the sad, sudden death of Kobe Bryant and his daughter Gigi. Or the death of a star like Michael Jackson. Some people cry when their favourite politician wins an election, even though they have never met them in person. Complete strangers can affect us deeply. And those tears can be contagious. When we see someone in tears, we may find ourselves feeling sad or happy even though we have no idea why they are crying. It should be no surprise then that emotion influences our preference for public figures. Often in these turbulent times our public and political discourse is dominated by emotionality and the effects of emotional contagion. This is dangerous because the contagion has scooped reasoning and fact in search of the truth. But emotions don't think and cannot determine what is true. In conjunction with effective thinking, though, emotions and thoughts can be harmonious and can give us wise thinking.

Many people are emotionally independent, deciding for themselves what to think and feel, some go too far with this, ignoring the media completely and believing in conspiracy theories. Others may believe the mainstream media completely. Some search for reputable news sources, such as PBS, which seems to avoid the limelight. Then there are many who don't follow much of it anywhere. This independence can be developed, strengthened, and generalized to the social and political arena, as it should, in order to strengthen ourselves, our society, and our democracy. We don't have to do as others do.

The problem is that emotions don't think. Many people make many of these daily decisions about which media outlet to follow or ignore based on automatic reactions, based on tradition and emotion. Even tradition has an emotional basis, involving sentiment. Outlets that convey emotion and drama attract viewers, because people are attracted to emotion, especially if there is a dearth of it in their own lives. News outlets have become the new reality show, except they are actually real. Or is reality itself based on reality shows, conveying fake news? It is hard to know what is real—we never really know for sure. We can check the facts, but how many of us were actually there to see the news unfold in real time? Thankfully people take videos of news events now so we can see it for ourselves. People like Darnella Fraser, the 17-year-old young woman who videoed George Floyd's murder with her smart phone, is now called a hero (Treisman, 2021). How do you know what is really happening and what causes it? You can't be everywhere at once. Then we get anxious and uncertain, panicky and erratic. Violence starts to erupt in many places. We are worried. Darnella and the people who enabled videos to be included on smart phones give us hope.

Emotions are very good at feeling and tend to want more feelings. They carry messages based on those feelings, but don't think. Feelings are food for emotions. Emotions attract other emotions. It becomes cyclical. At this time of the turmoil, our emotional antennae go up and we catch the anxiety around us and absorb it into ourselves without realizing what we have done. Catching emotions bypasses our thinking mechanism and often leads to trouble. It can infect our beliefs. Anxiety easily travels and spreads, but we have to check the details of what the anxiety is about before we know whether we should accept any message from that anxiety. It is natural to be anxious during this time of turmoil, but don't automatically take the message from anxiety that you should fear things. Anxiety can make us fear things that are realistically unworthy of being feared— like spiders. This can get a lot worse in a pandemic, not because of reality but because of irrational fears. The coronavirus may signify automatic death to some, although we know rationally there is an excellent chance that many with the virus will not die from it.

Receiving emotionality about social problems

When a politician or public figure speaks in an angry manner, they often automatically arouse angry emotions inside of us that trigger an immediate reaction or emotion. There appears to be a direct emotion-to-emotion type of appeal. The emotion inside us that receives this input is then often triggered which explains social phenomena such as public shaming or cancel culture. This in turn triggers either behaviour or thinking on our part that may be undesirable such as getting even, shaming someone, or cancelling things that people value. This is a type of emotional contagion. It is as if the reasoning apparatus inside us that produces decency is being circumvented.

We need to be aware of these ongoing interactions between the emotional flow as it impacts us and our own emotional reaction. This includes recognizing the importance of it being tempered and regulated by our own cognitive processes, including our wisdom and rationality, so that the wisdom-less emotional flow doesn't take over. At times of emotionality, when opinions on controversial topics are exchanged with emotion, some people feel challenged by the power of the incoming emotion attached to the speaker's opinion. It is the emotion that is affecting you and not the opinion; you may feel surprised or even shocked at the strength of the person's emotion. The other person may be subconsciously expressing the emotion at a particularly high degree of strength in order to be domineering, guessing that the strength of the emotion will overpower you as the receiver. Don't feel intimidated by the emotion; it does not usually suggest force or possible aggression towards you unless the person has this type of behaviour in their history. Let the emotion bounce off you like a dodge ball. Don't let the person trigger some of your own feelings that you hold inside you. The person may have some unconscious reason for the strength of their emotion, maybe something in their history that has nothing to do with you. It is when you react automatically to the emotion by being defensive or angry in return that problems can occur, and arguments and fights happen. Automatic reactions happen because something inside you has been triggered. You could be assertive and neutral in your emotion if you wish to disagree, stating your differing opinion in a neutral tone to de-escalate the emotional exchange. Don't worry about losing the argument; it should mean nothing to you unless something crucial is at stake, as defined by rational thought.

Many of us likely have some suppressed resentments that we carry within us. They can be released when a powerful figure triggers it by appearing to side with us emotionally, tapping into an emotional need we may have suppressed, like recognition or validation. For example, when some people see a minority group being given privileges or opportunities that they themselves don't feel they've received, they may perceive their emotional needs as being ignored. We can mistakenly project our anger onto them because we see them as favoured, if we feel our needs are not being met. This stokes our emotions. Whether the "others" in question are refugees or one of various minority groups, or just very different from us, these privileges produce a form of jealousy that is converted into hatred of those groups perceived to be favoured without merit. We project our insecurities by deciding that someone unlike us is being favoured, and we do this because we feel insecure and ignored. This is emotional thinking based on suppressed resentments.

Perhaps we really are being ignored, or perhaps this is tunnel thinking that ignores other perspectives or facts. Our feeling of insecurity can be so strong as to blind us from seeing things we do not want to see. This is confirmation bias. If we widen our perspective, we would probably see that we are not being ignored. Often, we may not wish to accept offers from the government due to distrust, shame, cynicism, or pride. So we may blind ourselves to these opportunities, pretending they are not real or just a trick. Recently arrived refugees are of course quick to say yes to government assistance; partly because they have no shame but also because they have a deep need and trust in their new country.

There are many issues that creep through society, stirring up emotions that can be contagious. Issues like incoming refugees. For example, we may believe that refugees are stealing our jobs in Canada, although they aren't (Grant, 2016). This would be painful; people naturally react quickly to avoid the risk of pain. Kahneman discusses the phenomenon of loss aversion, in which "the psychological impact of experiencing losses is roughly twice as strongly felt as that of experiencing gains."(Fernando, 2019) This is natural and emotional. The brain responds very quickly to threats, even symbolic ones. Pain hurts, even emotional pain, and its effects are quick, so naturally we strive to avoid it at all costs. Jealousy and resentment produce quick decisions instead of letting us study all the outcomes. Therefore some people can quickly get upset at refugees if they listen to the simple message that refugees steal our jobs, instead of looking at it from all sides. Being automatically risk-averse doesn't pay off. It involves the influx of fear that infects the reasoning process. Although it may not make logical sense, the irrational, emotional fear of being overtaken by an "outsider" is not uncommon.

Through vicarious empathy, others may catch these contagious emotions of jealousy and resentment. We may think that certain racial, ethnic, or religious groups are weird when really, they're just different from us. The word *weird* has emotional, judgmental undertones to it. *Different* is not emotional, it is objective and rational. Using emotional words spreads emotional contagion. Some of us feel like reacting right away to the emotional statements we hear, like "refugees stealing our jobs," if we are having trouble getting work. We may then become infected by it. They are not stealing jobs; in reality they take the jobs that few of us want.

This is where the gatekeeper comes in. Its job is to ask, "Do we really want to catch the suspicion automatically and let it affect us?" Probably not. It thinks systematically. Systematic thinking means checking the evidence. The gatekeeper would ask questions, check the facts from an objective source, and see if refugees are really stealing our jobs. *Stealing* is taking away something that belongs to us. What evidence is there that this is actually happening? How would it happen? Is there evidence that immigrants really want these jobs and get them before current citizens? If so, is that a trend or just one case? What are the details? We can't let the answer just be an automatic reflex to confirm our bias. Asking these questions is what your mind does. The mind is your gatekeeper. The answers should come from facts and details, not from the anxiety itself, because it is biased.

We need to learn how and when to inoculate ourselves against these emotional thoughts. We can catch an emotional feeling impulsively, probably an infection, and believe its message automatically. It could be a message related to social problems. But feelings are not facts, and emotions don't think. It is much better to stop instinctively catching these suspicious infectious emotions and consider them before we catch them and believe their message. It would help decrease the division in society if we think thoughts through.

Social media and cancel culture

Emotional contagion is particularly rampant when social media is involved. On social media, we see that one post usually begins with an emotional opinion on a controversial topic, related to an individual's sense of safety and security. Then many others follow, usually spurred on by the emotional feeling aroused by the initial comment. At this point, the emotion that is aroused by the comments appears to direct the flow of the dialogue, so that a one-directional flavour, akin to tunnel vision, occurs. The emotion that may be experienced by a participant will usually be reinforcing for that person and spur on a greater degree of emotion, as the foregoing emotional experiences have probably been contagious.

These experiences infect the reader so that they continue with even more emotional dialogue. This dialogue will go in the same direction, or it may be a counter-contagion taking the opposite direction, in which case the emotions are inflamed. The emotions that take over are then reinforcing a flow occurring in one direction or resulting in significant dichotomy and alienation so that the reader is vehemently opposing the comments made. In this way the emotion has become primary because of the effects of a phenomenon similar to emotional contagion in that emotions just carry the flow of the dialogue. Emotion has little structure, unlike logic. This flow often involves an implicit emotion, so that the participant of social media isn't aware that emotion is spurring them on. Social media, because it is anonymous and because there is no real, live person sitting across from us, easily serves as a springboard for our expression of emotion. It feels safe—but it isn't. We are accustomed to the immediate feedback we used to get from live, in-person conversations in the here-and-now. Social media fools us, since the other person may be a real, live person but they are anonymous, in the "there-and-now," far away in another city or country, although answering in real time.

On social media, various comments come quickly at us. We seem to take in their emotional messages automatically, especially if we are feeling spontaneous, casual, sociable, in the mood to connect, and are not in a state of psychological awareness about whether it is wise to do so. This lack of awareness occurs early in life, which is why it is usually not conscious. It is best to make it more conscious as we mature, to gain control over it. As a child, when our feelings are hurt we cry; as we get older, we realize that we have to stop letting our feelings get hurt. We distract ourselves, steel ourselves, change our behaviour, find new friends, or realize there are other ways to think about what has happened.

Calling people names on social media is how children behave. Yet this is common on social media, and it contributes significantly to the emotional contagion and divisions in society. Calling people cowards, pathetic, weak, traitors, or stupid is going to make many people defensive and angry. In this way it is divisive. As the recipient, don't fall for the bait. Prepare for it; it is better to not react to these comments emotionally, because emotional comments split us apart. In fact, that is probably what the online aggressor is trying to do.

The effect of emotional contagion has been found in research to occur from watching video on TV and social media, including YouTube.

Rosenbusch, Evans, and Zeelenberg (2019) found that "an immediate emotion transfer [...] occurs when audience members watch a vlogger[15] express emotion in a video." This is interpreted by the authors as emotional contagion via video. Emotions expressed on video will arouse emotion in the viewer, because of emotional contagion. As well, these researchers "demonstrated a situational spread of emotions by experimentally manipulating people's Facebook newsfeeds, with the finding that people express more positive emotions when they are presented with more positive emotions of other users." This offers some research support to our argument that emotional contagion can spread through social media without direct in-person human contact being necessary.

Emotions don't think, they just react. Emotional comments trigger personal responses; many people react immediately and urgently. For them, it may hurt to be called names, and in that way the emotional contagion can occur as counter-contagion—unless the recipient blocks it by recognizing that this is not a literal name that should be taken as personally accurate, but rather as a method the other person is using to get a reaction. The aggressor knows intuitively that this reaction will be an emotional one, likely knocking the victim down emotionally, their mind possibly having temporarily lost its ability to reason. The speaker then gets more power, since the recipient may get flustered and become irrational. Emotion mind takes over and the recipient is suddenly reacting to an insult personally, indicating that they are off their usual mark of being rational and cognizant. The other person's initial emotional insult statement provided the suggestion of urgency, a need to quickly defend oneself, in a game of emotional ping-pong, but they must ignore that urgency because it is false. If they identify the emotion from the other person as a cue not to respond emotionally, they, the recipient, comes out ahead. See the emotional attack for what it is: a weapon to weaken the recipient. Ignoring it by being silent and not immediately reacting gives you more control over the other person.

Psychopathological symptoms become contagious also. Conspiracy theories become attractive and appealing as suspicion, cynicism and probably delusions become contagious. Those people who have not had mental health issues or psychological problems may start to catch it, and those who have these issues and problems may find them worsened. It starts

---

15   A vlog is a type of blog for which the medium is video.

to affect everyone. We know that suspicion and cynicism have spread a lot over the decades, with people resigned to the idea that we have lost all control. Many people feel like they have lost control, and desperately want to get it back. Conspiracy theories are a wild way for people to imagine they have regained that control, when they usually haven't.

The trends of public shaming, cynicism, authoritarianism, and conspiracy theories have morphed, as trends involving emotions tend to do, into the popular "cancel culture," which would seem to be caused by emotional and social contagion. We know that emotions attract and pull for each other, ramping their power up as they feed off of each other. The power of one emotion joins with the power of another emotion, multiplying the power of the emotional and social contagion, perhaps through some type of social kindling phenomenon. The power from the emotional flow involved in public shaming, cynicism, authoritarianism, and conspiracy theories gets stronger. It happens slowly but surely, like a slow burn and kindling that can easily turn into a fire, figuratively, when it suddenly seems easier for some to accept that it is right to "cancel" people by firing them. This would appear to give those who "cancel" others the attractive feeling of social power many crave. They don't take into account the slippery slope into demoralization and helplessness that this likely causes as it affects the well-being of other citizens.

The effect of public shaming and cancel culture is undoubtedly transforming into the darkness of depression and ostracism. It evokes hopelessness for some people who view this occurrence as being moved to the bottom of the social hierarchy, which is only bothersome for those who believe in the authenticity and accuracy of that ranking system. And that also probably comes through social contagion, which is susceptible to immature judgments of an emotional nature, where individuals do not consider the social status of others, like a person with different principles.

The movement caused by social contagion occurs in shifts, likely from pessimism to cynicism to depression. Some then find relief from that depression by moving to social contact over social media. The contact occurs as some individuals will catch the contagious emotions flowing from others on social media platforms. People will again feel accepted (and therefore important) and valued socially and perhaps emotionally. These positive feelings may again disappear under cancel culture.

The social contagion part of this phenomenon is prominent because of the dominance of social media. The leading definition on Urban Dictionary (n.d.) says cancel culture is defined as "a desire to cancel out a person or community from social media platforms." (Although Urban Dictionary is not an official dictionary, it gives insight into the mood of society). It is not hard to see how the emotions of revenge, power, and control come into play in this desire, initially stemming from anger, as we see from the rest of Urban Dictionary's definition: people on social media "will call on their followers to report the social media accounts of the person or group that did the criticizing rather than discussing the criticism or showing by evidence where the criticism is incorrect." They go on to say that "narcissists make up the majority of the people who engage in cancel culture, and others who do this would include immature individuals." They come together for social support and power, which is likely important for these people. If they feel left out, they want to come together, as we all do. Social media provides an anonymous platform for like-minded people to join forces and commiserate, without face-to-face contact; it is an important venue for people who may have, in the past, felt less appreciated socially in real life. They would feel powerful, outlawing others from joining them in a non-democratic move. The power is reinforcing and addictive and contributes to emotional and social contagion, as people believe they have been accepted and belong to an apparently powerful group. Social power feels reinforcing when others are outlawed from joining. This may be a false feeling, however, as it depends on whether the excluded individual cares if they have been outlawed. Some people are not concerned about being "cancelled," and in fact may take it as an improvement in their social well-being if they then downplay the significance of the outlawing group.

However, this seems to be a slippery slope for some unfortunate people who lose perspective on what is happening to them, as the positive emotion they feel from cancelling others blinds them to possible pitfalls, like the actual loss of control that comes from shaming or excluding others—one might be banning a future employer who will remember this. The false consensus effect, "the tendency to assume that one's own opinions, beliefs, attributes, or behaviours are more widely shared than is actually the case, [...] is often attributed to a desire to view one's thoughts and actions as appropriate, normal, and correct" (APA, n.d.). This effect comes forth through emotional contagion, like birds who flock together stay together, because they feel mutual reinforcement through the social power that they perceive occurs through "cancelling" others. They miss the "false" part, whereby they make assumptions that these things have consensus, when they may not. This comes from emotional contagion and incomplete thinking in that it feels so good to these people to belong to such a group that they can't afford to think critically about it, lest they see how fragile their position is.

The slippery slope continues as the downward movement has a mild effect on society as whole. Some people who are rejected, or "cancelled," are likely to become depressed and suicidal, or aggressive and vengeful—or both. The power that those participating in cancel culture feel is likely to end getting them in "hot water," or even legal trouble. Such power usually finds that it breaks the boundary of what the law allows. They are "testing the limits" of society. It would, and probably already has, coloured the mood of society, making it negative as darkness and demoralization gradually oozes into the zeitgeist, the mood in society at any given moment, through emotional and social contagion. It is invisible to most people, but felt and experienced nevertheless. This is part of how emotional contagion contributes to the turmoil. When it moves slowly, many people don't notice it consciously—but it continues to move, like a creepy crawl. Cancel culture is one of the eventual outcomes of long-term demoralization, and in turn contributes to stronger short-term demoralization in society, as part of the creepy crawl downwards.

As cancel culture expands, as the *Washington Post* reports in their article "The Real Problem with 'Cancel Culture,'" it is "pressuring mainstream institutions, which serve as society's idea curators, to adopt a much narrower definition of 'reasonable' opinion." (McArdle, 2020). The *Post* reports that the new rules would exclude the viewpoints of many Americans, and develop an intellectual monoculture, which is inherently unhealthy with destructive tactics. The real problem here is the word *culture*. Cancelling things that are controversial has become a culture, as if we are not going to pay attention to any of the issues involved and will just sweep them under the rug. This is emotional contagion, as the emotions sweep through society deciding what the perceived "right thing to do" is on an emotional basis, rather than a logical approach, which would be to examine the issue at hand. No one is in charge of cancel culture, as Benjamin Wallace-Wells (2020) says. This would include the issue of how it is that obliterating things is thought of as the right course of action to please a certain group, without examining why this is thought of as the correct way to handle something. We are becoming the ostrich society, a society of people who bury their heads in the sand because they don't want to know what's going on and are happy obliterating things.

It is very demoralizing to see how people can take advantage of others. Feeling "cancelled" can leave some people depressed or suicidal. Those who have exerted the power can end up in jail or being homeless themselves, and depressed when they realize how false the power is. Power is fleeting. No one wins from cancel culture. It gives too much power to popularity, too much power to trends. Even political parties adopt its tactics. It is a subtle, underground civil war where empathy is lost and people are rewarded for taking power away from others; development of an authoritarian personality can occur in this way. Authoritarian leaders use other people. Fear and hate appear to underlie these developments psychologically, as hate dominates, controls, and produces fear, and this makes many people vulnerable and anxious. Emotions don't think but they can be very powerful. If it truly is an underground civil war, we could be in for a lot of trouble if it breaks through, controlled by an authoritarian force who loves the power. In this case, the positive emotion that power induces could end up being destructive.

There are many explicit emotions also, especially at a time of turmoil when the implicit ones break through into consciousness and awareness. Sometimes in life, feelings overwhelm us and we may cry, scream, yell, or curse. We may break something, punch someone, run away, or drive too fast. Bad things can happen. Sometimes people absorb feelings which they cannot tolerate, like jealousy or envy of someone perceived to have more favourable qualities. Sometimes we can then have a reaction to this inability to tolerate the internal emotion, a reaction which often produces counter emotions such as anger, hate, or depression. In a heightened emotional state people can act impulsively and irrationally on these feelings. We need a gatekeeper. We really need to know what's going on with our feelings so that we are not overwhelmed. We need to know how to keep the right balance, how to let ourselves have plenty of positive feelings, how to keep them as our own, how to stop taking on other's feelings or to letting ourselves be affected by other's feelings in ways that we really don't want to be. We also need to know how to own our feelings, and how to balance them so they give us those positive feelings we cherish without letting them overwhelm us and take over. If this happens and we are overwhelmed, we really can't function very well anymore. We may end up in a weaker position, or even in some danger; the worst case is that we could find ourselves doing things we regret later, even serious things.

Public shaming

Let's take a deeper look at the societal impact of emotional contagion. It seems widespread and is becoming more deep-seated, as seen in emotionally based political decisions and impulsive actions in Western society over the past few years, if not decades. Feelings and emotions spread fast. People under a state of constant stress, fear, and anxiety easily get into a state of emotional thinking, with quick, emotionally laden thinking characteristic of Kahneman's System 1, rather than slow, logical, reasoned thinking of System 2.

Fearful people tend to vote with their emotions. When they do so, especially with angry ones, they tend to get desperate and impulsive, and make irrational choices. Emotions are high. Emotional contagion is rampant. People forget that emotions don't think while the media raises our emotions to overwhelming heights. We are consuming news about real-life drama unfolding almost daily in 2020. Life has become a reality show.

We see the impact of emotional contagion on society when we see how emotions impact people in public life. Many people are on edge. When emotions spread, they get very powerful, as has public shaming, according to Max (2020). Social media has been front and centre in this phenomenon, according to the *New Yorker* article, which describes the phenomenon of emotional contagion without defining it. Max gives examples, including one where a man took a picture of himself in a mall in front of the fictional Star Wars character Darth Vader for his children to see and ended up receiving death threats because someone thought he was a predator targeting her children and posted this on social media. It was shared 20,000 times. This is contagious fear and suspicion, where there was no second thought, just action driven by fear. When we read this example, watch what you feel, and do not let your emotions about it get the best of you and put you into System 1. Fear about predators and other dangers seems high in the collective subconscious. It is unfortunate, and we can learn a lesson from this not to let our emotions drive us to action without thinking first, in this case realizing possible undesirable consequences, a realization that comes from System 2 logic. Emotions don't think. In this case, they just acted, harming a person's reputation.

Jon Ronson, in his book about public shaming (2015a), said about a different incident that "a life had been ruined. What was it for: just some social media drama?[...] What are we getting out of it?" He said that we are in "a great renaissance of public shaming." The media inflames controversial issues because they know their audience is upset about it and attracted to emotion. It is addictive and the media feeds into it. So what are we getting out of it? Emotion. People want emotion in public life because they don't seem to get enough authentic positive emotion in their ongoing lives, possibly an effect of family breakdown. What kind of emotion are they getting from social media? The chance to get power and revenge in an anonymous way? Social contagion runs wild. Negative emotional contagion runs wild. But what else are we getting out of it? Acute, serious demoralization in society. An increase in anxiety, cynicism, and angst. A decrease in trust and respect.

Negative emotional contagion has spread so far that it has significantly infected people's emotions in a detrimental way. This is especially true in instances of public shaming, where culprits are fired from their jobs without, it would seem, a full investigation.

Let's look at these issues. A woman in Central Park in New York aroused strong emotions when she called the police on a Black man who was birdwatching. He had complained to her about her dog not being on a leash. She ended up being publicly shamed. There were over twenty-five million views of the video in the first few days of the incident. She was out for a walk when the incident happened. The woman said that "there was an African-American man threatening [her] life." (Ruiz-Grossman, 2020) She called 911 and asked the dispatcher to send the police. As far as we know, there was no threat to her. The mayor of New York called it "racism, plain and simple."(Cook, 2020) No, it is not simple, it is complex, but it is racism. In the heat of the moment the emotions pull for a quick, easy answer, including from a political leader, although there is no easy answer.

Racism is a hot topic. It should be. But whatever the current "hot topic" in society is, it automatically arouses emotions related to it. These are "hot" emotions, which are contagious, and stir up quick emotional reactions. It seems automatic. These emotions evoke more support on the side of the victim, in this case the birdwatcher, almost like a magnet. He must have been scared knowing that the police were coming, given the history of the police in dealing with Black people. As a result of this rush to judgment, the woman was fired from her job and gave up her dog. Emotional contagion works quickly; we rush to judgment because of the hot emotions. We just react. We feel his pain, in a way. It would seem that emotional contagion resulted in her being fired as revenge, without that punishment having been thought through. It was said "she was trying to frame him." The woman was vilified.

It takes slow, reasoned, logical thinking to dispute the emotion implied through emotional contagion's influence in spreading "hot topics," as emotion can carry simple irrational messages. This story quickly morphed into a symbol of racism and white privilege. Some of us feel that we better not challenge it at all, or we will be caught up ourselves in the swirling voices of emotional contagion via public shaming.

This is the emergence of the collective subconscious into consciousness, since bitterness and anger between races had understandably been simmering below the surface. It likely emerged into consciousness when the opportunity came up. Feelings were now allowed to erupt. This is an understandable reaction as an outlet for this bitterness. It validates the reason for the anger and bitterness, since the anger is genuine and specifies the nature of the anger, in an emotional way, towards privileged white people who have not known the trials of racism. It is a creative way of handling anger, much better than violence.

These comments that create public shaming, although they have some validity, lack context. This is typical with emotional contagion. They only give one side of the story, shaming the Central Park woman without really knowing her. This woman appeared to my trained eye as having an anxiety attack, and may have developed an anxiety disorder, diagnosed or not, prior to this event.[16] People with anxiety magnify the danger of an event, and they can become irrational. They are in System 1, while in the midst of the event, while people reading about it later are in System 2. It is possible that she is afraid of spiders, storms, thieves, and she lives in constant fear. This may be just one more thing she reacted to irrationally. Other people reacted to her in an emotional manner. Contagious emotions in one person often pull out emotions in other people, automatically, even different emotions. The emotion she showed probably triggered extreme emotions in other people automatically. Systematic reasoning and critical thinking were not in significant evidence in the media reports during this

---

16 Comments about this case are my speculation and conjecture, as I have neither met either person, nor know of them, other than through media. It raises awareness of their personhood and humanness, which are often minimized in these events.

situation, because the media pulls for emotions also. But these are needed in these instances.

With emotional contagion, some readers may think I am defending this woman, as if there is only one side of the story to be told. But it is only fair that her side of the story be told. She deserves empathy also. To be thrust into the public spotlight can be tough for anyone. She is a real person with a life. She may have lost friends, lost a mate, or lost her house if she couldn't pay rent or make the mortgage as a result of being fired. When I say this, do you get angry and think I am taking her side? Or favouring white people? I am not. Showing empathy does not necessarily mean taking sides. I am trying to be objective. The Black man may have needed time off also, as he may be fearful about the police or about white people. He may also have lost a significant role in his job.[17]

Public shaming shows how strong emotions have become. Although every now and then emotions were expressed publicly in the past, such as when people spoke at speakers' corners or wrote letters to the editor, this is stronger, there are more of these situations making the news. Each side's situation has tragedy, and each side deserves respect, empathy, and compassion. This dilemma indicates the alienation many of us are feeling in our society from people, from feelings, from humanness. All parties involved need compassion, not judgment.

Public shaming shows the effect of emotional and social contagion on the reasoning process of individuals reacting to an event by spreading rumours and emotions. Lazy, incomplete thinking resulting in poor decisions is evident in public shaming. Judgments are made very quickly, without systematic reasoning and critical thinking. It's like we dare not question an emotion produced by a hot topic because we are worried that we would be vilified for taking the wrong side. And we could be when we see what happens in an age of demoralization. It is better to think it through over a few days after things cool down to ensure fairness.

There are many events of public shaming that have resulted in job loss. In 2013, a woman was fired from her corporate director position at a New York communications company for having sent out a tweet linking AIDS

---

17 Comments about real situations means I am showing empathy while trying to stay neutral. Some readers may feel that commenting about others' emotions is a way of putting someone into a weak position. That is not so. Others say that showing empathy to a person in a situation is a way of taking sides. That is not so either. These opinions can be the effect of assumptions based on emotional infection. Such effects are not intended here.

with being Black right before boarding an eleven-hour flight. This was after having tweeted similar acerbic jokes while travelling about people needing deodorant or having bad teeth (Ronson, 2015b). She showed bad taste, but perhaps these things happened because she was tense from work and this was her way of handling it, albeit it not a good one. It demonstrates a bad underlying attitude, which can come out when you are least expecting it in this atmosphere of social media, and especially when you are tense about life's issues. It is better to work on changing the underlying attitudes and handling the issues. Various people have been fired for their social media posts (Herman, n.d.). In Canada, two men were fired after yelling a vulgar, sexist slur at a female TV interviewer, one of them saying that it was "hilarious." (Canadian Press, 2015) These incidents may be behaviour modification in real life, where an adverse consequence is given for behaviour that is likely reflecting inappropriate feelings of entitlement. CNN reports that during the pandemic, runners have been berated for exercising without masks, city dwellers have been criticized for congregating in parks, and beachgoers have been condemned for hitting the sand (Kaur, n.d.). Emotions are flying high and affecting the mind's ability to think clearly. Emotions are now in the public spotlight, and it is causing havoc as toxic emotions and related public shaming infect our well-being and produce demoralization. No wonder some people have social phobia and social anxiety.

Emotional contagion has gradually increased and become an emotional pandemic

"We're in a vortex just being whipped around. Pandemic. Wildfires. Economic devastation. It's just crazy man!" Eddie Glaude of Princeton University said this recently on MSNBC (2020). Some people carry this tension close to the surface, sometimes boiling over. It affects us. There is a cost to society emotionally. Some people are quick to blame and judge. Anxiety is rising. People are tense. It is contagious. It may even be addictive, because some people are attracted to it and like to get their "fix" of emotions. The media provides it easily, not considering that they are contributing to a harmful emotional pandemic. It is not just the coronavirus pandemic we need to be concerned about—it is the emotional pandemic too.

Usually when things happen gradually, we do not notice the change. The public's attention span for news is not very long, as people have their own lives to live, but we still manage to soak up the negative effects. When the latest short-term news item of some similarity comes up, the negative effects society has previously absorbed hooks into the new event and adds to the emotional residue, adding to demoralization and cynicism. We hardly notice it.

Emotional contagion is like this, regarding negative news events. It builds up slowly, creeping in without our being aware of it. For many years now, cynicism, mistrust, and rancour has gradually increased in politics, building on previous milder days. It has festered. This has turned into situations where not only is there a lack of respect, but where this disrespect seems to have been absorbed by others.

Having a lower degree of respect includes distrust and suspicion and carries a sense of getting even or taking revenge, but subtly, so that it does not become inappropriate or obvious. Eventually bullying, dominating behaviour is demonstrated by political parties. This was evident in recent U.S. Supreme Court appointments, when one party did not put forward a new judge for many months, leaving the seat empty until the election, after which they hoped to have the deciding power. Then, recently, they took the reverse approach, wanting to fill an empty seat as soon as possible before the next election, hoping to get their way before falling out of power. This contemptuousness would arguably not have happened many years ago. This is a result of gradually increasing emotional contagion, which is growing to the point worry that a civil war or insurgency will eventually break forth (Harte, 2019). A mob attacked the U.S. Capitol building. There was an alleged plot to kidnap Michigan's governor and overthrow the government (Carrega et al., 2020). There are reports that vigilante group activity is on the rise in the U.S. (Shortell et al., 2020). Although these people are criminals, this does not happen without it being nudged by emotional and social contagion; the effect of disrespect and contempt shown by politicians, especially the former president, is so strong that when it rubs off on the criminal element, they already feel similarly, and so take it as permission to act on it. This does not happen in a time without turmoil, but when the turmoil is already present, it provides the energy and the scope for it.

These actions and the recent turmoil have been the culmination of the gradual upward creep of anger, as seen in the many shootings, the mass murders, the riots, the police brutality, and episodes of white supremacy. Earlier it may have been triggered by 9/11, by the war in Iraq, or the ENRON conspiracy. Looking back over the last few decades, demoralization or low-grade depressiveness and pessimism seem to have become more prominent in society—although in the collective subconscious—as various episodes of violence and corruption seem to have been more frequent. Perhaps right-wing people felt shunted aside when the previous president was elected in 2008. It must be hard for them if they feel disenfranchised. People say the scene was ripe for the former president to be elected, and these factors seem to be what they were referring to. This population's emotional needs may have been ignored, their grievances festering within. This, along with many other events, subconsciously or consciously built up their ideas into potential action, perhaps to the point of overthrowing government with violence. This is likely the result of gradual contagious emotions over the years related to a felt need for rebellion and control being absorbed by susceptible individuals who are prone to gradually ramp up the emotion to a point of actual events. If there were no gradual increase of turmoil, they would not have been in the position where they felt their actions were acceptable.

There is no doubt that emotions have a great impact on society, and much of this is communicated through social and emotional contagion. We pick up feelings and emotions from others that we can relate with, and this strengthens and magnifies the emotion in some people. Public shaming, cancel culture, and many negative social trends stem from the residue of previous negative experiences in the social realm, such as displacement, homelessness, lack of opportunity, loss of privacy in a digital age, helplessness in making changes, and medicalization of social problems. In a slippery slope downward we wait for the next downward step that contributes to further demoralization.

Things are getting better for us in society. Look at the evidence. After discrete, time-limited tragic events when people come together, there is recovery. But after events that stretch out over time, with controversy, like the mass murders and gun shootings in the U.S., recovery is slow and sparse. The effects of mass murders add to ongoing worry about our safety as well as to demoralization. When we see it is happening, we experience the reality of it and realize that it could happen to us. Cynicism and pessimism rule. That contributes to the negativity.

Impact on Politics

Emotional contagion was involved in the case of U.S. Senator Al Franken, as it influenced his decision to resign. Many senators later stated that their decision to support Franken's resignation had been made "in the heat of the moment," and that the process was a "rush to judgment" without due process. Emotional contagion is one of the most powerful forces in life; it runs through society when a "hot topic" like this erupts, infecting people's rational abilities and political thinking. Emotions are prone to divide people, as various labels are interpreted with a bias. The emotion of humility is missing in politics. Candidates who use emotion properly usually win elections. Politics is like a horse race, because of the emotion, and election races are framed this way, to the detriment of democracy. Lazy thinking and cognitive ease are some of the culprits.

We all have emotions. In the important arena of politics, we are especially subject to the impact of emotions and emotional contagion.

Emotional contagion in the political world of Al Franken

Let's illustrate the power of emotional contagion by looking at a political example of allegations of sexual assault where emotional contagion likely played a powerful role in its ending.

The #MeToo movement began in 2006 as an effort to bring about social change, organized primarily through social media. It really emerged into public consciousness in 2017, when several high-profile actresses opened up about their experiences with sexual harassment in the film industry. It became an important factor in how society judged what was acceptable behaviour by those in power. In October 2017, the *New York Times* and the *New Yorker* reported, according to the BBC, that many women accused American film producer Harvey Weinstein of sexually harassing, assaulting, or raping them (BBC, 2021). The reactions to these stories moved through society and became front and centre in the national and international mood. Suspicion about men being sexually inappropriate spread. It became contagious; people become cynical about famous men.[18] Bill Cosby, formerly loved as a comedian, was convicted of a sexual crime. The effects of emotional contagion at that time from the Weinstein and Cosby cases may have spilled over to subconsciously affect the public's judgment of Senator Al Franken.[19] After several allegations of sexual misconduct were made against him (Mayer, 2019), and after having been a U.S. senator for about ten years, Al Franken resigned from the U.S. Senate on January 2, 2018.

It could be that Franken lost his position out of fear that his situation was just as bad as those of Weinstein and Cosby. This is irrational, as they are completely separate cases, but strong suspicious emotions about high-profile cases can be irrational and contagious and subconsciously affect our reasoning ability. The emotional tinge runs through the story as the mood of the #MeToo movement was also involved and affected society significantly. Emotional contagion runs through society when a "hot topic" like this erupts, and there have been many in the last few years.

This is the background: In November 2017, Leeann Tweeden, a conservative talk-radio host, alleged in a blog post and a radio interview that Franken forcibly kissed her on a 2006 USO tour during a rehearsal for a skit. This was during the early days of the #MeToo movement.

In the blog post she wrote of how he aggressively kissed her. She said she had said 'OK' "so he would stop badgering me" (Monyak, 2017). She said she pushed him away, feeling "disgusted and violated." There was also a photograph of Franken appearing to place his hands on Tweeden's breasts while she was asleep (Garber, 2017). In Franken's defence, CNBC's John Harwood said on Twitter, "That pic was obviously a joke, not groping, just like LeeAnn Tweeden wrapping her leg around Robin Williams and smacking his butt."(Harwood, 2018). The picture does look like a purposeful pose for PR purposes, but is inappropriate nevertheless, looked at in the framework of the current zeitgeist. In the context of the reports of various other sexual assaults perpetrated by Franken, the photo from

---

18 This is not a defence of men, nor is it favouring one side or another. Some people may subconsciously interpret comments such as this one in this way. Emotional contagion could produce such a bias.

19 This is no way suggests that Mr. Franken should not have resigned. This does raise the possibility that there may have been emotional contagion involved in the public attitude towards him.

eleven years before took on a different flavour, possibly influenced by the emotional carryover.

In response to Leeann Tweeden's allegations, Franken said, "I certainly don't remember the rehearsal for the skit in the same way, but I send my sincerest apologies to Leeann..." (CNN Politics, 2017). He said that "anyone who wanted to read the photo as confirming what I was accused of could do that." True. But Leeann Tweeden felt that Al Franken's behaviour was "disgusting." Behaviour thought of as disgusting has a strong psychological aversiveness. Very few people feel comfortable when they are disgusted. Disgust is pervasive and enduring. It seems to paralyze the ability to reason.

In the days that followed, seven additional women came forward with allegations of inappropriate behaviour by Franken during photo-ops. Franken was accused of touching a woman's buttocks, giving a woman a wet, open-mouthed kiss, and holding a CNN reporter's breast, ostensibly through her clothing, for several seconds. These are all inappropriate, invasive, and troubling actions. Other similar revelations involving Franken came fast and had a powerful effect.

Subsequent reporting in 2019 by *New Yorker* journalist Jane Mayer (2019) revealed controversies about Tweeden's allegations. It shows how emotion can colour our judgment of something when it is a "hot topic" circulating in the media, and carries a lot of emotion and controversy, and when it is widely known and popular. Society's disgust was real.

Reactions change over time. The following quotes from Mayer in the *New Yorker* and in the *Guardian* (Bryant, 2019) regarding the Al Franken situation came a year and a half after his resignation. These quotes are from U.S. senators, most of them in Franken's party. Six of the eight senators were men, indicating a possibility of bias. These quotes are significantly different from their immediate, earlier reactions to the story when it was breaking. This seems to give us an idea how emotion is contagious and spreads, even amongst U.S. senators in a political debate about a contentious issue. Emotions take over people's rational abilities very soon after an event, infecting their mind and disrupting their ability to think rationally. As seen by the following quotes, this subsides a few weeks or months later. Emotions dominated at the time of the event and governed aspects of their rational mind at that time, but disappeared later, when the mind was thinking rationally again.

Senator Patrick Leahy said that supporting Franken's resignation without first getting all the facts was "one of the biggest mistakes [he'd] made" in forty-five years in the Senate. "If there's one decision I've made that I would take back, it's the decision to call for [Franken's] resignation. It was made in the heat of the moment, without concern for exactly what this was." Senator Tammy Duckworth told the *New Yorker* that the Senate Ethics Committee hearing "should have been allowed to move forward," adding, "that due process didn't happen and this is not good for our democracy." Independent senator Angus King said he'd "regretted [joining calls for resignation] ever since." He added, "There's no excuse for sexual assault, but Al deserved more of a process. I don't denigrate the allegations, but this was the political equivalent of capital punishment." "This was a rush to judgment that didn't allow any of us to fully explore what this was about. I took the judgment of my peers rather than independently examining the circumstances," Senator Jeff Merkley said. "In my heart, I've not felt right about it." "I realized almost right away I'd made a mistake. I felt terrible. I should have stood up for due process to render what it's supposed to—the truth," Former senator Bill Nelson said. "I made a mistake. I started having second thoughts shortly after he stepped down. He had the right to be heard by an independent investigative body," Senator Tom Udall said. "I've heard from people around my state, and around the country, saying that they think he got railroaded. It doesn't seem fair. I'm a lawyer. I really believe in due process." Former Senate Minority Leader Harry Reid, who was retired at time, told the *New Yorker*, "It's terrible what happened to him. It was unfair. It took the legs out from under him. He was a very fine senator."

These quotes give us an idea of the power of emotional contagion, how emotion can spread and be contagious, taking over people's rational abilities, although temporarily. When the dust settles, they have a different perspective than they did originally. Even then, the phenomenon of "group-think," which contains significant elements of emotional contagion itself, may have been at play at this later time. It is possible that Al Franken lost his seat in the Senate because of the contagious effects of the strong cynical emotions that contributed to his being found guilty.

When people talk about the "heat of the moment" or a "rush to judgment," they are talking about the strong effect of the emotion at the time it was experienced. This emotional phenomenon clouded their thinking when the potential for contagion was strong and hard to resist. Everyone seemed to be on the same page. The emotion of disgust likely played a role in contributing to the onset of emotional contagion at the initial decision. It appeared to be very strong at the beginning, seeming to take over the function of the mind in making decisions. In this way the emotion was contagious, and infectious, as if it were so captivating to the mind that the mind couldn't refuse its offerings. The effect of the disgust that came from Tweeden's described imagery made the emotion powerful and difficult to withstand. The contagious effect may have been multiplied by the number of people involved. The fact that it was expressed by women who were vulnerable, and the implication that thousands more felt it, the presence of other cases such as Weinstein's, and the #MeToo movement were social factors in contributing to the contagious effect. When it is socially and emotionally contagious, others catch it, and it is strengthened even more. Strong contagious emotions in a high-profile social or political setting are difficult to resist. Franken relented. Most decent people would. It became clear that what he did was wrong when viewed through a new lens provided by the #MeToo movement, a lens that should have been available much earlier.

There was likely an unwillingness to challenge or confront these strong emotions, which is not uncommon among people who feel uncomfortable around open emotions. This unwillingness can also be contagious. Emotions like disgust and fear are rarely questioned, especially when there are many similar emotions impacting people and running through society. They are assumed to be legitimate reasons for a decision. Their strength and contagion seem to temporarily overtake the ability to reason. Was there a need to "punish" Franken for the sexual misconduct by pushing for and supporting the resignation? Maybe. Somehow that question didn't seem appropriate to ask at the time.

The thing that we forget about emotional contagion is that it will pass. The disgust emotion no longer seemed to have its effect after some time; it was only there in the present moment. It is not possible to maintain disgust as a current feeling for a long time, because feelings by their nature do not last long. But they can be renewed or refreshed. The feeling of disgust over sexual assault cases lingers in the collective subconscious, and it is renewed every time relevant news hits. There are many incidents in life that produce various emotions and feelings, and we cannot afford to extend the psychological energy to maintain that current experience for a longer period of time. It is more of a cognitive fact than an ongoing living emotional memory, which, if it were, would sap energy from us day by day. We may no longer feel that exact emotion years later. As a cognitive fact, we now may have a different opinion about it. When the emotion is only a memory, the contagious effect wears down; the opinion changes, as it did for the senators. We can then use our reasoning abilities objectively. But although there is no more contagion, there is a subconscious emotional residue, as there is with most serious, public occasions of emotional contagion. It colours our judgment. Many women and some men have recurrent active images of disgusting scenes of sexual violation that would retain its currency and keep it active in their memory. So the controversy lingers.

There are two sides to this story, as there are to every story. To what extent does emotional contagion colour the perception of each side? Does it really distort the truth? It would seem that the experience of disgust is a legitimate source of evidence that colours our perception of a situation, as is pain and other negative emotional reactions to events. Just because the time has passed does not remove the facts of the matter. But it takes time to think about it all and consider both sides; use the slow thinking of System 2. Emotional contagion seems to be present to a significant degree on both sides in the heat of the moment.

Emotional voting

Emotional contagion has affected our democratic process more now than ever. It seems that many people vote with their emotions now instead of thinking through the pros and cons of each candidate. Voting should be based on a rational decision. Being well-informed is an asset when contributing to political and social dialogue. We have come to the point where emotion runs so strong in political debates that at times it takes over our reasoning abilities, our political discourse, and our votes. While this phenomenon may have always been present, it tends to have become so much larger and stronger and contributed to the recent times of turmoil.

Society's leaders are seen by different people in a positive, a negative, or a neutral way. Although the leader is the same person behaving the same way and saying the same thing, they are received differently by different audiences. Therefore the leader described in a positive way by one person may have a negative impact on another. That is human nature.

People with an emotional bent usually appeal to others' emotions, and such people often win elections. Intellectual people who are less entertaining or appealing rarely win elections with logical, reasoned-out policy. But when some personal meaning is added to this logical policy, the heart, or sentiment, provides the necessary type of emotion that adds perspective and often drives the words home appropriately. Reasoning doesn't speak for itself. Emotion speaks instead. It is when emotion is over the top that emotional infection of the mind can occur, becoming destructive. Policies need to be coloured with emotion and personal appeal to voters; if the emotion follows from the thought, is mild to moderate, and is expressed as emotion, it works. Emotions are more appealing than thoughts and logic. This is a winning style. Poetry usually wins in elections, not policy.

We know that in emotional contagion, the emotions seem to bypass one's reasoning ability or mental faculties. Instead, they directly impact the emotions. When a matter is meaningful to someone, it impinges on their emotions. The phenomenon is vulnerability, and it becomes problematic when an emotional leader has too strongly used their emotion. They may instill fear, dread, darkness, anxiety, despair, and general negativity into their followers. This strengthens their followers' attachment. When emotion brings this force into the rational mind and takes over, it can't be defeated easily. Emotions have no rationality, so the emotion that one feels when a leader makes a loud, powerful statement with simple language cuts right to the gut. When a candidate says in a strong way that "It's all done wrong!!" or "I am very intelligent!" then if there is even the slightest inkling in the voter that significant matters have been handled wrongly and that this person can right it, that message can feel so strong that it can take over some listeners' decision-making abilities. It compensates for any weakness the voter feels in themselves, and in this way the voter feels strong. Falsely. Because emotions don't think but many people use their emotions to arrive at a conclusion. This is attractive to people who are insecure and unsure of what is causing their problems. They are looking for an answer, even if they don't recognize this. The inkling that something has been done wrong somewhere becomes a certainty in their mind because the force of emotion the speaker portrays convinces the listener of wrongdoing and overtakes their reasoning process. The person likely used their emotion to think as a habit so they were ripe for this. So the listener allows this takeover, likely feeling relief. This is a reinforcing emotion and the emotional contagion spreads. People don't have to think. The former president thinks for them, saying "I am your voice!" When it is repeated over and over in strong emotional language—complete with swearing and name-calling and other powerful manipulative techniques—the emotional contagion is almost complete. The emotion from another person has been contagious, the person has absorbed it and that emotion has powerfully taken over their willing mind. But the message is still false. Voters often vote with their emotions based on who is the most favourable or likeable candidate. That is why the most emotional person often wins.

The idea of emotional contagion influencing political thinking may cause cognitive dissonance because it may make no sense to the logical mind. We have to remember how active the subconscious mind is. Some authors think that affective contagion is the underlying process that drives motivated reasoning and rationalization in political thinking (Erisen et al. 2012). They state that emotional cues are embedded in the political message through implicit emotion, whether incidental or deliberately embedded, and produce strong affective contagion. These implicit emotions are an important contributor to the unconscious emotional contagion passed on to voters in political campaigns.

The emotional contagion infects the rational mind so strongly that sometimes it just feels wrong to have an argument based on facts and logic, which feel emotionally weak. Nothing could be further from the truth. Logic and facts are not weak; they may just feel that way because they are not usually exciting or colourful. Feelings can dominate, even though they shouldn't. Emotions don't think; they can't reason things out and look for cause-and-effect. We need a way to be inoculated against such infectious, toxic emotional contagion so we can make a rational choice instead, using systematic reasoning, critical thinking, and wisdom. Feelings have a role in the choice, but not one of domination.

Emotions and feelings need to be guided by logic and facts in a real but gentle way. Then the emotions will listen to the mind. Emotions don't listen to force and domination from one's own mind. They rebel if they feel clamped down, causing emotional or behavioural distress to the person. The mind adds perspective and can complete the faulty thinking brought about by an incomplete emotional message. The emotions know that thinking is the duty of the mind and will listen and follow the mind's guidance, but only if the mind is gentle and empathic with its feelings and has the feelings' needs at the uppermost most of the time. The mind needs to try and meet the emotion's needs, or tell it in a simple, understandable way what it is doing to meet its needs. They are partners—the mind and the emotions.

It makes sense that a successful politician would have a good balance between their mind and their emotions. This involves resisting various emotional appeals. The contagion from the emotion in these cases can be so infectious that they are blinded by it. The emotional appeal is usually short-term and blinds the person to the long-term implications when the pending pleasure is within reach.

It is easy for the emotions to try to think. They think quickly, with distorted thoughts, and just give simple messages. Lisa Barrett (2017) says that "affective realism, the phenomenon that you experience what you believe," give us "body-[budgeting] predictions laden with affect, not logic or reason, [that are] the main drivers of [our] experience and behaviour." She says when you hear some news that you immediately believe, that is affective realism. In other words, it feels real because of the effect of emotion, also called affect. It keeps you believing something even when the evidence makes it highly doubtful. Simple messages provided by emotion can give a label to something, prompting you to automatically move to where the label points you, probably because it feels good. Affective realism is one of the serious problems causing emotional turmoil of our times and seems to occur when toxic emotions infect our thinking.

When it comes to voting in an election, no matter how important that choice is, many say that our choice should be emotional. Yes and no. There could be an emotional connection you have with the person you are choosing that is based on reasoning. But the emotion shouldn't dominate the reason for your choice; thought should. Otherwise we get emotional voting. Emotion dominates if you vote against a person or party based on one thing you dislike and end up not really knowing what position you are voting for. That is impulsive, emotional voting and it is occurring more often now. Predictions about how the politician will govern based on reasoning, knowledge, and experience, as well as knowledge of non-specific factors like personality, all count. Since emotions don't think, if we vote emotionally we are not considering all the factors we should.

Some politicians may want us to make our choice based on emotional thinking. They know emotion works. Their election campaigns are likely to use emotional verbiage verging on the extreme. Others may want us to vote rationally, to make our choice based on systematic reasoning and critical thinking, letting any emotions follow from the conclusions that these approaches help us arrive at. That would not constitute emotional contagion, but it is usually not appealing to most voters.

Politicians can be like a magnet in that they attract and absorb some of the angry emotions and frustrations that people have with life in general. This can flare up during a crisis. Because we rarely interact with politicians face-to-face, it is easy to vent our angry feelings towards them; this anger can lead to emotional voting in future elections. When you vote emotionally against someone, you want that "idiot" not to win the office. Negative emotional voting only occurs from anger when you want to vote against the candidate without considering the alternative. So you vote for someone else who will also have weak points, that you may discover later, if they are elected. The opposing candidate's strengths will seem more visible and encouraging when you only compare them against a weakness of the person you want to lose. That is the contrast effect; the contrast appears greater when seen in limited scope than it really is with a wider perspective. You need to research the candidates realistically and neutrally. You may be experiencing confirmation bias, where you perceive someone the way you want to see them only because of your negative emotions about the other candidate. While thinking emotionally, you forget the strengths of the candidate you dislike, while simultaneously forgetting the weaknesses of your other option. But emotions don't think. You might be satisfied temporarily because you feel better, but if you didn't compare each candidate's strengths against their weaknesses in a systematic, cost-benefit analysis, you are probably not thinking rationally and objectively about your vote. Do this objectively and not emotionally. Unfortunately, we tend to approach elections with confirmation bias, looking for what we already believe in.

Televised political debates highlight weak moments of a candidate, making gaffes and misstatements. Some media lead viewers to assume that this moment accurately portrays the candidate by continually replaying it. Such moments induce emotional reactions. In reality, we all have our strong and weak moments; we all make mistakes and misspeak. The emotional contagion caused by a photo or clip colours our opinion about the candidate with the halo effect. The halo effect is a type of cognitive bias in which our evaluation of a person on one dimension influences how we feel and think about the person on other dimensions, such as their character, so that perceptions of one of the person's qualities lead to biased judgments of the rest of their character (APA, n.d.).

Because the first appraisal of a photo is usually quick, from System 1 (quick, impulsive, gut reactions), the second appraisal, slowly reasoned out, may never be done, as emotional contagion and incomplete thinking from System 1 take over in affecting our judgments of the photo. This is emotional contagion from the effects of implicit emotion from others' voice tones being contagious and infecting the recipient's reasoning. The second appraisal, if it would be done, would be from System 2 (slow, reasoned thinking). It would take logical, reasoned thinking about the nature of photography, human movements and various possible situations and movements we could find ourselves being photographed in, especially in the days when everyone has video cameras in their smart phones. We know that a single photo of someone we know at a weak moment in their personal life doesn't usually portray the whole truth about who they really are, so why do we accept this about a candidate?

Emotional voting occurs when you vote against someone because you are angry at something they have done. You are so angry that you want to get back at them. In this era, with technology sending out emotions, messages and images to millions of people simultaneously, it doesn't take long for the contagious effect to occur, and for that anger to build up. You might catch it from others. Emotional voting also occurs with contentious political issues that stir up strong emotions of disgust, such as abortion and same-sex marriage. People may vote for or against a candidate based on their emotion surrounding such an issue, forgetting that there are many other issues to consider.

Many of us become emotionally involved in political and social issues when we take political statements personally. This affects our vote. We vote emotionally, instead of recognizing the emotion we're feeling about a candidate and whether it is reasonable to let that emotion influence our vote. When we vote emotionally, we vote blindly. With the halo effect, the strength of the disgust we feel about a controversial topic can stay with us in a visceral sense. Disgust is a major factor in emotional voting, especially when life or death topics, such as abortions or guns, are on the table. Political parties that are supported by emotional voters will often base their policies on the leanings of their base, and what results is a policy based on voters' quick, emotional judgments. Hence we have wars, bombs, jails, border walls, guns, police brutality, and the list goes on. Any or all of these situations may appeal to the base instincts of the voters, like revenge, judgment, control, and punishment (which can be traced back to a need for power in people who feel otherwise disenfranchised). Such voters prefer extreme positions and are likely to be impatient with nuanced, reasoned positions, which take time. These are all emotional positions more appealing to the gut.

If people vote emotionally, impulsively, without using systematic reasoning or critical thinking, then should the elected official base their policies on what they think their voters want, when that is based on quick, impulsive emotional reactions, rather than reasoned, thought out responses? Emotional contagion has probably infected them also, and the future of a government or even a country. Democracy did not intend for a leader to be elected this way. This is one reason why emotional contagion is one of the most powerful forces in life.

Let's look at the labels *left wing* and *right wing*. *Left wing* could be interpreted as, "let's take a lot of money from the taxpayers for the government to provide a lot of programs to help all the needy people." *Right wing* could be interpreted as, "we don't need so much government assistance because all these people should help themselves instead of relying on programs paid for by taxpayers." These positions are at extremes, as we see by the use of the word *all*, and so are prone to emotional thinking and likely to get emotional reactions, which cause divisiveness. Remember that all-or-nothing thinking is a cognitive distortion and a sign of emotional thinking. Implicit emotion is powerful. If a party or its voters go further towards the extreme, more emotional turmoil is likely to result. Although it may be the extremists who become more emotional, the media often designates an entire political party in this manner, through emotional contagion colouring judgment and hence its portrayal in the news.

Most mainstream voters usually avoid extremes when voting. It is the people at the extremes that attract the attention of the press because they are emotional and dramatic, and this sells papers and attracts viewers. Viewers like emotional stimulation. The emotional contagion has appealed to viewers emotionally, but only when emotional voting subsides will we return closer to the norm and lower the turmoil in society.

Embedded emotions determine political choices

Political thinking itself is influenced by emotions. Political psychologists say it is "biased systematically by the feelings that are aroused in the earliest stages of processing" and development of political thought. "This underlying affective bias in processing drives motivated reasoning and rationalization in political thinking."(Erisen et al., 2012) Emotions are embedded in a political stance taken by a politician. Political scientists think we make choices based on the policies of politicians and whether they are right- or left-leaning. But our choices are determined significantly by affect as well. Political psychologists say that when "citizens form and express their political preferences," they are influenced by symbols such as "judicial robes, physical characteristics of people, like skin color or height, and myriad contextual factors," which trigger our biases. They are strengthened by the subconscious. Our response to politicians is also influenced by how deep their voice is (Burkley, 2018), if they have easy-to-pronounce names (Laham et al., 2012), how tall they are (Fleming, 2011), or the shape of their face (Konnikova, 2013). As well, the candidate whose name appears first on the ballot earns 2–3 percent more of the vote, on average, and 90 percent of candidates benefit from having their name listed first (Miller & Krosnick, 1998). All of these may influence behaviour outside the awareness of citizens. In fact, in his first election, the former president was listed first in all states he won with narrow margins. Weir says this probably delivered the presidency to him (Weir, 2019). Names with few syllables win. Oval-shaped faces win. Deep voices and tall politicians win. That doesn't sound like policy, it's more like poetry.

These factors and others trigger emotions in us that can make us like or dislike the politician. It appears automatic and subconscious. Few people would say that they vote for someone because they are tall and have a deep voice, but people rarely can report on their subconscious motivations for their choices in life. According to the *New York Times,* "new studies reveal a subconscious brain that is far more active, purposeful, and independent than previously known."(Carey, 2007) Again according to the political psychologists, "both affective [emotional] and cognitive [thought] reactions to external and internal events are triggered unconsciously and spread activation in memory through associative pathways that link feelings to thoughts to behaviours." (Erisen et al., 2012). These are unconscious processes. There is no reason those unconscious triggers don't also apply to voting. In moment-by-moment interactions, when we hear comments being made and see video of politicians, our internal emotions sometimes seem to take over[20] in the way that they do when we

---

20 As in other examples in the book, I say "seem to take over," rather than state it as a fact, because it cannot be verified or proven, but is based on my knowledge of psychological and emotional factors and behaviour in human beings.

see subtle synchronization and mimicking of movements that produces contagion. With 4K definition and surround sound, politicians, musicians, and athletes now seem close and real right in our own homes, and we pick up real vibes that can produce contagious effects.

Our subconscious mind notices these things. Unconscious stimuli, those aspects of our visual, auditory, tactile, and aromatic environment not registered by our conscious mind, are ubiquitous and abundant in the real world (Erisen et al., 2012). Advertisers routinely manipulate implicit influences, whether selling motorcycles or presidential candidates. Indeed, evidence dates back to Vance Packard's classic best-selling book, *Hidden Persuaders*, in 1957 (Packard, 1957). It sold over a million copies in the late fifties and early sixties. This quote from Wikipedia summarizes the book: Packard "explored advertisers' use of consumer motivational research and other psychological techniques, including depth psychology and subliminal tactics, to manipulate expectations [...] including manipulative techniques of promoting politicians to the electorate."(Packard, 2021)

Domination of emotional thinking

We saw emotional contagion in full force during the 2016 U.S. presidential race when the former president, while still a candidate for the presidency, used the phrase "lock her up" about his opponent, the first female presidential candidate ever nominated by a major party. Never before has a candidate for president threatened to lock up his opponent. This phrase became attached to emotions of anger, power, control, and authoritarianism. His followers, mistakenly but understandably because of their emotional needs, perceived this rhetoric as their own because of the absolute power of emotional contagion. They identified with the authoritarian characteristics because they wanted someone in charge to reduce their opponent's power because they couldn't do it themselves. Theoretically, they may have had authoritarian maternal figures in childhood and wanted the authoritarian father figure (represented by the former president) to take away their opponent's power, because their fathers couldn't. So these emotions may have been very infectious for the people prone to catching them. They feel left out, ignored, and powerless in a competitive society, one that rewards power, and so the powerful emotions are very appealing and alluring to them.

This authoritarian approach continued to describe the former president's approach throughout his presidency. It is his personality style. This strategy alarmed many people who were concerned about the future of democracy, as this approach was only ever taken in authoritarian countries (Tucker, 2016). It permeated American politics, reaching its pinnacle in early 2021 with his supporters' undemocratic attack on the U.S. Capitol building. This was a result of emotions heightened to a level rarely seen in Western politics, as emotional contagion swept through the country and around the world (although unrecognized for what it was). Emotions spread the leader's message to his mob.

Without emotion, there is no passion to whatever meaning was being given, and without meaning there is no action. His followers finally had a strong, long-awaited leader, and became very emotional, showering him with adoration and blind devotion. They may have been relieved, finally, that there was a man with whom they could identify, who claimed to recognize them and would, in their minds, represent their needs and lead them to a hallowed land. He said early in his candidacy, "I am your voice." Who was he speaking to when he said that? It was to those who ended up wanting him as their leader. We know that relief takes the lid off long held and chronically repressed emotions. They have finally been released without scorn or rejection (from their leader). These repressed emotions become very contagious when met by a strong person seen as accepting and representative of their needs, performing in a very loud, vociferous, apparently genuine way. This was backwards empathy: meeting their needs by providing them with power, fake power that turned out to be false. Little did they know that the apparently genuine nature of this candidate was actually a narcissistic, delusional belief that he alone could fix everything, in a way that only he saw. This genuine nature would explain his open sincerity but also a delusional disorder reflective of some form of mental illness.

Delusional disorder is a serious mental illness where you can't tell the difference between what's real and what's not. No one alone can fix everything or know more than others about so many topics. Delusions of grandeur occur when you believe that you have more power, wealth, smarts, or other grand traits than you really do. People truly believe they have these characteristics and so will come across as genuine—but this does not mean, in fact, that their beliefs are true. Genuineness does not equal truth, but his followers appreciated his genuineness, a characteristic unfortunately not common to politicians. This appears to be a textbook case of delusion of grandeur. It is also the result of years of cynicism about politicians telling the truth. People assume genuineness equals the truth when it doesn't.

It is a cause for alarm that many authoritarian leaders have attracted large numbers of followers (Dean & Altemeyer, 2020). They use strategy to heighten and use emotional contagion to its fullest, as people can identify with a person they perceive to be a strong man. Perceived strength with perceived genuineness are emotionally reinforcing to the voter, but, in fact, this can be an emotional infection of one's mental faculties.

We saw emotional contagion in Canada when the Canadian prime minister had the public frustrated and angry at him for going to his vacation second home to see his wife and kids who were living there as the pandemic wore on. His wife had been diagnosed with COVID-19 (she later recovered). For at least two weeks, including weekends, he was giving a daily update on national television on developments in Canada regarding the pandemic and the government's various programs to provide financial assistance. He was still working while worried about his wife. When she recovered and went to their second home with their children, he stayed behind to work and stay in touch with the public. When he finally joined his family, many people were angry and cynical because they felt like he was breaking rules, going to the second home when they were supposed to stay home because of the pandemic lockdown. This cynicism coloured their perception, blinding them to the reality of the actual situation. This is reality of the situation as seen from another perspective. They may have failed to help Canadian citizens to see that he had been socially isolated at home while still working for long hours seven days a week, overseeing the government's response to the pandemic, all while his wife had been ill. That would stress most of us to the max. Some people felt that going to his second home was elitism and were angry at him. But the Prime Minister needed a break from stress so that he could relax and then return to leading his country through a crucial time. This would be true no matter which party was in power. He is human.

Intellectual humility

The emotion of humility is absent in the heightened atmosphere of intense political competition. Insecure people seem to have difficulty being humble. It is difficult for them to accept compliments, acknowledge their strengths, or realize that being humble does not mean being inferior. Humility is not the same as humiliation. Showing humility requires good self-esteem and the confidence to acknowledge that you are not perfect, at the same time as not putting yourself down.

This is important because with the lack of respect among political parties, and with the lack of decency in politics, it is difficult—if not impossible—for some people to agree that the political opposition has some good points, or some strengths. This comes out of irrational fear of losing something crucial to one's identity or one's party, or the fear that something extremely negative will take over the country, should they acknowledge the strengths of the opposition and should the other party get elected.

Bowes (2021) describes affective polarization as occurring when "people tend to perceive members of other political groups who hold opposing political views as immoral or unintelligent." Affective polarization is different from ideological polarization, which refers to intellectual differences on policies and issues while regarding the opposition with respect and dignity. Affective polarization is related to emotions and indicates that emotions have taken over; they have hijacked the mind and decided to substitute emotional judgments in their evaluation of the opposition. These judgments can be severe, seeing others as evil, disgusting, or despicable. In order to maintain respect, decency, and dignity, we have to be able to trust that the political opposition is decent and respectful of us as human beings, and that they are not going to treat us like wild animals or attack our legislative body, or even threaten to kill legislative members during riots.

In order to change our beliefs at the height of a political storm, Bowes insightfully makes the point that intellectual humility is required. This reflects "the degree to which people evaluate the accuracy of their beliefs and are willing to change their beliefs when presented with compelling evidence that they are wrong" Bowes (2021). This would produce "greater respectfulness, tolerance, and open-mindedness." The author correctly points out that people can still hold specific beliefs intellectually that they have no intention of changing, while still maintaining a willingness perhaps to reflect on their beliefs or to think about how they may affect others. They would have a lesser degree of affective polarization. This usually requires some emotional realization, which we may have seen in the after-effects of the Capitol riots: some participants changed their position, realizing the impact of the attack as dangerous and threatening to peoples' lives—actually having resulted in the tragic deaths of five people. Emotion is usually required to make significant changes in one's deeper beliefs, and that emotion usually has to be strong and stem from unfortunate, tragic events. The same emotional dynamic may occur when someone who is against abortion, euthanasia or even vaccination suddenly changes their mind when a family member is confronted with one of these dilemmas. This is the power of emotional contagion in influencing others and their own intellectual positions. In this case, it may not always technically be emotional contagion, as the mind may accept the input of the emotion by using logical thought, assessing a cost-benefit analysis and considering the emotion felt regarding the topic at hand. Emotional infection occurs when the emotion dominates the mind, the emotion having initially been absorbed through emotional contagion, so that it is unable to do this rational analysis.

Horse-race politics

The daily news is often presented as if it were a combination of entertainment, tragedy, drama, and sports. It is horse-race politics. Continually breaking news. Anticipation. Fake news. Scandals. What might happen? How bad will it be? Much of what is going on constitutes and exacerbates emotional contagion. We need to slow this down. Elaine Hatfield and her associates (1993) warned us about emotional contagion. We need to stop immediately catching emotions.

Horse-race politics treats elections like sports, where teams are in a pennant race. Viewers love the excitement of sports. Teams vie for the top spot. Horse-race politics gives us the same kind of feeling. There is a lot of excitement over the competition. Polls tell us who's winning, just like sports standings. Viewers, who generally are the voters, seem to be caught up in the emotional contagion they are catching or magnifying through exaggerated thoughts in election "races."

The major news outlets present politics like horse races. Politico highlights critics of horse-race politics, who say that "horse-race coverage trivializes politics into a game or a sporting event. [...] It nudges substantive policy coverage out of the public eye and encourages voters to board the leader's bandwagon" (Shafer, 2019). Emotional contagion thrives on bandwagons. "When journalists covering elections focus primarily on who's winning or losing—instead of on policy issues—voters, candidates, and the news industry itself suffer, a growing body of research has found" (Ordway, n.d.). Horse-race politics is clearly contaminated by emotional contagion because emotional words abound in the media's coverage. The former president has oft been quoted using emotional words, although Thomas E. Patterson of the Harvard Kennedy School says that "[the former president's] stand on undocumented immigrants was not all that different in its provisions than that of several other Republican contenders." (Patterson 2016a). His words made it newsworthy, Patterson said, [not the ideas], and the mainstream media picked it up. The words only appeared to have that effect because of the emotion they aroused. He used extreme words to arouse people's emotions like *rapists, murderers,* and *terrorists.* This is prime territory for those who are not inoculated against emotional contagion. They soak up these extreme words because they elicit fear that matches their internal fear and anxiety. They want someone who protects them from that fear, a person they perceive as strong. Like a judge or policeman—even a bully—because they are perceived as powerful. Strong, powerful men are attractive candidates to the scared voter who votes emotionally.

Awareness of how to prevent absorbing emotional contagion from the news can start with the realization that we need to figure out what the people who present the news are trying to accomplish by using this sensational method. Are they really trying to present the news in the fairest way possible, or are they trying to present it in a way that attracts viewers and readers? It seems to be the latter, proving again that Marshall McLuhan was right when he said, "The medium is the message." Mark Federman describes it thus: "McLuhan was concerned with the observation that we tend to focus on the obvious. In doing so, we largely miss the structural changes in our affairs that are introduced subtly, or over long periods of time." (in Pyatt, 2010). McLuhan said that the media set the tone of society's mood more with their presentation style than the actual news they present. We often react to media headlines, in-your-face video, breaking news, tragedies, and excitement with System 1 thinking: quick, sudden reactions. The news networks are aware that drama attracts viewers, which makes them money through increasing viewership and commercials. They often heighten the drama in the news in a way that is emotionally contagious (Bridge, 2021). Emotions attract more emotions, and people want and need more emotional fulfillment. If the media broadcast can spread emotion to other people, more viewers will tune in and boost the network's ratings.

In the news, we often see a close-up of someone who is distressed. Most people continue to tune in, wanting more because they subconsciously or unconsciously like the drama and emotion, even though they may be consciously commenting on how horrible the person's plight is. Democratic principles do not seem to handle this idea well: that the subconscious or unconscious may like drama, hence we want more and turn to the news for it although it is not good for us. Popular reality shows are more abundant, perhaps reducing the possible effect of vicarious satisfaction through desensitization. This phenomenon can produce suspicion, cynicism, depression, anxiety, fear and panic and is part of the gradual creep toward demoralization.

The broadcast news has a stake in this. There is a financial advantage to broadcast drama that attracts viewers: it brings in commercials. American commercials also are different from those in other countries. *HuffPost* wrote, "These days, it seems impossible to sell anything on U.S. TV networks without the use of explosions, interpersonal violence, gratuitous sex, car wrecks, or gunplay. It's almost a flip image of Canadian TV, where you see elements sadly lacking on American spots: humour, whimsy, subtlety, cleverness, intelligence" (Mann, 2013). It would seem then that emotional contagion is strengthened in the U.S. by commercials, which are probably appealing to individuals using System 1, and not so much in Canada, where commercials may be appealing to individuals using System 2.

Journalists may be subconsciously, or perhaps consciously, using emotional contagion to attract viewers and readers. They could instead responsibly disseminate balanced information to help viewers develop a wider perspective. They could make them aware of the infectious effect of toxic emotions via emotional contagion. We need to be aware of these factors in order to judge the situation. We cannot easily stop automatically catching the emotions and feelings that flow towards us if they are purposely directed our way by the mainstream media.

Patterson (2016b) wrote a report on the serious consequences of horse-race elections. In the 2016 U.S. election, he says that policy issues accounted for 10 percent of news coverage of the 2016 general presidential election. He says that "Election news is framed in the context of winning and losing rather than what's at stake in the choice of a president." In other words, it is coverage for sports pages. Substantive concerns, such as policy positions, were last in terms of the coverage allocation, accounting for "roughly a tenth of the primary coverage." He says that the psychological impact of the developments in the horse-race election campaigns is a major factor. It is a sport although supposedly more sophisticated with psychological factors, emotional factors, competitive edges, winners, and losers. It is clear then that horse-race politics, eliciting excitement over competition, heightening drama with name-calling, and magnifying aspects of character like language, health, and gender—all begets emotional contagion and sends cognitive factors like policy positions to the back burner. No wonder we get controversial winners; it's a popularity contest, especially when we remember that voters pick people who are tall, with long faces, deep voices, and easy-to-remember names. Democracy loses as a result.

The politician knows, possibly subconsciously, that contagion of their brand is what they want to be popular, since contagion spreads like wildfire if there is no psychological inoculation. They don't want inoculation for the voters. That would lower the emotional reactions that bring them votes. They know about emotional voting. Emotion always wins elections. Create the perception of a poison and then come up with an antidote: themselves. They want the toxic emotions to spread, so they can be the ones to rise above and defeat the perceived toxicity. They are the antidote for the poison. Often the leaders seem to swing from one persona to another—strongman to soother. This is the connection between populism and success: emotional and social contagion, which brings votes, and the factors that create the emotions that bring votes. If their brand becomes contagious, based on underlying factors like fear or pride, then they are well on their way to an election victory, with no articulation and without much focus on policy.

Emotional contagion can develop from writings like poetry—where figurative language, the colour used to amplify our writing, is used to make the emotions flow in a way that makes the feelings jump off the page towards the reader (or in the case of video, the viewer). There are five distinct categories of figurative language: metaphor, simile, personification, hyperbole, and symbolism (Your Dictionary, n.d.). These are excellent techniques to use in advertising and speeches. Elections are supposed to be about choosing the person or the party with the best policies. Instead the viewers are making their choice based on the poetry of the candidate's words, not policy: the most compelling figurative language wins. As a result, the best-qualified candidate does not always win.

The emotions invoked by figurative language, the competitive win-lose atmosphere, the entertainment provided by the drama and various personalities all spread emotional contagion. Emotions infect many voters, driving the most rhythmic candidate to a win. It may also meet some people's needs for more emotion and meaning in their lives. When we consider that poetry invokes rhythm, charm, and emotion, and that public policy invokes boredom and dullness, we see that the winner of elections wins using poetry, not policy. Poetry is strengthened by emotional contagion.

The elephant in the room: the need for power

Underlying all this seems to be the emotional need of some politicians (as well as many other people) for power and recognition. These politicians demonstrate a neurotic need which speaks of possible underlying insecurity in childhood, and a consequential lack of emotional validation. They have the inability to delay gratification, instead choosing the quick fix of the power surge. They take in the power of the voter and that meets the unfulfilled psychological need they have, fulfilling it by being elected. This is the result of emotional contagion, since the power and strength of the emotion overrides the need for a leader to be logical and use evidence-based information to make rational decisions. When this type of leader is so hungry for the emotion, they let that emotion take over any ability they have for logical thinking.

What they need to do is blend in the emotion with the cognitive aspects. This would result in perspective, empathy, wisdom, and balanced decisions. The parties at the extremes, whether politically left or right, are often infused with infected emotional contagion, which results in their decisions being out of balance, emotional and irrational (van Prooijen & Krouwel, 2019). The emotion infects the thought with contagious toxins. The insecure voters who used emotional voting feel a lot better if their candidate wins. They feel recognized and powerful. But these results are temporary when the winner makes their decisions based on intrinsic, internalized emotion they are attached to rather than on facts and logic. It has negative consequences for the country.

The wise voter has to see these things and not vote based on raw emotions such as fear and revenge, but instead use balanced judgment. Emotion at a time of turmoil tends to be related to greed: having one's unfulfilled needs met; instead it should be based on love: giving and not receiving. A vote is the citizen's way of giving to the country. In an age of insecurity, however, people do not feel like giving; they feel like taking.

Lazy thinking and cognitive ease

Martin Luther King, Jr., who was assassinated in 1968, said "Rarely do we find men[21] who willingly engage in hard, solid thinking. There is an almost universal quest for easy answers and half-baked solutions. Nothing pains some people more than having to think."

Lazy thinking, or incomplete thinking, where the individual doesn't put out the required mental energy to think through an issue, preferring cognitive ease, becomes a problem which contributes to emotional contagion. The term *lazy thinking* is used in the professional literature, but, because of the negative, demeaning connotation of the word *lazy*, the more objective term used in this book is *incomplete thinking*.

Kahneman, the Nobel-winning psychologist, says that the phenomenon called cognitive ease appears to be associated with good feelings (Kahneman, 2011). This helps the fluent processing of sentences, helps you to trust your intuitions, and helps you to feel that your current situation is familiar. He states that cognitive ease will bias beliefs. The ease of rhyming seems to produce a cognitive ease, good feelings, and a feeling of familiarity. Ideas in verse, he says, are more likely to be taken as the truth, presumably when compared with a phrase with cumbersome wording. There is an emotional connotation involved, and since emotions flow, it makes sense that emotional flow contributes to acceptance of ideas and thoughts. The rhyme makes the words flow like a poem. Poetry flows inside the person; that is its feature. There is what Kahneman would call cognitive ease in poetry. To flow like this requires emotion, tapping into personal energy and meaningfulness. This flow, internal to the person, is very powerful and trumps reason. This may be why poetry trumps policy in election campaigns.

Emotional contagion depends on incomplete, automatic thinking that fails to deconstruct the content of the fallacious assumptions behind the contagious emotion. This happens because of the strength of the emotion, and also because of the appeal of the simplistic concept of the point. This simplistic concept appeals to our primitive instincts—fear of extinction or genocide—which are emotional in nature. It overrides our reasoning and so sets it aside in favour of the distorted, fallacious thought; then we react to it. When the amygdala is active, it overwhelms our cerebral cortex and its ability to think because it involves an effort to do so.

---

21 Note the sexism, even from such an esteemed man. It was typical of the times. It was corrected two sentences later with use of the word "people."

This has been called "neural hijacking" or amygdala arousal by Daniel Goleman (1994). We default to cognitive ease, or incomplete thinking, which is easier because it requires less effort. It provides a channel for the impact of emotion, helped by cognitive ease since it doesn't take the mental effort necessary to scrutinize the basis of the fear and dispute its errors. This results in emotional contagion. It is much easier to accept a simple thought driven by emotion because it takes less effort. When others accept it, we feel we can do it too without fear of criticism. It becomes easier to accept it even though the consequences can be disastrous. Instead, we need an inoculation against emotional contagion.

Incomplete thinking seemed to worsen when personal computers appeared, and then worsened further with the development of surfing the web, texting, commenting on websites and forums, and social media. Social media has produced fast scanning and its associated characteristic, incomplete thinking, in people already so inclined. They may have attention problems, and an inability to think through an issue. These problems are cousins of headline news. It can become a significant problem contributing to emotional contagion, which depends on incomplete, automatic thinking.

Incomplete thinking appears to be a corollary of cognitive ease. Pennycook and Rand's research (2019) found that "analytic thinking is used to assess the plausibility of headlines" and that "susceptibility to fake news is driven more by lazy thinking." These authors say that "the dominant explanation for why people believe fake news has been that their reasoning is held captive by partisan biases—their thinking gets hijacked." (as reported by Weir, 2020). Although it was not stated that emotional contagion or emotional thinking is part of this phenomenon, because it was not part of a study reported by Weir, the possibility was left open by implication: "Where ideological bias exists, this bias is typically caused by intuitive processes rather than by reasoning." Professor Peter Ditto, as reported by Weir, found that liberals and conservatives were both likely to evaluate information more favourably when it supported their own political beliefs. He says that "Whether or not people believe fake news isn't just a cognitive process. It's socially reinforced. It's a team effort...," he says (Weir, 2020). Social reinforcement and team efforts often includes components of emotional contagion, as they are often involved in social dialogue. Recent research by Martel, Pennycook and Rand (2020), in fact, showed that "reliance on emotion increases belief in fake news."

The internal emotional flow can be facilitated, magnified, and expanded by the external emotional flow impacting on it. Think about what the emotions do coming from another person using voice, gestures, and movement. The contagious emotions impact on the part of us that wants to put out less cognitive effort to understand it. In human interactions, the most meaning seems to be imparted when there is easy, comfortable emotional flow instead of reason and rationale. The emotion is powerful. You see this clearly in crowds, and in emotional and social contagion. Elections can be lost because of the effect of cognitive ease. It is essential for us to stop automatically catching emotions! What brings good feelings through cognitive ease via incomplete thinking could easily turn out to be democracy's downfall. It is apparent that poetry can trump policy if we let it.

Linked to the association between cognitive ease, lazy thinking, and reliance on emotion is the observation by van Prooijen and Krouwel (2019) that "political extremism is fueled by feelings of distress and is reflected in the cognitive simplicity, overconfidence, and intolerance, likely of many of the members of the political extreme group." They state that "these insights are important to understanding how political polarization increases political instability and the likelihood of conflict between groups in society." How true. Now we have to apply it.

Emotions don't think. Thinking clearly and logically instead will clear up many fears people have about others who are not like them. Violence tragically happens to people of all groups, countries, races, and religions. True, it may happen in some places and to some people more than to others, but this is related to social factors such as poverty, poor housing, and family disruption, not to mention unpredictable social and political forces in many countries. These are part of the social and cultural forces that contribute to severe psychological maladjustment in people. Society has to bear responsibility for the lack of integration of diverse individuals into mainstream society.

We see in this chapter the crucial role that emotions play in politics. Emotions are not a "soft" factor in inducing political affiliations and votes, instead it seems to be the most crucial factor.

Cynicism, Hate, and Related Issues

Suspicion is contagious, even appealing, in a time when corruption is plentiful and our lives are constantly monitored. Many are disillusioned, apathetic, and cynical, and these emotions lead to suspicion that builds like a slow burn until it explodes: in society, in killings, riots, and protests, or in individuals, in serious health problems. Cynicism is associated with depression, heart attacks, cancer, dementia, and even lower incomes. We can overcome cynicism with balance, flexibility, and relativity. The collective subconscious and psychological underground are powerful. Emotional infections occur—hate has been able to infect minds to the point that it has killed hundreds of millions in many wars. Hate comes from accrued, contagious negative emotions; instead we need contagious positive emotions like gratitude and compassion.

Interpersonal trust is down, especially in those who are prone to emotional thinking. Most people in the U.S., regardless of thinking style, distrust the federal government. The Pew Research Center (2021) finds that public trust in governments is near historic lows, now around 24 percent. The same is true in Canada, to a lesser degree, where only 36 percent of the population say that politicians can be trusted (Angus Reid Institute, 2019). Many people do not know who or what to believe about government, politicians, and policies, so they believe no one. Many feel that politicians lie and as a result have become turned off by politicians, to the detriment of democracy. Some voters suspect that all politicians lie, so they reject them and vote for people who are politically inexperienced. The same trend is apparent in many Western countries. A few decades ago, people felt that politicians were all the same, regardless of party, but no longer. Now they have become so far apart that there is turmoil and divisiveness in society, and the emotional and logistical side effects of the coronavirus appear to have escalated this difference.

When operating in System 2, a person may say that they are not suspicious. However, when in System 1 (where quick, impulsive thoughts are expressed), it seems many people these days can quickly become suspicious. The Pew Research Center says that interpersonal trust has declined significantly in the U.S., to the point that there is a widespread perception that people are not as reliable as they once were (Pew Research Center 2021). This is the result of cynicism and divisiveness. They say that "many ascribe shrinking trust to a political culture they believe is broken and spawns suspicion, even cynicism, about the ability of others to distinguish fact from fiction."

Some people may develop suspiciousness independently. They may also be affected and their suspicion reinforced through emotional contagion in ways they are unaware of. Those who tend to blame others for their problems are especially prone to catch contagious suspicion and distrust from others, setting the stage for more contagious conspiracy theories at a time of turmoil. When someone says they are suspicious of something, and the listener has tendencies to think emotionally and suspect the same, then hearing the first person's thoughts is likely to reinforce and strengthen the suspicions in the listener. Consequently, the listener may move from having a potential thought to having a firm belief by catching and absorbing the emotional tone from the speaker through emotional contagion.

Emotional contagion has played a large role in all of this. It seems to have become appealing to catch feelings of suspicion from others and find that they are escalating within oneself. Sometimes this has been automatic contagion, where fast, automatic thoughts occur before they have had a chance to be subjected to one's critical thinking and systematic reasoning. Stories of corruption automatically activate and strengthen underlying feelings of suspicion that many already have towards government. Emotional reasoning and quick thinking, related to the type of thinking characteristic of horse-race politics and headline news, override critical thinking and systematic reasoning to produce more suspicion and cynicism.

Scandals and corruption give us reason to be suspicious and cynical, and think things are happening around us that we don't know about. Corruption is plentiful. For example, when the Cambridge Analytica story broke, we learned that 50 million Facebook profiles were harvested for the British consulting firm in a major data breach (Westby, 2019). People couldn't really process it emotionally because of its great scope. They seemed numbed. That is a huge number. 50,000,000. The Netflix movie *The Great Hack* tells the story, and "[opens] our eyes to the way our lives are constantly monitored—and controlled—through digital technology" (Westby, 2019). Some people feel society is helpless in dealing with this.

Since we can't change the issues like corruption and scandal quickly, we have to use effective, constructive thinking to handle their effect on us. For example, when we see advertising on television, we filter it using constructive thinking. We don't buy everything we see advertised. In the Facebook situation, we know that people have had our data before; although it isn't great, and we don't like it, it doesn't mean that someone is coming to scam us. If we handle these situations like we deal with advertising, we judge that it couldn't be that bad. Sadly, some people are being taken advantage of by the theft of their personal data. We may not feel adequately protected by government, so we become more cynical and disillusioned.

Another example is cheating in baseball. The Houston Astros, a Major League Baseball team, were found guilty of stealing signs in a very elaborate plot. Their manager and general manager were involved in covering this up. They were both suspended and then fired; the team was fined $5 million (Vigdor, 2020). The manager of the Boston Red Sox was also fired after being implicated in the Astros' scandal (although he was rehired a year later). Baseball fans felt cheated, used, taken for granted, ignored, and tricked. It was as if fans didn't count. Some people felt even more strongly: that all teams cheat, so there's nothing new in this. This is all-or-nothing thinking typical of cynicism and emotion mind. Do you think that all teams cheat in baseball or other sports? If so, you are probably a victim of contagious cynicism.

The baseball situation was uncertain as the public couldn't really know the truth. Uncertainty brings an opening for suspicion to enter the fray. That is okay; it should enter the fray. But it is still uncertain because suspicion needs evidence. Some people default to thinking that all sports teams cheat, without looking for logic or evidence. That is lazy thinking. That is cynicism. That is all-or-nothing. Are you afraid of being called naïve if you don't agree that all teams cheat? Are you concerned with being smart and wise? Naïve and cynical are two opposite ends of the spectrum; smart and wise are in the middle. That's the place to be.

Rampant cynicism means that many people assume the world is falling apart. How often have you heard "What is the world coming to?" Our emotions cause us to believe the worst is happening. World events may seem, at a quick glance, to strengthen this belief, but the worst is defined as "the most unpleasant, difficult, or severe."(*The Cambridge Dictionary*, 2010). When something is called the worst, it usually isn't. This is a cognitive distortion that comes from quick thinking. When we talk about "the world" falling apart, we recognize that there is a climate crisis, but the planet isn't crumbling. We must also recognize that we can change our behaviour to mitigate the climate crisis. The exaggerated expressions about the world falling apart or going crazy allow us an outlet for our feelings. But the unfortunate fact is that they spread in a contagious way when we don't stop and think it through. Emotional contagion has made this outlook seem much more severe than it really is and has produced cognitive distortions, including overgeneralization and catastrophizing (Casabianca, 2021). Cognitive distortions are inaccurate thoughts that "are simply ways that our mind convinces us of something that isn't really true" (PsychCentral, n.d.). It is actually not as bad as it seems. When we line all the bad things up in a row, we forget the many positive things that happen.

These situations of cheating and climate change are depersonalizing, demoralizing, and objectifying. Some people feel like objects because that's how they are treated. Some of us feel like data, as if we don't count as human beings. We feel like we are here to be taken advantage of, only required for our money. Our feelings and needs are often ignored. We need to correct these distorted thoughts. But they are often true. Those emotions seem to spread through society and add to our suppressed anger, depression, and cynicism. We are hurt. Now we are in a cynicism pandemic. It has spread to many people through emotional contagion, and all these situations only add to it, letting it build cumulatively and increase our demoralization, and brings down the country's mood. Maybe that is what the public is trying to say when they ask, "What is the world coming to?"

In a time of turmoil, people catch cynical attitudes very easily. Cynicism feeds the turmoil as too many people become more and more demoralized, and less and less optimistic. Cynicism is defined as "an inclination to believe that people are motivated purely by self-interest"; or "an inclination to question whether something will happen or whether it is worthwhile"(Oxford, n.d.).

How bad are the effects of cynicism? We think things are worse than they are. We think things are rampant when they aren't. We don't have to absorb these depersonalized feelings that make us feel like we don't count. We don't have to give power to the instigator by taking on a feeling that they are sending through their tendencies towards sociopathy, where we are treated as data or sources of money.

Kindling: the slippery slope downward into a crisis

One mechanism that increases emotional contagion is the spread of emotions caused by kindling. Kindling is a term used to describe how some people slip down into the psychological rabbit hole of a mental health crisis in shorter periods of time and with less extreme triggers, as their emotions become inflamed like a fire. This happens with slow burning. A slow burn and kindling can easily turn into a major fire that spreads. Society seems to have been figuratively slipping slowly into a deep rabbit hole over the past few years. Negative emotions related to feeling ignored, hurt, resentful, fearful, and angry occur and build; misperceptions and cognitive distortions also occur more often, as situations may be read incorrectly, adding to cynicism and demoralization. It builds up—a slow burn. It simmers, and slowly becomes stronger and more intense until it explodes like it did in 2020–21.

For example, there could be a perception that other people are not contributing to society and yet are favoured by politicians, a perception that probably comes while you are in pain and feel tired and disrespected. This could be a distortion, (perhaps a vast overgeneralization referring to a select group of a few people), or it could be mostly true (referring to more than a few people but not everyone). It is likely an extension of cynicism. Many people may perceive that it is true that they are being ignored, regardless of a lack of evidence. Some will accept it as truth due to confirmation bias, and others may agree with it on an emotional basis, although in both cases the perception may be false. The irritation from feeling ignored and the associated emotions of feeling hurt, fearful, or angry can produce the slow burn of resentment and can be inflamed through kindling. Long-term amygdala kindling has been shown to increase general behavioral hyperactivity and fearful behaviour (Fournier et al., 2020). Previous episodes may have raised expectations of negative events and made it easier for consequential negative emotions to occur. Hence it might only take a weak emotion to trigger another associated emotion in a shorter period of time. This happens as one emotion, having no boundaries, moves into the space of an adjoining emotion and adds something to it. It mixes in, making it stronger and helping it to flare up quickly. It may initiate some mechanism which enables contagion to move in a quicker, stronger manner. After all, emotions move and blend a little like fluids do, and have no boundaries other than the receiving person's gatekeeper.

Through kindling, it is easier for an emotion to be attracted by another nearby emotion similar to it. If a cynical emotion is lingering within us, close to the surface, related to a previous incident, or as an ongoing predisposition of someone, it doesn't take much to produce a strengthening or an uprising of the lingering cynicism. It was ready to erupt, spilling over and becoming active again. This is the collective subconscious in action, just like a volcano ready to blow. It could be activated when someone cheats or tricks us, or when a skeptical person tells a cynical story, and so we need a gatekeeper to protect ourselves from it. That is where rational thinking comes in, to correct the false alarm of emotion. Your emotional part will thank you for correcting its errors.

It doesn't take as much to produce a feeling related to one you've had before, even if it was months or years ago. Feelings flow easily and affect neighbouring feelings, since they do not have real boundaries. You might have subconscious memories, so there is already a starting point for the depressed, angry, or cynical feelings to kick in. This time, you feel them sooner and more easily. Feelings are attracted to lingering emotional residue. A similar dynamic occurs in situations in the public mind, as there are conscious and subconscious memories among members of society. With an emotional predisposition the next time they are aroused, there is not as far to go to wake those feelings up and carry them further than last time. We need to be careful about letting this happen, by using constructive self-talk so that we don't go downward quickly. We learn to tolerate a lower standard. Although we are still traumatized, if we see something troubling in the news, we are less shocked by its occurrence because we have seen it before, so it adds to the previous residue of cynicism by building up the cynical process. This is what has set society on the slippery slope over the past few years or even decades.

Cynicism and depression

Feelings of hopelessness, helplessness, and lack of control are plentiful in society these days. No wonder people get depressed. And then Big Pharma gets rich off the medication costs for antidepressants. Market research says that the "increase in awareness regarding the disease state [i.e., depression] and rise in number of patients suffering from stress are expected to create lucrative opportunities for the market players in the future" (Allied Market Research, 2018). That was written before the pandemic, but emotional distress, depression, and anxiety have greatly increased since the pandemic began (Berman, 2020). Psychoanalysts used to say that depression came from repressed hostility. There must be a lot of that now, since anger is close to the surface and a lot of people feel helpless and cynical, so it makes sense that depression rates have gone through the roof. Anxiety and depression were already costing the Canadian economy $50 billion a year before the pandemic (Carmichael, 2021), and at least $210 billion a year in the U.S. (Analysis Group, 2015). Although medical doctors will tell you depression is a disease or illness, coming from an ostensible biochemical imbalance, it also comes from absorbing dark contagious emotions in a society in emotional turmoil.

It is not one thing that causes depression. It is biopsychosocial, a combination of biochemical, psychological, and social factors. The biochemical imbalance theory of depression is yet to be proved scientifically. Those dark contagious emotions of pessimism, cynicism, and hopelessness, sometimes related to lack of control over corruption and dishonesty in society, will lower our mood, especially in those without an inoculation to the contagion. Learned helplessness is a phenomenon in which individuals learn that they lack behavioural control over environmental events. This, in turn, undermines their motivation to make attempts to alter situations. Repeated exposure to uncontrollable stressors is thought to result in individuals failing to use any control options that may later become available, due to learned helplessness and cynicism. It makes more sense to combat the factors that lower our mood than just to treat the mood with medication. Both are sometimes necessary, but one without the other is often an incomplete treatment, especially with the dark emotions in society that are absorbed by many people.

A person with a cynical mindset may find that it spirals out of control and leads to depression. A study by Nabi, Singh-Manoux, Ferrie, and associates (2009) found that cynical hostility is a strong and robust predictor of depressive mood. Individuals who expressed a cynical personality were at a five times higher risk of developing depression than those who did not express such a personality trait. They suggest that people recognize their cynicism so they can take steps to recover. It is important to monitor your thoughts and consider them only as hunches or possibilities, rather than definite fact. This allows you to consider alternative thoughts. Since we have 60,000 thoughts a day, it is not possible for all of our thoughts to be correct. Try appreciating different perspectives; make an attempt to recognize when situations make you cynical and see if that is the only way to think about it. Compare the cynical approach to the reality of the objective. Sometimes things came to an ending after a whole sequence of unfortunate events that make that ending inevitable. That doesn't make it a trend.

This negativity bias can have a powerful effect on your life (Cherry, 2020). A study by Ito, Larsen, Smith, et al. (1998) found that negative images produced a much stronger response in the cerebral cortex than did positive or neutral images. They recommend cognitive methods to overcome this, such as stopping negative self-talk, reframing events in a positive light, paying more attention to positive events and remembering them frequently, and being aware of your own tendencies to be negative and instead raising positive interpretation of events to the forefront of your awareness. Learned optimism and learned hopefulness are other methods to overcome hopelessness and helplessness and provide that inoculation (Seligman, 2006; Tomasulo, 2020). These methods, as well as traditional cognitive behavioural therapy, help challenge those cognitive distortions of personalization, pervasiveness, and permanence, which lead to false beliefs that widespread negativity is a permanent part of life (Moore, 2020), as well as providing methods to increase feelings of motivation, resiliency and wellness. These methods would all apply to the cynicism and negativity that flows through society in a time of turmoil.

There is no medication for cynicism, just for depression, which can be a symptom and effect of prolonged cynicism. Unless cynicism is abated, depression will continue. Antidepressants are a false cure when used alone since they only cure the symptom. Adding these psychological and social therapies together is often a part that is missing and needs to be included to treat depression.

It can be a vicious cycle. People with depression often need to have their medication dosage increased as the symptoms of depression return, complicated by rampant cynicism. We have been damaged by cynicism for decades as it spreads unchecked and becomes stronger. It is time for those in charge to do their work in preventing this abuse of the public. But it is not either-or. We the public also have to do our part by working on overcoming cynicism rather than accepting it.

Many people feed off each other to the point that they even defend their cynicism. It is rewarding for some people who tend to feel that their deeper cynical beliefs and feelings are validated when someone else is also cynical, thereby reinforcing it and strengthening it. Reinforcement of the cynicism by others' cynicism would encourage contagion, overcome doubt, and strengthen the cynicism feeling. We need to drop these social influences and stop jumping to conclusions. We can jump to conclusions because of the way emotions affect us. A cognitive distortion called mental filter says that we get depressed when we see everything around us in a negative light, as if we are looking through a dark filter of cynicism. So, many will assume people cheat or steal when they don't, or are unfaithful or corrupt when they aren't.

Confirmation bias and negativity bias

People who are cynical choose to link negative events together, overlooking positive events, confirming their cynicism, in a case of confirmation bias associated with negativity bias. These people get together and commiserate about the corruption in society they've decided is already there. It is there but focusing on it exclusively without balancing it with positive events will strengthen a cynical outlook. This is likely brought upon by emotional contagion, where people reinforce each other's distrust and strengthen the negative emotion.

This is likely related to a growth of pessimism and depression, in conjunction with a reluctance to be trusting and naïve, lest one be taken advantage of (which would be their expectation). This would suggest an excessive sense of toughness possibly related to a strong attempt at showing resistance and resisting gullibility. This is associated with suppressed anger, perhaps from having been hurt earlier in life when one was trusting. It is important to deal with that hurt feeling by working at overcoming it and not letting it control you to the point of becoming cynical.

Cynicism occurs because people feel hurt, betrayed, and helpless in the face of unfair practices. They prepare themselves for it to happen again by adapting cynicism as a form of defence so that they do not get hurt again. It involves preparing a tough mental defense of negativity bias to protect one from hurt upon the discovery of unfair practices. There seems to be a sense of a subconscious commiseration about this, like a collective subconscious. Thoughts about unfair practices being abundant these days are probably exaggerated in comparison to reality, but nevertheless flow through the psychological underground of society via social contagion and on social media. They are not necessarily being talked about openly among people and are not usually reported in the regular media but are seemingly familiar to various others. As a result, cynicism flows strongly.

Consider relativity and perspective to broaden thinking and overcome cynicism

A person may believe that they are vulnerable to being hurt if they are naïve or overly trusting, so they use cynicism as a defensive mechanism. They may feel tough that way, but it is a false toughness. It is better to acknowledge the negativity in the issue at hand and accept that it came to be that way through many factors beyond yourself. For your part, take responsibility, but don't condemn or blame yourself. It is not necessarily dysfunctional to take a negative view of things, but we should be reasonably accurate and consider things in their relativity to other topics. There are other ways of interpreting what happens in society rather than looking for something that confirms an implicit or explicit bias. Sometimes, as they say, s--t happens—to all of us. But often it doesn't. It is difficult to consider things with relativity and flexibility if people hold on to a fixed way of seeing things.

To overcome cynicism, we need to consider the relativity of things. Simply put, it is a matter not of accepting the permanence or extensiveness of a negative situation, or its pervasiveness, but to acknowledge that it exists under certain conditions. For example, we may think things "never work out," but it is more accurate to say that sometimes things don't work out, and sometimes they do. This also allows us to make changes by moving pieces around, changing conditions and situations to make them more palatable. This takes time, so we need to think long-term and see progress as it occurs.

A good place to use reason, knowledge, and perspective as inoculation against cynicism would be to combat the emotionally contagious distrust of experts' knowledge and the power we perceive them to have. Too many people are skeptical of medical and scientific experts in the pandemic atmosphere. There seems to be a fear of authority, usually reflected in a person's lack of social power, defined by their perceived lower place in society's pecking order. It may stem from a perception of undue power exercised in legal matters, without flexibility or empathy, by someone that is like a father figure (a police officer, a judge, a lawyer, a correctional officer). Authoritarian figures are likely to have compartmentalized thinking and spread rigid, dogmatic social power, likely feeling positive feelings from their exercise of control over others in the legal arena (Dean & Altemeyer, 2020). In reality, only some people in these fields have these characteristics to an extreme, while others might have them more moderately.

Generalized suspicion and distrust of those in authority appears to occur from emotional contagion. Without cognitive skills to discern between various sources of domination, some people will default to perceiving all types of perceived domination, including experts, with suspicion and cynicism regarding authority. Some may have felt emotional contagion from one source earlier in life (problematic father figure) and transferred it to another (experts with cold personalities). So they reject medical or scientific advice because of the strong effects of the angry emotion they are feeling. This reaction should not be automatic, as an automatic response is likely to be fueled by the emotion impinging in a disruptive way on the thought processes. Instead, people need a cognitive filter, their gatekeeper, to discern if all experts are really cut from the same cloth—for example, if they are all cold and uncaring, which they are not.

It may also be a good idea to take a closer look at your group of friends. It is often recommended that we avoid being around negative people, but this same advice should be applied to being around people who are cynical. If your friends tend to be negative, thinking that the world expects something from them all the time, and constantly complaining that they are shortchanged, then you might want to reconsider whether they are good for you. If you absorb the negative emotion attached to their beliefs, your cynicism is probably increased by their contagious emotion. Solid relationships and good social structure are more likely to be meaningful and have a greater emotional support with actual trusting relationships. Trusting may be a risk, but an important one.

Cynicism is toxic and is bad for your health

Cynicism can be toxic. It is associated with poor health, poor habits, chronic depression, and has even been found to be associated with heart attacks. The BBC reported in 2007 (BBC, 2007) that a study from the Archives of Internal Medicine of 6,814 people "found that cynical distrust was associated with signs of inflammation which in turn increase the risk of heart disease." The study suggested that cynical people may be more likely to lead unhealthy lifestyles, like smoking or suffering from obesity, which creates more risk factors for heart disease. The cynicism may also be fixed as its proponents likely do not tolerate ambiguity very well, which is necessary when dealing with stress. A study by Lepore found an effect of social support on cardiovascular activity. Low cynicism people with social support had significantly smaller increases in blood pressure during a stressful task than high cynicism people with social support during the same task. Less cynical people are likely to have lower blood pressure and respond more positively to social support (Lepore, 1995).

A study by Tindle, Chang, Kuller, and associates (2009) found that cynicism was associated with an increased risk of total mortality and cancer-related mortality, with these effects a little stronger for Black people, although also present for white people. As well, people with high levels of cynical distrust may be more likely to develop dementia, according to a study by Neuvonen, Rusanaen, Solomon, and associates (2014). Cynical distrust, which is defined as the belief that others are mainly motivated by selfish concerns, has been associated with other health problems, such as heart disease, but this study was the first to look at the relationship between cynicism and dementia.

Psychologists Stavrova and Ehlebracht (2016) found that "people who reported cynical views of human nature had smaller incomes (by thousands of dollars) [...], compared with their more optimistic peers. Cynical people are suspicious, and suspicion prevents cooperation, which is more effective than competition. It turns out that suspicious people make less money.

Is cynicism our default position on life?

Cynicism seems to continue, unabated. It's got to the point where, as actor Tom Hanks recently said when being interviewed for his role in the Mr. Rogers movie *A Beautiful Day in The Neighborhood*, "cynicism has become the default position for so much of daily structure and daily intercourse"(McIntosh, 2019). He says that "we have become so inured to that, that when we are met with as simple a message as 'Hey you know what, it's a beautiful day in the neighbourhood!' we get slapped a little bit. We are allowed, I think, to feel good. There's a place for cynicism, but why begin with it right off the bat?" No one has actually stated publicly that maybe this contagious attitude of cynicism is killing us. If we put together the results from the research named above predisposing some people to an early death, as well as Tom Hanks' comment, this conclusion could be viable. Did Mr. Rogers have the recipe for life and good health? Probably. Is the opposite of cynicism—concepts like trust, innocence, naïveté, cheerfulness, romance, positivity, sentimentality —the recipe for life and good health? Probably. Do we think of them as too childish to accept? Let's hope not. Cynicism may seem more mature or wise but, in fact, it isn't. But it is contagious.

We shouldn't let cynicism rule us. Being affected by too many occasions of mistrust and hurt feelings can stay with a person, and without psychological intervention it develops the all-or-nothing rigid thinking typical of embedded cynicism. In this way cynicism tends to be permanent and may define an important part of the personality of the individual. The individual may always be looking for the negative side of any topic and exaggerating it. Some people just tend to look for the negative view automatically. There is always something negative, and you can find it if you look. That is tunnel vision, ignoring all the beauty around and just seeing the dirt. We need to guard against cynicism becoming permanent or ingrained into our personality. That can be a difficult undertaking for some, particularly if it means accepting something that the person feels is hurtful. The person will tend to protect themselves by being cynical to avoid being hurt or feeling betrayed. The question is will they actually be hurt? Or can they prevent themselves from being hurt by taking a wider view of things and appreciating other aspects of life and living, like the positive things all around? Positive self-talk and feeling gratitude for the good things can balance this out.

Some people are cynical about governments and people in authority. They may feel those in charge do not show empathy or compassion towards those who are not as well off, and so they may believe that they cannot trust any positive statements from the government about helping them. They think if they do, they will only end up let down. Think of a government's positive statements only as possibilities. Hope for it, don't expect it. But don't expect it not to happen, either. Just anticipate possibilities. That is not cynicism. Perhaps the government would be more open about an upcoming decision than a cynic would allow them to be. It is better to recognize that governments may vary in their degree of yielding positive or negative attitudes towards people, as opposed to perceiving that governments are always untrustworthy in every situation. Anticipate, rather than expect, that a government will take a negative position because that will allow you to have some flexibility in your appraisal of the government's potential actions. That perspective allows for a slight possibility that the government could take a positive approach. This is a movement forward for the hardened cynic.

Thwarting and reversing cynicism

Thwarting and reversing cynicism is an important goal to achieve in order to lessen the political and emotional turmoil which affects society. It is important to find a middle-of-the-road approach between being cynical and being gullible. Extreme, black-or-white approaches attract emotional contagion, as the emotions associated with extreme positions are met either with contagion or counter-contagion. Emotions easily inflame each other. Moderate approaches tend to be more cognitive in orientation, since they take more thought, and therefore are more resistant to emotional contagion. Building resilience to cynicism may pull people in opposite directions, as if people stick to cynicism because they feel it will give them protection. They are afraid that if they give it up, they will instead become innocent and gullible, thereby being vulnerable to being tricked, cheated, or defrauded. This is indeed possible, so it seems that an important way to resist cynicism and develop resilience is to accept that it is also important to resist being innocent and gullible. Being innocent seems akin to wearing rose-coloured glasses: always seeing the positive even where it doesn't exist. That seems to be a dilemma facing many of us. We need a middle-of-the-road approach, like being smart and wise.

We need to focus on the attributes necessary to overcome cynicism, like being aware, smart, and discerning, as well as being astute, selective, and able to differentiate between options. We can be cheerful, positive, and sentimental while still being aware smart, and discerning. We can also deal effectively with the unfairness and self-centredness that people perceive to be occurring in society. Feeling empowered and working on overcoming the issues, rather than feeling helpless and unempowered, will add to resilience. Being tough is only relevant if you are tough-minded, not giving in on your opinions and sticking to your guns in spite of any emotion, as long as the evidence supports it. Reality involves recognizing the positive, the negative and the neutral. Act with persistence, in coming up with solutions, achieving different perspectives, using wise thinking, and avoiding catastrophic thinking.

One way to handle cynicism is accepting reality in spite of its negativity. This involves radical acceptance, meaning that we have to accept something that we do not like, or do not approve of, because it is real and actual and came to exist for many reasons. We could just wish things away. But if we do, we live in fantasy, and this leads to problems. "Radical acceptance is about accepting life on life's terms and not resisting what you cannot or choose not to change. [It] is about saying yes to life, just as it is." (Hall, 2012) It doesn't mean you endorse whatever you don't like. Of course you don't, and you shouldn't. It means you are accepting what is real. Marsha Linehan (n.d.), who developed the concept, says that "radical acceptance rests on letting go of the illusion of control and a willingness to notice and accept things as they are right now, without judging." Accepting reality is a way of overcoming cynicism. Things are not as bad as you think. This doesn't mean we approve of whatever we don't like, or that we have to like it. We can still work at changing it or adapting to it, and yet enjoy the rest of life.

We need a boundary between emotions and emotional states, so that the kindling of emotions is held behind a "fireproof" wall. It is part of the gatekeeper's job to build this wall in your mind. Having ready-made thoughts and awareness to prevent this kindling would include thoughts which would differentiate one situation from the other. We need to feel some power in our judgment of different people to be sure that we can believe a thought like, "Just because person A tricked us it doesn't mean person B would do it too."

This process is not straightforward, as much of it is unconscious. Studies indicate that "certain non-verbal gestures trigger emotional reactions we're not consciously aware of, and these reactions are enormously important for understanding how interpersonal relationships develop" (DeSteno et al., 2012). But this doesn't mean we are at a loss for reading non-verbal cues. Segal, Smith, et al. (2020) provide an online help guide on how to read non-verbal cues, such as consistency between verbal and non-verbal behaviour, tension or lack of tension in eye contact, body posture, and tone of voice. The website Inc.com identifies fifteen cues and traits of trustworthiness, including consistency, compassion, humility, a lack of bullying, transparency, an ability to confide, an ability to compromise, and avoidance of gossip (Thibodeaux, n.d.). Having good, comfortable, eye contact, a comfortable, flexible rhythm to one's voice, and a commitment to these qualities are all important.

Being positive and cheerful are likely to entice individuals to see the positive aspects going on in society instead of looking at a list of trends that selectively choose only the negative. Being suspicious while aware and flexible, is important. We need to let both the positive and negative exist, as they are part of life. This is not an either-or attitude, common to cynical people looking only at the negative and naïve positive people looking only at the positive, both because of confirmation bias. In reality, both negative and positive exist together. We accept and build on the positives and work on overcoming the negatives. We need to experience the positives and allow them to affect us emotionally through positive emotional contagion, without taking an undue rosy attitude to life. A realistic attitude is important, involving positive, negative, and neutral perceptions.

Many of us can be hungry for the drama in society

Perceptions can be challenged by events and facts. Recent events of police brutality against Black people in the U.S. and Indigenous people in Canada suggest that the perception of safety in our environment does not feel real. It is not real. There are enough events in both countries to confirm the idea that the safety of Black and Indigenous people has been compromised in both countries. Some police officers may actually hide behind the perception of safety while in fact using it as a shield for brutality and racial bias. They may have authoritarian issues in their personality. The authoritarian personality believes in complete power, "a type of person who prefers a social system with a strong ruler—the authoritarian person is comfortable being the strong ruler but if the individual is not the strong ruler then he or she will demonstrate complete obedience to another strong authority figure [...] [with] complete obedience to rules and regulations." They often harbour "antagonistic feelings towards minority groups, whether religious, ethnic, or otherwise" (Iresearchnet, n.d.). These are emotional types of decisions, involving implicit emotion, producing drama in action. Domineering, overpowering individuals cause a rise in compassion towards the underdog, often members of a minority group.

We can be attracted to such drama like nails to a magnet. Many of us seem to need its emotional fix, perhaps to replace the intimate, personal emotional connection that is missing or weak in our lives. Emotional contagion of negative emotions can cause a person to absorb another's negative emotions too much, too quickly, too deeply, particularly in real life, and can leave them too emotionally connected to the wrong person, organization, cause, or business.

Some people believe that they need fear to keep from feeling vulnerable, that being afraid protects them. This doesn't make sense to the logical mind, but this irrational thinking that fear protects them is the effect of emotional contagion. They think fear is important; they have absorbed the fear to the point that having it is important to them. Instead, if we think more rationally about ongoing social and political situations, we will be safer. Look at the facts. In the months after 9/11, the *Guardian* says that "passenger miles on the main American airlines fell by between 12 and 20 percent, while road use jumped. The change is widely believed to have been caused by concerned passengers opting to drive rather than fly" (Ball, 2011) because of fear of further hijacking, according to Professor Gird Gigerenzer, a German academic specializing in risk. Flying suddenly seemed quite dangerous and this emotion became contagious and infected many people, especially around New York. It is true that planes were grounded for a short while on government's orders, but it is likely that fear overtook the population's rational thinking when these orders lifted, and they refused to fly. This is a natural human occurrence and again points to the power of fear in society and its role in emotional contagion.

Psychologist David Myers (n.d.) pointed out that "from 1990 through 2000 there were 1.4 deaths per ten million passengers on American scheduled airlines. Flying understandably feels dangerous. But we have actually been less likely to crash and die on any flight than, when coin tossing, to flip twenty-two heads in a row." The *Guardian* article went on to say that "travelling long distances by car is more dangerous than travelling the same distance by plane" (Ball, 2011). Gigerenzer "has estimated that an extra 1,595 Americans died in car accidents in the year after the [9/11] attacks—indirect victims of the tragedy." He attributed these deaths to "people's poor understanding of danger." In the words of Gigerenzer and his colleague Gaissmaier (Gaissmaier and Gigerenzer, 2012) "Terrorists can strike twice—first, by directly killing people, and second, through dangerous behaviors induced by fear in people's minds." This "poor understanding" seems to be partly associated with an overriding of knowledge and logic by emotional factors related to the power of fear and illustrates a likely role in inducing emotional infection. It seems that such understanding may exist but was surpassed by the effects of fear. Emotion trumped reason. It should remind us that the safest time to undertake an activity is the time immediately after an incident because everyone is watching for related risks and dangers, safeguarding against it. In this case, emotional contagion, catching contagious emotions of fear from others, infecting one's mind, seemed to have infected many people and sadly contributed to their death.

The collective subconscious runs through the psychological underground

There is a type of collective subconscious running through the psychological underground of society and it often emerges, especially during times of riots and protests. The psychological underground is a little-known concept closely related to the collective subconscious. It often includes suppressed emotions when similar thoughts are suppressed consciously in individuals even as they circulate in society. However, they overlap according to individuals' characteristics and whether they use repression (which make the issues unconscious), or suppression (which make the issues subconscious). They are accessible to consciousness when necessary. It relates to largely unspoken feelings, issues, and trends among people in society and is usually only shared on those occasions where an event may trigger it, like in private informal gatherings of trusted people with common interests, perspectives, and personalities. One example is the masses of people who gather to protest. People will acknowledge that previously they had their own private thoughts about the issue. Police brutality and the authoritarian personality are good examples of topics that have lingered in the underground for decades. The book *The Authoritarian Personality* describing this was written by psychologists in 1950 (T.W. Adorno and Else Frenkel-Brunswik). Now, some seventy years later, concerns regarding authoritarianism in society have risen again, having long been ignored by journalists, politicians, governments, and many political scientists.

The number of people present is often underestimated when large crowds gather, triggered by an incident such as George Floyd's death at the hands of a police officer. The huge degree of protest involved the vast release of emotion, as seen in the summer of 2020. Most governments are poor at recognizing this, unfamiliar and inept at addressing it, preferring instead to suppress it. As a result, the psychological underground with its collective subconscious is usually kept bubbling below the surface, ready to erupt into consciousness when triggered by a public incident. Such public incidents usually involve death, destruction, and tragedy, the type which arouse the emotion of the people.

If, somehow, a designated person in society were trained to be a "listener," to listen to people to see what they were feeling and thinking, to click into the collective subconscious and then work to address grievances, then perhaps we wouldn't have the issues we do. We have "horse whisperers" and "pet whisperers" who can somehow communicate with and understand animals, but that there seems to be only a few "people whisperers": those who can communicate with and understand people, especially those who feel neglected and are possibly simmering with hidden anger.

Part of the problem is that governments rely largely on police, security, and enforcement to keep the lid on issues in society. These enforcers are focused on the criminal element, by training and necessity. Because of this, they miss much of what goes on in the psychological underworld of mainstream society. They are just looking at behaviour, which is superficial. As a result, they are usually unprepared for events like mass shootings that are largely related to untreated mental illness in paranoid white men with little or no criminal record and associated toxic masculinity (another area that is ignored), who likely have poor coping skills. The enforcers are unprepared for protests and resulting riots, and erroneously default to the opinion that they are criminally motivated, probably due to confirmation bias and tunnel vision in some police and security personnel.

We were affected by this lack of preparation and anticipation from the government in the spring of 2020. The authorities have typically regarded the social upheaval as criminal in composition, needing police, courts, correction, and even military intervention, rather than regarding it as the sociological and psychological breakdown that it really is, made up of feelings of demoralization, alienation and marginalization. It is likely that the collective subconscious involves a feeling of apathy which, while not an emotion, is a state of being that is a disguise for feelings of helplessness and alienation. Apathy is a cousin of suspicion, pessimism, and cynicism; it may appear earlier in the developmental chain than the others. It can also be subject to emotional contagion as apathy can mimic depression and helplessness; it can spread through a crowd as easily as these other emotions do, often not identified as an emotion but more apparent in behaviour (or lack thereof), often manifesting in depression. Such apathy may manifest in the form of addiction and avoidance, as individuals in their twenties and even into their thirties find themselves underemployed and directionless, leaving it difficult to find the motivation to seek employment and purpose in our competitive, status-seeking society.

When suppressed feelings are released

A larger degree of emotional contagion occurs when like-minded people start to realize out loud that they have similar thoughts, feelings, needs, and perspectives that are being ignored. Because of the lack of direct connection between the masses and those in power, it is a chronic problem. The suppressed emotions from the collective subconscious erupt regularly and will continue to do so unless the issues are addressed. Without action, the time is ripe for complete and thorough emotional contagion to completely overtake reason and produce semi-organized riots, like in 2020 and early 2021 in the U.S. The emotions may spread like wildfire throughout Western society, and we know that emotions don't think; they often produce turmoil.

The BLM protests in 2020 were indicative of emotional contagion at its strongest: resentment towards police and centuries of Black suppression was released and chaos occurred. When suppressed feelings are released, the emotions emerge quickly, strongly, and actively. They become contagious as the collective subconscious becomes conscious. The psychological underground comes above ground.

Emotional contagion allowed people to catch and absorb the emotions that were released by each other. This strengthened the awareness of how important this issue was on an emotional level, so they came together in crowds to commiserate; they experienced a form of mass empathy and activism as they protested. Their activism and protests reflected activated emotion.

Underlying this seemed to be a fear of annihilation or racial genocide. Embedded in the phrase "Black Lives Matter" is the fear that they don't matter, that genocide may be the only ending. When Black people are killed by the police, they think, naturally, that Black lives don't matter, since people with authority kill them for no apparent reason. It is an excuse. Black lives matter; of course they matter. The colour of a person's skin has nothing to do with their worth. Nor should their gender, or whether they are gender-neutral, non-binary, or trans. Nor should their age, their nationality, their citizenship, their abilities, their intelligence, their birthplace, their wealth or lack thereof, their religious beliefs, their sexuality, their place of residence, their size, their health, their ability or disability. We all need to work to reach our potential and to help each other do the same. We live in an ecosystem. We are all on this planet together.

Suppressed emotions relate to a power imbalance that has spread too far out of proportion. So many people are homeless while the very rich now includes almost 3,000 billionaires in the world. Simply put, being homeless makes people feel they are one step away from annihilation or extinction, and that their lives don't matter. With automation eliminating many of the less-skilled jobs in society, many of the unfortunate are jobless and homeless, and this contributes in a major way to the demoralization that has been contagious among many of society's disadvantaged people.

Much of the homeless population in the U.S. is Black. ABC reported in 2020 that Black people accounted for an astonishingly disproportionate amount of the country's 568,000 homeless Americans. (Allen, 2020) The police who protect upscale businesses are seen as being on the side of the powerful oppressors. The actual killing of Black people seemed to confirm that the helplessness and powerlessness experienced by the disadvantaged was a catalyst when the lid came off suppressed feelings.

Hate is the greatest power in dominating systematic reasoning

When we consider the power that negative emotional contagion has when it infects our systematic reasoning abilities, one has to suspect that the power of hate is probably the greatest power of all the negative emotions in influencing and dominating systematic reasoning (closely followed by its cousin, fear). Although there are no microscopic germs in the infection produced by emotional contagion, the power of infection generated by hate is just as great, if not greater, than a virus. It has the ability to infect people's minds to the extent that it can kill hundreds of millions of people, as evidenced by the many wars throughout the world's history (Hedges, 2003). The Second World War alone killed around 75 million people, of whom 40 million were civilians (Casualties of World War II, n.d.).

We see hate's ability to infect the minds of people in the irrational and destructive effects of racism prevalent around the world. The hate associated with racial prejudice is turned towards individuals with skin of a different colour—in many countries, but particularly in the U.S. The irrational fear and reactive hate within the individuals who killed Ahmaud Arbery, a young Black man out jogging in Georgia, and the hate within the former police officer who killed George Floyd in Minnesota by kneeling on his neck, took over and infected their common sense and systematic reasoning so that they made an emotionally based decision to kill. They may think that they thought about it, but the underlying emotion of hate and power drove those thoughts to action.

The action by the killers was purely emotional when wise, thoughtful decisions were required. This is the power of emotional contagion when one's own emotion infects one's own mind. The hate is so strong at that time, and the mind so weak and culpable, that the emotional infection takes right over and produces the fatal action. The weakness of the mind has likely been there for years and decades. It has likely been taught, trained, and educated through systematic bias and prejudice against people of colour. There is no awareness of alternative ways of thinking, otherwise taught through critical thinking, leaving them to surrender to their weak thinking. These people don't recognize their thinking as weak; they falsely believe that it is strong thinking because they perceive aggression as strength. It is a false strength. This is tunnel, telescopic vison: one targeted idea in mind, and blinders on so that all other possibilities are not even considered. The power of hate is so strong, so blinding, and so perpetual over months, years, and decades, and even centuries and millennia, that it has infected their ability to think logically when the topic of race is the focus.

Society has long tried to eliminate hate, but it is a complex act. There can be no doubt that its emergence has been the result of years of emotionally contagious emotions of cynicism, fear, anger, helplessness, depression, prejudice, and demoralization, in conjunction with a lack of awareness of its lengthy simmering in the collective subconscious. We need to work on reducing hate not in a greater societal focus but in a focus on smaller groups so that we can harness positive emotional contagion to do so, by teaching skills of gratitude, compassion, and other positive contagious emotions. Focus on targeted groups starting with methods of reducing cynicism, anger, and reducing prejudice against outside groups will be of immense help in this regard.

11

Disgust, Controversies, and Politics

Disgust is a major factor in deciding how our emotions affect our social and political beliefs and our judgment of a political candidate. It induces fear and bypasses reason. When a politician discusses a controversial topic with emotion and conviction that we relate to, we can become attached to that person, spreading emotional contagion. Learning how to handle emotions can regulate behaviour in ways that laws don't. Some previously "law-abiding" individuals have committed explosive, emotional crimes, due to difficulty handling emotions. Medication and laws do not cure negative emotional and social contagion. We need moderate, flexible, rational, and critical thinking to balance the effects of emotion, including fear. As a political movement, populism has an emotional base, spreading its message through emotional and social contagion.

The way we process the emotion of disgust influences our political thinking. "Our political beliefs may derive from a specific aspect of our biological makeup: our propensity to feel physical revulsion," writes the *Atlantic* (McAuliffe, 2019). Disgust is interesting as it is: a mild, low-level emotion that we tend to isolate and disregard, but it is sneaky. It actually is a major subconscious factor in deciding if or how emotions affect our social and political beliefs. A study found that the brain's response to a single disgusting image was enough to predict an individual's political ideology (Ahn et al., 2014). The *Atlantic* article goes on to say that "at a deep, symbolic level, some researchers speculate, disgust may be bound up with ideas about "them" versus "us," about whom we instinctively trust and don't trust." Those are crucial emotions in our early development as a person.

Disgust is a strong emotion that can affect our political beliefs

How would our attitudes towards disgust affect our opinions on social issues? They could influence beliefs about whether governments should help those we consider to be "dirty." There is no reason why that should be the case logically, but it happens. Since disgust brings up emotional reactions that overtake reasoning, this is a case of emotional contagion. Disgust may generalize and colour judgment through quick emotional thinking.

Being prone to react with disgust to distasteful images and generalizing social or political topics is fast, quick, impulsive, System 1 thinking. It is technically acceptable to do so since we have freedom of thought; it is not wrong. It would be wiser, however, to practise System 2 thinking, which involves slow, logical, systematic reasoning. We have a responsibility to think things through with reasoned thinking when choosing our positions on contentious topics. Otherwise, we are practicing emotional voting. We should not rely on being disgusted with an idea as the basis for any position on any given issue. Freedom of speech does not give us licence to be reckless with our thinking and speaking. What disgusts us may not disgust others. Our feelings of disgust can produce visceral emotional reactions. In politics, disgust can be so strong that it unduly affects a voter's judgment of a candidate. The contagious effects from this emotion clouds a person's judgment of the candidate's overall suitability.

People who think emotionally tend to perceive situations as being at one extreme end of the spectrum or the other, whereas those people who use systematic reasoning tend to perceive situations as falling at various points along a spectrum—including in the middle. To place someone somewhere in the middle of their political leanings takes some cognitive effort. Some people unfortunately prefer to avoid making this effort, by using cognitive ease rather than systematic reasoning, simply dropping a position to the extreme right or left without any thought process.

Professor Paul Rozin and his colleagues have studied disgust (2016). They contend that a central property of core disgust is that the object deemed offensive has to be thought capable of "contaminating" other objects—even if the person sensing this contamination knows that it's just an illusion and there is no scientific or logical reason why it could happen. They discuss that when the law "once in contact, always in contact" applies, even without logical or scientific proof, a core disgust has likely been triggered. It is controversial, then, as to whether it is justified to avoid something that is disgusting because that tends to be irrational, and yet it is often given as a reason for avoidance.

To gain membership in the core disgust club, Rozin says, the candidate must meet all of the following criteria: something you could eat; something that has or had a life of its own; and something that has the power to make other things disgusting. Our behaviour then becomes irrational, emotional, and illogical. There is contagion there; the feeling of disgust has infected our mind, inducing fear and bypassing the need to reason something out.

Controversial topics are susceptible to emotional contagion

Controversial topics like war, the pandemic, and abortion are susceptible to social and emotional contagion, where the associated emotion is caught and transferred to others. Our feelings about such topics can easily be distorted and are susceptible to overgeneralization. These can be stimulated by similar situations or related controversies and contribute to emotional contagion, particularly if there is no moderation offered. Moderation could be from fact checking, alternative arguments made by others in an emotionally neutral or emotionally supportive manner, or by engaging in face-to-face contact rather than over the internet. We need to overcome the bubble characterized by the anonymous, impersonal medium of social media, which, in fact, encourages emotional contagion because of the anonymity. Don't wait for someone else to do it. Do it yourself. Try to understand social media's psychological impact on you.

You may react to an esteemed public figure you see on social media. You may be subconsciously wanting your emotional needs to be met by that person who is esteemed in your eyes, who is espousing a particular stand on a topic that you identify with in a personal way. But that public figure is not actually there with you because you see them only on social media. They may represent something to you emotionally. When an esteemed public figure presents a position on a controversial topic with emotion and conviction, we may feel understood and appreciated. This arouses our emotions and we may become attached to that figure. The impact is particularly strong for people who are prone to automatically catching the emotional part of an argument and act on it, thereby catching and spreading the emotional contagion. Be aware of the pitfalls of the situation; don't let yourself get too caught up in them emotionally. Keep your reactions at a hypothetical, curious level. Remember that wise people do not react impulsively and automatically.

Fear, anger, and cynicism especially are infectious in a social environment, easily passing from one person to another, especially through social media. Social media is primarily anonymous and yet it is intensely personal, and prone to emotional contagion. We can somehow feel our inner emotional needs being met if someone discusses a topic meaningful to us. You can be immediately infected by the emotions, absorb them deeply inside yourself, and feel them (sometimes intensely), and so you act on them quickly. For many people this is an automatic process. Just because they feel the fear, anger, and cynicism from that other person, they mistakenly assume there is a genuine reason for it and then do something they later regret.

During the pandemic, we are swamped with emotions of fear, anxiety, and depression from social isolation. Then these emotions attract other stronger or similar emotions like dread, panic, and hate. Those people who cannot understand or control the emotional buildup are overwhelmed with emotions which take over their actions. Mass shootings increase, police brutality continues, and certainly depression, anxiety, and contagious demoralization worsen.

Learning how to handle emotions effectively can regulate behaviour in ways that imposition of laws do not. Laws only address the symptoms. This is why the "law-abiding" concept is mostly irrelevant. It fails to consider that an individual's cognitive abilities and emotions need to be under control in order to obey the law. It fails to consider the power and strength of an underlying motivational drive and the consequent emotional contagion infecting and supplanting one's cognitive abilities, in spite of an individual's favourable "law-abiding" history. Some previously law-abiding people commit explosive crimes, emotional in nature. Their violent actions are the result of problems caused by unfamiliarity or unwillingness to focus on learning how to recognize, manage, and regulate emotions and see the connection between emotions and actions.

Emotional and social contagion are invisible. Quick action taken through enacting laws and policing is deceiving in its apparent thoroughness because it doesn't account for the invisible contagion. The contagion still goes on in spite of the law. We need a psychological inoculation. With social and emotional contagion, there are no bacteria, no viruses, no medical doctors, and no judges. It can't be measured on a blood test or an MRI; it can't be sentenced to jail. Laws don't stop it. Medical tests don't pick it up. It can't be arrested. There is no medication for it. Society certainly tries to use medication, by prescribing anti-anxiety and anti-depressant medication to settle emotional issues without addressing the social or psychological cause. Medication doesn't cure emotional and social contagion.

But you can lower it by being aware when you might give it off to others, that is, when you might emit, exude or express it, and if so, whether you are giving off healthy, positive feelings to others. If the feelings and emotions you are exuding outward are negative or unhealthy, then you need to work on holding them back, or keep them to yourself. If this is difficult, and you want to hold them back, but cannot (for example if you are depressed or anxious), then it is best to talk about what the feeling is to others and acknowledge that you do not want to share those feelings, unless the other person gives you permission.

We cannot rely on others, however, to stop giving off feelings. Politicians, singers, journalists, and many others will still do so. So you can also lower it by setting in place your gatekeeper to stop absorbing other peoples' negative unhealthy feelings when they are emitted or expressed.

Society and our biochemistry are off balance

Our society is clearly off balance and in turmoil. This has an impact on people's biochemistry. It is not a surprise that many people have a so-called biochemical imbalance, as contagious, infectious negative emotions we have discussed here impact our bodies and minds, throwing them off balance. Serotonin, norepinephrine, and dopamine levels are off balance as a result, producing anxiety and depression, which are rampant.

There is no medication for cynicism, which spreads through emotional contagion. And this was true prior to the pandemic. Since then, more than 42 percent of people surveyed by the US Census Bureau reported symptoms of anxiety or depression in December 2020, an increase from 11 percent from the previous year (Abbott, 2021). This is the result of demoralization building up more and more over the years, topped off by the tumultuous 2020 and the pandemic. It is expected to continue past the end of the pandemic. But there are many psychological, cognitive, emotional, and social solutions to depression and anxiety.

The effects of emotional contagion can be bad. Fights occur, arguments happen, relationships end, and property can be destroyed. When people just react to the emotion without taking time to appraise the situation and the character of the person involved, there can be problems. Sometimes, sadly and tragically, people die as a result of quick, emotional reactions. Emotional and social contagion often play an important role.

Many people find that after a negative event, when it is too late, their reactive and sometimes aggressive, dangerous actions were in fact contrary to their beliefs and values. They may be genuinely surprised by this. Much behaviour is produced by subconscious thinking and associated emotionality that may be opposed to a person's conscious principles. Many people are surprised at the power their inner emotions have on their lives. They have a hard time tolerating the emotion they have automatically absorbed, so they may quickly and impulsively—sometimes recklessly—have an aggressive, defensive, or even violent reaction against the person they perceive has triggered them. Sometimes feeling emotionally attracted to an individual who had displayed such an explosive emotion, who they soon decide consciously is inappropriate to be attracted to, leads to a strong internal disgust. This prompts a strong behavioural reaction of aggression towards that person. Emotions don't think.

We need to achieve emotional distance by cognitively attributing problematic behaviour to some dysfunctional state in the other person, then expressing this quietly rather than accusingly or forcefully. That would lessen the emotional contagion. But it seems that being heard and seen expressing anger by a crowd serves a psychological and emotional need for some people. This may be psychological compensation for being or feeling ignored or powerless. It is important to prevent this behaviour by reflecting on the hidden, deeper motivation causing it. The strength of the anger expressed towards a public figure can reflect an underlying psychological issue. Working on resolving that issue can prevent emotional contagion in the future. Emotional contagion can run amok and cause havoc. It is up to us to prevent it.

Implicit emotion is embedded in many political beliefs

Emotion is embedded in many political viewpoints, beliefs, and values. It can be implicit or subtle, and still play a very strong, if not defining, role in discussions about social, political, and economic issues. For democracy to be effective, we need to use systematic, rational thinking to compare alternatives and define strengths and weaknesses when we vote.

When a belief with an emotion embedded in it forms a person's psychological identity, and when they are validated for it by others, that validation usually means a lot to them. This is important because it reflects how vital the emotion is, and how key the role that emotional contagion plays in influencing others. We saw how politicians tend to arouse emotions which trigger votes. The emotional feel dictates their choice. This produces emotional voting. The effects of emotional and social contagion become negative and detrimental to society when people use the emotional, reactive part of their brain, rather than the cognitive, thinking part, when deciding how to vote. Amygdala arousal may affect their votes.

A reaction can be irrational if only narrow parts of a situation are considered. The individual does not take the total situation into account. It requires intellectual curiosity, awareness, and tolerance to investigate an opposing viewpoint. Such tolerance is not normally present in people harbouring strong, forceful emotions and needs within them; this strengthens the incoming emotion and magnifies it when it is expressed. These people are driven by their inner emotion to hold a more absolute, and usually extreme, position.

Psychological inoculation against emotional contagion

An important part of inoculation against emotional contagion as a citizen and voter is to use reason, knowledge, and facts. Our ability to incorporate emotionally laden information into our thinking, using pre-existing knowledge of the facts, is critical. If the facts support it, we can remind ourselves that yes, this "(emotionally laden information) we have just been made aware of sounds like it is a real concern, but let's gather more information and consider it further to see what it is about, rather than acting impulsively on gut instinct and emotion." Take it in only a little and think about it.

We can tell ourselves that there is usually a more moderate way to approach it. We can use reasonable, rational thinking and logic, check the evidence, question our assumptions, see what has happened before in similar situations, and think about other ways to interpret the evidence. We need to use flexible thinking, rather than absolutist thinking: remembering that sometimes different things can happen in different ways, from different causes, rather than deciding that negative things always happen in the same negative way, for the same reason.

For example, if there is a bombing or a shooting by a person of a specific religion, the emotion we feel may come from the belief that there is a connection between that religion and the violence. This thought may be appealing to those who think this way, who like to connect events with a group of people unfamiliar to them based on fear. It may not be true, though. One person's fear ramps up the next person's fear and it becomes contagious; feeling the emotion tends to easily spread to the next person, circumventing their critical thinking capacity, and then to another, and so on. They are naturally attracted to the commotion involved in the emotion without knowing what it is about, as we all are. If there is another violent incident, we may assume the violence is caused by the same group of people from the same religious group, without looking for any evidence. Emotion, particularly fear, suspicion, unfamiliarity, and insecurity, makes us jump to a conclusion that may not be true, and because of the power of the emotion we may mistakenly assume our conclusion is correct. This is an example of how cognitive distortions are involved when psychological contagion affects us. But flexible, reasonable thinking gives us the ability to be moderate. Violence is caused by extreme psychological maladjustment, so the people who are involved in committing violence are psychologically disturbed, no matter which religion they belong to. This may be challenging for some people to accept. Usually, any person who commits violence in a normal political environment is experiencing severe psychological maladjustment.

The media is likely to interview people who have heightened fears because it is, in their opinion, newsworthy. They may focus excessively on the fears. This can spread emotional contagion because drama is infectious. It makes us feel like the anxiety and danger levels are truly high, even if that is not the case. It seems understandable: there is often some reasonable fear, and people need to express it. But it is often then ramped up even more. If they feel like their fear isn't being heard, or understood, or recognized as valid, they will often subconsciously exaggerate it to a level that is so high that they know someone will listen and tell them that their fear is valid. This may hit the media and there it can seem more prevalent in society than it really is. This makes the fearful person feel heard and understood. They think that now someone will take action to make them safe. But the action they want might not be taken to the degree they think it should, so emotional contagion strengthens, and some people then get more upset, fearful, and anxious.

Because the reactions are emotional, there is limited room for reason if there is no psychological inoculation. This comes from thinking what event should be happening to justify this much fear. There is probably no justification for it, such as would be present if a kidnapper, terrorist, or shooter were coming around the corner with a gun. Most people know that this is not likely to be the case, and yet still feel fear. They know it is always possible, so they increase their fear to protect themselves. They have anxiety in subtle, abstract ways, and it rises. By being emotional and catching emotions, or by feeling empathic with the victims of a tragedy, people may be worried about things going wrong, whether they are connected to the original situation or not. This is emotional contagion. It raises fears in areas where no actual cause for fear exists. There is not a shooter around every corner. It spills over to the other issues, like relationships, finances, and health, even though they may not be logically related to the original fear of terrorism, active shooters, or viruses. Just because you read or hear about these issues doesn't automatically mean they will happen to you. Tell yourself that.

Prevention of the spread of emotional contagion would lower anxiety and reduce its chances of spilling over into unrelated areas. It can be prevented by recognizing from the heightened emotion that a statement is likely irrational and exaggerated, and that includes many cognitive distortions. Use "I language" by validating a true emotion with an accurate "I statement," a statement in the first person starting with the word "I" as described below. This will help validate the emotion because it is more accurate and personal. Validating the emotion will lower the heightened aspect. Validating the emotion doesn't mean that there is a real reason to be anxious; it doesn't say that yes, there is indeed a shooter around the corner, but rather it says, yes, it is understandable that you feel anxious about the possibility of there being a shooter close by, especially if there has been a number of such incidents recently. You can, however, calculate the odds of this happening as extremely low. This validation may settle the emotional contagion and make it more open to rational discussion. Rational discussion makes the emotional part less strong and the cognitive part stronger.

To be rational, a person needs to accept that some degree of fear is reasonable if the facts suggest it. And the facts do seem to suggest it, if we go by the media reports: in the fifty years before the 1966 Texas tower shooting, there were just twenty-five mass shootings in which four or more people were killed. Since then, the number has risen dramatically, and many of the deadliest shootings have occurred within the past fifteen years, starting with the Virginia Tech shooting in 2007. They are unpredictable, and this as well as the large numbers raise the fear. That seems somewhat rational, and also emotional. They account for fewer than 2 percent of the annual 39,000 gun deaths in the U.S. (Palmer, 2018). Nevertheless, it is a serious phenomenon that needs to be addressed. It is likely that the mass shootings reflect some underlying issues in the psychological underground that is not being clearly identified and dealt with, possibly related to toxic masculinity.

Being rational prevents fear from spreading by correcting cognitive distortions such as, "the world is going crazy" or, "what is the world coming to?" Those are sayings that express our emotions and feelings. They are distorted because the whole world or country is not crazy. Rather than expressing fears in the third person, like, "The world is crazy," it would be better to say, "I am scared." Try, "I am worried about the direction things are going," or, "I am very worried right now." This is a realistic, personal way of putting it. It brings the person back down to earth and combats the exaggeration effects of emotional and social contagion by making it specific to one person: the "I" in the phrase "I am very worried." It invites discussion of specific, actual possible worries and solutions. That way, even if there is a real, credible worry, the person is expressing it with an emphasis on their cognitions; the statement is made with a realistic component that keeps the emotion at a workable level, amenable to finding solutions, instead of saying something emotionally contagious, such as "The whole world is going to pot," which blocks this ability.

Populism's roots are truly emotional

Wirz' article (2018) points to the important role of emotion in populist appeals, which elicit stronger emotions in the populace. In some ways, the rise of populism appears to occur as a psychological reaction to feared domination or even annihilation of people who feel powerless. The powerless feelings they may possess about a perceived threat to their survival will trigger a psychological reaction to defend against this perceived threat of takeover by the powerful. It may feel like it is real, due to emotional contagion, and it may be true for an unfortunate few, but often it is an irrational fear. Since this is a pervasive but often unrecognized psychological feeling, those involved who are feeling powerless and threatened are likely to come out in droves to fight it off. For this reason, it is important for empathic candidates to address this need by offering reassurances that the needs of the populist class will be met whenever possible and describe how that can be accomplished in a realistic, believable manner, thereby empowering them.

The media picks up the needs of the populist class, sensing that it needs power. Their coverage produces the emotional reactions being spread through emotional contagion, in turn producing a strong effect where logic and reason are unfortunately easily abandoned in favour of the emotional experience embedded in the pursuit of power. This can be a rewarding experience for the powerless individual who may now feel understood and reassured. But this may be a detriment, since logic and reason and objectivity may not be maintained.

This inner emotional experience also has a strong physiological basis. It triggers the common reward pathway in the human brain, which is composed of both central nervous system structures and endogenous neurotransmitters such as dopamine communicating between these structures. "Dopamine biases memory towards events that are of motivational significance" to the individual and is "an essential element in the brain reward system" (Arias-Carrion et al., 2010). The Institute for Behavioral Genetics in Colorado wrote (n.d.) that "the reward pathway evolved to promote activities that are essential to the survival of the human race."

The drive for survival is one of the strongest energies available to the human being. When it is strengthened by the impact of emotional and social contagion, it may become so strong that it influences the defining spirit or mood of the times. This seems to be the case during a time of turmoil. The populism that affected the world in 2015-2019, and into the 2020s, as seen particularly in the U.S. and the U.K., seemed to reflect the rise of these psychological needs being met by a powerful leader in a socio-political setting. This was true particularly for some underprivileged white people, those who wrongly felt misrepresented by the previous American president. Perception of skin colour wrongly defines a person's allegiance and vote in many countries.

Mistaken as purely a sociological movement, populism's roots are truly emotional, as shown in the need to resist feelings of powerlessness by domination and annihilation. Along with that is the physiologically based reward system fueled by dopamine, which fuels the drive for survival.

One example is Brexit in the United Kingdom (U.K.), where many people seemed to vote on the basis of pride in their country, renewing feelings of power and identity, feelings of nationalism and independence. An underlying fear of domination by Europe was probably involved. These are strong emotional factors appealing to the need for survival, one of the greatest needs we have as a people. We see it in nationalism. People are afraid of losing their identity, an identity which gives them meaning. This is emotional, and they make their decisions about how to vote based on these feelings. During the referendum, the people seemed to ignore reason, knowledge, and logic behind rational economic decisions and the benefits of free trade for their country's economy. It must have been a hard decision for everyone. Voters' decisions were enhanced by poetry more than policy; that is, by the emotion flowing inside them in poetic-like comfort when they thought of the issue, rather than by comparing and contrasting facts and details that had been considered. We have to feel good about our vote and about the person or position we are voting for; it has to resonate inside us, so in a sense when a candidate's position flows like poetry to our ears, it easily connects inside us. But it has to be both—emotion as well as reason—that we use to decide how to vote. Using emotion by itself is not a good thing. Emotions don't think.

The time was ripe for the power of emotional contagion to take root in the U.S. and the U.K. People needed to have their voices heard or, at least, perceived as being heard. They felt oppressed and insecure. There is nothing wrong, vulnerable, or weak about being insecure. We all go through it at times. Candidates with emotional power, sociopathic characteristics, and the ability to use emotional contagion in their favour have been elected in both countries. British citizens who supported Brexit wanted to maintain their identity as Britons, which, if lost by membership in the European Union, was the equivalent to annihilation for them. The population was ripe for influencing by emotional contagion, as used by their successful candidate for prime minister who exploited this vulnerability. Emotional contagion being one of the most powerful forces available to human beings, it was bound to succeed, at least in achieving power for the so-called underclass. In the U.S., the issue was unfortunately race, and the perceived need for white supremacy among some people. This reflects a perceived threat of risk to the survival of white people, who felt their endurance as a race was at risk, hence the need to feel "supreme" again.

True empowerment

This often brings up what we as psychologists call "catastrophic thinking," in which we can imagine our country being conquered by a stronger, neighbouring country. What is needed instead is true empowerment, rather than a strive for power, which is often obtained by numbers or by affiliation with a perceived powerful persona. The strive for power is understandable, but false, since power really means domination and inequality. True power comes from only personal empowerment, which involves equality and cooperation.

The former U.S. president, when he was initially running for president, said "I am your voice," as if he spoke for the voiceless. In reality, he appeared to want to take over their voice (Cannon & Goodin, 2016) instead of giving them one. Since he had a dominant persona, which seemed to have a magnetic, hypnotic effect on even those in his own party, as if he was putting them under his spell, he was able to connect with the inner emotion of the insecure, the powerless, the undereducated, by promising to be their voice. When that did not happen, it was natural for them to be let down. For many, this wouldn't be the first time. It is almost tragic when someone's hopes are diminished this much. We need to let ourselves feel sad for them. This doesn't mean we support their beliefs, as emotional contagion would have us believe. We don't. But they are people whose hopes are diminished and that is sad.

By appealing to the emotional needs of the powerless, the astute politician with sociopathic tendencies is able to get elected. In the long run, though, the most powerful and effective leader is a benevolent, empathic, well-adjusted person who is effective at carrying out their duties, while at the same time speaking to and empowering the people. This brings a balance to society. The controversial topics can be contagious as they often have an excess of emotion attached to them. We need to be aware of this and use our abilities to lower our emotional reactions to them without compromising our perspectives. This takes patience, wisdom, and the ability to affect social change in an assertive manner while maintaining respect and empathy for all.

12

Overcoming Emotional Contagion: Handling Incoming Emotions

Specific solutions with examples are offered to overcome negative emotional contagion. Being aware of its existence is a start to resisting it. You can't resist what you don't recognize. Don't catch emotions from others immediately, just let them connect briefly. When feeling an emotion coming on, don't act on it right away. Think it through, even for a few moments. Stop automatically catching emotions. Using rational, systematic reasoning, critical thinking, and flexible thinking and considering various perspectives is helpful, including a good perspective on whether a feeling from elsewhere belongs with you. Filter out the negative infectious emotions. Strong emotions can produce automatic reactions that you need to ask yourself questions about before acting on them. Social media proliferates and contributes to divisiveness.

We have talked a lot about emotional and social contagion. Let's talk about how you stop, block, and overcome negative emotional contagion, and apply it to our life in society. Let's focus on this with an emphasis on interpersonal, social, and political situations. We need to apply these methods not just in an interpersonal setting but also in impersonal settings, as when we absorb emotions from political, entertainment, or sports figures. While it is acceptable to absorb them, don't do it blindly or automatically. In a time of turmoil, we need an effective gatekeeper who uses thoughts and behaviours to recognize when to open the gate and allow incoming emotions to be absorbed, and when to close the gate to block them. We need to *Stop Automatically Catching Emotions* when they are contagious. This inoculates us against emotional contagion.

Being aware that we have an inoculation against emotional and social contagion reassures us that we don't have to absorb it. We can resist contagious emotions others express or emit. Awareness of negative emotional contagion is a start to blocking or resisting it. You can't block what you don't recognize. If you are aware of it and can identify it when it happens, you can learn to block it. It gives us the ability to stop catching emotions from others automatically. We can instruct ourselves with awareness of whether or not to catch and absorb emotions coming towards us when we notice what is happening.

For example, if someone is too dramatic, we can stop getting drawn in. Don't catch the emotion, just let it connect briefly. This can happen if the other person is overly emotional about a small thing, where, in your assessment, the emotion seems too much for the situation. If strong feelings are expressed by someone regarding a controversial topic that you haven't thought through, ask for more information about it; tell them that you are curious. You may not want to let yourself get too emotional right away. If you do, tell yourself that's okay. Connect briefly, but don't catch the other person's emotions or let them come on too strongly or immediately affect what you think about the topic. Buy yourself some time. Look around, distract yourself, ask questions, or think about something you enjoy. You are free to have your own opinion, but you need to make sure you think the subject through first. Tell them that. If you catch too many emotions about it right away, those emotions may try and think for you. Emotions don't think. They give simple messages, so they may solidify your beliefs too soon, before you have done your own research about the topic and have a chance to consider both sides. There are always two sides, and they both need to be considered.

We need to first be aware of our own emotional reaction. We have to make sure it is not automatic. Then we need to assess emotionally laden information and feelings from others. Begin by taking a moment to evaluate what the information is about before accepting the emotion. When you hear a story and feel someone's emotion about a situation, but are not involved yourself, try not to absorb that emotion—especially if you suspect the emotion is too strong, overdone, or negative, or if it doesn't seem to fit the situation. For example, remember the person in Chapter 2 who cried a lot about a dead bird? You can connect with their emotion for a few seconds, but it is best not to catch and absorb it.

The first step to overcome the contagion is to recognize it for what it is and firmly tell yourself that you are not automatically allowing yourself to have that feeling. Just because someone else has a feeling doesn't mean you should have it, too. We are all different. By first assessing feelings that others are expressing and deciding if they fit you and the situation, you will stop automatically catching emotions. It just takes a few seconds to do this. For example, if someone is frantic about accidentally breaking a glass on the floor, ask yourself a few questions (e.g., was anyone hurt? was it an expensive glass? how did it happen?) before you get emotional, and decide quickly whether you need to feel emotion, and, if so, what emotion you should feel (angry? calm? worried?). You could even practise this now through imagery and self-talk as you read this chapter.

Thinking rationally using, for example, systematic reasoning, critical thinking, and wisdom will help you get a handle on things. It provides you with a good perspective on whether the feeling belongs with you in whatever situation you are in. But consider the context: whether you are at a reception, a picnic, or a dance, it probably doesn't call for a bucket of tears, so tell yourself to hold them back. They can come on automatically, and if that happens, if it seems called for, you can still tell yourself to hold them back. (Don't say to yourself: "don't cry." This may remind you what your mother told you as a youngster, and it sets in play a parental rule, and we are not recommending parental rules.) Thinking rationally involves using reason, logic, evidence-checking, and flexible, moderate, and wise (rather than absolutist) thinking. It is important when accounting for individual differences and putting things into perspective. Checking the evidence reminds you that everyone breaks stuff now and then. We know people are different, so account for that in your mind, your gatekeeper. Some people cry at the drop of a hat; if you do that, change your focus, change the thought, think of a happy memory, and think of your momentary tears as a gift of sensitivity.

Blocking emotional contagion can be a difficult undertaking because emotions are generally pleasant and enjoyable, whether we express them or receive them. Positive emotions, however, should come from undertaking safe, acceptable, and socially and interpersonally appropriate activities. Use systematic reasoning and critical thinking to judge if this is the case before deciding whether to receive them. Emotions are the zest of life: they give us meaning, they make us feel good, and they help us enjoy things. Emotions can also bring us tears, shakes, worries, cynicism, and other uncomfortable feelings. They let us grieve and remember. Although feeling sad is uncomfortable, it is positive if it gives us a release. It is if the feeling is overdone, or not appropriate to the situation, that determines its acceptability. A lawyer probably shouldn't cry when he or she picks up a client's sad emotions, even though he or she may feel sad, because the client may then feel uncomfortable.

Handling unexpected emotions

Emotions can be expressed by others around us at any time, even if we are not prepared. They also happen inside us, sometimes surprisingly. They warn us if there is something wrong by making us feel anxious and scared. We are not recommending that you stop feeling emotional or stop absorbing emotions from others at all times. Instead, hopefully you can learn how to do the following:

- identify when an emotion you feel is giving you a meaningful warning.
  (Hint—probably not too often).[22]
- identify when you are absorbing someone's emotion in the moment.
  (Hint—are you feeling a similar feeling to someone else?)
- recognize situations when emotions are being expressed or emanated.
  (Hint—it may not be obvious)
- recognize implicit emotions.
  (Hint—check the voice inflections as they speak)
- separate emotions from words and statements, in person, online, or in text.
  (Hint—what they say they feel may not be what they feel emotionally)
- decide if and when you should stop absorbing others' emotions.
  (Hint—absorbing them means taking them inside as if they were yours)
- decide which emotions are destructive and which ones aren't.
  (Hint—think of both yourself and someone else)
- decide which occasions are likely to elicit these kinds of emotions.
  (Hint—does this happen in the same place or with the same person?)
- know how to stop enticing emotions from others.
  (Hint—do you leave feeling points hanging for others to finish?)
- know how to stop absorbing them.
  (Hint—own your own feelings)

---

22 These hints are given to stimulate the readers' thinking. Many of these points are also addressed further elsewhere in the book.

The point here is that emotions can infect the mind in a negative way, and you need to filter that out. Identify if a feeling is newly present. If it is, that is okay: monitor it because it could be contagious if appealing and attractive to you. Remember that it can be a false appeal; it is up to the mind to appraise what might happen if you let yourself absorb an emotion by using knowledge of cause-and-effect in many potential situations. If it connects with you, which it probably will, and you feel it—that's good. Just leave it at that, and don't absorb it inside you if this is a first meeting with someone.

When you feel a strong emotion, being expressed by another person, and related to a situation involving that person, it could feel good to do a lot of different things:

- kiss that person
- take that drug
- get too close
- swear out loud
- have a casual sexual encounter
- argue back
- leave the scene
- run away
- shoot that gun
- drive fast
- have too many drinks
- be cynical
- give up a goal
- quit a job
- punch the person
- quickly change residences

All these possibilities are based solely on the quick emotion you pick up unexpectedly from another person. You would be in System 1, reacting automatically to what the other person is feeling and the emotions they are giving off. You need to stop these reactions, take a few seconds, and move into System 2.

To move into System 2, ask yourself these questions:

In the longer term, is doing this good for you

- at this time,
- to do this act,
- to or with this person?

Stop and ask yourself these other questions:

- What will happen next if I do this?
- Is that the only thing I can do?
- Do I really, truly have to do it?
- Would another different or milder act be better?
- What could that be?

The life situations involved could range from fairly common to very risky. Don't rely on your feelings for an answer. If your answer is that it would feel good, then that is not a good answer. Use systematic reasoning or critical thinking to get your answer. Be objective. Use cause-and-effect predictions. Here are some more questions to ask yourself:

- What is the situation?
- What is at stake?
- What could be the cost?
- Is it safe?
- Could someone be hurt?
- Could I be hurt?
- Is this the best thing to do?
- What else could I do instead?
- What is the worst that could happen?
- What is the best that could happen?

By answering these questions honestly, you are preventing negative emotions, or potentially destructive emotions, that could come from your next action in this situation. Answering these questions correctly forces you to confront the situation. Some positive emotions could also end up producing actions that could be destructive or dangerous; don't disregard that possibility. You need to appraise them as well.

Appraising the emotion's message

To prevent emotional contagion when feeling an emotion coming in on its own, perhaps as a warning, don't act on it right away. Be curious about it, but don't believe anything about it at first. Don't take any message from it until you've appraised it. For example, if the emotion is general anxiety, don't automatically assume you are right to be anxious. The situation may not warrant it. But if it is a feeling of urgency, listen to it. You could be unsafe; the emotions could be trying to warn you. Take a few moments to appraise the feeling and the situation.[23] This—not acting right away—is your inoculation against the damage that impulsive actions from contagious emotions can do. Think first. Don't give in to any doing any action that the emotion coming towards you seems to trigger, unless you have thought about it earlier and agree with it, or unless it is urgent. Even then, take a few moments to appraise it and make sure it really is urgent, in fact, and not just in feeling. Use your mind. Ask questions to assess it. Look for evidence around you. Is the situation you are in unsafe? Look around. Define it. Be specific. Use your mind to assess it objectively. The anxiety may be justified; it may be urgent. Urgent situations usually have something concrete, definite, and real about them. If not, ask yourself if someone around you is anxious. If there is, ask the person what are they noticing. Ask them if they are often anxious. Consider that as evidence that you may be absorbing their possibly unfounded anxiety. If there is nothing you can see that is urgent, then you are probably absorbing their anxiety, so you can ignore your anxious feeling and tell it to leave. Don't panic; if you do, you are feeding it. Often you can just accept the anxiety is there without accepting any message accompanying it, such as something being wrong, or that something bad is going to happen. You can take some deep breaths to let go of it.

Let's continue. If you have an anxious feeling but you're not sure why, you might have either picked it up through emotional contagion, or you felt it from within yourself. The emotion has helped you by alerting you about this; you need to thank it and promise it a quick follow up from the mind. The emotion listens. Use simple words and brief phrases. Thanking the emotion doesn't mean admitting it is correct; the warning could be false. The mind is in charge of systematic reasoning. The mind decides

---

23 When I refer to taking a few moments, I usually mean a few seconds, about forty seconds – at most. The word *moments* does not mean *minutes.*

if it is correct. You need a moment or two to consider the situation before you say something or undertake some behaviour that starts with the emotion. That is okay; the emotion needn't be upset about that because the mind is just doing its job.

For example: the mind remembers now that your mother is coming over and you had forgotten. That's why you had the anxious feeling. Emotions cannot think: they only feel and give simple messages. They can give you advance notice like this. Feelings are important because they give us guidance, in partnership with the mind. The mind and the emotions are equal partners working together. That's how you get wisdom. Because emotions can be contagious, don't react right away. It could get you in trouble. The emotion blends with the mind to come up with a wise thought. Give it a chance to do that. So you remember now that you forgot to prepare supper for your mom, and you'd better do it now so as not to disappoint her and then feel guilty.

The way you react to the guidance from your emotion is up to your mind. The emotion can infect your mind through emotional contagion. Your mind has to let it in; it has a choice about whether it can be infected or not. The executive part of your brain is your mind, and it is in charge. Your mind may agree with your inner emotion that your mother's imminent arrival is urgent and important, and that you need to react. The mind will walk you through your thought process:

"Okay, emotion, you're right. I need to prepare for her visit. This is important, I agree. Let's see, what shall I get (for her to eat).... *(pause)*. Okay, that's an option.... *(pause)* That could work.... *(pause)* That could work, too."[24]

Meanwhile, the mind is not letting the anxiety's contagion come in and infect it because then it won't think straight. If you talk inwardly to the emotion and accept its urgency, and promise you are working on it, and show it the evidence by coming up with some ideas, the emotion will let you have a few moments to react, and may help the mind. By acting, you are validating the anxious emotion, and the anxiety will slowly disappear. The mind continues to be inoculated against the emotional contagion, while accepting the urgency. It doesn't panic.

---

24 The pauses and ellipses (short line of a few periods), here and in later examples, means that you pause for a few seconds, continue, maybe have a couple of similar thoughts, and go on in the same direction of thinking, followed by action in the same direction.

"Steady as it goes," the mind thinks. "We want to handle this right. Let's see... (pause)"

The mind then takes a few more seconds and continues the process, coming up with a few more options. These should be options to avoid risk while taking action: to do something effective and positive to plan for your mom's visit. Announce to yourself the initial option you've chosen. When the mind handles it steadily, a few extra seconds will pay off in the long run—in comparison to begin impulsive and panicky, letting the emotions take charge. You will feel calm and relief. The mind and the emotion have worked together as partners. If the mind needs more time, if perhaps it isn't thinking quite right, then you can recommend some simple ideas from basic knowledge.

"Let's just stay safe, avoid a risk, take a few breaths. What ingredients do I have in the house?" You take a few deep breaths, slowly exhaling each time. Remind yourself that you are an adult and don't need to stress about pleasing your mother.

The mind is buying time to do more thinking. You don't need to be perfect and if your mom wants you to be, then that is her issue. If you practice lazy thinking, your emotion probably won't trust your mind any longer; it may take over and get you into trouble. Emotions don't think. But they do tend to get impatient and impulsive if the mind dilly-dallies too long.

You may become angry, depressed, or anxious. Your mind can instead make a deal with the emotion and say it needs some time to de-stress and think more clearly. The emotion will usually let it, as it wants the mind to think clearly and solve the issue at hand. But the emotion wants the mind to stick to its deal. The emotion isn't patient, but does have good faith in the mind—as long as the mind follows through. Remember that the idea doesn't have to be perfect. The mind is flexible. So are the emotions as long as it knows the mind is working on it. Mom will probably take that tea she likes that you always have on hand, and something like a store-bought cookie and an apology for not baking her favourite pastry or making her a meal. But if this is a dinner arrangement, then be glad you have a microwave. If your Mom is supportive and knows you have a hectic life, you should be ok. If not, you still don't have to please her.

Perhaps a situation is more tense: your boss calls you and leaves an important question about your future with the company on your voice mail. She has some tension in her voice and asks you to call back. There are a few things you can initially tell yourself:

"The boss' message is incomplete, so we will continue to assess it as we get more information... We want to handle it in the best way we can right now to lower risk... We want to show that we are serious about this." Your mind needs to not absorb the boss' tension, but just notice it, take it into account. Reiterate why you are thinking this way and take a stance in your internal thinking as to whether or not this development is truly risky.

Next, come up with a reason in your private thoughts as to why it could be risky. Has there been a negative outcome in the past, and what was its impact on you? Try to be specific. If yes, consider the cost if this were to happen again. If you want to keep this job, is that the cost you need to avoid?

Allow some emotion that goes hand in hand with the words you are saying. Emotion is your partner, but remember to allow the emotion only to accentuate the words. Don't let your emotions choose the words.

Now you call back your boss. She is still tense; she has an idea, shares it with you, and asks for your opinion. Let's say you disagree with the idea. It would be wiser to say, "I have a different idea," instead of telling her that hers is stupid (even if that's what you really think).

Your emotions will co-operate if they are confident your words are genuine. Otherwise, if you tell your boss that you like her idea, but you don't really believe what you're saying, you have probably absorbed the boss's tension, and just want to impress her. Her tension may have been contagious; your inner emotion may take over and get you into trouble. It could start to make you nervous, or stutter, or show other signs of anxiety because it knows you are lying. Your boss could pick up on that and ask about it. Your mind and your emotion are partners in this. Speak slowly. Take a couple of deep breaths and proceed. At that point, you could be brave and tell your boss about your idea. "Well actually, what about..." Call it brainstorming.

As this goes on, we recognize that we can probably endure any upsetting or impatient emotion inside us temporarily and may not have to regard it as a reason to react instantly. You can recover. Just tell the emotion you realize it needs something and that you, the mind, are working on it.

Maybe you worry about how the boss will react. This is the mind's job, and the emotion will usually wait for the mind to think it through if necessary. This will include using the information your emotion has given you, so you can use wise thinking. Consider your knowledge, ask yourself how the situation has been handled before and how that went, and try to predict, based on your memories and knowledge, what would happen if you made a certain choice. Remember that the best way to make a prediction is to base it on how people have behaved previously. We need to realize also that we don't have to prove ourselves by reacting quickly or brilliantly, and that we are not a loser or weak if we don't. Not many of us are brilliant and we still do well. In fact, we are smart if we know that we don't need to prove ourselves. That is confidence, but it needs to be based on reality: past successes, even if small.

We can manage it by being smart enough to predict situations where these things are more likely to happen, and to brace ourselves by having these coping thoughts at the ready when such an event happens to prevent an impulsive reaction. A coping thought could be sensing that the other person's mood may be unusual, and that they are likely affected by an emotional flow inside them. Knowing that, we might be better off not reacting right away and thinking it through first. We may decide not to take a comment from the boss personally. Maybe she is under stress, trying to be perfect, just like most of us. This is an example of cognitive re-appraisal. You realize the boss has been tense because she wants to be perfect. It isn't because of you. That's a relief. This all doesn't take too long to think through. Rehearse it in your mind, add in your own helpful thoughts.

In cognitive reappraisal, we assess the cause of an event in another way—a way that is honest and true, but likely more objective and less subjective. "Cognitive reappraisal involves recognizing the negative pattern your thoughts have fallen into, and changing that pattern to one that is more effective. Changing the course of your thoughts, or how you're making sense of things, can in turn change the course of your emotions, turning the dial down a couple of notches" (Cognitive Behavioral Therapy: Los Angeles, n.d.). These are "reality-based ways of reappraising the situation."

This was one situation. We discussed it in detail hoping that you can hopefully apply it to similar situations you may encounter, not necessarily involving a boss. Other situations could involve a politician speaking to a crowd, or a group and their emotions.

If you think the reason for an action in a group is acceptable, but are unsure about catching the group's accompanying emotion, then just hang around the people whose reason you agree with and who are expressing their feelings. Check the situation out. For example, maybe you are at a protest and others are clapping their hands. You want to join the clapping, and agree with the crowd's reason by mimicking their behaviour. You may start to feel their feeling of happiness and delight through emotional and social contagion by just being near them. Let their feelings connect with you. You are riding on top of their feelings, not mixing right in, but on the periphery. You could decide to clap your hands the next time they do (clapping hands would be an action), if you agree, since it joins you with their feelings and, by implication, with their reason for clapping. It pulls you more deeply into their feelings and you slowly start to absorb them. Some people clap their hands louder or longer than others do. You could go slow and test it out. (If this situation doesn't apply to you, think of similar situations that might, where others are behaving in a way that you are thinking of copying. These are meant as suggestions of certain behaviours which could arouse certain feelings.) If it feels okay, and the cause is okay, then gradually increase it. Actions brings out feelings. That is alright if you are okay with their reason, and if you can predict what will happen and how you will react from being drawn into their feelings. This can be positive emotional contagion.

If you are not sure of the validity of their reason, such as at a discussion on an important topic, then when they are clapping at an idea you are unsure about, don't clap your hands. Listen to their words some more to see if there are any significant things being said that seem risky or dangerous. If so, then pull back. Clapping your hands will pull you into joining emotionally with the cause even if you haven't established its validity for yourself. That's where emotional contagion can affect you in ways you don't want. The emotion can validate it, which is not desirable, because emotions can't think. Instead, your mind takes on its role as gatekeeper and has to make this decision. It is up to you. Remember the saying, "Put brain into gear before opening mouth" (or in this case, before clapping your hands).

We know that when someone emanates or gives off an emotion and you find yourself experiencing the same emotion, you don't need to actually catch the emotion yourself. Stop automatically catching emotions. You can just connect, without catching. You may assess it as not beneficial for you; even if it is, it needs to be appraised for a few moments first. Don't use your emotion to assess it. Use your mind to make the appraisal. If it is not beneficial for you to absorb this feeling, then tell yourself that this is not yours. The next decision may be whether to let it bounce off you or to only connect with it and keep it for a short while. You could say to yourself, "This feeling is not mine," followed by a more assertive "I don't want it (or you)." If you have to, silently say, "Get away" to the feeling, as if you are talking to an unwanted insect that has landed on you.[25] You are not accepting the feeling. It is not yours and you are not allowing it in. On the other hand, if you assess it as beneficial, but are reluctant to actually bring it in, you could say something approving to yourself that is welcoming and encouraging, and let the feeling connect for a short while.

Feelings like anger, worry, and anxiety are more prone to be contagious. They are louder, more visible, more intense, and seem to flow more easily. They can be accepted by the receiver because of apparent empathy or understanding[26] and can be emotionally contagious. Emotional contagion relies on the quick, fast thinking in these relatively superficial social situations. There is little or no slow thinking or reasoned thinking, no contemplation of which is the best choice to make. We might literally "go with the flow" when often we should not. But you can slow the thinking down.

It is better for slow, reasoned thinking to occur in quieter, personal realms where reflective thought is possible, rather than in noisy realms, where reactions are more impulsive and not thought out, yet may be formed more deeply because of the flow of emotion and social approval. For empathy to be real, you have to take the "as if" approach we discussed earlier to keep a boundary between you and the other person. When reasoned thinking doesn't occur, many people, after they have had time to think things through, will indicate that they made errors of judgment, connected too much, and later revised their conclusions. It is difficult to resist the flow of the emotional contagion because of its power and influence, but what is not observable publicly are one's private thoughts. It is best to defer any conclusions about contentious issues until you get a chance to think about it independently and reflect when things are cooler.

---

25 It may feel strange or awkward talking silently to a feeling, but we all talk to ourselves silently, and doing so has some power over our feelings.

26 If another person shares your angry feelings, not if you are angry at the other person.

Tell yourself to do this later if the timing is tough because of the quick flow of emotion. This provides time for slow, reasoned thinking that is not susceptible to emotional contagion.

Handling social media

Let's talk about blocking the effects of emotional contagion on social media. In my experience, emotional contagion is particularly present on Twitter, as well as on Facebook and other sites and forums. However, this is not a comparison of social media sites to determine which ones are more susceptible to emotional contagion, but is a comment on how social media is very susceptible to the phenomenon in general.

For example: someone in public life says X and there is some emotion there in what that person says. Then, if someone else on social media, or in the news, or in real life has a reaction to it that is quick, impulsive, and emotional, and they say Y, then we probably have the effect of emotional contagion. There could be an alternative response that the second person could have used instead, a response using cognitive, reflective, objective, or intellectual faculties, usually facts; they could have resisted an emotional response, thereby curtailing emotional contagion. A reaction is a sign of impulsivity, likely provoked by emotional contagion, but a response is usually a thoughtful comment, not provoked by emotional contagion. We tend to see reactions on social media. Social media has become a place for emotions to be exchanged, not information. Because of the anonymity, some people take risks, and delight in provoking emotion to make others upset. This is their way of being passive-aggressive, provoking hostility anonymously without taking responsibility for it.

The original author of a post may have purposely said something emotional as a trigger, knowing that it would induce a quick, emotional reaction in a second person, and that this would have a chain effect, triggering others. Because of this, it is best not to reply emotionally. Otherwise this spreads the post's message using emotional and social contagion, as each person responding triggers the next person in a downward chain reaction. More emotional words are used, giving the initial post more attention. People usually respond to emotions and emotional comments quickly, impulsively, emotionally, and without thinking. This is what trolls on the internet do, making emotional, controversial comments to stir others up on purpose. They seem to know that emotions don't think. They love wreaking havoc. This assumes the emotional response is not well thought-out and is impulsive and reactionary, likely to inflame further people down the line via emotional and social contagion.

Let's look at a real example. If we do this in "real time" then we pick up the emotion in a tweet. At time of writing, the former (then current) U.S. president said on Twitter: "WARRANTLESS SURVEILLANCE OF AMER-ICANS IS WRONG!" Let's ignore the content to make the point. Note his use of capital letters and the exclamation mark, as if he were speaking loudly and emotionally. If retyped in usual upper and lower case with a period at the end, his implicit emotion is ignored, and it may feel good to do so. Someone else replies, "No idea what you're ranting about." This person also ignores his capital letters and the exclamation mark, which is good, as it defuses the emotion. Someone else then replies with eight lines of his own contrary opinions, but with all capital letters. The first comment, the "No idea…" comment, of one line without caps got 41 retweets, the second, all-caps comment got 115 retweets, almost three times as many, both after about fifteen minutes. The first responder has not risen to the emotional bait; in fact, by ignoring the caps and the implied emotion in the capital letters, he downplays the content of original tweet. The second comment is more likely to attract more retweets with eight lines of capital letters, which in Twitter land is a good accomplishment, and supposedly better than the other comment. But the second comment is what the original tweet was trying to attract, since by using all-caps emotion in the original tweet, there was an implied hook for people to respond emotionally. This second responder took the bait. People are prone to do this, impulsively and emotionally, trapped by emotional contagion—probably because it feels good to get something off your chest and have others retweet it. It is not really the good thing that Twitter would have you believe, as it promotes emotional reactions. We forget that emotions don't think. Emotional contagion is very powerful on social media, and it takes a lot to resist. Many people reply with counter-contagion equally quickly and emotionally, perpetuating divisive emotion. Emotions automatically pull for other emotions.

The person initiating it comes out ahead, since the person responding with very strong emotion is usually being impulsive. Others will react emotionally, prompting a social media ping-pong game that does noth-ing other than give people a temporary outlet for their pent-up emotions, knowing that the other person doesn't live next door and won't come over to harass them. They will likely continue to retweet this, producing more emotional responses which other people will reply to with equally emotional comments, resulting in divisiveness and contributing to the turmoil in present-day life.

The proliferation of social media contributes to divisiveness. It is a tough situation because people will say that we are entitled to comment as a result of freedom of speech, and that this will get our message across in a meaningful way. This reply is likely to be filled with implicit emotion which can be picked up by others who either agree or disagree. There are many ways of expressing emotion, ranging from capital letters to emojis to cartoons. The problem here is that if the original emotional post had been ignored, the divisiveness and turmoil would have subsided. The former president liked to divide and conquer, and emotional contagion contributed to this and enabled the division to occur. Although we must of course have freedom of speech, the issue here is truly about expression of emotion, implicit emotion in the words, in ways that are responsible.

This is where the former president got his reinforcement. He got the attention he craved and continued using his trademark capital letters in following tweets. The emotion he triggered spread, carrying its contagious effects to those who were susceptible and took the bait. His messages were usually laden with capital letters, emotional phrases, and strong words, all conveying heightened emotionality. His voter base likes emotion, so he provided it and then they voted for him. The candidate providing emotional experience usually wins. How can opposing candidates argue with emotion? Only by pointing this fact out: that what he was doing was using emotion to stir people up and divide them. Part of what he said that was genuine because he honestly thought what he was saying was true. Genuine emotional statements are appealing to those who think politicians always lie. If leaders really think their words are true, then they don't feel the need to cover them up, and they will seem remarkably genuine.

13

Overcoming Emotional Contagion in Interactions

More examples and methods of handling contagious negative emotions are given. Try to understand what is going on with others emitting or expressing emotions before absorbing them. Actively think about what the person is trying to say and do and why. Don't rely on gut instinct; carefully analyzing incoming information works better. Don't be suspicious, just appraise the situation, asking yourself ordinary questions about it. Use conditional, partial acceptances before committing. Talk with your inner, wiser self about it. Recognize emotional triggers, disconnect the emotional link to them, avoid emotional ping-pong games. See the other person objectively. Question your feelings by looking for evidence to justify them. Realize that reality is positive, negative, and neutral. It is not likely as bad as the emotion tells you. Recognize implicit emotion.

Interactions with other people produce a lot of the emotional contagion that occurs in life. Personal energy and emotion are expressed, given, and received in interactions, both knowingly and unknowingly.

Active thinking, systematic reasoning, appraisals, and wisdom

In order to prevent and overcome negative emotional contagion, we need to be able to understand and handle its movement and energy. You may act irresponsibly if you act upon these things immediately. When someone expresses negative emotions, we do not want to immediately absorb them, so that first we can better understand what is going on with the other person or group of people emitting or expressing them. We want a temporary inoculation so that we do not become immediately infected by possibly toxic feelings.

Let's say a person is speaking energetically and making motions with their arms. This means they are expressing a lot of emotion, perhaps intentionally or spontaneously. They are swearing and accusing. We need to ask ourselves many questions when you come across this behaviour. Don't react right away automatically, unless they are starting to fight. Figure out what the person is trying to say and do and why. This is active thinking. What are they expressing? Is the person speaking directly to us? Are they quoting someone else? Are they serious? Is this just a story? Is there any danger here? Are they just excited? Is this their usual manner? We appraise the feelings, the energy, and the emotion. We realize that they are toxic and infectious, and possibly even dangerous and harmful. So we bypass the emotions by avoiding eye contact, and we consider the facts. We do not allow the emotions from the other person inside ourselves; they may have no positive value. We close ourselves off. To do that, think of this moment as if it were a movie and this person were in the movie. By not permitting the emotions access, they are not likely to make us angry. We can deflect, change the topic, give only a general agreement, disagree assertively, or point to a disadvantage—but not argue. Even if they are talking to you directly. Ask the person calmly to lower their voice. Repeat their words calmly. That means not raising your voice or getting emotional. Arguing emits emotion, and you could get infected.

Appraising someone when they interact with you means that you need to try and figure out what is going on with the other person, what they are feeling, why they are feeling that way, what they have been experiencing or doing recently, rather than just reacting. Many people believe that relying on gut instinct is the best way to read and understand others. Recent research, however, shows that "systematic reasoning beats gut instinct for working out what other people are thinking and feeling" (PSYBLOG, 2016). Analytical thought is shown to be more helpful than intuitive thought in reading other people (Ma-Kellams & Lerner, 2016). This is important because it validates our approach of undertaking systematic reasoning: gut instinct involves emotional contagion, where emotion overtakes reasoning to arrive at a conclusion. This would apply when listening to politicians' speeches or an influencer's persuasive spiel. You need to use active thinking when you hear them speak. Developing some expertise, even taking some time to use systematic reasoning and wisdom to appraise the characteristics of others and their emotions, makes us better at deciding whether or not to absorb their feelings. We are developing our gatekeeper. The American Psychological Association (2016) produces a podcast with an episode about understanding and reading non-verbal behaviour. There are many other resources available to do this. This is our inoculation against contamination from emotional contagion. Even though it takes a few seconds, and there may be some primitive emotional contagion coming through, you can stop, think, and decide to buy some time before making this decision.

Scientific research shows that carefully analyzing information works better. It makes sense that careful analysis would also be wise when choosing employers, professors, political leaders, friends, and even life partners. This is a more nuanced, reflective position similar to what is available when an individual uses a wise mind, blending emotion with thought. Maybe there's a perspective you could take that would let you accept some of the feeling coming your way. Perhaps you'll walk into the pub and enjoy the music, the conversation, and the emotional atmosphere—but you won't take a drink or a drug. And you won't absorb any emotion from others that you don't like or that comes from a wrong place. Thinking things through, even for a few moments, produces better decisions in interpersonal situations. This prevents automatically catching another's emotions and helps you arrive at better decisions.

Sometimes, though, it is difficult to do this. The flow of strong, vibrant, personal energy coming from another person, whatever they are expressing, anger or enthusiasm, can have an automatic effect on us that makes us pull the emotion in. If it is in a crowd, accompanied by energetic music—like in a sales pitch or at a political rally—you may feel like diving right in, following the feeling, wanting to experience it inside you because of its energy. It is contagious. When the vibrant emotion is right there in front of you, radiating from someone who is interacting with you or speaking in a crowd, it often pulls you right in. We merge with it and feel it too—automatically. This is especially so if we are attracted to the flow of personal energy and don't understand what purpose it serves. We need to work at understanding this. It is important to put that pull on hold while you appraise it. We can feel enthusiasm surprisingly strongly; it's almost like we can touch it. That is a flow of contagious energy and invisible emotion. The force of the attraction can be so strong and magnetic.

If you find yourself being pulled in at the first instance of meeting someone, feeling an incoming emotion, and reacting to it right away, then there will likely be an issue. You may find that you do not actually want to be involved. For example, if someone exudes dynamism, charisma, and emotion, it could be contagious. You may also absorb a primitive message attached to the emotion. You start to become closer to this person and do what the person does. When the person accepts your slight movement forward, they exude more charm and charisma. You take this as a sign that the person really does want you to participate, and so you take another step, feeling attracted like a magnet. If you have not appraised the individual, and are not practicing active thinking, you just go with the flow. You accept the contagion. You may end up discovering this person is not really good for you, and hoping it is not too late and that you don't wind up in an unfortunate, even dangerous situation. It could, however, be a good thing for you; you don't want to pull back and miss a good thing, either. This is why appraisal of the situation is so important.

Think of the pros and cons, and if you deem this situation a bad fit for you, then don't participate. Learning to resist means that for a few moments you have to temporarily give up the temptation of a good feeling while you make the appraisal about its desirability. If it is truly good, you'll make a wise decision.

It is important to let yourself have conditional acceptances so that you don't make commitments at that moment based solely on the contagious emotion you feel. You can then use systematic reasoning instead, over moments, hours, or even a couple of days. This means we have to work hard, sometimes very hard, at understanding what lies behind that flow. What purpose does it serve the person speaking? Ask yourself, what would it mean to really accept this flow? What would you have to do? Would you have to change anything? By seeing behind the flow, discovering its motivation and purpose, you can decide if you want to accept or resist its contagious appeal. But first you have to recognize it is a flow that has a real potential impact on you that will pull you in magnetically if you don't act. This is using active thinking. Evaluate why the feeling is being emanated and make a tentative decision.

If it is only a temporary decision, you need to appraise it over a few hours or a couple of days and decide if it is right for you. It may not be. If it is not, resist it. If you are actively thinking, and it feels like it fits you and who you are, only then can you allow it. And so you join them at that bar; listen to the music, absorb the feelings, learn interestedly about their perspective, and get closer emotionally. You are in control. You have thought about it. It means something to you since you want to have the experience. It has to seem right for you. If it does, let it come inside you. If this is a politician, or an influencer, or someone appealing to you because of their stand on an issue, then their beliefs and style need to feel right. There needs to be information supporting that feeling that you appraise cognitively. The cognitive appraisal you are doing can block emotional contagion, unless of course you accept it, and they blend together into unity.

To make an appraisal you have to give up a potentially gratifying feeling for a few seconds or moments while you do the work. This means getting to know the person, checking his non-verbal movements, his words, his attitude, his likes and dislikes. It is not just whether it feels good emotionally, but whether you sense that this person fits you and your values. If you are unsure, but have a sense that the other person's values are not vastly different from yours, then take a step further. Gradually. Sensing their values means discerning if you both view life and the world around you in a similar way.

We assess internally whether experiencing the excitement outweighs the risks to our values or our safety. This assessment is cognitive, often conscious. Then when we catch and absorb emotions, we are really approving of them as consistent with our values. It's just that the approval is very quick and often subconscious because it strikes a preexisting chord within us. It's often best to make that final approval in gradual stages, as feelings usually have a belief or desire attached to them that you can deduce as you appraise the person. There are many valuable experiences of incoming personal energy and affect that are rich in positivity and health, and a delight to be taken in and absorbed. They can enrich us, and move us, and have a profoundly positive impact on our lives. It is very exhilarating, and worthwhile waiting to see what it is about.

The impact of the contagious emotion will lessen or disappear after a trusting talk with your wiser self. The wiser self may recognize and validate the inner self's need, where the inner self is the part within you that is more instinctual and visceral. The inner self then gets some information to put things into perspective and choose more wisely. The inner self is trusting our wiser self. That magnetic grip comes from the inner self because it is steeped in visceral emotion. The wiser self includes logical reasoning and also some emotional sentiment regarding the self. It compares this new, potential experience with similar past experiences to assess it. When the inner self trusts and listens to the wiser self, the magnetic grip is lessened and the person makes a wiser choice, as it allows the "magnet" to pull it in, or weakens the "magnet" so that it doesn't pull it in, because the wiser self knows what it is. It sees the situation for what it is; it knows that just because it looks good doesn't mean it is good. Remember that your inside has to deal with it, and your inside is counting on you to treat it in a tender, gentle, wise way. It is the inside that hurts and then causes you to feel the hurt on your outside, so you feel the pain and suffer. Your inside is also counting on you to give it warmth, love, and energy, which can happen if the energy is actually positive. The inner self values the love that would come with a loving, positive experience.

It is important to resist an immediate pull by being aware of these aspects and of your internal dynamics. They can regulate and manage that pull and make a wise choice that fits you. This all includes being aware of our internal emotional drives, feelings, and needs, which is where the contagious emotions land in the body and the magnet has its impact. To do this, we have to talk to our inner self in its own language. Talking in its language helps communicate with it because it can convey trust and understanding. The inner self cannot develop another language or a better vocabulary, so we have to understand and accept that and talk in its language. Use short, simple, words and be a little childlike. Be caring and use some fantasy type of images and comparisons. That shows good consideration for it.

If we have decided that this temptation should be resisted, then when we talk to our inner self we have to explain why we made that choice. We need to reassure our inner self that this particular pull from this particular flow is not good for us, that it will not complete us in the way that the inner self is feeling or hoping that it might. It would be good to explain in its language why we feel this way about this particular flow. We can gently explain cause-and-effect, from the wise part of ourselves, joining with them because this is all you. You could say, "This choice will not be good for us." This appeal to the inner self to care for the wiser self is powerful. You are in this together. We should also tell it that we could meet our emotional need for self-completion in another way, by bringing in another pull instead—one that is safer and more likely to do the real job.

Talking to the inner self in its own language means to get in touch with it in a more primitive way. Our inner self is visceral, so we need to use simple, basic, language to communicate with it gently and softly. There needs to be a working empathy, a trust and understanding between our two selves to make all this happen. Our inner self needs to be able to trust our wiser self's judgment, because it is wisdom, warmth, and intuition that our wiser self offers, not cold logic and fact. Our inner self is more likely to trust our wiser self, which feels empathy for our inner self. It is in touch with our inner self and feels its pain. Our wiser self speaks in our inner self's language. Our wiser self hurts when our inner self does. They are in it together. This trust and explanation will settle our inner self's need to have this void filled at this time. Once the need is recognized by our wiser self, who addresses it, our inner self trusts our wiser self and usually agrees to wait. But our inner self may still be impatient for the need to be met, especially after it has tasted it. Our inner self trusts our wiser self that it will have its need fulfilled, but it tends to be impatient. Our inner self trusts that the wiser self will fill that need by allowing in the right flow at the right time.

So when we see that piece of cake, or that shot of whiskey, or the exciting love interest, or a new exciting, risky place to visit, or the salesman or politician offering something we have been longing for—when anything tempting presents itself, our wise self can talk to our inner self and say gently, but firmly, "I know you want this, but we're not sure yet if this is what we think it is. It might be the real thing, but we need to check it out first." Or even, "We need to think about it carefully... it will be better later... when you get another thing... it will make you feel truly better inside." It might be something firmer, like "This sounds too good to be true; it won't work out the way you think." You may say, after a few minutes' reflection, "This is really good... it all falls into place... let's go for it." That wiser self needs a few minutes. It is essential to provide that time. Because you trust the wiser self, and know it loves you, you will probably decide to follow it. It doesn't want you to be harmed because it is you, and as you feel better, it also feels better.

Recognize when situations are emotional to avoid automatic reactions

Sometimes you may realize that you are sharing a strong negative feeling with someone when you are talking with them, but then you catch yourself doing this and want to stop doing it. You don't want to catch a negative feeling like hate, depression, or fear. There are a few things you can do if this is happening:

- Work on taking different perspectives and say to yourself, "Whoa, just a minute!"
- And then you may say it out loud, something like, "Just a sec here, what do you mean?"
- You could follow it with something like, "this is pretty strong."
- Perhaps you say this last thought silently to yourself if you suspect the other person may be offended. This allows you to buy some time and reflect on what is being said so that you can take another look at it.
- If you say this last thought out loud, the person's response would be interesting because they could say, "What do you mean?" This may suggest that they don't think their statement is strong, or that they feel challenged.
- If so, just answer calmly. Do not argue.
- Perhaps they innocently say, "Do you think so?" This may suggest they are open to a different way of making their point that tones down the strength.
- You may say something like, "I'm not sure about..." or, "What about..." And then change your perspective or focus to an idea or recommendation for a milder phrasing as you complete those sentences.

You have different internal concepts and ideas than the person speaking and may have some other ways to think about it. Thoughts usually come before feelings. You are doing this for yourself and for the other person.

Much of the work, though, would be internal, so that you work on changing the feelings that you're experiencing in the moment. That can be difficult, so you need to practise that technique ahead of time by questioning your values and beliefs about contentious topics that you think could come up with this person, based on what you know about that person's interests and opinions. Try to determine how strongly you hold an opinion, or if you are flexible about it, so that you get an idea of where you sit in case it comes up. Be aware of a topic's potential controversy and take a look at different opinions to see if or how you might change your opinion. You need to be aware of different perspectives rather than just accept one as if it were the only true option. The only things that are true when looking at them from one perspective are obvious facts of physics, like gravity.

We are drawn to others' emotions almost instinctively. People usually let the feelings in subconsciously and automatically, often because they strike something meaningful or emotional inside of us. It seems automatic, but it's really not. We can control it.

Blocking absorption of emotion

By beginning to block the absorption of emotions in interpersonal inter-action, you will then improve your chances of doing so successfully with practice and time. It is a skill you develop, and it is not possible to develop it all at once. It is necessary to keep on doing it purposefully. It takes time. Eventually it will be habitual, and if you do it purposefully most of the time, it becomes automatic. You will become better at differentiating between feelings: which kind to block, when not to, and which feelings to accept and absorb.

Blocking emotional contagion is a moment-by-moment situational decision, a learning process that eventually becomes habitual. If you didn't block a feeling that would have been good to block the first time, you just have to tell yourself you would like to block the emotion the next time. Expand on the reason why you made the mistake. Tell yourself that you don't want the feeling you absorbed.

Perhaps someone close to us says, in an angry way: "You are stupid." You can block the negative emotion by doing some of the following:

- Recognize that these words and phrases are triggers. Recognize that this is an emotional and irrational time for the other person.
- Don't take it personally. The other person has chosen to use these words. Even if irrational, they are still the author of their own words. It is their style. They probably do this to others, also. You may have done something unfortunate or inappropriate, but it is their style to respond this way. They could respond differently.
- Don't become inflamed by their emotion; don't get angry and swear back. If you have that inclination, that is just automatic. Ignore that urge. Don't act on it. It doesn't mean you lose. Some-times the other person is looking for reason to have a fight or an argument. Don't give it to them.
- Just let them say it; it doesn't mean anything bad about you. We can't say or do everything perfectly, and neither can they. It reflects

what emotional state they are in or how bad their temper is. Just let it bounce off you.

- Recognize that people get into these states. These things happen. When someone is in this state, we have to pull our emotions back from its effect to prevent a major emotional explosion in both parties.

You are avoiding an emotional ping-pong game by blocking the spreading contagion of the negative emotion, and the resulting counter-contagion from you if you were to react quickly and emotionally.

- If you feel that you have made an error or misspoke, you can apologize. Remember the apologizing doesn't mean you are admitting guilt or fault. You can qualify it by apologizing because something unfortunate happened and that the other person felt they had a bad experience.
- Let the other person vent their feelings some more. Use empathy to verbally acknowledge that they felt they had a bad experience.
- Be general in your admission or apology by saying that sometimes you don't do or say things in the right way. (None of us does that every time.)
- If you did say or do something bad or wrong, admit it and apologize. Take responsibility for it. That is maturity.

These negative comments are likely to affect us in a strong way because they hit us in a sensitive spot. Our natural instinct is to get emotional as a matter of retaliation. In order to combat this, we can get objective and see the other person, while this is going on, as outside of us. Try to temporarily depersonalize them. Let's say a woman's husband is angry at her. They normally have a fairly good relationship.

- See the person objectively: "A 42-year-old man with brown hair standing 5 feet, 10 inches. Lives at 32 Brown Street, discussing his interpretation of his wife's behaviour." Use that language in your self-talk, not out loud, instead of: "My angry husband, what a bastard." This objective temporarily makes him feel like an outsider to you, which is what you want now.

- Say something to yourself like, "He is going through something right now." "He is having a tough day."
- Don't listen to his words, but hear his words to appraise the situation. To listen means to agree and take the words as instruction, or to take the words as true and believe them. To hear the words means that you hear them and know what they mean, but that you may or may not agree with them, react to them, or act accordingly.
- You can do disarming, which means reflect to the angry person something affirmative but non-committal. Perhaps, "Okay, I hear you telling me that I am stupid. Maybe I did something wrong." (Saying "maybe" does not mean you are admitting guilt, it means you are ready to negotiate.)
- At this point you can recognize, probably silently, that their words are vast overgeneralizations, and that happens when people are emotional. You cannot be stupid, since stupid is defined as "lacking thought or intelligence" (Cambridge Dictionary, n.d.), and you are reading a book now without pictures—you do not lack intelligence.
- However, you may have forgotten, as we all do sometimes, to "put brain in gear before opening mouth." You may have said something inappropriate because your emotion got the best of you.
- So admit that you were not thinking at that moment, and validate that the other person was upset for a good reason. You could realize that the word stupid is here meant as "forgetting to think." You made an unfortunate comment or decision, but that does not mean you are an unintelligent person. You do not need to accept or absorb the demeaning put-down.
- Say to yourself, "Just because they are loudly calling me stupid, and just because I forgot to think, does not mean I am an inferior, undeserving, or unworthy person."

Accepting the put-down is often an automatic, subconscious reaction and needs to be challenged in your own mind. Otherwise it is an automatic absorption of emotion. To avoid this, you can accept that the person is yelling this word loudly, but do not accept it as meaning anything about yourself. If the person yelled that you were the ugliest person on Mars, would you accept that? This is really the same thing. It doesn't apply to you unless you let it.

You need to disconnect that link between the triggering event and your automatic emotional thoughts and the subsequent erratic behaviour that may be an automatic reaction for you. Hence the phrase, "pushing your buttons" about getting a reaction out of someone: it's like pushing a button for the elevator to come, and then the elevator automatically arrives. You do not want to be like an automatic elevator doing what it is told.

We can do the same thing with politicians, athletes, movie stars, business people, or journalists—anyone in the public eye. They are usually pushing our buttons or triggering us to get emotional because that's what they want us to do. When they make public statements on live TV or social media, the resulting emotions pull in viewers, readers, and followers. We may automatically react negatively when we hear a public figure make a pronouncement; we may label them, or automatically put them in one camp or another and be prepared to have an internal war with them. We start calling them an "idiot" or something worse. This is displaced emotional contagion, since the other person is not physically present in your immediate environment, but the person's appearance and voice via video triggers an emotional reaction, suggesting there is infectious emotional contagion. It is acceptable to be emotional, and you have a right to your emotions, but you also have a responsibility to ensure that your emotion is not aggravating some kind of internal war inside you. That is bad for your health, both physical and emotional. And if you carry these feelings into a discussion with others, then you may be contributing to the turmoil within society. It is not worth it. If you want to do it, be rational about it; point to behaviours that happen and the effects they may cause.

Handling fear and cynicism

Fear, panic, cynicism, anger, hate, and pessimism can dominate our reasoning when it comes to social and political events. Fear especially produces the fight, flight, or freeze syndrome, the "Triple F," which produces severely distorted, all-or-nothing thinking. This is emotionally contagious, tending to strengthen from person to person, especially when personal situations become involved. But the knowledge that emotional contagion comes from fear should cue us into thinking about what we are doing if we find ourselves becoming automatically fearful. We then need to reassess our reaction and rethink our positions on the topic being considered. Decide whether the fear is justified, rather than coming to an automatic conclusion based on the fear. Just thinking things through this way can lower the feeling of dread. The same thing can be done for the emotions of panic, cynicism, anger, hate, and pessimism.

If we feel cynical about a political, social, or economic issue, believing that bad things will happen, we need to stop and think rationally about how dangerous this issue really is, or whether it's even dangerous at all. Is it permanent? Is it part of a negative trend or does it stand alone? Using our gut feelings to answer these questions is unhelpful, since we know that the effects of fear can produce an irrational answer. There is a difference between saying that bad things will happen, and that some bad things could potentially happen, but only under certain conditions. Emotional thinking will give us the former statement, rational thinking the latter.

These feelings, especially fear, panic, anger, and hate, tend to be automatic. Cynicism and pessimism can be chronic, colouring a depressive personality. Fear needs to be based on facts instead, so we can rationally estimate whether danger exists—and if so, the probability of said danger actually occurring. It is important to not rely on our feeling of fear to provide us the answer. Instead, pause: consider what we have been told, put your immediate reaction on the back burner, and tell yourself that maybe there's another way to think about it (just to buy time to allow us to think about it some more). Pause for a few more seconds. Be skeptical about the fear; maybe it isn't as bad, or maybe it is, we aren't sure. Maybe it deserves anxiety, or concern, but not fear. Look at it from a different perspective. We aren't automatically saying the situation isn't bad and that you should dismiss the fear. We are assessing it and thinking about it for a few more moments, in a slower, more reasonable way, using Kahneman's System 2 instead of the fast, quick way of System 1.

We use skills from cognitive behavioural therapy, which can be adapted for use by everyone, not just people with mental health issues. Ask a few questions of yourself and others. "What is the evidence that things are as bad as we are feeling?" Remember that a feeling isn't evidence. Look for the facts, the perspective, the figures. Brainstorm, think outside the box, and find your own answer from more than one source. Ask different people for different ways to think about it. Maybe the evidence isn't there. If that is the case, let yourself change your thoughts about it to account for that aspect. Maybe you are exaggerating the danger. Maybe there should be just a caution. Remember that people have their own biases and histories and may have been hurt in their lives. They may be reacting based on that bias or hurt, so they may be emotional. If you have a hunch that this is the case, then take caution. Unless they can blend their emotion and thought into wisdom or take a fresh perspective from an emotional distance, then don't use that source. Make this a habit. This is your inoculation against emotional and social contagion.

A well-developed appraisal apparatus will help overcome fear. You can develop one. It is better to develop it so that it contains, and can be driven by, intuitive wisdom. This is the type of wisdom that has merged emotional experience with good judgment and rational thought relying on experience and knowledge of cause-and-effect. It is a matter of anticipating what could happen based on a combination of good intuitive sense and logical thinking rather than an automatic fear. Just because you feel fear doesn't mean that there is really something to be afraid of. Susan Jeffers, a psychologist and self-help author, wrote the best-selling book *Feel the Fear and Do It Anyway*. This will, in fact, help overcome that fear.

Having an inoculation against emotional and social contagion gives us the ability to moderate its impact. Unfortunately, if we react quickly without thinking, the consequential Triple F is triggered and strengthens our emotions. But this syndrome was developed to handle a wild animal chasing our ancestors in humankind's primitive days. It is not good at handling complex situations, so we have to combat the Triple F syndrome and its automatic reaction. Stop automatically catching emotions and using them exclusively to arrive at conclusions. Emotions don't think. This way we are inoculating ourselves against irrational feelings.

Rational thinking can overcome irrational, fearful thinking

Anxiety was strong in American society in the latter half of the 2010s, and at the start of the following decade. Most people are anxious about safety, health, and politics. Emotional contagion is playing an active role in spreading fear. It often obstructs rational thinking. Cognitive behavioural therapy can lower anxiety and depression by helping people think more effectively. Otherwise, emotions can infect peoples' thought processes and contaminate their ability to think rationally. Emotional thinking heightens and perpetuates the emotional domination of the cognitive processes.

Reality is likely not as scary as it seems based on the emotion being expressed. There is probably not acute fear, like if a terrorist were coming around the corner. But some people tell themselves that it's always possible, and so they raise their fear levels to protect themselves. They end up having anxiety in subtle, abstract ways. Anxiety rises, that is natural. Being emotional, and catching emotions by feeling empathic with victims, can cause others to be very worried about things going wrong, whether it's justified or not. This is emotional contagion. It raises fears where no actual cause for fear may exist. It can spill over into other issues, like relationships, finances, and health (even though they may not be logically related to the original fear). Just because you read about or hear about these issues doesn't mean they will happen to you.

Prevention of the spread of emotional contagion would lower anxiety in society and reduce its chances of spilling over into unrelated areas. It could be prevented by recognizing a heightened emotion, understanding that it is likely irrational and exaggerated and includes many cognitive distortions. One could deal with it by making a truly accurate statement using "I language": validating a true emotion with a statement in the first person beginning with "I." This validates the emotion because it is more accurate and personal, lowering the heightened aspect. Validating the emotion doesn't mean that there is an actual reason to be anxious; it means it is understandable that you feel anxious. This validation may settle the emotional contagion and leave you more open to rational discussion. Rational discussion makes the emotional part less strong and the cognitive part stronger.

To be rational, the individual needs to accept that some degree of fear is reasonable if the facts suggest it. Emotional thinking is akin to childlike thinking where fantasies are thought of as reality. We know how powerful this is from the abundance of superhero movies. In some people emotional thinking can override the power of their conscious mind when the emotions flow at the height of the moment. The fantasy of an elaborate web involving accomplices and terror groups is accepted as reality by the emotional mind. Conspiracy theories create a safe place for the person who feels vulnerable; they feel safer because it maintains their fantasy that one person could not overpower them. If they accepted that possibility in reality, even venturing outside could be scary. This is, again, not logical, so the executive, conscious part of the mind would realize this and overrule it, much as we deem our dreams fictional. But the emotional, fearful mind could overrule the logical mind in a weak or hectic moment when it feels our safety and survival are at stake. We need to ensure that the stakes are really that high, and that it is not just our anxiety telling us this. Otherwise, the anxiety has taken the brain right over.

Review interactions to see how to improve

Practise these methods of rational thinking by reviewing a recent interaction you had with someone when there was something meaningful taking place. When you practise, see the event in your mind like watching a video, one section after another. Pick an event that, although meaningful, wasn't too difficult an experience; you are just practicing how to do this. Practise with the easier situations first to get an idea of how to do it, and try the more difficult situation later.

Try and slow the event down in your mind and take these steps:

- See if you can feel the feelings the other person was expressing or exuding while they were speaking.
- Make sure you recall as best you can the scene, the room, the colour of the walls, any items that were visible, any sounds, the position of the other person, their posture, and so on. These details will help you recall what was going on.
- What do you sense the person was feeling?
- What did they seem to want?
- What were they doing?
- What did they say?
- How did they say it?
- Did they make any gestures?
- Did they hesitate? Were they fast or slow?
- Let the awareness come to you, slowly.
- Now ask yourself again: what might they have been feeling? You are not looking for a "right" answer, just hunches and awareness.
- What emotion do they seem to be exuding? Remember that the emotion they exude or emit is usually not conscious. You won't be perfect at it.

If it was a person making a persuasive speech, like a politician, then there are a few things to consider. Did the person seem to be expressing a lot of emotion in trying to convey a message stronger than their words? If so, then you know they are using emotion, consciously or subconsciously, as their primary way of communicating. If not, and their emotion was conveying a message that fit their words, then the emotion is a secondary way of communicating, used only for emphasis. That's what you want. If they seemed to be showing little or no emotion, then the person may not be personally invested in what they are saying and are going through the motions. In any of these cases, you may get a hunch of what was being expressed and can analyze how you responded to it.

Ask yourself some questions. You can't answer them all; this just gives you choices from which to choose two or three. This will prepare you to be aware of the emotion or feeling the other person is radiating or emanating next time.

- What were you feeling?
- What did you feel in your body? Any different than usual?
    (Look for vague changes. Sensations, awarenesses, hunches? It doesn't have to be definite or coming from a specific location in your body.)
- What was your posture? Were you leaning forward or backward?
    (Forward means you were receptive; backward means you were not receptive.)
- Did you like the message? Did you feel happier? Angrier? Bored?
- If you felt bored, did you understand the message? What did it say?
- Do you think you took in any ideas? If so, to what extent do you agree with the idea now?
- Do you think you absorbed any emotions?
- If so, did you want to accept that emotion? Let it come deeper?
- Why or why not?
- Do you think you might have picked up emotions that quickly triggered you to be emotional also?
- If so, was that okay?
- If it wasn't okay, how could you have had a different emotional reaction?
- Sometimes another person reacts according to their personal style and it affects you through contagious emotions. Was that the case here?

A fun and effective way to practise this analysis is to do this with movies, impromptu interviews, performances, speeches, presentations, or just watching other people interacting. Ask yourself these questions about the people you're watching. You likely won't be able to feel the feelings, but it lets you practise. It especially works well when you are the third person in an actual discussion where the other two talk more.

To stop automatically catching emotions, you have to be aware of the existence of the implicit or explicit emotions being expressed along with spoken words, and the power they have. It is easier to notice the phenomenon when someone is giving a speech or presentation because you are passive and not required to respond or take part. So you can notice voice inflections, gestures, the implicit and explicit emotions, and look for emotions that are being emitted. The speaker may be giving off emotions as they speak.

When you are in a one-on-one conversation with someone, it can be more difficult to notice these things, since it is difficult to attend to two things at once. We notice the stronger signs, but it is important to notice the moderate and milder ones also. It is important to try and notice some of these markers while conversing:

- Ask yourself whether this expressed emotion is attracting you to attend to the person, or their position on whatever they are talking about.
- Do you want that? You can't respond to something like an emotion with purpose or intention if you don't notice it being there. Otherwise, it has an automatic impact, just like the air circulating around you or the temperature in the building.
- When you notice it, and you will, be aware that this emotion is elusive: indefinable, harder to pin down.
- Don't worry about defining it. Just notice its presence once or twice. You can work at defining it later.
- How does it affect you?
- Does it make you want to agree, disagree, or does it have no effect?

It is better to only connect at first, instead of catching emotions from a person you hardly know. When feeling an emotional connection being made, you can still easily disconnect if the feelings become undesirable. You probably haven't absorbed the feelings yet. It is only a connection; it is not made through emotional contagion. But when the feelings are absorbed through emotional contagion, the ability to disconnect becomes more difficult because the emotion is already inside you. It may not be tough for all the different kinds of emotions caught through contagion, but it does involve some release from inside you, as opposed to shaking off negative emotions felt through only a tenuous connection. You should always reconnect if the relationship looks promising and you can catch the emotions the next time.

Overcoming Emotional Contagion: Interpersonal Boundaries and Interactional Components

To overcome negative emotional contagion, stay purposeful and alert.
Ask yourself questions, be curious about the person's behaviour.
Let emotions bounce off you as if you were a duck handling rainfall.
In this way, set emotional boundaries, strengthening your inner
self to allow only compatible feelings to enter. Be skeptical about
exaggerations from others. Use empathy while maintaining boundaries
between yourself and the other person. Don't give a lot of superficial
attention to the person expressing emotion, unless you fully attend
to and talk with them, since either (avoiding superficial attention or
fully attending) can prevent emotional contagion. Change your posture,
don't copy other people's postures or movements. Use opposite
emotions.

In addition to this book, articles by various authors give good recommendations on how to handle emotional contagion.

Stay purposeful

Sigal Barsade (2020b) recommends staying "alert and purposeful in both [...] words and actions" as you interact with others. This would apply to conversations with others as well as information you are taking in. Being aware of the phenomenon of emotional contagion and how it can affect you is important, as you do not want to let it affect you automatically. We need to manage and regulate emotions effectively when they come towards us from others, especially jealousy, hate, and anger. As Barsade points out, "If you're feeling incredibly anxious or fearful, ask yourself: Do you really have a reason to feel this way? Or is it your friends, your social media feeds, or news from non-expert sources that is leading you to feel that way?" Do you catch another person's emotions? You need to be able to handle them and know whether to absorb them or not depending on if its source is credible and knowledgeable. Is their information legitimate, and not exclusively something that just makes you feel good?

Look for the types of events, comments, or behaviours that are likely to trigger your emotional response. When others express emotions in an emotional state, this is your cue to not react automatically in an emotional manner. This applies just as much when watching politicians or speakers who are in an emotional state; don't have a quick emotional thought that agrees absolutely with what they say. That is the effect of emotional contagion.

Many people tend to react quickly and emotionally when others are emotional, especially if irritated or irate. Other people sometimes subconsciously want to get an emotional reaction from us. We are likely to be triggered, for example, when someone calls us a bad name, possibly referencing something that we are sensitive about. When that happens, that person is probably trying to get us aroused in an emotional way; they may be trying to make us vulnerable because then we are likely to respond emotionally. Instead, try to integrate your emotions and thoughts when responding. That's why it's important to be alert in words and actions. Recognize what is being done and think of it as possibly a subconscious strategy from the person. If the person had spoken in a softer, more respectful way, with a decent rhythm of the voice, and not too high or low pitched, we could trust that flow and go with it, after a brief appraisal.

When someone expresses, emits, or exudes a certain emotion, you can decide that you don't have to let that emotion strike you if you think it could be harmful. This is the job of the gatekeeper. If you think it may be harmful, then just say no, like a cop stopping traffic. You can hold your hand up in a stop motion (or just visualize yourself doing this if you are around others), or just say it under your breath. Perhaps you take a deep breath. It can be difficult to identify which emotion may be harmful, and it can also be difficult to block that emotion from striking you. It is not a simple step-by-step procedure. It takes time, work, and patience as you are learning it. If you are not sure, you can try one method the first time (stop the emotion or not), and the other the next time (unless you liked your first choice and it worked, then do it again). See what happens, and then just go with whatever direction the results take you.

Rempala (2013) supports the idea that emotional regulation strategies like these can have an impact on emotional contagion. This means that the implicit emotions we contain within ourselves must be managed and regulated so that we don't let ourselves become vulnerable to emotional contagion.

As soon as you realize that a destructive type of emotion is being emitted, like irritation or blame, then you realize that you need to block it from striking you—in the same way that you would block rain if you were wearing a raincoat. You need to wear a "psychological raincoat" to block the difficult emotions that land in drips and drops on you like rain. Or think of how a duck's feathers let rain bounce off them. Be like a duck in this way, let them bounce off. Anger is an easy one to identify, and so is fear. See the emotion as belonging to the person expressing it. Practice being objective, as you would by observing someone being verbally angry at another person.

There are other difficult ones to identify, like cynicism, pessimism, depression, panic, and hate, which are often involved in implicit emotion that is vulnerable to emotional contagion. They're not difficult to identify if you are objective, thinking in System 2 mind and observing from the outside like watching a movie. But they are difficult to identify if you are in the middle of the situation and in your subjective, System 1 mode. In that state you are not watching for the emotion, feeling, or even the mood; instead you are listening and responding to what is being said. You are following the words consciously, but the emotions and feelings have your subconscious attention.

You have to train yourself to always be shifting back and forth between the words and the accompanying emotions. You have to train yourself to be curious about why the person is acting the way they are, as the psychologist Lisa Feldman Barrett recommends (Barrett, 2017). This way you back up from the emotions and are able to observe and consider the person's actions, and what they are getting from their tactics. Use your curious mind to figure them out. Without this process, you are just reacting from the emotional part of yourself and judging the person. Keep an open mind. You pay attention to the words, but then you realize that the person speaking may be pessimistic, or hateful, or any number of negative qualities. Using your rational mind, you are curious about why this person has that strong emotion instead of just being frustrated or annoyed. It is difficult because you have to stay in the moment to take part in the conversation, but every now and then you need to back up and observe for a few seconds: what feelings is the person expressing, and what is carrying their true message: their words or their emotions.

Setting your emotional boundaries

Resisting the influence of emotional contagion involves setting emotional boundaries and fostering emotional independence. It also means developing and strengthening your own responsibility. You are in charge of yourself; you are the author of your own thoughts and feelings. You are responsible for them. They have an impact on you, so you have to develop them in a way that is best for you, giving you your best chance to be your true self while still being responsible to yourself. This means learning to regulate the emotions inside yourself: give yourself the emotions that best fit you, your personality, and your beliefs. It also means managing your thoughts, preventing "hot" thoughts that trigger hot emotions—like thinking of someone as an "idiot."

To give yourself these true emotions, you have to set emotional boundaries that foster your emotional independence (meaning you don't take on someone else's feelings or style if they don't fit). You define who you are and what feelings fit you best in order to convey the kind of person you truly are inside. When you do this, then you will absorb only those feelings that accentuate you, ones that will not create new feelings within you that are foreign and ill-fitting. Instead, you only allow feelings to enter you if they add to whatever is already inside you, to enhance and highlight who you already are.

Setting emotional boundaries means preparing your gatekeeper to evaluate incoming emotions before allowing them in and deciding whether to keep them at surface level or let them come in deeper. Being aware of incoming emotions helps you get some control of them. If you suspect the emotion is too negative and not good to absorb, be wary about taking it in. We are not talking about the words. We are talking about the emotion, whether implicit or explicit, that accompanies the words. It may be harmful or toxic to you. If you don't want to accept a message spoken in an emotional way, then look at the emotion just as a person's style for getting the message through. Just recognize the emotion as being there, like an advertisement with a lot of bright colours, not as the main message. See the emotion as just an attention-grabber; try and ignore it, and definitely don't take any message from it. Don't let the person's emotion trigger you to accept the message. If you can, look at the message in print and then see if you agree with it. Try and figure out what makes the person sending the message have this emotion that they are showing. A reaction to emotional behaviour is often an automatic one. It won't be automatic if you are aware of it and decide not to react to the emotion the other person is expressing. If the other person is speaking to you loudly, that doesn't really mean their message is any more valid. The person is usually using volume to make it seem that way. If you maintain a calm emotional exposure, you are not getting triggered by the emotional behaviour.

Think about it this way. When you buy a car, do you check out the mechanics, the specifications? Do you take it for a test drive? Or do you just buy it because of the commercials? Do you listen to the emotions expressed in the advertisement? Maybe you do. The emotions expressed are conveying a message. We are moved to accept the message that goes with it based on the emotion, without really evaluating the content of the message. as long as the words seem good. That is ineffective, incomplete thinking, and subject to emotional contagion. You have to evaluate the fact of the message, as if they were in print. The emotions expressed in a message can be very powerful—more so than the actual words—as long as the words sound right. They make you feel good. But really, should you buy that car and not take a test drive, listen to and look at the motor? If you do it with a car, you can do it with persuasive messages from people.

It is the same in political messages. Sounding good isn't enough. They have to actually be correct and precise, otherwise we are accepting something as correct without really knowing if it is. We don't want to accept a comment like, "This is the best car ever made," or, "I am really the best person to do this job" as correct simply because it was spoken by an emotional person who uses hyperbole like "the best." It may feel good and be alright to say it socially; we know the speaker feels good about it, but we don't take their words literally. Do we really know what it takes for a car or person to be "the best"? There is no real way to measure "best" since there are no objective measurements to prove it. So if a politician says, "I am your voice"—do we really believe him? Or is he taking over our voice, leaving us without one?

Emotional independence means having awareness of who you are inside yourself: what feelings you like and enjoy, and what feelings you do not like or enjoy. This develops emotional awareness. You would not want to welcome in a feeling that you would not enjoy. Sometimes a chronically upset stomach can mean you are allowing them in. If, however, you are met by a feeling that is very close in quality to a feeling that you already have inside of you, perhaps bigger or better, then you would probably want to allow that feeling in to strengthen the one that you already have inside you. Because it has the quality that you already have, and it just may be a bit stronger in its feel, so it blends in very well. It enhances you and forms a bit of a defence against other feelings that are more foreign to you. You would not then allow a foreign contagious feeling inside you because you are building resistance to it. Why would you want to take it in if it is foreign to you? If you want to improve yourself, that's fine, but you do so by improving the quality you already have inside you. Because that is what makes you, you. Qualities are permanent; they do not change. You cannot add a different quality, it won't take. It won't feel right.

Using mimicry to "feel yourself" into the person's state

Elaine Hatfield, the originator of the emotional contagion concept, suggests that "if people pay careful attention to the emotions they experience in the company of others, they may well gain an extra edge into 'feeling themselves' "into the emotional states of others"(Hatfield et al., 2003). By using mimicry, people can "feel themselves" into the emotional states of others, as she suggests, or insert themselves emotionally into the other's emotions without them knowing it. This is a form of empathy. This way, as long as you keep an "as if" quality to maintain emotional independence, you can predict what might come next and prepare yourself to handle it. This is difficult to do, but it gives you an advantage over the other person. You get predictability and hence are unlikely to absorb contagious emotions. However, if the other person is aggressive and dominant, you have to be very careful when you do this so as not to pick up their feelings and mimic their aggression to your detriment. We talk about avoiding mimicry in such situations in the next chapter.

To resist the influence of emotional contagion, see the emotional expression as belonging to that person only. That other person is not you. The way you see it will determine whether you absorb it or not. In other words, although the emotion may be expressed in a strong way, possibly loudly with emotional words, it is not yours unless you want to take it. And that would be a decision to make after an appraisal. If it seems like it is a cousin to your own feeling, then it probably has the same quality. It will feel right and then you can take it in. That is not truly emotional contagion because contagion suggests that the other emotion does not really belong inside you, that it is infectious and could harm you. Think of it as belonging to the person expressing it. That doesn't mean you don't like it at all; it just means it isn't you, so you rebuff it. Your gatekeeper can think these thoughts to block the contagion. When you build this resistance inside yourself, you build your gatekeeper. You do not present a warm welcome to this contagious feeling and are already setting the stage to repel it.

As resisting negative emotional contagion gradually becomes more habitual, you may need to take a few seconds to respond to an emotional comment. That's okay. Those old sayings of counting to ten or putting your brain in gear before opening your mouth are like gold. Thinking about what to say (or whether to say anything at all) in order to refrain from using someone's implicit emotion as a basis for a response is wise. By responding first from an analytical or logical position instead of an emotional place within you, you are doing your part to interrupt the chain of emotional contagion. This gives you time to appraise the emotion.

You are developing emotional awareness, becoming aware of how and why emotions are expressed. You are developing resistance to emotional impact and building resilience, while at the same time fostering your social responsibility.

Don't attend to the person and change the topic

Barsade developed some strategies to combat emotional contagion. Extrapolating from her suggestions we see that an obvious way to handle it is to not attend to the event or person producing emotional contagion. Her research, as cited in Dahl's article (2015), has shown that emotional contagion "relies a lot on attention." We have discussed how people who exude contagious emotion seem to attract other people to them. The emotion fools you into thinking that you want it or need it. But you will appraise it yourself to determine that. If it is positive, of course you attend to it. But otherwise, avoid it: don't look at the person, don't listen to the voice, and, as Barsade suggests in the article, "try not to even let this person cross your line of vision." Rather than focus on people who are negative, walk away. It is like an addiction when we seek out a negative person to absorb their emotion. Don't let that negative emotion come to you. Why would you want it? It may feel familiar, but turn away, change the topic. Familiarity is not a reason to participate. Even turning sideways will help so that it doesn't come full force onto you. Don't listen to it, just let it bounce off your ears; it's just noise. Changing your behaviour is crucial because you are not reinforcing the tendency you have had to attend to this negative emotion. Don't see that person as much if they are always negative. You have to change something within yourself to actually avoid it and just walk away. Now you are not feeding that part of you that seems to need it.

If this is a friend or relative, and you can't walk away in the moment, you can change the topic. Make sure you avoid eye contact, get up, and walk around. You could always walk away later. Sometimes it takes courage and determination. Remember to ask yourself what is going on with you that makes you want it. What is there about that negative emotion that attracts you to it? Is it criticism, abuse, loud noise?

Think of how this may pertain to someone in your life. Does it represent something to you? Does it remind you of someone who tried to give you some affection but ended up yelling or criticizing you? At a time when you really needed affection? Is it affection you are looking for? Then you will have to work on that issue.

Use an opposite emotion

Another method Barsade suggests is to counterattack negative emotion with an opposite contagious emotion, a positive one of calm serenity. Take a deep breath, do some quick mindfulness meditation, quote the serenity prayer, visualize something from nature, pet your cat or dog, or just distract yourself by looking at something interesting or pleasing in the room—anything that suggests something more positive than the negative emotion being expressed. Speak calmly and smile pleasantly. You are not so much trying to convince the other person not to express the contagious emotions as you are giving yourself a different, opposite emotion to feel inside. Remember that you are responsible for your own feelings. It overrides the contagious emotion you might otherwise take in. If you are in an audience, you can give yourself an opposing emotion to feel by using imagery to conjure it up. Think of a joke, a favourite song or a nice flower. Even if the real thing isn't there, it can help override or minimize the emotional contagion.

Active listening reduces emotional contagion

Active listening is a psychotherapeutic technique which can be adapted to everyday life communication. It involves listening fairly intently to what the other person is saying in order to grasp and understand the full meaning of their statement. The APA (n.d.) says, in a psychotherapeutic setting, the person "listens to a client closely, asking questions as needed, in order to fully understand the content of the message and the depth of the client's emotion." Listening to a person as an individual, fully attending to them in the present moment, and the emotion in their message, and subconsciously assessing how that emotion and message fits with the personality of the individual, is, interestingly enough, a way to prevent emotional contagion from affecting you. If you fully understand the individual and the message you are not likely to absorb the emotion in a contagious kind of way. In doing so you are getting a fuller sense of the individual, allowing you to appraise them and what seems to motivate them to make the statement they are making, and express the emotion they are expressing. This, in turn, gives you a few moments to decide if you want to absorb the emotion, because, in a sense, you have decided whether it is something that fits with you, your style and how you see things, or not. Then, if so, you can absorb the emotion they are expressing or emitting. In other words, it is your gatekeeper appraising the individual as you listen. You may decide that you only want to connect for a few brief moments with the individual and their emotion, because they don't fit your style, hence not catching and absorbing their emotion.

"Listening can transform your understanding of the people and the world around you, which inevitably enriches and elevates your experience and existence," says Kate Murphy (2019), a journalist who wrote a comprehensive book on listening. She says that "our collective listening, or the lack thereof, profoundly affects us politically, societally and culturally." Listening directs us to what feelings and emotions to absorb. How we listen to a leader affects us—do we listen skeptically, critically, or with automatic adoration, just absorbing it all? As we listen, do we imagine ourselves questioning this person as if we were conversing with them?

When we listen to a person we are speaking with, you "guide" them to a certain area of conversation without them knowing you are guiding. You communicate this to the person by virtue of selective active listening, responding more to things they say that are positive and less to those that are negative. In turn, this person may feel more positive about themselves.

Active listening can prevent emotional contagion. If you really listen to the speaker and try to understand where they're coming from, what their needs are, what they are truly feeling, what they may be missing in life, and why they express themselves in the way they do, then you would be less likely to end up infected by their emotions. Even if you just get a sense of these aspects, you will know the person a little more and be able to evaluate what that emotion was all about. You would be less likely to absorb it automatically, and more likely to use cognitive appraisal. Then you could make the decisions to absorb it or not, as you have appraised its safety and value and whether it is likely to enhance your emotional wellbeing.

It works both ways. Murphy also points out that when people don't listen to others, as in not hearing what they have to say and not caring to understand it, then the people who are not listened to feel cut off, lonely, ignored, or alienated. They have a deep need for a positive emotional experience that comes from someone else, one that could be filled if their peer practised active listening. When they are left unfulfilled, which sadly often happens, they become like a sponge: absorbing emotion and feelings from others indiscriminately to compensate for what they don't receive elsewhere in life. They can then be susceptible to emotional contagion, liable to be infected by toxic emotions. Part of the solution then would be to try active listening; and engage with them so that they don't feel cut off (Indeed Editorial Team, 2021). This does not mean you agree with them, but it does mean you understand deeply what they are saying. People will then be more likely to listen to you when you are the speaker. They will respect you. You can also be clearer and more assertive, using good eye contact and other interpersonal speaking skills to connect with the listener emotionally. That way they won't feel alienated, needing to pull in and absorb feelings from others, prompting more emotional contagion.

Overcoming Emotional Contagion: Dealing with Hate, Prejudice, and Various Situations

Overcoming hate, prejudice, and other contagious negative emotions is possible. Understanding someone tells you if it is alright to absorb their emotions. If a person expresses hate, assess if they are just troubled or whether they value being hateful. When you hate someone it kills you emotionally and can kill you physically through cardiac issues, so change it to dislike. Some people with these issues may lack emotional affection internally. Don't commiserate. They may have personality quirks that mean you could let their emotions bounce off you. Avoid people who value being hateful, as well as eye contact if you are anxious around them. Move your body in a different way. Use rational language, keep calm, talk lowly and firmly to an aggressive or negative person, detach yourself from the situation emotionally by viewing the other person in an objective way.

Prejudice and hate usually are aimed at people based on superficial qualities like skin colour or religion. It is important to remember not to judge a book by its cover. You must assess your reactions. That's why most people test drive a new car: to test how well it suits them. Why not "test drive" a person? When difficult emotions like hate and disdain infect us, we have to deal with them by lowering the severity of the feelings.

Dealing with hate with cognitive and emotional empathy

You don't know what the emotion really represents unless you know where it comes from. You may understand why someone hates someone else, but you probably don't think that it is right. To understand it is not to agree with it, or to approve of their feelings. But you recognize what makes them feel and act a certain way. When you understand someone, it automatically gives you a wise gatekeeper that tells you whether or not to absorb the emotions they emit. This gives you an intact emotional boundary. If their hate is dystonic, meaning they don't identify with being hateful and do not want to hate, this may help you deal with it more effectively and permit you to continue interacting with that person. But if their hate is syntonic, meaning they want to hate and they value it, then after you do your appraisal, you may want to limit or end your interaction with that person.

Just because you reject their words or feelings doesn't mean you reject the person. You probably wouldn't want to absorb hateful or even angry and distrustful feelings just because a person had an emotionally dysfunctional upbringing. That person likely emits their feelings subconsciously as they are talking to you. Don't even connect with them emotionally. Just let them come to ear level; don't take them inside or you'll begin to feel the same way. Treat them the way you treat the dodge ball: let it bounce off you. They may have little personal awareness and are unaware of what they are doing.

To handle these situations, you can use cognitive empathy, as Bloom (2016) describes, instead of emotional empathy. Chris Thomas (2013) describes emotional empathy as "our automatic drive to respond appropriately to another's emotions," which occurs if you are not using the "as if" quality. He says, "this kind of empathy happens automatically, and often unconsciously." It is "the subjective state resulting from emotional contagion." You are perhaps sharing and absorbing another's feelings simultaneously, which leads to emotional contagion. To prevent that, you could use emotional empathy, and balance it out with cognitive empathy. Emotional empathy is more genuine and likely to connect with the other person emotionally, and cognitive empathy is taking another perspective intellectually, "a largely conscious drive to recognize accurately and understand another's emotional state" Thomas says.

In cognitive empathy, you "stay in their head" with their ideas and do not connect emotionally. You do this at a cerebral, analytical level—involved, but not with your heart or gut, which is emotional empathy. You think logically and objectively about what the best thing is to say so that you do not get drawn into absorbing their feelings and become overpowered by them. It is best to not respond to their emotional behaviour: don't mimic their behaviour, don't attend to whatever their feeling is. Make sure when you reply that you do not use the same tone, rhythm, words, or style as the other person. To do so would be mimicking them and would likely draw their feelings into yourself. If the other person calls Martians "stupid," you could say something describing their negative actions, without a label,[27] indicating the problematic behaviour the other person or group has done or said could be seen as troubling. This will give you some emotional distance from their inner hateful emotion but allow you to see some things intellectually from their perspective and prevent a conflict. If they keep on insisting they are "stupid," you can agree to disagree with that person about the label, and refer to some possibly harmful things they have done, if you agree. Remember there is always an ounce of truth in what someone says, and they want recognition for that.

Dealing with your own feelings of hate

It is good to work on letting go of any hatred you feel inside yourself. Remember that we often feel inclined to move to an opposite emotion if we want to enact change. You don't have to, and you shouldn't. Letting go of hate doesn't mean you have to like the hated person or approve of their behaviour. You can change hate to dislike, even a strong dislike. That is easier to do. When we feel hate in ourselves and start to work on eliminating it, it will free us up to live a better life. It allows us to enjoy beauty and love again. Hate is a more common experience than we think. At some time in our lives, we probably hated someone. We may have forgotten or repressed it because we didn't want to admit that we used to hate someone.

If we got over the old hate, we can do the same for a new one, even if it is politically focused. Overcoming hate doesn't mean you are letting the person win, or that you are giving in. Sometimes hate gives you a false feeling of power, and it is hard to give that up. Hate may make you think you have power when you really don't. Steve Andreas (Andreas, n.d.) points out that "everyone has had an experience of hating someone and later somehow finding a comfortable resolution, but we often don't realize that we've done that." You do that as time goes by and something better replaces it. He says that "experience [...] holds the unconscious key to changing a present hate in a useful way."

It is not possible to "just let go" of hate, since there must be something reinforcing about holding a feeling of hate—likely that feeling of power

---

27 As before, we do not want to name actual groups that xenophobic individuals could be triggered by, but are naming a fictitious group to stay neutral.

and revenge and a desire to get even, to get control, and to recover power. Andreas says if we "find a memory in which [we've] already succeeded in unconsciously resolving hate," it will help. Most of us have done that earlier in life, moving on from a hated rival in adolescence. If you picture the current target of your hate, you probably have a clear image of that person in your mind. Now look at a mental image of another person you used to hate. That image is probably not as clear. It may be foggy or muted. Make the image of the person you have recently felt hate for foggy and muted like the older memory. That is okay; it doesn't give the other person power. You still dislike that person or their opinion. Andreas says that the sensory images of the person are important; if you reduce them so they are smaller, foggier, and subdued, your unconscious will take care of the rest. You are giving permission for the unconscious to do so when you create the image in your mind. Some people even create a small cartoon image of that person in a picture in their mind which can help you move along in this process.

You will also need to tell your unconscious the reasons why you are letting go of the hate. The reason is probably because that hate is killing you inside, and you don't want to let the person you hate get back at you internally that way, by carrying around that lethal feeling of repressed hostility and cynicism. That can literally kill you later in life through cardiac issues. Hate wears you down and eats away at you. You suffer. It blocks out your ability to be free inside to love someone. That way the hated person wins even if you haven't seen them for a long time.

Dealing with prejudice

One of the reasons that we have emotional contagion is because people who have been alienated earlier in life have a strong need for other people's feelings and affections. It runs so deep that they absorb other's feelings unconsciously and automatically. They may not even stop to consider the actual intended message; they want the feeling that comes with it so much they pull in all the implicit emotion. Some relate with the emotion so strongly that they take in the associated message by default, even though they may not really agree with it. But the message may be one that is negative and filled with prejudice: racism, misogyny, or xenophobia. They take it in because it makes them feel better to be part of a group (even if that group is racist). They like to belong and feel emotional validation.

What seems to happen is that some people express emotions as a kind of subconscious appeal for emotional affection or validation. This does not justify their racist or prejudicial behaviour in a logical way, but it does help understand their inner psychological makeup. This is important because if we listen to their inner needs and validate them, if we recognize them and their possible internal strengths, then they are less likely to exude the types of emotions that are contagious. We are less likely to accept their contagious feelings because we know intrinsically that what they need is emotional acceptance as an individual, not acceptance of their apparent racist, misogynistic, or xenophobic beliefs.

They will deny this if confronted with it, and that will likely alienate them even more, so it is best to keep this in mind and speak to them in a way that has a qualifying attitude, as opposed to an absolute attitude.

When racist white people meet a person of colour, they are often surprised to find them likeable and pleasant, smart, and enjoyable. They have already put the person into a negative group because there is a lot of distance between them. They judged them negatively because it made them feel better about the respect they receive from the racist group to which they belong. They may have been approved of by their racist group at a time when they felt lonely, ignored, and inadequate. They got approval for agreeing with intolerant sentiment, which they perhaps did to be liked and accepted. They mimic the message giver, whom they admired because they feel heard and understood. They start to emit contagious emotions themselves. The negative message they agreed with came along with the emotion and was accepted without being understood. They didn't think it through and are now surprised when the truth is the opposite: that people of colour are, in fact, good people. If they can't comprehend that, it becomes cognitive dissonance, which causes anxiety.

It seems that some of these prejudiced people will at times subconsciously exude contagious emotions to like-minded people in a way that will automatically give them the validation they seek. They appear to never really have been appreciated as an individual emotionally.[28] Many

---

28 No comment in this book, including this comment, provides an excuse for racism or other prejudice, or any dysfunctional emotional contagion, nor do they seek to absolve or justify this attitude. It is an attempt to understand and explain the underlying factors behind the attitude to help make change happen.

people feel alienated and emotionally alone. Rather than holding back, some will exude emotions in an attempt to connect. But they do so impersonally, like to an audience. Not succeeding in individual attempts, feeling lonely and alienated but wanting emotional attention anyway, they may give talks to an audience or lead a group from whom they can absorb the emotional adoration. This seems to happen automatically, without them thinking about whether this is a good thing to do. They may not have been listened to enough in their life, so that they haven't really been validated by others, as Kate Murphy (2019) says. In this case no one has really taken a true interest in who they are, what they like, and what they are doing. They were never truly known and accepted unconditionally as a youngster.

Possibly having been deprived of emotional affection as a child, they are short of the internal emotion people need to keep them substantial, strong, and viable. Many such individuals would deny this as an adult because they think they are strong inside. But that may be a strength of principles gained from other sources such as through the military, or even strength from an external source, like money or guns. It's not an internal strength that stands on its own. They may be compensating as a defence against the shortage they feel inside. They may express more emotion than the average person who is better adjusted emotionally. They seem to do this because they unconsciously want emotional validation in return.

Their beliefs exist apart from their existence. A person's beliefs do not define them as a viable, functioning individual. They may be an intrinsic part of them, but we have to remember that when a human being is gravely ill, we empathize with them. We appreciate their value, and if we talk to them we will probably appreciate various memories together—none of which relate to their beliefs, but which may relate to empathy for their struggle, or common interests. That's why baseball, golf, and music are so important. They, like other popular interests, unite us—not politics.

Usually when an idea that is generally accepted only as irrational and controversial (such as conspiracy theories) appeals to someone, there is an ounce of truth in the idea that the person wants acknowledged. But their emotional needs take over their thinking and they exaggerate the idea into something greater than reality. We get caught up in counter-contagion when we angrily refute it.

When we listen to them and validate small, specific truths in their beliefs, then we are really blocking and derailing the strong, contagious emotions, while at the same time validating them and their personal need for recognition and appreciation. This way they feel listened to and respected. That's all they seem to want. If we let anger and contempt get in the way of these feelings and seek revenge, we are letting negative emotional contagion affect us. Validation does not mean that we have to agree with their points, it just means that we have to confirm their points as interesting and possibly meaningful. Sometimes validation may come if we include milder or smaller parts of their positions in our feedback to make it truly valid, and accept that ounce of truth. If we accept the ounce of truth, it will probably make a large difference. All the person wants is respect and empathy. They may not insist on the rest of the ounces in the pound being accepted.

Others may feel that by doing this, we are reinforcing them and making things worse. That may be the case for a few of the rebels, and those are the ones that need to be separated, isolated, and punished by law enforcement if they break laws. They are more likely to be true anti-social personalities or psychopathic individuals as compared to the majority of the rebels who are protesting socio-political causes. This does not mean we are saying their socio-political causes are invalid and reducing it to a psychological problem. Many of the causes are valid. They are so used to rejection, sadly, that they may perceive this to be the case when it is not. There is always truth and merit in a socio-political protest, but the time and place may not always be right. People were once ridiculed for advocating that women should vote. By listening to people and accepting their ideas as having some degree of merit, society eventually arrived at the right conclusion. Listening gives them the respect they are looking for and reduces the chance that their implicit or expressed emotions will be contagious.[29] Make this a non-judgmental approach; it is negative judgment and disrespect that they react to. In this way you are avoiding emotional contagion: refusing to argue with the person when they are expressing emotional needs. People are really looking for respect not for

---

29 I am attempting to remain neutral in this book. As an example, consider the Hollow Earth Society, where some people have theories that the Earth is hollow. Even though this is false, we would not argue with them, to avoid the emotionality, and would say that would be an interesting possibility, because many people do not explore the inside of the planet and are more interested in outer space. They probably feel alienated in life, and this puts the person, and not their idea, first.

their idea, but for themselves emotionally. Many people are unaware of this unconscious need and stick with their conscious idea, but by addressing the unconscious need for respect the contagious effect is turned back. Avoid calling it that because people may feel you are dismissing their idea.

Essentially, emotional contagion can be minimized by instilling a healthy mixture of emotional and cognitive empathy; listen to and understand people who express emotional contagion.

Personality quirks allow us to overlook emotional comments

One way to be objective is to imagine that the other person has a little quirk in their brain, like a mini-stroke or something that affects the way they think or act or show emotions. In nursing homes or psychiatric wards there are, sadly, people who have poor memories or distorted perceptions. They confuse one person with another and never realize their mistake because of their illness or brain damage. If you have ever visited one of those places, you may have passed by a patient standing in the hallway who thought that you were their son or daughter, their neighbour, or a famous athlete or movie star, when in fact you are an unrelated stranger and have never been famous.[30] If one of these people became angry with you because they thought you were the baseball player who cost the Boston Red Sox the World Series title in 1986 by making an error in an important game,[31] would you start to feel guilty about making that error, or get angry with the other person for picking on you or mixing you up with a famous baseball player? Why not? Your answer to this question could give you some clues as to what your thoughts should be about how to handle other people. Your answer was probably that it doesn't apply to you so you don't need to be upset; that you see it as an unfortunate mental health or cognitive problem in the other person that you could be compassionate about. You would probably realize that the person's illness sadly caused them to lose their judgment and say these unfortunate things. You would realize that it was not their true opinion, and that they would not have said it if they had been in their right mind. You ignore it, do not take it personally and so do not absorb their emotion.

Think along these lines when dealing with a difficult person. They do not have a mental illness or brain damage, but think of them as having

---

30 When visiting my elderly father in a nursing home, another resident I didn't know thought I was a famous movie star.

31 Apologies to Boston Red Sox player Bill Buckner, who made this famous error.

some sort of quirk. They are similar things. Difficult people may have an idiosyncrasy that could be from a minor abnormality and is beyond their voluntary control. Maybe they experienced trauma a long time ago and it affects them unconsciously. Maybe they have mild brain damage or a touch of dementia; some people do and still function alright. Knowing this could stop you from getting angry or defensive; this is more likely to happen if you absorb a contagious emotion from a person in their "right" mind. Maybe they have controversial opinions; maybe they are critical or dominating and it's affecting you to the point that you are taking on related feelings. Maybe you are thinking that the person might be right because it sounds good on the surface; sometimes simple people are strong with their opinions because they don't appreciate the complexities or subtleties of an issue. This is not a knock or criticism against them, but they may have a personality quirk.

Regard their personality quirk as having maybe been caused by a small tumour or a mini-stroke that makes them do or say these things. Their quirk is probably not caused by these things, but a quirk probably exists somewhere in their mind, cause unknown, so you don't have to take their words literally. It is just them being them. This will give you good motivation to not automatically absorb their comments and their feelings. They may, however, have a minor point; you could say that and then think about it later. Buying time like this also prevents emotional contagion. When talking with them, you could change the subject, respond vaguely, or even answer assertively. Do this without being angry. Perhaps gently give them examples of how they are wrong. You will still interact with them but do so without letting it affect you so much. You might end up being a bit sad, but you will not feel angry about their comments.

Stopping mimicry

When another person seems dominant or forceful, some people on the receiving end can take on similar characteristics themselves, or even opposite characteristics, through emotional or social contagion, or counter-contagion. To overcome the effect of emotional contagion, you need to examine it. Emotional contagion happens through mimicry. To block the emotional contagion in these situations, make sure you don't subconsciously mimic the other person's style, posture, or phrasing. The dominant person's emotion can be quite powerful, so tell yourself: "I don't want the strength of that emotion." Without these proactive methods, the contagion can have the effect of captivating you, and if you absorb the emotion you will be more easily persuaded by this person to agree with their ideas because a message tags along with the emotion. If you start to feel the same emotion they do, or possibly an exact opposite emotion, then the emotional contagion has had an impact.

For example, a dominant person may want the recipient to be submissive and fearful, which is opposite. Or they may want the recipient to prevail over others, which is dominant, while remaining subservient to them. If you find yourself treating your friends in a way that is not your style, but rather the style of this person, that is a sign that you have taken on the other person's emotional style due to emotional contagion. You may also unwittingly take on their message as a tag-along. If so, you need to change the way you are interacting. If you find yourself being fearful, anxious, and afraid when you are around this person, that is another signal to change the way you are interacting or behaving around this person. Consider not being around this person as often.

To avoid mimicking them and to resist this emotional contagion, move your body in a different way from the dominant person. When you interact with them, move your body so that it is not obvious to the dominant person. Moving your body in a manner opposite to the other person, purposely not mimicking them, will thwart emotional contagion and make it easier to have your own feeling instead of the other person's.

This can also be true when this person is on stage or making a speech. Sitting mesmerized, watching and listening to the person will open you to emotional contagion, but moving around, assuming different positions in your chair, and avoiding eye contact will minimize this. This is important in cases when the speaker may be using emotional contagion to push disagreeable opinions on the audience. Watch out for automatic mimicry and prevent yourself from engaging even in small ways. The advantage is that you will start to feel more independent and less influenced by the other person. Ensuring that you are actually agreeing with the spoken words, not the attached emotion, is also important.

Using rational language and recognizing emotion

Rational language allows you to be more objective with others and get some psychological distance from them. It will deter emotional contagion from being received. Otherwise you could be smothered or enmeshed, pulled in too close to the negative person when it is not good for you. This can come from using too much emotional language. For example, thinking or saying the other person is *vicious* brings you closer to the aggressive person emotionally in a negative way; you feel very afraid of her, whereas if you used a more objective word like *dysfunctional* to describe their behaviour, it creates some emotional distance between you. The term *vicious* brings out an emotional reaction of fear. If the other person has actually been vicious, it is best to describe the behaviour, such as "they beat someone up...," in a way that fits the definition of vicious. Be literal and avoid exaggeration. A plain description is more objective and less likely to attract contagion. If the person has not committed such an act, then the word *vicious* should not be used. Remember that the feeling does not make the description correct. A more objective word is better, like *dysfunctional*, or perhaps *dominant*, again describing the other person's actions. This can be done through self-talk as well as by describing others' characteristics. Using emotional words opens the channels, encouraging emotions to be absorbed. If you want to accept someone's emotions, just use emotional language.

Another way to avoid emotional contagion is to recognize the other person's emotions and acknowledge their origin. Recognize the dominant person's emotion and that it originated in this other person because that person has a need for it. It belongs with them, not you. See it objectively. One of the needs that person has is to influence you; they need to have power, which they enjoy, and they are using emotion to influence and dominate you. This is subconscious and they are likely not aware of this. This emotion has developed in an emotional-behaviour pattern in the person's life because the emotion has likely helped them influence others who were unaware of it. See this other emotion as separate from you. It is not yours. You do not have to absorb it, nor do you have to let the other person influence you with it. When you move differently and avoid mimicking their movements, you will likely discover other feelings and emotions inside yourself that are true to you and not a result of emotional contagion.

"Keep Calm and Tame Lions"

You can use the lion tamer's methods to help deal with an aggressive person. The lion tamer never fights with the lion, they would lose; they are calm around the lion but still in charge. As that person is talking in a loud, emotional way, tell yourself that you don't have to react to their loudness or their emotionality. Keep on being you. Keep calm and talk softly but firmly. Remaining calm is key to overcoming emotional contagion because the other person subconsciously wants you to get worked up, just like lions do. If you are worked up, you get emotional and irrational, and that gives the other person an advantage. It may not make sense intuitively but remember that calmness gives you control; being calm allows you to think. Secretly within themselves the other person likes being relaxed—as we all do, even if we don't realize or acknowledge it. They may then let their guard down and trust you, as the lion trusts the lion tamer.

Understand the importance of the aggressive person's inner psychology. That other person may be loud, emotional, or aggressive—but why? The aggressive person may actually be fearful, so they try and become powerful to compensate. Accepting them, but not their behaviour, will help. Their behaviour is just bluster, like a gust of wind, trying to be powerful. That person behaves this way for some reason they are not telling you about. Look beyond the behaviour you see and try figure out what is driving them to be that way. When they are loud, overpowering, and dominating, you know that in reality they are probably afraid of you. Why else would they try to be overpowering? It is a defence. Demonstrate that you are not dangerous, that they have nothing to fear. That's what lion tamers do.

These methods are not foolproof and are not guaranteed to work, especially if the other person is mentally ill or psychotic or paranoid, and if they are in front of you, interacting with you personally, and not in touch with basic reality.

Detachment and disconnection reduce emotional contagion

Another way to reduce emotional contagion may be to purposely use a mild form of detachment from an emotional situation. This is another form of calmness, although detachment is different; calmness still involves some attachment. An experiment by Rempala (2013) found that dissociation worked in lowering emotional contagion when people were watching videos of happy or sad people. In a lab experiment, people were asked to remain detached while watching videos of people interacting. They were told to imagine themselves sitting in a movie theatre. They pictured all the components as though they were an outside observer. This is a way you can detach yourself from a situation. When the study participants did this, they didn't absorb as much emotion. When you go to a scary movie, sit back and observe, imagining the crew making the movie, how the actors have that makeup applied, and how the director creates the scary effects. Remain detached and know you are safe in your seat. It is an intellectual approach which distances you emotionally.

Rempala's experiment was in in a lab, and it is awkward to do in real life because if you try it, you may find that you are automatically distancing yourself from life in general. Only use it in specific situations, like dealing with dominant people who use emotional force. Do it by seeing the situation objectively, as if you were an outsider. In a way, the experiment was saying that as you see things happening and listen to people talking, you can distance yourself from your emotions by telling yourself to pretend that this is a movie. The trick is to be detached emotionally but stay alert cognitively. Or it could be like playing a game of chess where you are detached emotionally but present cognitively and intellectually, strategizing your next move, and knowing that anxiety would impede your ability to think clearly. Just pay attention to the words and ignore the rest.

The goal is to disconnect yourself from the emotion in the scene but stay alert cognitively so you can use these strategies. You could also ignore your previous knowledge and experience with that person just during this exercise. Instead, you could be objective by using the beginner's mind approach (Buggy, 2020). This calls for you to pretend you are seeing this person for the first time, to see the other person as objectively as you can, instead of relying on your old negative feelings and judgments about the person. See the person as someone you have never met before, creating a fresh kind of experience. This sets you ready to be open to a new appraisal. You don't know if they are okay or not, so you see them and appraise them in a fresh way. It may be the same, or it may be different.

Maybe they are okay in a way you never realized. Start by seeing them only as a whatever-aged person, wearing a whatever-coloured article of clothing, however tall or short, with a whatever-shaped face. By doing this, you are seeing the person for what they truly are: another human being, like yourself, with these particular physical characteristics. As you do so, you are disconnecting from any emotion coming from this person. You may not even notice it, since your focus is solely on their physical characteristics. At the same time, you could cognitively appraise what this person is doing or saying and stay aware.

Through these methods we are finding ways of blocking, resisting and limiting feelings of hate, prejudice, and handling forceful people so that we do not need to automatically catch negative emotions as they come toward you. By doing so, we are able to live in a better society by handling ourselves and others in a more positive, constructive manner.

Overcoming Emotional Contagion by Understanding Your Inner Emotions

Get adequate sleep, eat healthily, exercise regularly, and cultivate your own sense of self, purpose, and direction in life. Separate the person's emotion from their words when they speak, to identify and recognize their implicit emotion. Identify when others exaggerate to express emotion. Your inner emotions are relevant; if you have a feeling you will likely attract the same feeling from outside you. Have a gentle, guiding conversation with your inner self to understand what is going on with your feelings that may make them want to attract contagious negative emotions. Meeting and filling your inner emotions' needs is a healthy way to block the temptation to absorb contagious emotion. When you are true to yourself, in its wholesome, healthy form, then you will resist the incoming emotion that is not wholesome or healthy for you. This is your inoculation.

A basic approach to preventing emotional contagion is to maintain your physical and emotional health, including getting adequate sleep, eating healthily, and exercising regularly. This is necessary for making good decisions towards inoculating yourself against emotional contagion. It also means cultivating your own sense of self, your own sense of purpose and direction in life. It means preparing your underlying principles and beliefs: the things you will and won't do, the kind of people you like to be around, and the kind you don't. Make sure to state, to yourself and trusted friends, your reasons why. This will increase the chances of them cultivating a similar sense of purpose, so you will welcome their contagious emotions to join with you, as well as sharing your emotions with them.

Separate others' emotions and gestures from their words

To overcome emotional contagion, you have to separate the emotion from the words. You can only overcome emotional contagion in the moment by blocking it. We said earlier that to appraise the incoming emotion from a person when you make the appraisal, you have to check his or her non-verbal movements, their body language. This can be difficult. It is not just recognizing the importance of body language, but it is noticing it as it happens, and noticing the tone of voice and the flow of energy that may be emitted as the person speaks. This is how the emotion is expressed. Ask yourself how much this is contributing to the verbal message you are hearing, and whether you really want to accept the message because of it. Maybe you do, or maybe not. Do the words themselves actually deserve those gestures and tone of voice?

Look for these non-verbal or para-verbal features; notice the voice instead of just the words. The voice uses tone, volume, rhythm, pitch, sharpness, and softness. Listen not only to the voice but also to the manner of speaking: pauses, inflections, and hesitations. Sometimes the inflections also contain some emotion, which can be noted by some depth or softness or emphasis. A specific word or phrase can be emphasized this way, and we sense that the meaning being conveyed really comes from that emotion and not the semantic meaning of the word. Para-verbal refers to some noises made with the voice, such as grunts and moans, apart from the actual words. These are all methods of expression of emotion. Look at the movements and gestures, whether fast, slow, rhythmic, or swaying. Look for head gestures, look at the hands, fingers, arms, shoulders, as well as— of course—the type of eye contact. These are all vehicles to express feelings. They are how the message is delivered. They look silly by themselves but they fuse with words and deliver an impact, even overriding the actual meaning of the words.

Psychologists call it fusion if we have fused the gestures to the words. It is automatic, making two separate things into one (Bach & Moran, 2008). We need to defuse, or separate, the gestures and words coming from other people so they are truly the two separate factors they are. They can be difficult to separate, so you can practise by watching TV and putting it on mute: while you watch people talking, especially when the talk is spontaneous (rather than scripted), this allows you to take in the visual without the sound so you can follow the gestures and try to figure out what the person is feeling. If you can then rewind the program and play it with the sound, you can compare your reactions. If you can, try recording the audio so that you hear the sound without the visual. This way you can literally separate the verbal from the visual. Then ask someone else to repeat the same words in a dull way (or simply imagine it). The words can then truly speak for themselves.

In these ways you practise and get used to recognizing the emotion. Then you may start to apply these methods in real life. Observe people talking to other people to get the hang of it. It will start to come naturally to you after you practice in these ways.

Part of the way the other person may use to express emotion is hyperbole, or exaggeration, saying, "this is horrible," or "this is fantastic" about an accomplishment that really may not be. These words, said with emphasis, bypass the thinking part of the mind and strike the emotional, uncritical part of the mind. Strong emotion can now be delivered automatically. Emotions don't think. The implicit emotion itself then carries the force of the message that came before, so that the "this" in the phrase "this is fantastic" is then regarded as less far-fetched and much more astonishing than it really is. It is crucial to be aware of and even identify the implicit emotion being produced and radiated as the medium through which the message is being conveyed. The emotion is the message. The awareness of this as it happens blocks the emotion from impacting you directly, because the thinking part of your mind, the executive brain, intervenes. The executive brain includes working memory, flexible thinking, and self-control (Low, 2020). It enables you to focus your attention, inhibit impulses, tune out irrelevant information, and switch mental tasks like deciding to regulate and be aware of your and others' emotions. You can decide in your own way whether you want to accept the implied message attached to the implicit emotion, instead of it being automatic and unconscious. This is how you can be active while receiving a message, staying alert as you interact with the message in your own mind. This stops emotional contagion.

If the other person is overbearing or negative, then as a listener you should try and limit your spontaneity. Hatfield says that if one is stiff and withdrawn when encountering strangers or people whose emotions one doesn't want to absorb, a clear message is being sent, communicated only through body language: "I don't like you, I don't want to be like you, and we are very different people" (Hatfield et al., 2020). A stiff stance, however, can be an obvious stance that others will see, so try to discreetly look natural while behaving in a formal and disinterested way.

When emotional contagion hits, it is helpful to use the wise mind because it involves emotion and wisdom. This emotion can merge with or combat the incoming emotion. Wise mind is backed up by cognitive skills that the incoming contagious feelings do not have: logic (looking for evidence and facts to establish meaning and relevance), knowledge (pertaining to the situation at hand to help assess the information being provided), perspective (a quick look back in your memory to check the other person's history and reputation), and behaviour (ensuring not to mirror the other person's behaviour as they speak).

Wisdom involves blending knowledge with experience and intuition, using balanced, nuanced thought to allow for subtleties and exceptions. The internal visceral juices will integrate the meaningfulness of the moment and protect the internal body. Deep wisdom from meaningful experiences, accompanied by a reflection on those experiences, will prevent the incoming negative feelings from being absorbed automatically. Through wisdom you develop a strong inner philosophy which develops into a mental library to protect you, assuming that it includes valid verified information from external sources.

Handling contagious feelings of anxiety and fear

Suppose that you are interacting with someone who is anxious and pick up their anxiety through emotional contagion. This could relate to the anxiety felt during the time of turmoil being experienced in society. It's not too late to handle it. You are likely to pick up a little, but you can stop yourself from picking up the rest. It can be overcome.

Someone anxious is talking to you about the pandemic, and you start feeling a little anxious even though you don't want to. You don't feel that the feeling is justified. This means you have probably picked it up through emotional contagion because anxiety is contagious. That's natural, especially if specific examples were given. You are probably feeling concerned these days (or at times when many people are anxious about a situation) and are subconsciously open to anxiety. Your amygdala picks it up automatically since it looks for cues. Don't feel helpless—you're not. In this case, the reason why another person is anxious should be relevant to you, so first you ask yourself, or maybe the other person, whether the degree of anxiety is warranted. Maybe it should just be a mild cause for concern, or maybe it is not even that. Remember that you need details. Could the example apply to you? Maybe there is some uncertainty in a time of danger. Look around, think about it. It is usually the anxiety itself that is contagious, as opposed to the reason. So your gatekeeper doesn't let it in; your gatekeeper talks to the anxiety and says, "I'm not taking you in, you don't apply to me." At this point, make sure the mind is correct in its appraisal. Talk back to the anxiety you feel: "No, that anxiety belongs to him, not me. I don't want it. It is his, and I'm not taking it." The feeling will likely disappear or weaken.

It is natural to feel anxious at a time of turmoil in society. It is a time to be wise, to be smart, to be aware. Sometimes it is correct to be anxious, like during a global pandemic. But you still need to check on specific situations. Think for yourself. Is your mask up across your nose? Is it safe to not wear a mask just because someone else isn't? Is it okay to remove the mask now? What is the rate of infection over the last few days? Are we in another wave? Talk to yourself based on facts. "Maybe it's safer to wear the mask right now; there's nothing to lose. But if nobody is wearing one now, and there is no longer a risk, then maybe I don't need to wear one either" (unless you are immuno-compromised).

It doesn't mean that the other person deserves the anxiety; you can talk to them about letting it go, that they don't need it, that they could relax by taking deep breaths or visualizing relaxing scenes. Try teaching them to challenge their anxious thoughts and put things in perspective. Throughout it all, you are not taking that emotion. (If you do take a little, you could also use these methods). When anxiety is contagious it is like it is being transferred to you, even though you don't agree with it and don't have any anxious thoughts yourself. You do not have to accept the transfer. You say that to it, under your breath, "I'm not taking it, it's not mine."

You can also notice these incoming thoughts and feelings as mental events, which is what they are. That is all they are. They are not yours. It is hard to do but it doesn't have to be perfect. Just because they are in your mind doesn't mean they belong to you. Don't own them. When we say that they are not yours, and after declaring "I'm not taking it," they may still enter your mind because they can be powerful. But they're still not yours; they don't have to be in your mind, so you can drop them back out. Shift your focus onto something else. This is defusion; it allows you to back up and get some distance from your thoughts and feelings. They are just words in your mind, you don't have to believe them. You can change them with Cognitive-Behavioral Therapy, Dialectical Behavioral Therapy, or Acceptance and Commitment Therapy. But eventually, if they still stay in your mind, they are yours, even if you don't want them. You are holding onto them for some unconscious reason. Maybe it's for some unusual kind of comfort. You can consider letting go of that.

Anxiety and fear are similar. Fear is more urgent, anxiety more general. How do we deal with fear? Psychologist David Myers (n.d.) says that "we fear what's immediate." Myers points out that teens are, mistakenly, "indifferent to smoking's toxicity because they live more for the present than the distant future." Some young people don't fear the coronavirus, or many other fatal diseases because to them death is not imminent, so they think it doesn't count. To them, it is as though a risk isn't a risk if it's not imminent. That is not true, as we know from the risks taken by people who smoke and then have lung disease later.

Unless something is imminent, it is not worth fearing. But you can feel anxious, if it is justified, and prepare for it. Fear is only for things that are impending, but you can be concerned about things that are risky but far off. We need to be sure that the fear is realistic. Something like a tornado ripping through town, only moments away from your house—that's true fear. Otherwise, it's probably not worth feeling fear for something that's not looming. You can drop it to being aware and concerned, or anxious, and deal with it that way. Some people may even worry. Just tell yourself, if so, that it is not an immediate threat but make plans for handling it when it happens. This is called awareness.

Krishnamurti, an Indian philosopher, said that in order to overcome fear, we need to understand fear: learn about it, not how to escape it, not how to fight it, not how to resist it. We can accept fear, meaning we can accept that it is present, but we do not need to accept any meaning from it unless we have verified it; for example, unless we have made sure that there really is a dangerous tiger and that it really is chasing us. Fear is often irrational, and so can escalate since there is no logic behind it. We can accept that the fear is there because accepting it takes the wind out of it, but this is not accepting that there is, in fact, something to fear. That is the brain's job, and emotions don't think.

Emotional contagion can also be regulated and controlled through synchronicity. Lisa Barrett (in Flora, 2019) says that using emotional contagion works with babies, since they synchronize their breathing with their parents, and it calms them down. Matching our breathing to that of an upset person or baby, who may be breathing fast, and then slowing our breathing down without them being aware of it, will help slow down the other person's breathing, including babies' breathing. Managing your own behaviour means you can manage emotional contagion by synchronizing it with others and then taking control from there. For example, talking fast with a person who talks fast to synchronize with their pace of talking and then slowing down will sway the other person to also slow their pace—even though they probably aren't aware of it. This way you can influence fast or loud talkers to change their pace through synchronicity, which brings emotional contagion under your control.

Anxious people often breathe quickly and shallowly, and matching an anxious person's breath, fast speech, and other anxious behaviour can often get them to change their anxious behaviour. Start where they are at and slowly change your behaviour to where you want both of you to be. If they slowly revert back to their anxious style, match them and then slow down again: they will likely follow you. The advantage of this is they probably do not know what you are doing but you are in control. If they catch on just tell them about it in a gentle way, and let them decide what to do.

Internal emotions play a role

We seem, as a society, to like emotional stimulation from an impersonal source, often someone like a public figure. Some people are hungry for emotional stimulation while at the same time avoiding it in their personal life, preferring to be proper and polite without being emotional and genuine. People who are hungry for emotional stimulation or affection often haven't had enough inner emotional nourishing in their own lives. Their needs for warmth and stimulation may go relatively unmet in their daily interactions and be met by impersonal sources instead. This increased receptiveness for emotional stimulation on both the part of the giver and the receiver in a social environment through social media and hyped-up news can contribute significantly to emotional and social contagion.

Some people may be trying to get their emotional needs met by impersonal sources in the media, including reality shows, athletes, entertainment figures, or politicians. This isn't new but may be exaggerated more recently. Sometimes people may project their inner emotional needs onto a politician who is appealing and decide to vote for that politician. That is fine; you can vote for whoever you like. But remember voting is a serious responsibility. If you do, be sure he or she has some genuine substance and can give you what you want and need in the form of policies. To do this, remember that the best way to predict someone's behaviour is to look to the past because they will likely repeat their past behaviour. See if they have done something close to what they are promising now in a similar environment in the past. They will likely do the same in the future. Can they take that to where they will be performing in the future? Did they notice something wrong or missing in their previous work and want to correct it now? Don't let your emotions answer the question by themselves. This is not a popularity contest. Liking someone is not the best way to judge a candidate. Look at the facts. If the answer fits, there is a good chance they could get the job done. If not, there could be a problem.

One way to achieve psychological inoculation against emotional contagion is to take a deep breath and reflect. Look and see if you might be experiencing strong emotions generally. Is someone expressing a lot of emotion in their messages around you, or in the media? Are you feeling that you may be influenced by it, with little regard to logic? Be aware of it and reflect on the emotion. Learn from it but do not let it take over your thoughts or actions. Take a deep breath and slowly exhale. The cause may be good, but you don't want to let the emotions get too strong or they could take over your judgment. Let the mind do the thinking. It can merge with the emotion and provide wisdom, giving it perspective and realizing that it may vary in strength and application depending on people and places.

When we accept our inner emotions as present, we can deal with them. Those inner emotions can be very powerful. They contribute to emotional contagion because they can subconsciously attract the contagious emotion. Even if you disagree with something, you may still agree to some extent, and want to feel the emotion which is contagious. It's kind of like eating a delicious dessert you know is not good for you. Sometimes it's not really good to eat that dessert, although it feels good, and sometimes it's not best to absorb the incoming feelings and emotions just because they feel good. You need to appraise them to decide whether you can bring them in or not.

Understanding and communicating with your feelings

We need to understand our feelings in order to deal with them. When you are unsure which contagious, appealing feelings to keep, you can rely on the strength and power of your natural self to be honest about the emotion's fit inside you. This comes from the subconscious mind, which cannot lie. It is important to be aware of and trust the healing power and energy of the subconscious mind. The subconscious mind is very powerful and can do the work of the healing and strengthening. When you trust your subconscious, it induces an inner realization of health and harmonic mentality in the unconscious, beyond your awareness. Your subconscious will speak to you in ways that you may not be familiar with: in body sensations, in dreams, in feelings of peace when things are just right. It is letting you know that all is well by giving you this awareness. When you are true to yourself, in its wholesome, healthy form, then you will automatically resist what is not wholesome or healthy to you, as you define it.

This helps you resist emotional contagion by allowing you to decide on the framework of when to take in feelings, which ones, from whom, and in what context. Your framework fits your true nature in its wholesome and healthy form, as known only to you. It allows you to deflect any feeling of emotional contagion which does not fit your true self because you already have your true feelings of strength and resilience inside you. This may have become more clear to you as you have worked at combating emotional contagion. You can identify the true, real feelings that belong with you because they feel right. Just right. You were born with them and they are yours. Attend to them. Honour them. This is your inoculation.

When you gain an awareness of this framework inside you, you start to resist emotional contagion because you don't need anyone else's feelings that don't fit; you can rely on your own. You only take in the feelings that fit, and that reinforce your own, because when you take in any contagious feelings, they blend with those aspects already inside you. You can resist emotional contagion when the other feelings do not fit you or are not needed, or you can absorb them when they do fit your true inner self and inner core. You can now make the choice to accept or deflect the other feelings. That choice is now available to you when you sense someone else's feelings potentially mixing with yours in a social gathering.

You can help this process by having a conversation with your subconscious. You can talk in a gentle way to your subconscious, and you can listen to your inner emotion. You can resist emotional contagion by having the inoculation that comes from within yourself, from your own true self's feelings. You might want to invite in other feelings that complement yours without changing them, otherwise the addition wouldn't be your own true feelings. You can tell which are very similar to yours, but maybe of a little better quality, so you invite them in. You know they will take. They blend with yours.

For example, if you are usually angry and suspicious about things but want to tone it down, it would be healthier to be assertive and specific. Anger is a normal emotion, but it can be toned down by being specific about who you are angry at. Try to lower it to a milder, temporary emotion, like annoyance or frustration, that is specific to a few people or causes. Then you can be assertive towards them. Assertive does not mean anger but it can feel similar, so you are toning it down without blaming others.

Communicating with your inner emotions

To prevent these problems, or to deal with them after occurring, it is important to have a gentle, guiding conversation with your inner self. You need to understand what the inner emotion needs and what makes the outside emotions so appealing, even if logically you don't want to feel them. Feelings exist inside of you and they communicate with you. Respond to them by talking gently with them and listen to them in order to connect.

It may seem silly to talk to our inner emotions, but it works. Be patient with it. There is nothing wrong with it. But there is a lot "wrong with it" if your unmet emotional needs get you into trouble with people or with the law. Talking to your feelings is easy, and can prevent those things from happening. It doesn't make you stupid, weak, or soft. Those are learned misconceptions. The reality is quite the opposite: it makes you smart.

Listening to your internal feelings does not mean you have to agree with them, it means you are hearing them non-judgmentally in order to understand what they are saying. They may be wrong, but they also may contain an important truth or uncovered need that would be good for you to understand. Maybe there is a misconception somewhere there on your mind's part. This does not mean you are criticizing or finding fault. It means you are educating all parts of yourself.

If you work on meeting and filling the needs of your inner emotions in a healthy way, you won't feel the subconscious temptation to absorb contagious emotion. Healthy eating, aerobic (including cardiovascular) and anaerobic exercises, therapeutic massage, deep relaxation exercises, therapeutic breathing, bubble baths, a walk in a park, mindfulness meditation, and love and acceptance are other ways to communicate with them—so if you find conversation with them difficult, try some of these other things to take care of them.

Let's talk about communicating with the internal emotions through inner conversations. Your emotions are letting you know what they need. Listen to your emotions. Tune into yourself and ask, "What am I feeling?" You may not know right away, but just listen for a little voice inside you answering the question. Don't try and answer it with your mind because the answer doesn't come from your mind. The answer will come from deep inside. The emotions will feel better just knowing you are listening and caring. You care because they are part of you. Communicate with them as described here and see what happens.

If listening to your emotions seems so silly that you do not want to do it, then you can skip this part, since to try it would probably cause you to be too upset or anxious. Thinking it is silly could make you anxious and jittery. But then again—if you want to avoid this exercise because you are anxious about it, then you are already listening to your emotions because you're feeling the anxiety and are taking instructions from it to avoid the exercise. Maybe you could just listen to them some more and have a conversation with them about it. You could ask, "Why should I avoid this exercise?" Not a challenging or skeptical kind of why, but a curious, interested kind of why. You need to be interested in the answer so the emotions trust you and your mind. Maybe they are right. Or maybe you could clear up whatever they are anxious about because the anxiety may be unwarranted. You could clarify it in an inner conversation with them; for example, tell the anxiety that you appreciate its presence because it is trying to warn you of something, but point out to it, in a supportive way, that it is okay for you to listen and talk with them. Tell them that it is not silly, and that you are in fact communicating with them now. Many people don't realize themselves that they're already doing this. You could listen to your body and see if the anxiety is telling you something you had forgotten, some old, buried hurt that you don't want to uncover. Don't worry about being foolish because you don't need to do this in front of anyone, and you don't have to tell them about it. You could do this alone, but you could also try this with a therapist, or with understanding and perceptive friends or loved ones.

We all listen to our bodies every day: we feed ourselves if our stomachs say they are hungry and rest if we feel sleepy. This is the same thing. The emotions are often left out while our body parts get attention. You would attend to a sore arm or pain in your chest, right? In the same way you can listen to your emotions and talk meaningfully with them. If not, they may convert into physical pain (likely without a physical cause), causing headaches or stomach aches because they know that physical sensations get attention. Emotions are smart that way, and this actually happens a lot.

When dealing with inner emotions and feelings that are hurting, bubbling just below the surface, it is important to connect with them to see what they need or feel. Sometimes it is a recurring physical twinge that is really a converted emotion, or a troubling hunch that brings unease or discomfort. Even if it feels physical, it could still be an emotional feeling converted to a physical sensation. Of course, it may be physical, and it is always important to get a medical checkup to ensure there is no medical issue or physical cause.

If there is a buried hurt that you don't want to uncover because it may be painful, then it is important to deal with it slowly and gradually. Maybe leave the bulk of it for now and work on just a piece of it. Ask in a curious way what it is about. Communicate with it because it wants to come out, but know that it would be too much to come out all at once. Tell it that; explain that you know it wants to be released and that you will help it come out gradually, because it would be hard for your equilibrium to handle it all at once.

It is important to try working out a compromise with the emotions so that their needs can be met while reasonable needs of the mind are also being met. The emotions want to tell you something in the hopes that you will take action to fulfill them or ease their pain. The mind wants to tell you that it has some logical factor to consider, some idea or prediction. It is important to listen non-judgmentally to each side. It is also important to tell each side that you are working on meeting their needs, but they may also have to relinquish something. After all, they are part of you and they each want the others to be healthy too since your body, your mind, and your personhood are all involved.

Learning what makes your internal emotions want to attract contagious emotions

The point to these methods is to understand what is going on with your feelings that makes them want to attract contagious emotions automatically and unconsciously. Maybe they are taking in contagious emotions because they feel ignored or empty. Maybe your affectionate needs are not being met so you try through other means. Perhaps the emotions are trying to get around the mind because it is too strong, exacting, or unforgiving. Maybe your mind needs to let go and let things happen. Or maybe they shouldn't, and your mind needs to have a heart-to-heart with your emotions because what they are taking in may be dysfunctional. If you resolve this and create harmony between your mind and your feelings, you won't find yourself as willing to attract or absorb contagious emotions automatically.

Your inner feelings want you to pay attention to their message. They want you to notice, like checking the warning lights on your car's dashboard that tell you what is going on inside the car—but instead of seeing a "change oil" symbol, you feel an unusual or novel feeling inside yourself. Take guidance from it, but do not just take it as a message. You feel the feeling. It is an awareness. The feeling is something to experience in its own right. Especially when it is joy, happiness, curiosity, or another positive feeling. The feelings bring the true rewards and energy of life. It is not what happens to you, it is the feeling you get that counts. But if the feeling is worry or anxiety or sadness, listen to it and get a sense of where it comes from and what it may be about. Don't take its message literally, just use it as guidance.

The reasonable mind

Having this conversation means attending, hearing, feeling, sensing, and listening to your inner emotions. It does not mean lecturing or instructing them. You can talk to them softly and gently after you listen to them, otherwise they won't listen to you. They want to start with telling you something. The inner emotions are like children; they do not have a significant degree of logic or structure, and so they do not really know what the most logical choices for behaviour are. Emotions don't think. Listen to them as they tell you what is going on with them and what they feel. They are looking to the parent for guidance, and that is you and your mind; use the executive part of your brain that can incorporate softness, wisdom, and gentleness as it uses logic, knowledge, and reason. They want to trust you. It is ideal when the emotions take guidance from the reasonable mind since it has logic, knowledge, perspectives, and reason on the one hand and wisdom, empathy, understanding, and compassion on the other. The reasonable mind balances them out.

As you listen to and feel the emotion, your reasonable mind works on coming to a compromise with your inner emotions. In this situation, the reasonable mind has three goals:

- to understand the emotions
- to receive something meaningful and perhaps treasured back from the emotions
- to have an important aspect of the emotion's needs met successfully, with professional guidance [32]

The mind is always in charge, and it has the discretion to reject any needs the emotions may have, as long as the mind is objective and reasonable in its judgment. You are talking to yourself from your reasonable mind, so you will probably find yourself treating yourself as you would like to be treated: being honest, clear, considerate, and compassionate.

---

[32] Such guidance is best coming from a therapist who follows a similar approach, or from this or another piece of literature that is compatible with this approach.

Your message to the inner emotion needs to start with empathy, understanding, and acceptance of their needs and perspectives as valid. Speak to your emotions privately, silently. For example, here are some examples of ways to speak to an inner emotion of anger:

- "I know that you'd like to just react and get angry. If you did, you feel that it would help you get even."
- "I can see you feel angry about what happened; it is natural to feel angry inside. You feel that you were wronged." (It is important to talk in feeling words to the emotions.)
- "You probably feel hurt inside." (It is important to include "you feel" because you are focusing on your feelings. If you say, "I know that you'd like to just react and be angry because it would help you get even," then you are encouraging yourself to actually do so.)
- Acknowledge what the inner emotion is. You are talking to the emotion, and it needs to be validated.
- After saying, "You feel that it would help you get even..." you can let the reasonable mind continue: "...but it could cause more problems and more hurt. It might not be worth it."

When you say it might not be worth it, you are meeting the anger's need with empathy because you are simultaneously implying that it might be worth it. The feeling responds to this empathy by paying attention to you.

- Go on to explain what you mean. The emotion can't think it through. Tell it that, "There could be a fight. There could be some tears. Someone could get hurt. There could be a ruined reputation—and all these things are not worth the anger."
- Conclude with "Feeling angry doesn't mean it is okay to do something angry. You're not that kind or person. I will help you handle it in a different way to make it better."

Your reasonable mind is being supportive and wise. By including "you feel," you are distancing yourself a little from the subjective feeling of it, thereby subtly discouraging yourself from reacting that way by separating the feeling from the action. Validating the emotion means that you are saying that it's understandable to feel that way. You focus on that part. It does not mean that you are allowed to actually get angry and be destructive. It is not understandable to fight, insult, or destroy anything. There could be negative consequences that we have discussed earlier. This is where the reasonable mind comes in. Your reasonable mind knows that, so you don't have to explain it. The reasonable mind just takes over. The reasonable mind uses compassion, logic, knowledge, empathy, and wisdom.

At this point, the emotion will listen to you because it knows you care about it, because you have been empathic and supportive, and because it needs some wisdom and guidance and knows it. It works especially well if you "join it" by saying these things in a soft, understanding way, like a wise parent who likes and respects you. After all, you are talking to yourself. (Try to create your own version; these words are given here as a framework). The emotion really wants to be validated and understood, and because it is fluid it can easily flow into a similar feeling next to it when validated. And you, your reasonable mind, joins together with it. The mental and the emotional, together. When the emotional part feels understood and accepted with your reasonable mind, it feels complete and whole. This will constitute the gatekeeper that decides when to allow contagious emotions to enter inside you.

In these ways you are meeting the need and validating the focus that the emotional part of you has while still being logical, reasonable, and wise in your mind. You are trusting yourself and integrating the logical and emotional parts. You are sensitively talking to your inner self, from your reasonable or wise mind. You are treating it as an equal and explaining to it that the mind is helping make changes, not rejecting the emotion's ideas. It is, in a sense, being affectionate and compassionate, taking care of it and meeting its needs in a way the inner emotions can trust. Remind them that they don't have to take care of things anymore. The two can merge in a healthy way, each yielding to the other when needed. When the inner emotions have their needs met, they won't be as easily influenced by emotional contagion from the outside. When the emotions feel fulfilled by the input and guidance from the mind, they will let the mind be in charge and won't try and overpower it.

The reason and wisdom of the mind shares its important principles and values with the emotions, giving priority to what is integral and pertinent to you as a true individual person on the way to being pure and wholesome in fulfillment and being.

We have in this book worked toward a development of your gatekeeper, your reasonable mind, to be able to wisely open and close the gates when incoming emotions are coming toward you, allowing positive contagious feelings to enter but closing the door to negative contagious feelings and emotions through using a psychological inoculation.

Afterword

This book has discussed the problem of negative contagious emotions in society and how many people seem to have an automatic absorption ability that results in the absorption of such negative emotions. It has been my wish to bring this to people's awareness so that they can find ways to recognize and manage this phenomenon to prevent destructiveness. However, it becomes more and more evident as we move into 2021 that significant destructiveness continues to be caused by people relying on emotions to think when, in reality, emotions don't think. Most people know this but easily forget this in daily life.

When people make decisions based purely on their emotions, things often go wrong. This happens especially in large group scenarios, amongst strangers, in crowds, malls, parades, arenas, marches, when people are walking and talking. Things happen spontaneously. People carry their lingering emotions, often suppressed, into these places, where, when moving about, they can easily be triggered by the emotions of other people when there are controversies. As well, in controversial areas of life, there are often actions brought upon by emotions like fear or hate. Somehow the ability to think ahead can be easily lost at these times.

We know it is important to think things through before acting on them, to think of the best way to do something, to prevent things that could go wrong. But we may forget to follow this advice when moving about in everyday life. Football teams design plays and think things through and are smart about it. If they simply acted on their emotions, and ran or passed without planning, while being excited about the chance to win, they would just play spontaneously and hope for the best. It would be mayhem. This is the kind of behaviour we need to avoid in our daily lives. Instead, plan how to handle challenging or uncertain situations. Remember —emotions don't think, so they can't plan. But positive emotions can occur as a result of proper planning and responsible actions. We need to think ahead when we enter these various situations and visualize planned situations to test them out in our mind's eye. Otherwise, many of us are just tempted to react instinctively, relying on emotions.

When we see certain situations unfold related to ongoing controversies in life, there can be real problems. People catch emotions from each other in crowds, through automatically mimicking others' movements, feeling the emotions coming from their voices, and, when they think the same way, absorbing others' emotions. This is the effect of emotional contagion. It doesn't have to be this way. Actions are driven by a lot of emotional energy. Emotional energy produces physical energy. The collective subconscious is active and stimulated in many of these situations. When we realize that this occurs in the destructive acts we read about, such as the storming of the Capitol building in Washington, on January 6, 2021, and others, like refusing a vaccine for covid-19 that could have prevented a person's own death in April 2021 (Reinstein, 2021), we should be stunned, stunned that people act purely on their emotions when emotions don't think. Many major decisions that many people make are produced and driven by underlying strong emotions, reinforced by the collective subconscious, instead of logical thinking, anticipating consequences and planning. It seems to be that the mind, as a result of its incomplete thinking, enables emotions to creep in and take over the body's actions, including engaging in destructive events, when, in fact, systematic reasoning and critical thinking by the mind would provide more effective results and nondestructive results.

The perpetrators of many of the problems encountered, in the case of the January 6 insurrection attempt on the Capitol in Washington, and other situations, seemed to have decided, subconsciously, that they had to let their emotions drive their behavior. They seemed to think, very quickly, simply that because an action feels good it should continue on, without considering possible consequences, other than what they anticipated would happen, which was that the previous president would be installed. For an action to occur, such as a storming of the Capitol building, there must be a thought, even if a very quick thought, driven by an emotion, propelling it to occur. And these types of actions occur regularly, especially when a person receives emotional input from another person or from within themselves persuading them to do it. They absorb the feeling that is very appealing, so the person wants to do it, without checking out whether it is realistic or without further planning.

Such people have a very strong need to feel good, likely because they haven't felt good, to a meaningful level, previously in their life.[33] And, for some irrational reason not apparent to most people, who perceive it differently than the participant, an upcoming or imminent event may be meaningful to the person who sees it their own way. Possibly it gives them a feeling of control or importance. This could occur if they previously haven't felt significant or important enough or they lacked the opportunity. Somewhere in there, they have likely decided that it is acceptable to not think things through before they act, likely deciding instead to take action subconsciously or unknowingly, because it is fun and rewarding to them. Plus it seems to feel good to act, especially doing something that people can see has a consequence.[34] It may mean (to them) that they are taking charge, which doubles the fun and reward, falsely. In these cases, they are choosing to do these actions because they anticipate feeling these rewarding emotions, without using critical thinking, systematic reasoning, or logically predicting the outcome based on past experience. Emotions don't think.

People acted on the emotion triggered by the previous U.S. president, while he was still in power, with the presidential seal plainly in sight while he spoke, failing to see that what was proposed was destructive, regardless of the president proposing it, and likely to cause mayhem, which it did. This was incomplete thinking, driven by the emotion of receiving recognition and approval, as they perceived it, from the president. They seemed to have a strong need to follow the direct orders of an authoritarian man, the previous president.

It may not have been evident to them consciously that the consequence would be destructive to them and to others. Taking charge requires an efficient, effective decision by the executive in charge of the brain, the mind, not the emotion, which likes to enjoy things and have fun. Many people are trained to think that fun is only reasonable and positive if the person is responsible to oneself and others. This situation of incomplete thinking may have come to be because their minds have not been trained to think things through this way, and because of the gratification they

---

33 Does this make you think that I approve of an action that would result? In general I do not. I am being descriptive, analytical, and as neutral as possible in this discussion in order to understand the dynamics..

34 Not all people can see this, as some people may have had some type of diagnostic cognitive defect preventing them from systematic thinking or thinking things through, or lack of opportunity to learn this in the educational system or in family life.

likely felt from the power and authority they felt they had from the president, infecting their ability to think logically. They likely had such a need for years, and emotions are very powerful in driving our behaviour.

Action alone does not mean they are taking charge, because they would not have thought it through. They have not gained the reward of being satisfied by the mind's effectiveness, so the reward system that encourages and makes more likely the recurrence of action will be filled by hedonistic emotional pleasure rather than by solving problems. This is the emotional pleasure that comes with gratification that could be based on what they interpret to be decisive action, due to an intolerance for the ambiguity that is necessary to handle complicated situations. By spending the time and effort, and possibly using paper and pen, or a computer program, some people could have seen that what seems ambiguous and complicated could be delineated into a more understandable situation, hence negating their actions.

In vaccine hesitancy, we see a different type of reaction where emotions take charge.

We see in the fear of blood clotting from the vaccine the tragic effect of emotional contagion. People read about blood clotting from a vaccination and panic that it could happen to them. This is the effect of thinking emotionally because the emotion of fear overrules the ability to think effectively. When we think effectively we see that in Canada, the event rate appears to be 1 in 250,000 doses (Hamilton Health Sciences, n.d.). The same article suggests that high COVID exposure risk situation (defined as 20 cases per 10,000, for example, like Ontario has been), the benefits of the AstraZeneca vaccine far outweigh its risks. But we should word it differently, because emotions need simple messages and large numbers. Many use implicit emotion for an internal reference when they read. So we should say that there is a 249,999 chance in 250,000 that a person will be safe if they take an Astra Zeneca vaccination. That is a 99.999 percent chance that the person will be safe. Not only that but with the vaccine they will be safe from COVID-19. Although other regular medication such as aspirin and even birth control pills are accepted without question, data shows that they are, in fact, more dangerous than the vaccine used to prevent COVID. We take aspirin for granted, and yet people worry about a much safer process that saves lives. In fact, research shows that aspirin isn't always beneficial for our health and can be associated with a higher risk of severe bleeding. In spite of medical guidelines from the Mayo Clinic that clearly state that adults older than 70 who haven't had a heart attack and people who have a higher bleeding risk shouldn't take daily low-dose aspirin, because of the bleeding risk, many people continue to take aspirin daily to prevent heart attacks. (Mayo Clinic, n.d.) And yet many will refuse vaccinations that have a good chance of saving their lives.

The power of fear is very strong and underlies the hesitation of people to allow vaccine to be injected into their arm which would save their lives and possibly many others, by deadening the effect of the lethal covid-19 coronavirus. The fear, which seems to work from a major distrust of government, science, or medicine, dominates the rationality involved. These are abstract entities to many people, and this may produce distrust. Most of the same people have likely attended real medical appointments from time to time, or even a hospital, when they have an urgent medical need, such as an acute pain. When there is a real qualified person involved offering services and reassurances, people will often trust that person. But they don't trust abstract entities.

To illustrate the power of fear of ambiguity, MDs say that people who have resisted the vaccination against COVID, due to fear, are dying of COVID, after refusing the medication that would have saved them. Reinstein (2021) tells the story of an elderly couple who ignored science and died of COVID-19. She says that about 1 in 5 Americans are refusing vaccinations that could save their lives. They don't seem to understand that this is a serious issue and is actually lethal and could cause death. Contagious emotions of distrust and fear would seem to have infected this elderly couple's thought processes, as both were in the sciences in their careers, one an engineer and the other a nurse, according to Reinstein. Emotional contagion appears to have infected their reasoning processes, as suspiciousness is a contagious emotion liberally spread through the vulnerable in the media. It has to be asked if these deaths are a passive suicide that speak to other unresolved issues in society, in the collective subconscious or psychological underground, such as lack of fulfillment in life, lack of recognition, demoralization, cynicism and similar issues that circulate through emotional contagion and which were discussed in this book.

Glossary

The expressions herein are limited to definitions and descriptions of some psychological terminologies used in this book. Some such terms are developed for this book, while others are adapted from the psychological literature. Some are adapted from the source indicated; others are defined by myself for the purpose of this book. Terms from the psychological literature are referenced accordingly. Terms that are related to a primary term are "nested" under that primary term and described in that location, and cross-referenced in their proper alphabetical place with reference to the primary term for its location. Definitions give a brief introductory description of the term. Expressions and terminology in the public realm related to politics or social trends are not included in this glossary.

I cite numerous definitions from the American Psychological Association *Dictionary of Psychology* on the APA's website. Further information can be found by searching the American Psychological Association's online dictionary at https://dictionary.apa.org/. Together with the source link, these definitions (for example, active listening, affect, cognitive dissonance, etc.) are listed alphabetically in the references under "American Psychological Association (APA) (n.d.)." The letters "n.d." included with any reference indicate that no date of publication is available.

Acceptance and commitment therapy (ACT) is a form of cognitive behaviour therapy that helps clients to abandon restrictive strategies and instead experience and accept their difficult thoughts without their meaning, conceived as just words put together in a certain way, and feelings as a necessary part of a worthy life. Clients then clarify their personal values and life goals, learn to make life-enhancing behavioural changes accordingly, and develop new and more flexible ways of responding to challenges (APA, n.d.).

Active listening is a psychotherapeutic technique that can be adapted to communication in everyday life. It involves listening fairly intently to what the other person is saying in order to grasp and understand the full meaning of the speaker's statement as well as their emotion (APA, n.d.). Listening to a person as an individual, fully attending to them in the present moment, and the emotion in their message, and subconsciously assessing how that emotion and message fits with the personality of the individual, is, interestingly enough, a way to prevent emotional contagion from affecting you. If you fully understand the individual and the message, you are not likely to absorb the emotion in a contagious kind of way.

The term **affect** is a more general term that is often cited. Affect is defined by the American Psychological Association (n.d.) as "any experience of feeling or emotion, ranging from suffering to elation, from the simplest to the most complex sensations of feeling, and from the most normal to the most pathological emotional reactions. It is often described in terms of positive affect or negative affect."
See also **feeling** and **emotion.**

Affective is defined by the American Psychological Association (n.d.) as an adjective demonstrating, capable of producing, or otherwise pertaining to emotion or feelings. For example, an affective disorder is an emotional disorder.

Affective realism, the phenomenon that you "experience what you believe," gives us "body-[budgeting] predictions laden with affect, not logic or reason, [that are] the main drivers of [our] experience and behaviour," according to Lisa Barrett (2017). She says when you hear some news that you immediately believe, that is affective realism. In other words, it feels real because of the effect of emotion, also called affect. It keeps you believing something even when the evidence makes it highly doubtful.

Long-term **amygdala kindling** has been shown to increase general behavioural hyperactivity and fearful behaviour (Fournier et al, 2020). Previous episodes may have raised expectations of negative events and made it easier for consequential negative emotions to occur. We may perceive them more easily although erroneously through confirmation bias. It might only take a weak emotion to trigger another associated emotion in a shorter period.

Appraising someone when they interact with you means that you are trying to figure out what is going on with the other person—what they are feeling, why they are feeling that way, what they have been experiencing or doing recently—rather than just reacting. Appraising applies objectivity, or the lack of moral judgment to the individual being appraised in terms of right or wrong, due to the appraiser's objectivity or disinterest in the outcome of the appraisal.

See also **cognitive re-appraisal.**

Automatic absorption ability. When emotions flow between us, the adjoining party (the group or person) with this ability often quickly catches and absorbs the emotion expressed by another individual or group automatically, without realizing it or thinking about it, just because of the strength and appeal of the emotion to them.

Beginner's mind approach (Buggy, 2020). This refers to doing an exercise where you visualize and regard the person, event, or object you are encountering as if you are seeing it for the first time. The goal is to see the other person as objectively as you can, instead of relying on your old negative feelings and judgments about the person. See the person as someone you have never met before, creating a fresh kind of experience. This enables you to be open to a new appraisal.

Cognition is defined by the American Psychological Association (APA, n.d.) as a component of the mind, referring to all forms of knowing and awareness, such as perceiving, conceiving, remembering, reasoning, judging, imagining, and problem-solving. Along with affect and conation, it is one of the three traditionally identified components of mind. A **cognition** is often referred to as a thought or an image in the mind.

Cognitive is an adjective connected with thinking, knowing, or conscious mental processes. A person has **cognitive** functions, referring to their style and type of thinking.

Cognitive-behavioral therapy (CBT) is defined by the American Psychological Association as a form of psychotherapy that integrates theories of cognition and learning with treatment techniques derived from cognitive therapy and behaviour therapy. CBT assumes that cognitive, emotional, and behavioral variables are functionally interrelated. Treatment is aimed at identifying and modifying the client's maladaptive thought processes and problematic behaviors through cognitive restructuring and behavioral techniques to achieve change.

The American Psychological Association Dictionary (n.d.) defines **cognitive dissonance** as "an unpleasant psychological state resulting from inconsistency between two or more elements in a person's cognitive system. It is presumed to involve a state of heightened arousal and to have characteristics similar to physiological drives. [...] [It] creates a motivational drive in an individual to reduce the dissonance." It produces emotional distress when there is a consequence of a person's performing an action that contradicts their personal beliefs, ideals, and values; it also occurs when confronted with new information that contradicts those beliefs, ideals, and values.

Cognitive distortions are inaccurate thoughts that "are simply ways that our mind convinces us of something that isn't really true" (PsychCentral, n.d.).

See **cognitive empathy** under **emotional empathy**.

See **cognitive ease** under **lazy thinking**.

Cognitive reappraisal involves recognizing the negative pattern your thoughts have fallen into, and changing that pattern to one that is more effective. [...] Changing the course of your thoughts, or how you're making sense of things, can in turn change the course of your emotions, turning the dial down a couple of notches" (Cognitive Behavioral Therapy, 2014). **Cognitive reappraisal** means the person identifies their cognitive distortions and then will reappraise, or reconsider more reasonable, accurate ways of describing their inner thoughts, through constructive self-talk, which is talking to yourself from your logical mind.

An unspoken feeling, such as feeling hurt and resentful about being an underdog, may exist in what we will call, with apologies to Jung, the **collective subconscious**. A belief, and its associated feeling, appears to be widespread in society but is largely unspoken, running through the psychological underground of society, circulating through trusted subdued sources and on social media. It emerges at times of unexpected riots or

protests. The collective subconscious contains a type of recurring but largely unspoken belief, occasionally conscious and acknowledged in society but usually kept silent verbally. Related contagious emotion spreads through the collective subconscious amongst people with unspoken common issues.
See also **psychological underground.**

The Merriam-Webster Dictionary (n.d.) reports that a **conspiracy theory** is a theory that explains an event or set of circumstances as the result of a secret plot by usually powerful conspirators, or a theory asserting that a secret of great importance is being kept from the public. *Psychology Today* quotes Daniel Jolley, a psychologist and conspiracy theory researcher, who says (in Muller, 2020): "**Conspiracy theories** bloom in periods of uncertainty and threat, where we seek to make sense of a chaotic world. They often provide a simple answer to a complex problem [...] which can make them very appealing. [...] research shows that conspiracy theories satisfy unmet psychological needs and provide security of knowledge in a time of uncertainty."

See also **contagion** under **Emotional contagion**

The **contrast effect** is the perception of an intensified or heightened difference between two stimuli or sensations when they are juxtaposed or when one immediately follows the other (APA, n.d.). For example, an opposing candidate's strengths will seem more visible and encouraging when you only compare them against a weakness of the person you want to lose an election. That is the **contrast effect**; the contrast appears greater when seen in limited scope than it really is with a wider perspective. You need to research the candidates realistically and neutrally.

Confirmation bias is the tendency to gather evidence that confirms pre-existing expectations, typically by emphasizing or pursuing supporting evidence while dismissing or failing to seek contradictory evidence. Our feeling of insecurity can be so strong as to blind us from seeing things we do not want to see. For example, you perceive someone the way you want to see them only because of your perceived pre-existing negative emotions about the other candidate. In this case it may co-exist with the contrast effect.

Defusion—Think of it this way: Fusion is a state that occurs when two things are stuck or glued together, or "fused," so that they are inseparable. Defusion is the result of the opposite action, when this is undone, e.g., by being pulled apart so that they are now "defused," or are no longer fused together. In psychology, it is the separation of an emotion-provoking stimulus from the unwanted emotional response as part of a therapeutic process, similar to when a bomb is "defused." (Your Dictionary, n.d.). For example, if your young child sees a barking dog for the first time, they may start to cry automatically and say, "The dog might bite me!" You, as the parent, may say, "No, nice doggy," and demonstrate that the dog is safe by patting it without showing fear. In acceptance and commitment therapy (ACT), **cognitive defusion** is an attempt to change the way one interacts with or relates to one's thoughts by creating contexts in which their unhelpful functions are diminished (Hayes n.d.).

Delusional disorder is a serious mental illness characterized by at least one month of delusions but no other psychotic symptoms; delusions are false beliefs based on incorrect inference about external reality that persist despite the evidence to the contrary (Bourgeois, 2017).

Dialectical behavior therapy (DBT) is defined by the American Psychological Association (n.d.) as a flexible, stage-based therapy that combines principles of behavior therapy, cognitive behavior therapy, and mindfulness. It establishes a "dialectic" between helping individuals to accept the reality of their lives and their own behaviors on the one hand and helping them learn to change their lives, including dysfunctional behaviors, on the other. Its underlying emphasis is on helping individuals learn both to regulate and to tolerate their emotions. DBT is designed for especially difficult-to-treat patients, such as those with borderline personality disorder.

An emotion is defined by the American Psychological Association (n.d.) as a "complex reaction pattern, involving experiential, behavioral, and physiological elements, by which an individual attempts to deal with a personally significant matter or event. The specific quality of the emotion (e.g., fear, shame) is determined by the specific significance of the event. For example, if the significance involves threat, fear is likely to be generated; if the significance involves disapproval from another, shame is likely

to be generated. Emotion typically involves feeling but differs from feeling in having an overt or implicit engagement with the world."
See also **feeling** and **affect**.

Emotion mind is a concept developed by clinical psychologist Marsha Linehan (2015) and described as your state of mind when your emotions are in control and are not balanced by reason. In this state, emotions control your thinking and behavior; you are ruled by your moods, feelings, and urges to do or say things.

Emotional contagion has been defined by Elaine Hatfield, the research psychologist who coined the term, as "the tendency to automatically mimic and synchronize facial expressions, vocalizations, postures, and movements with those of another person, and, consequently, to converge emotionally" (Hatfield et al., 1994). Hatfield says emotional contagion comprises "social, psychophysiological, and behavioral phenomena," and is "comprised of many components—including conscious awareness, facial, vocal, and postural expression, neurophysiological and autonomic nervous system activity, and instrumental behaviors" (Hatfield et al., 2009). **Emotional contagion** is defined by the American Psychological Association (n.d.) as a rapid spread of an emotion from one or a few individuals to others. For example, fear of catching a disease can spread rapidly through a community.

Hatfield says **primitive emotional contagion** is "relatively automatic, unintentional, uncontrollable and largely inaccessible to conversant (conscious, verbal) awareness." We can all feel primitive contagion. This may be the case when viewed from a perspective of comparatively primitive situations like crowds and groups in spontaneous situations at sports events, celebrations or political rallies or protests, involving varying degrees of raw, unbridled emotions. But **emotional contagion in more mature-like situations**, like individual or group meetings, where people sit on chairs to talk, seems to indeed be able to be controlled, slowed, guided, regulated and even stopped by individuals who receive its impact, partly because the impact itself is weaker because of the setting, if those individuals were aware of methods to do so and motivated to use them.

Other than the spreading of disease, the term **contagion** is also defined as "the spreading of a harmful idea or practice" (Lexico, n.d.). An emotion or feeling can infect a person, taking over their rational, logical thought.

The APA (n.d.) describes the concept of **social contagion** as referring to emotional effects that happen in a social environment, heightening emotional reactions. It involves the spread of behaviours, attitudes, and affect through crowds and other types of social aggregates from one member to another. It is sustained by relatively mundane, superficial interpersonal processes, such as imitation, conformity, and mimicry, in predominantly social environments such as crowds, parties, and malls, where more intimate, personal communication is less likely to occur. It occurs also in the electronic media, on social media, and through gossip and rumours.

Emotional counter-contagion is a quick emotional reaction against a contagious emotional effect, where the emotion is thought of as disgusting and is immediately repelled. Counter-contagion usually has the effect of keeping us in a contagious emotional state but switches the emotion over quickly to either fear or to more anger in retaliation to the initial contagious effect.

Emotional infection, like the dangerous viruses that spread germs, spread toxic and harmful thoughts carried by emotions received through emotional contagion.

The emotion enters into the person receiving it, priming the person for the quickly following simple message that it sometimes carries with it. When it does this then we have a version of **emotional infection**, caused by the initial emotional contagion, carrying an implicit or explicit emotion with a simple message which infects the person's thought processes, taking over the essence of those processes and the objectivity of the thought, powered by the strength, force and appeal of the emotion. The power of the emotion is appealing to the receiver, dominating the reasoning process, rendering it less effective. As Sigal Barsade says (2020a), the term "infectious" comes when through a variety of physiological and neurological processes, we actually feel the emotions we mimicked—and then act on them.

Chris Thomas describes **emotional empathy** as "our automatic drive to respond appropriately to another's emotions," which occurs if you are not using the "as if" quality (Thomas, 2013). He says, "this kind of empathy happens automatically, and often unconsciously." It is "the subjective state resulting from emotional contagion." In **cognitive empathy**, you "stay in their head" with their ideas and do not connect emotionally. You do this at a cerebral, analytical level—involved, but not with your heart or gut, which is emotional empathy. You think logically and objectively about what the best thing is to say so that you do not get drawn into absorbing their feelings and become overpowered by them. **Emotional empathy** is more genuine and likely to connect with the other person emotionally, and **cognitive empathy** is taking another perspective intellectually, "a largely conscious drive to recognize accurately and understand another's emotional state," according to Thomas.

In **emotional ping-pong**, quick emotional arguments occur with very quick retorts and volleys, like in a ping-pong game where returns and retorts are quick.

The **false consensus effect**, "the tendency to assume that one's own opinions, beliefs, attributes, or behaviours are more widely shared than is actually the case, [...] is often attributed to a desire to view one's thoughts and actions as appropriate, normal, and correct" (APA, n.d.). This effect comes forth through emotional infection.

A **feeling** is defined by the American Psychological Association (n.d.) as a "self-contained phenomenal experience. Feelings are subjective, evaluative, and independent of the sensations, thoughts, or images evoking them. They are inevitably evaluated as pleasant or unpleasant, but they can have more specific intrapsychic qualities, so that, for example, the affective tone of fear is experienced as different from that of anger. Feelings differ from emotions in being purely mental, whereas emotions are designed to engage with the world."
See also **emotion** and **affect.**

Under acute stress, people **fight, flee (take flight), or freeze.** This is the **Triple F.** This is the classical fight-or-flight response, with an additional

F word added: freeze. Some people freeze when under stress, when fight or flight are not possible, like a driver who freezes and does not move or respond at all when stressed in a traffic jam, experiencing uncertainty, even though a traffic police officer is directing him or her to move quickly.

The **fight-or-flight response** is an automatic physiological reaction to an event that prepares the body to fight or flee when faced with a situation perceived as stressful or frightening (Psychology Tools, n.d.).

The term **flow**, as we use it,[1] is a perception, a feeling, or an occurrence of movement of emotional energy between people, or even within a person. It is a crucial component of emotional contagion. As we experience it, flow is an intangible but definite quality that seems to be transmitted by people at a vaguely perceptible level, independent of the content of a message. When we talk about emotional contagion, we are referring to the contagious or infectious influences that this flow of emotional energy has on others, as if it seeps into another person and affects their emotions, often without them realizing it.

A **gatekeeper** is the part of your mind that decides whether or not to accept an incoming feeling or emotion, rather than letting it happen automatically. We need to think carefully, using logic, facts, and knowledge to make executive decisions as to when it is alright to open the gates and allow incoming emotions to be caught and absorbed, or whether to just connect or let them bounce off you. This is the job of the mind, to decide when this is constructive and when it isn't. The mind gives the instructions, and the rest is automatic, as the body responds automatically to the mind's instructions.

The **halo effect** is a type of cognitive bias in which our evaluation of a person on one dimension influences how we feel and think about the person on other dimensions, such as their character, so that perceptions of one of the person's qualities lead to biased judgments of the rest of their character (APA, n.d.).

---

1   Our use of the term "flow" in this context does not refer to the type of flow described by the psychologist Csikszentmihalyi: an internal flow state, inside the person, in which the person is completely immersed in an activity with intense focus and creative engagement, deep concentration.

Implicit emotion is an emotion that is experienced or expressed under-the-surface and is not readily noticeable. Implicit emotions are not necessarily obvious to the eye or ear, or conscious to the mind of the speaker or listener, but they have a significant effect on them. Emotional contagion can be implicit, beyond immediate awareness. People can be affected by an implicit emotion. It is what prompts the impact and the spread of the opinion of the speaker because it is the emotion that is more readily caught by the observer, often subconsciously, and not the words themselves.

Implicit emotion regulation can be broadly defined as any process that operates without the need for conscious supervision or explicit intentions, and aims at modifying the quality, intensity, or duration of an emotional response" (Koole & Rothermund, 2011). It is an automatic unconscious or subconscious process regulating emotions to keep them balanced. Implicit emotion regulation is vital in offsetting the impact of impulsive emotional responses that are triggered automatically by events. Since environmental events often bring on some degree of emotional contagion that needs to be offset, implicit emotional regulation will do so.

Interpersonal psychotherapy (IPT) is a time-limited form of psychotherapy, originally based on the interpersonal theory of Harry Stack Sullivan, positing that relations with others constitute the primary force motivating human behaviour. A central feature of IPT is the clarification of the client's interpersonal interactions with significant others, including the therapist. The therapist helps the client explore current and past experiences in detail, relating not only to interpersonal reaction but also to general environmental influences on personal adaptive and maladaptive thinking and behaviour (APA, n.d.).

Lazy thinking, or incomplete thinking occurs where the individual doesn't put out the required mental energy to think through an issue, preferring cognitive ease instead. This helps the fluent processing of sentences, helps you to trust your intuitions, and helps you to feel that your current situation is familiar.

Cognitive ease will bias beliefs. We prefer the ease of rhyming, and a feeling of familiarity, which require less effort to think things through. It appears to be associated with good feelings (Kahneman, 2011), an experience largely of implicit emotion. Our comforting conviction that the world makes sense rests on our almost unlimited ability to ignore our ignorance, according to Kahneman.

A **mirror neuron system** is defined by Rajmohan and Mohandas (2007) as a group of specialized neurons that "mirror" the actions and behaviour of others. Avenson (n.d.) says that the mirror neurons activate the areas of the brain associated with the emotion of the speaker, thus conjuring up the emotion as if the receiver were experiencing it naturally. Humans utilize the mirror neuron system to understand and predict others' actions, according to Myowa-Yamakoshi (2014).

Modality is defined by the American Psychological Association (APA, n.d.) as any particular therapeutic technique or [therapeutic] process [among many]. It is also used in medicine in a similar way, as any [particular] type of treatment for a disease or medical condition [among many] (Cambridge dictionary, n.d.).

Motivational interviewing is a client-centred yet directive approach for facilitating change by helping people to resolve ambivalence and find intrinsic reasons for making needed behaviour change. Originally designed for people with substance use disorders, motivational interviewing is now broadly applied in health care, psychotherapy, correctional, and counseling settings. It is particularly applicable when low intrinsic motivation for change is an obstacle. Rather than advocating for and suggesting methods for change, this approach seeks to elicit the client's own goals, values, and motivation for change and to negotiate appropriate methods for achieving it (APA , n.d.).

See **primitive emotional contagion** under **emotional contagion**.

The **psychological underground** is a little-known concept closely related to the collective subconscious. It often includes suppressed emotions when similar thoughts are suppressed consciously in individuals even as they circulate in relative secret in society. However, they overlap according to individuals' characteristics and whether they use repression (which make the issues unconscious), or suppression (which make the issues subconscious). They are accessible to consciousness when necessary. It

relates to largely unspoken feelings, issues, and trends among people in society and is usually only shared on those occasions where an event may trigger it, like in private informal gatherings of trusted people with common interests, perspectives, and personalities. The suppressed emotions from the collective subconscious erupt regularly and will continue to do so unless the issues are addressed. When suppressed feelings are released, the emotions emerge quickly, strongly, and actively. They can become contagious as the collective subconscious becomes conscious and the psychological underground comes above ground.
See also **collective subconscious.**

PTSD or **Post-Traumatic Stress Disorder** is a disorder that may result when an individual experiences, or witnesses an upsetting traumatic event, or is exposed to effects of same through indirect but real exposure, resulting in distressing and disruptive symptoms such as avoidance, chronic, inappropriate arousal, and flashbacks.

Radical acceptance is about accepting life on life's terms and not resisting what you cannot or choose not to change. [It] is about saying yes to life, just as it is" (Hall, 2012). It doesn't mean you endorse whatever you don't like. It means you are accepting what is real. Marsha Linehan (n.d.), who developed the concept, says that "radical acceptance rests on letting go of the illusion of control and a willingness to notice and accept things as they are right now, without judging." Accepting reality is a way of overcoming cynicism. This doesn't mean we approve of whatever we don't like, or that we have to like it.

See **Reasonable mind** under **wisdom**

There are two components of **self-regulation**: behavioural self-regulation and emotional self-regulation. Manage and regulate your behaviour and manage and regulate your emotions. Both are important for managing emotional contagion. Arlin Cuncic (n.d.) writes that "self-regulation involves taking a pause between a feeling and an action," thinking things through, implicitly, in a way that "allows you to act in accordance with your deeply held values or social conscience and to express yourself appropriately."

See **social contagion** under **emotional contagion.**

Daniel Kahneman, a psychologist who won a Nobel Prize, talked about **two systems of the mind**, System 1 and System 2, in his best-selling book, *Thinking Fast and Slow* (Kahneman, 2011). System 1 is thought to operate automatically and quickly, with little or no effort to thinking and no sense of voluntary control. It is the fast system, where quick, emotionally laden thinking dominates. System 2 allocates attention to effortful mental activity, including complex computations, agency, choice and concentration. It is the slow system.

The **threshold for emotional explosion** is the level of tolerance for internal suppression of bottled-up emotion that is pushing to be expressed.

Wisdom is defined by the APA (n.d.) as "the ability of an individual to make sound decisions, to find the right—or at least good—answers to difficult and important life questions, and to give advice about the complex problems of everyday life and interpersonal relationships. The role of knowledge and life experience and the importance of applying knowledge toward a common good through balancing one's own, others', and institutional interests are two perspectives that have received significant psychological study." **Wisdom** as used in the book is an amalgamated balance of thoughts and feelings with various flexible perspectives used as a framework. Our emotions are often necessary to provide wisdom, which is an intermediate place between cold, hard fact and pure, emotion-based feedback. Wisdom comes from of a blend of rational and emotional input. When rationality integrates with an emotional message, it results in wisdom, which provides some good judgment.

Thanks go to Marsha Linehan (2020) and her use of wisdom and wise mind in her writings and videos, as she describes **wise mind** as an overlap between reasonable mind and emotion mind (Dietz, n.d.). As such, my use of reasonable mind is not identical with her description, as my use of **reasonable mind** includes wisdom, empathy, understanding, and compassion, which would blend with the reasoned thoughts to put a flexible perspective on them after taking these aspects into account but retaining the logic, reasoned-out thoughts as a primary aspect.

References

Abbott, A. (February 3, 2021). COVID's mental-health toll: how scientists are tracking a surge in depression. *Nature.* https://www.nature.com/articles/d41586-021-00175-z

Abramson, S. (2020). *Proof of corruption, bribery, impeachment and pandemic in the age of Trump.* St. Martin's

Ackerman, C. (n.d.). *What is self-regulation? (+95 skills and strategies).* https://positivepsychology.com/self-regulation/

Ahn, W., Kishida, K., Gu, X. et al. (2014, October) Non-political images evoke neural predictors of political ideology. *Current Biology.* . DOI: https://doi.org/10.1016/j.cub.2014.09.050

Allen, K. (January 2020). More than 50% of homeless families are black, government report finds. ABC News. https://abcnews.go.com/US/50-homeless-families-black-government-report-finds/story?id=68433643

@AllenFrancesMD on Twitter. https://www.brainyquote.com/quotes/martin_luther_king_jr_133813

Allied Market Research. (2018, November 21). Antidepressant drugs market to reach \$15.98 Bn by 2023. Cision PR Newswire. https://www.prnewswire.com/news-releases/antidepressant-drugs-market-to-reach-15-98-bn-by-2023-globally-at-2-1-cagr-says-allied-market-research-873540700.html

Almohammad, A. H. (2016). Toward a theory of political emotion causation. SAGE Open. https://doi.org/10.1177/2158244016662106

American Psychological Association (APA). (n.d.) *Dictionary of psychology.* https://dictionary.apa.org/acceptance and commitment therapy

American Psychological Association (APA). (n.d.) *Dictionary of psychology.* https://dictionary.apa.org/active-listening

American Psychological Association (APA). (n.d.). *Dictionary of psychology* . https://dictionary.apa.org/affect

American Psychological Association (APA). (n.d.). *Dictionary of psychology* . https://dictionary.apa.org/affective

American Psychological Association (APA). (n.d.). *Dictionary of psychology.* https://dictionary.apa.org/cognition

American Psychological Association (APA). (n.d.). *Dictionary of psychology.* https://dictionary.apa.org/cognitive-behavior-therapy.

American Psychological Association (APA). *Dictionary of psychology.* https://dictionary.apa.org/cognitive-dissonance

American Psychological Association (APA). (n.d.). *Dictionary of psychology.* https://dictionary.apa.org/confirmation-bias.

American Psychological Association (APA). (n.d.) *Dictionary of Psychology.* https://dictionary.apa.org/contrast-effect

American Psychological Association (APA). (n.d.). *Dictionary of psychology.* https://dictionary.apa.org/dialectical behavior therapy

American Psychological Association (n.d.). *Dictionary of psychology.* https://dictionary.apa.org/emotion

American Psychological Association (APA). (n.d.) *Dictionary of psychology.* https://dictionary.apa.org/emotional-contagion

American Psychological Association (APA). (n.d.). *Dictionary of psychology.* https://dictionary.apa.org/false-consensus-effect

American Psychological Association (APA). (n.d.). *Dictionary of psychology.* https://dictionary.apa.org/feeling

American Psychological Association (APA) (n.d.). *Dictionary of psychology.* https://dictionary.apa.org/halo-effect

American Psychological Association (APA) (n.d.). *Dictionary of psychology.* https://dictionary.apa.org/interpersonal therapy

American Psychological Association (APA) (n.d.). *Dictionary of psychology.* https://dictionary.apa.org/motivational interviewing

American Psychological Association (APA). (n.d.). *Dictionary of psychology.* https://dictionary.apa.org/social-contagion

American Psychological Association (APA). (n.d.). *Dictionary of psychology.* https://dictionary.apa.org/wisdom

American Psychological Association (APA). (February 2016). Speaking of psychology: Nonverbal communication speaks volumes. Episode 24. https://www.apa.org/research/action/speaking-of-psychology/nonverbal-communication

Analysis Group. (2015). The growing economic burden of depression in the United States. *Health Care Bulletin, Fall.* https://www.analysisgroup.com/the-growing-economic-burden-of-depression-in-the-united-states/

Andreas, S. (n.d.). *Letting go of hatred.* Psychotherapy Networker. https://www.psychotherapynetworker.org/blog/details/284/letting-go-of-hatred

Angus Reid Institute. (2019, June 24). Trust in government: Canadians wary of politicians and their intentions. http://angusreid.org/views-of-politicians/

App, B. McIntosh, D. N., Reed, C. L., & Hertenstein, M.J. (2011, June). Nonverbal channel use in communication of emotion: How may depend on why. *Emotion, Vol 11*(3), Jun 2011, 603—617

Arias-Carrion, O. et al. (2010). Dopaminergic reward system: A short integrative review. *Int Arch Med.* doi: 10.1186/1755-7682-3-24

Avenson, B. (n.d.). *Is your happiness (or sadness) contagious?* In Ornish. Living, feel better, love better. https://www.ornish.com/zine/are-emotions-contageous/

Azarian, B. (2020, September 23). They 'just want to watch the world burn': Psychological analysis reveals 14 key traits that explain Trump supporters. *Raw Story.* https://www.rawstory.com/2020/09/they-just-want-to-watch-the-world-burn-psychological-analysis-reveals-14-key-traits-that-explain-the-presidents-die-hard-supporters/

AZ Quotes. (n.d.). Eleanor Roosevelt quotes. https://www.azquotes.com/author/12603-Eleanor_Roosevel

Babiak, P., & Hare, R. (2006). Snakes in suits: When psychopaths go to work. *Harper Business*

Bach, P. & Moran, S. et al. (2008). *ACT in practice: Case conceptualization in acceptance and commitment therapy.* New Harbinger

Bailey, Rev. Dr. A., Pastor and Diversity and Racial Justice Trainer, Parkdale United Church, Ottawa, ON, Canada

Ball, J. (2011, September 5). September 11's indirect toll: Road deaths linked to fearful flyers. *The Guardian.* https://www.theguardian.com/world/2011/sep/05/september-11-road-deaths

Barrett, L. (2017). *How emotions are made: The secret life of the brain.* Mariner Books

Barry, D., McIntire, M., & Rosenberg, M. (2021, January 9). 'Our president wants us here': The mob that stormed the Capitol. *The New York Times.* https://www.nytimes.com/2021/01/09/us/capitol-rioters.html

Barsade, S. G. (2002). The ripple effect: Emotional contagion and its influence on group behaviour. *Administrative Science Quarterly, 47* (4), 644–675. http://dx.doi.org/10.2307/3094912

Barsade, S. (2014a). Faster than a speeding text: Emotional contagion at work. *Psychology Today.* https://www.psychologytoday.com/ca/blog/the-science-work/201410/faster-speeding-text-emotional-contagion-work

Barsade, S. (2014b). Feeling the love—At work *Psychology Today*. https://
www.psychologytoday.com/ca/blog/the-science-work/201408/
feeling-the-love-work

Barsade, S. (2018). Emotional contagion in organizational life. In *Research in
Organizational Behaviour*. https://doi.org/10.1016/j.riob.2018.11.005

Barsade, S. (2020a, March). The contagion we can control, *Harvard Business
Review*

Barsade, S. (2020b, March). *Coronavirus: How emotional contagion exacts
a toll*. Knowledge@Wharton. https://knowledge.wharton.upenn.edu/
article/coronavirus-how-emotional-contagion-exacts-a-toll/

BBC News. (2007, January). *Cynicism link with heart disease..* http://news.
bbc.co.uk/2/hi/6289847.stm

BBC News. (2020, March 17). *Coronavirus: US stocks see worst fall since 1987.*
https://www.bbc.com/news/business-51903195

BBC News. (2021, April 5). *Harvey Weinstein timeline: How the scandal
unfolded.* https://www.bbc.com/news/entertainment-arts-41594672

Bellis, M. (2019, October 2). *Biography of John Albert Burr: Black American
inventor improves rotary lawn mower.* ThoughtCo. https://www.thoughtco.
com/green-lawns-john-albert-burr-4072195

Bellis, M. (2020, January 13). *Biography of John Lee Love, portable pencil sharpener inventor.* ThoughtCo. https://www.thoughtco.com/
john-lee-love-profile-1992097

Berman, R. (2020, September 19). *US cases of depression have tripled during the COVID-19 pandemic.* Medical
News Today. https://www.medicalnewstoday.com/articles/
us-cases-of-depression-have-tripled-during-the-covid-19-pandemic

BillMoyers.com. (1993). *Healing and the mind.* Doctoroff Media Group.
https://billmoyers.com/series/healing-and-the-mind/

Bloom, P. (2016). *Against empathy: The case for rational compassion.*
HarperCollins

Bourgeois, J. (2017, November 14). *Delusional disorder.* Medscape. https://
emedicine.medscape.com/article/292991-overview

Bowes, S. (2021, January). Intellectual humility can reduce negative reactions to people who disagree with us, character and context, Society for
Personality and Social Psychology

Bridge, G. (2021, February 1). CNN primetime ratings fall back to
earth in first post-Trump week. *Variety.* https://variety.com/vip/
cnn-primetime-ratings-fall-post-trump-1234897869/

Bryant, M. (2019, July 22). Al Franken: Senators say they regret calling for his resignation. *The Guardian.*
https://www.theguardian.com/us-news/2019/jul/22/
al-franken-resignation-senators-regret

Buggy, P. (2020). *How to cultivate beginner's mind for a fresh perspective.* Mindful Ambition. https://mindfulambition.net/beginners-mind/

Burkley, M. (2018, September 11). Why deep voiced politicians get more votes. *Psychology Today.* The Deep Thinker. https://www.psychologytoday.com/us/blog/the-social-thinker/201809/why-deep-voiced-politicians-get-more-votes

Bush, G., Luu, P., & Posner, M. I. (2000, June). Cognitive and emotional influences in anterior cingulate cortex. *Trends in Cognitive Science, 4*(6), 215–222. doi: 10.1016/s1364-6613(00)01483-2

The Cambridge dictionary. https://dictionary.cambridge.org/us/dictionary/english/cognitive

The Cambridge dictionary. https://dictionary.cambridge.org/us/dictionary/english/stupid

The Cambridge dictionary. https://dictionary.cambridge.org/us/dictionary/english/worst

The Canadian Press (2015, May 12). Hydro One employee fired after FHRITP heckling of CityNews reporter Shauna Hunt. https://www.cbc.ca/news/trending/hydro-one-employee-fired-after-fhritp-heckling-of-citynews-reporter-shauna-hunt-1.3070948

Canadian Psychological Association. Webmaster. (2020, March 12). *"Psychology works" fact sheet: Coping with and preventing COVID-19.* https://cpa.ca/covid-19/

Cannon, C., & Goodin, E. (2016, July 22). *Trump to disaffected Americans: "I am your voice."* Real Clear Politics.https://www.realclearpolitics.com/articles/2016/07/22/trump_to_disaffected_americans_i_am_your_voice_131285.html

Carey, B. (2007, July 31). Who's minding them? *New York Times.* https://www.nytimes.com/2007/07/31/health/psychology/31subl.html

Carmichael, K. (2021, February 26). The hidden threat to Canada's economic recovery—our mental health. *Financial Post.* https://financialpost.com/news/economy/our-fragile-mental-health-is-the-hidden-threat-to-the-economic-recovery

Carrega, C., Stracqualursi, V., & and Campbell, J. (2020, October 8).*13 charged in plot to kidnap Michigan Gov. Gretchen Whitmer.* CNN. https://

www.cnn.com/2020/10/08/politics/fbi-plot-michigan-governor-gretchen-whitmer/index.html

Carroll, N. (2020, December 4). Backstory: Why do people deny the seriousness of COVID-19? I asked them. Here's what they said. *USA Today.* https://www.usatoday.com/story/opinion/2020/12/04/covid-conspiracy-why-people-dont-believe-deadly-pandemic-misinformation/3803737001/

Casabianca, S. reviewed by Gepp, K. (2021, May 6). *Stuck in the negatives? 15 cognitive distortions to blame.* PsychCentral. https://psychcentral.com/lib/15-common-cognitive-distortions/

Cassese, E., Farhart, C., & Miller, J. (2020). *Gender differences in COVID-19 conspiracy theory beliefs, politics and gender.* Cambridge Coronavirus Collection. DOI 10.1017/S1743923X20000409

Casualties of World War II. History of Western Civilization II. Lumen-Candela. https://courses.lumenlearning.com/suny-hccc-worldhistory2/chapter/casualties-of-world-war-ii/#:~:text=Some%2075%20million%20people%20died,bombings%2C%20disease%2C%20and%20starvation

Centers for Disease Control and Prevention. National Center for Health Statistics. (n.d.). https://www.cdc.gov/nchs/fastats/kidney-disease.htm

Centers for Disease Control and Prevention. National Center for Health Statistics. (n.d.). https://www.cdc.gov/nchs/fastats/deaths.htm

Cherry, K. (2020, April 29). *What is the negativity bias?* Very Well Mind. https://www.verywellmind.com/negative-bias-4589618

Chowdhury, M. (n.d.) *What is emotion regulation?* https://positivepsychology.com/emotion-regulation/

Clore, G., & Huntsinger, J. (2007, September). How emotions inform judgment and regulate thought. *Trends Cogn Sci., 11*(9), 393–399. doi: 10.1016/j.tics.2007.08.005

CNN Politics. (2017, November 17). *Read Al Franken's apology following accusation of groping and kissing without consent.* https://www.cnn.com/2017/11/16/politics/al-franken-apology" https://www.cnn.com/2017/11/16/politics/al-franken-apology

Cognitive Behavioral Therapy: Los Angeles (n.d.). *Improve your perspective: Cognitive reappraisal.* http://cogbtherapy.com/cbt-blog/2014/5/4/hhy104os08dekc537dlw7nvopzyi44

The Conversation. Canadian Edition. (2020, March 22). *Anxiety about coronavirus can increase the risk of infection—but exercise can help.* https://theconversation.com/anxiety-about-coronavirus-can-increase-the-risk-of-infection-but-exercise-can-help-133427

Cook, L. (2020, May 26). *Video of woman calling cops in Central Park 'racism, plain and simple': Mayor.* Pix11.com, New Yorkhttps://pix11.com/news/local-news/video-of-woman-calling-cops-in-central-park-racism-plain-and-simple-mayor/

Cowen, A., Elfenbein, H., Laukka, P., & Keltner, D. (2019, September). Mapping 24 emotions conveyed by brief human vocalization. *American Psychologist, 698–712.* DOI: 10.1037/amp0000399

Cuncic, A. (n.d.). *How to develop and practice self-regulation.* https://www.verywellmind.com/how-you-can-practice-self-regulation-4163536

Cure Violence Global. (n.d.). https://cvg.org/

Csikszentmihalyi, M. (1990). *Flow: The psychology of optimal experience.* Harper & Row

Dahl, M. (2015, April 29). *Is there an antidote for emotional contagion?* New York. https://www.thecut.com/2015/04/there-an-antidote-for-emotional-contagion.html

Dastagir, A. (2021, January 14). Anyone can fall for 'fake news,' conspiracy theories: The psychology of misinformation. *USA Today.* https://www.usatoday.com/story/life/health-wellness/2021/01/14/capitol-violence-fake-news-psychology-conspiracy-theories/6636395002

Dean, J., & Altemeyer, B. (2020). *Authoritarian nightmare.* Melville House Publishing

Decety, J., & Jackson, P. L. (2004). The functional architecture of human empathy. *Behavior and Cognitive Neuroscience Reviews, 3,* 71–100, as cited in Rempala, 2013

DeSteno, D., Breazeal, C., Frank, R. H., Pizarro, D., Baumann, J., Dickens, L., & Lee, J. J. (2012). Detecting the trustworthiness of novel partners in economic exchange. *Psychological Science, 23*(12), 1549–1556. https://doi.org/10.1177/0956797612448793

Dietz, L. (n.d.). DBT *self-help.* Wise Mind. https://www.dbtselfhelp.com/html/wise_mind.html

Dimberg, U., & Thunberg, M. (2012). Empathy, emotional contagion, and rapid facial reactions to angry and happy facial expressions. *Psych Journal, 1,* 118–127. doi:10.1002/pchj.4

Doherty, R. W. (1997). The emotional contagion scale: A measure of individual differences. *J. Nonverbal Behav, 21,* 131–154, 1997

Douglas, K. M., Sutton, R. R. M., & Cichocka, A. (2017). The psychology of conspiracy theories.. *Current Directions in Psychological Science, 26*(6), 538–542. https://doi.org/10.1177%2F0963721417718261

Durand F., Isaac C., & Januel, D. (2019). Emotional memory in post-traumatic stress disorder: A systematic PRISMA review of controlled studies. *Front Psychol, 10*, 303. doi:10.3389/fpsyg.2019.00303

The Economist. (2020, March 8–10). YouGov poll. https://docs.cdn.yougov.com/1ghnpqhhpu/econToplines.pdf

Ekman, P. (2003). *Voice revealed.* Time Books.

Erisen, C., Lodge, M., & Taber, C. (2012, December). Affective contagion in effortful political thinking. *Political Psychology.* https://doi.org/10.1111/j.1467-9221.2012.00937.x

Fan, R., Zhao, J., Chen, Y., & Xu, K. (2014). Anger is more influential than joy. *PLoS ONE 9*(10). e110184. https://arxiv.org/abs/1309.2402

Fernando, J. (2019, September). *Daniel Kahneman.* Investopedia. https://www.investopedia.com/terms/d/daniel-kahneman.asp

Fleming, M. (2017, March 22). *No. 15 'Hidden figures' box office profits—2016 most valuable movie blockbuster tournament .* Deadline. https://deadline.com/2017/03/hidden-figures-box-office-profit-2016-1202048264/

Fleming, N. (2011, October 18). Voters view tall people as better suited for leadership. https://www.theguardian.com/science/2011/oct/18/voters-tall-politicians-leadership

Flora, C. (2019, July). Protect yourself from emotional contagion. *Psychology Today.* https://www.psychologytoday.com/za/articles/201906/protect-yourself-emotional-contagion

Fokkinga, S. (2021). (n.d.). *Humiliation. Negative emotion typology.* Delft Institute of Positive Design. https://emotiontypology.com/typology/list/humiliation

Fournier, N. M., Brandt, L. E., & Kalynchuk, L. E. (2020, March). The effect of left and right long-term amygdala kindling on interictal emotionality and Fos expression. *Epilepsy Behav.,104* (Pt A),106910. doi: 10.1016/j.yebeh.2020.106910. Epub 2020 Jan 29. PMID: 32006790.

Frederickson, B. (2013). *Love 2.0: Creating happiness and health in moments of connection.* Penguin, p. 24

Frenkel, S., Decker, B., & Alba, D. (2020, May 21). How the 'plandemic' movie and its falsehoods spread widely online. *New York Times.* https://www.nytimes.com/2020/05/20/technology/plandemic-movie-youtube-facebook-coronavirus.html

Friedman, R. (2020, July 4). *Why humans are vulnerable to conspiracy theories.* American Psychiatric Association. Psychiatric Services. https://doi.org/10.1176/appi.ps.202000348

Frum, D. (2019, January 13). The mystery of the disappearing security clear-
    ance. *The Atlantic.* https://www.theatlantic.com/politics/archive/2019/01/
    does-john-brennan-have-security-clearance/579772/

Gaissmaier, W., & Gigerenzer, G. (2012). 9/11, Act II: A fine-grained analysis
    of regional variations in traffic fatalities in the aftermath of the terrorist
    attacks. *Psychological Science, 23*(12)

Garber, M. (November 17). Al Franken, that photo, and trusting the
    women. https://www.theatlantic.com/entertainment/archive/2017/11/
    al-franken-that-photo-and-trusting-the-women/545954/

Garfin, D. R., Silver, R. C., & Holman, E. A. (2020). The novel coronavirus
    (COVID-2019) outbreak: Amplification of public health consequences
    by media exposure. *Health Psychology, 39*(5), 355–357. http://dx.doi.
    org/10.1037/hea0000875

Goldbloom, D., & Bryden, P. (2016). *How can I help? A week in my life as a
    psychiatrist.* Simon & Schuster

Goleman, D. (1994). *Emotional intelligence.* Bantam Books

Grant, L. (2018, November 1). How a CBT thera-
    pist uses cost-benefit analysis. *Efficacy.* https://www.
    efficacy.org.uk/blog/cognitive-behavioural-therapy/
    how-a-cbt-therapist-uses-cost-benefit-analysis/

Grant, T. (2016, December 5). One year after arrival, Syrian refu-
    gees continue to face employment barriers. *Globe and Mail.*
    https://www.theglobeandmail.com/news/national/syrian-ref-
    ugees-facing-barriers-to-finding-work-one-year-after-arrival/
    article33204887/

Green, E. (2019, February 15). *How technology is harming our ability to feel
    empathy.* Street Roots. https://www.streetroots.org/news/2019/02/15/
    how-technology-harming-our-ability-feel-empathy

Hall, K. (2012, July 8). Radical acceptance: Sometimes problems can't be
    solved. *Psychology Today.* https://www.psychologytoday.com/ca/blog/
    pieces-mind/201207/radical-acceptance

Halton, C. (2021, March 31). *Wisdom of crowds.* Investopedia. https://www.
    investopedia.com/terms/w/wisdom-crowds.asp

Hamilton, D. R. (2011, July 19). Are your feelings infecting others? *HuffPost.*
    https://www.huffpost.com/entry/emotional-contagion_b_863197

Hamilton Health Sciences (n.d.). https://www.hamiltonhealthsciences.ca/
    share/blood-clot-astrazeneca-vaccine-safety/

Harrison, G. (2017). *Think before you like.* Prometheus Books

Harte, J. (2019, October 29). Trump tweet, political divisions fuel rising discourse about new U.S. civil war. Reuters. https://in.reuters.com/article/us-usa-civil-war/trump-tweet-political-divisions-fuel-rising-discourse-about-new-u-s-civil-war-idUSKBN1X812B

@JohnJHarwood, Twitter, Sept. 16, 2018

Hatfield, E., Cacioppo, J., & Rapson, R. (1993). Emotional contagion. In *Current Directions in Psychological Science, 2*(3), 96-99. https://doi.org/10.1111/1467-8721.ep10770953

Hatfield E., Cacioppo, J., & Rapson, R. (1994). *Emotional Contagion.* Cambridge University Press

Hatfield, E., Paige, S., & Rapson, R. (2003). Emotional contagion, intimate intercultural relationships, and intercultural training. In D. Landis & D. Bhawuk (Eds.) *Handbook of intercultural training.* 4th ed.

Hatfield, E., Rapson, R., & Le, Y-C. (2009). Emotional contagion and empathy. In *The social neuroscience of empathy.* Bradford. DOI:10.7551/mitpress/9780262012973.003.0003

Hatfield, E., Bensman, L., Thornton, P. D., & Rapson, R. L. (2014). New perspectives on emotional contagion: A review of classic and recent research on facial mimicry and contagion. *Interpersona, An International Journal of Personal Relationships, 8* (2), 159–179

Hatfield, E., Paige, S., & Rapson, R. (2020, September). *Emotional contagion, intimate intercultural relationships, and intercultural training. The Cambridge handbook of intercultural training.* Cambridge University Press. https://www.cambridge.org/core/books/cambridge-handbook-of-intercultural-training/emotional-contagion-intimate-intercultural-relationships-and-intercultural-training/9E2BFB5BB311D6C7C3D57A72D7F71C80

Hayes, S. Association for Contextual Behavioral Sciences. The Six Core Processes of ACT. https://contextualscience.org/the_six_core_processes_of_act#

Hedges, C. (2003, July 6). What every person should know about war. *New York Times.* https://www.nytimes.com/2003/07/06/books/chapters/what-every-person-should-know-about-war.html

Herman, L. (n.d.). *Yes, you can get fired for your social media posts: 9 times people learned this lesson the hard way.* The Muse. https://www.themuse.com/advice/yes-you-can-get-fired-for-your-social-media-posts-9-times-people-learned-this-lesson-the-hard-way

His Holiness the Dalai Lama & Archbishop Desmond Tutu, with Douglas Abrams. (2016). *The book of joy.* Penguin Random House

History.com editors. (2021, April 27). *Kent State shooting.* History.com. https://www.history.com/topics/vietnam-war/kent-state-shooting

Hopp, H., Troy, A. S., & Mauss, I. B. (2011) The unconscious pursuit of emotion regulation: Implications for psychological health, *Cognition and Emotion, 25*(30), 532–545. DOI: 10.1080/02699931.2010.532606

Hornsey, M., Harris E., & Fielding. K. (2018). The psychological roots of anti-vaccination attitudes, a 24-nation investigation. *Health Psychology, 37* (4), 307–315

Horsey, D. (2020, April 21). The contagion of conspiracy theories. *Seattle Times.* https://www.seattletimes.com/opinion/the-contagion-of-conspiracy-theories/

Howes, M. J., Hokanson, J. E., & Lowenstein, D. A. (1985). Induction of depressive affect after prolonged exposure to a mildly depressed individual. *Journal of Personality and Social Psychology, 49,* 1110–1113

Hruska, J. (2020, May 27). *Why do 44% of republicans believe Bill Gates will use coronavirus vaccines to inject them with microchips?* ExtremeTech. https://www.extremetech.com/extreme/310951-republicans-bill-gates-coronavirus-vaccines-microchips

Indeed Editorial Team. (2021, June 9) *Active listening skills: Definition and examples.* Indeed Career Guide. https://www.indeed.com/career-advice/career-development/active-listening-skills

Institute of Behavioral Genetics. (n.d.). Neuroanatomy and physiology of the "brain reward system" in substance abuse. University of Colorado. http://ibg.colorado.edu/cadd1/a_drug/essays/essay4.htm

Internet Hall of Fame. (n.d.). Inductees. https://www.internethalloffame.org/inductees/alan-emtageFN

Iresearchnet. (n.d.). *Authoritarian personality. Psychology.* Iresearchnet.com. http://psychology.iresearchnet.com/social-psychology/personality/authoritarian-personality/

Ito, T. A., Larsen, J. T., Smith, N. K., & Cacioppo, J. T. (1998). Negative information weighs more heavily on the brain: The negativity bias in evaluative categorizations. *J Pers Soc Psychol,*75(4), 887–. doi:10.1037//0022-3514.75.4.887-900

Johnson, J. E., Stout, R. L., Miller, T. R., Zlotnick, C., Cerbo, L. A., Andrade, J. T., Nargiso, J., Bonner, J., & Wiltsey-Stirman, S. (2019). Randomized cost-effectiveness trial of group interpersonal psychotherapy (IPT) for prisoners with major depression. *Journal of Consulting and Clinical Psychology, 87* (4), 392–406. https://doi.org/10.1037/ccp0000379

Jung, C. J. (1971). *The Archetypes and the Collective Unconscious*. Princeton University Press

Kahneman, D. (2011). *Thinking, fast and slow*. Random House Canada

Kaur, H. (n.d.). Public shaming has become a common pastime during the pandemic. But it doesn't really work. CNN. https://www.cnn.com/2020/06/06/us/pandemic-shaming-wellness-trnd/index.html

Kent State University (n.d.). M4Y. https://www.kent.edu/may-4-historical-accuracy

Konnikova, M. (2013, November 18). On the face of it: The psychology of electability. *New Yorker* . https://www.newyorker.com/tech/annals-of-technology/on-the-face-of-it-the-psychology-of-electability

Koole, S., & Rothermund, K. (2011, April). "I feel better but I don't know why." The psychology of implicit emotion regulation. *Cognition and Emotion*

Koole, S., Webb, T., & Sheeran, P. (2015). Implicit emotion regulation: Feeling better without knowing why. *Current Opinion in Psychology, 3*. https://www.sciencedirect.com/science/article/pii/S2352250X14000451

Laham, S., Koval, P., & Alter, A. (2012, May). The name-pronunciation effect: Why people like Mr. Smith more than Mr. Colquhoun. *Journal of Experimental Social Psychology*. https://www.sciencedirect.com/science/article/abs/pii/S0022103111002927

Lašas, A. (2012, April 11). *Bringing emotions into understanding revolutions*. United Nations University. https://unu.edu/publications/articles/the-role-of-emotions-in-politics.html

Lee, K. (2018). Metalligence: *A new psychology of thinking—learn what it takes to be more agile, mindful, and connected in today's world*. Health Communications Inc.

Lepore, S. (1995). Cynicism, social support and cardiovascular reactivity. *Health Psychology, 14*

Lerner, J., Li, Y., Valdesolo, P., & Kassam, K. (2015). Emotion and decision-making. *Annual Review of Psychology 66* (1), 799–823

Lewis, J. M., & Hensley, T. R. (n.d.). *The May 4 shootings at Kent State University: The search for historical accuracy*. Kent State University. M4Y https://www.kent.edu/may-4-historical-accuracy

Lexico, powered by Oxford. https://www.lexico.com/en/definition/contagion

Lexico, powered by Oxford. https://www.lexico.com/en/definition/cynicism

Lexico, powered by Oxford. https://www.lexico.com/en/definition/popularity

Linehan, M. (2015). *DBT skills training manual*. 2nd ed. Guilford Press

Linehan, M. (n.d.). On radical acceptance. Byron Clinic. https://byronclinic.
com/marsha-linehan-radical-acceptance/

Linehan, M. (2020, September). *Dr. Marsha Linehan teaches: Emotion, reasonable and wise mind.* You Tube. https://www.youtube.com/
watch?v=MLnUvxg_9p0

Low, K. Fact Checked by Chung, A. (2020, September 27). *What is executive function?* Very Well Mind. https://www.verywellmind.com/
what-are-executive-functions-20463

Ma-Kellams, C., & Lerner, J. (2016). Trust your gut or think carefully? Examining whether an intuitive, versus a systematic, mode of thought produces greater empathic accuracy. *Journal of Personality and Social Psychology, 111*(5), 674–685

McArdle, M. (2020, July 10). Opinion: The real problem with 'cancel culture.' *Washington Post.* https://www.washingtonpost.com/
opinions/2020/07/10/real-problem-with-cancel-culture/

McAuliffe, K. (2019, March). Liberals and conservatives react in wildly different ways to repulsive pictures. *The Atlantic.* https://www.theatlantic.
com/magazine/archive/2019/03/the-yuck-factor/580465/

McIntosh, S. (2019, September). Tom Hanks says cynicism 'has become our default' BBC News. https://www.bbc.com/news/entertainment-arts-49555613

McMahon, T., & Morrow, A. (2020, June 6). Fix the police: How the death of George Floyd is driving calls for reform in the U.S. and Canada. *Globe and Mail.* https://www.theglobeandmail.com/world/
article-fix-the-police-how-the-death-of-george-floyd-is-driving-calls-for/

Manera, V., Grandi, E., & Colle, L. (2013, March 18). Front. Hum. Neurosci. https://doi.org/10.3389/fnhum.2013.00006

Mann, B. (2013, October 13). The difference between American and Canadian tv commercials. *Huffington Post*

Marshall, L. (2017). *Racial disparities in police stops in Kingston, Ontario: Democratic racism and Canadian racial profiling in theoretical perspective.* PhD thesis. University of Toronto

Martel, C., Pennycook, G., & Rand, D. (2020). Reliance on emotion promotes belief in fake news. Cognitive Research: Principles and Implications, 5, 47. doi: 10.1186/s41235-020-00252-3

Max, D. T. (2020, September 21). The public shaming pandemic. *The New Yorker.* https://www.newyorker.com/magazine/2020/09/28/
the-public-shaming-pandemic?utm_source=NYR_REG_GATE

Mayer, J. (2019, July 29). The case of Al Franken. *New Yorker.* https://www.
newyorker.com/magazine/2019/07/29/the-case-of-al-franken

Mayo Clinic (n.d.). https://www.mayoclinic.org/diseases-conditions/
    heart-disease/in-depth/daily-aspirin-therapy/art-20046797

Merriam-Webster dictionary. (n.d.) https://www.merriam-webster.com/
    dictionary/conspiracy%20theory

Merriam-Webster dictionary. (n.d.). https://www.merriam-webster.com/
    dictionary/huge

Merriam-Webster dictionary. (n.d.). https://www.merriam-webster.com/
    dictionary/swath

Miller, J. M., & Krosnick, J. A. (1998). The impact of candidate name order
    on election outcomes. *Public Opinion Quarterly, 62,* 291–330

Monyak, S. (2017, November 16). Al Franken is in big trouble. *The New
    Republic.* https://newrepublic.com/article/145859/al-franken-big-trouble

Moore, C. (2020, December 10). *Learned optimism: Is Martin Seligman's
    glass half full?* PositivePsychology.com. https://positivepsychology.com/
    learned-optimism/

Morris, C. (2017, July 14). *Emotional contagion: Everything you need to know.*
    In Cognifit: Health, Brain and Neuroscience. https://blog.cognifit.com/
    emotional-contagion/

Moyers, B. (1993). *Healing and the mind.* Doctoroff Media Group. BillMoy-
    ers.com. https://billmoyers.com/series/healing-and-the-mind/

MSNBC. (2020, September 10)

Muller, R. (2020, April 4). COVID-19 brings a pandemic of
    conspiracy theories. *Psychology Today.* https://www.psy-
    chologytoday.com/us/blog/talking-about-trauma/202004/
    covid-19-brings-pandemic-conspiracy-theories

Murphy, K. (2019). *You're not listening.* Celadon Books

Myers, D. (n.d.). *Do we fear the right things?* https://www.psychologi-
    calscience.org/observer/1201/prescol.html

Myowa-Yamakoshi, M. (2014, June). The ontogeny of the mirror neuron sys-
    tem., *Brain Nerve, 66* (6)

"Mystery of Disgust" (2016). *Psychology Today.* Reviewed

Nabi, H., Singh-Manoux, A., Ferrie, J., Marmot, M., & Melchior, M. (2009).
    Hostility and depressive mood: Results from the Whitehall II prospective
    cohort study. *Psychological Medicine.* Cambridge University Press (CUP),,
    pp.1-9. doi 10.1017/S0033291709990432

Neuvonen, E., Rusanen, M., Solomon, A., et al. (2014, June). Late-life cynical distrust, risk of incident dementia, and mortality in a population-based cohort. *Neurology*

Ordway, D.-M. (n.d.).The consequences of 'horse race' reporting: What the research says. *Journalist's Resource.* https://journalistsresource.org/studies/society/news-media/horse-race-reporting-election/

Packard, V. (1957). *The hidden persuaders.* Igpublishing. igpub.com 1957. ISBN 0-671-53149-2

Packard, V. (2021, March 21). In *Wikipedia.* https://en.wikipedia.org/wiki/Vance_Packard" https://en.wikipedia.org/wiki/Vance_Packard

Palmer, C. (2018). Can making suicide more difficult save lives? *Monitor on Psychology.* American Psychological Association

Patterson, T. E. (2016a, December 7). *News coverage of the 2016 general election: How the press failed the voters.* Harvard Kennedy School at Shorenstein Center on Media, Politics and Public Policy. https://shorenstein-center.org/news-coverage-2016-general-election/

Patterson, T. E. (2016b, July 11). News coverage of the 2016 presidential primaries: Horse race reporting has consequences. Harvard Kennedy School at Shorenstein Center on Media, Politics and Public Policy. https://shorensteincenter.org/news-coverage-2016-presidential-primaries/

Pennycook, G., & Rand, D. (2019, July). Lazy, not biased: Susceptibility to partisan fake news is better explained by lack of reasoning than by motivated reasoning. *Cognition, 188,* 39–50

Pew Research Centre. (2021, May 17). Public trust in government: 1958–2021. https://www.pewresearch.org/politics/2021/05/17/public-trust-in-government-1958-2021/

Phillips, D. (2017, October 18). A marine attacked an Iraqi restaurant. But was it a hate crime or PTSD? *New York Times.* https://www.nytimes.com/2017/10/18/us/damien-rodriguez-marine-portland.html

Prochazkova, E., & Kret, M. (2017). Connecting minds and sharing emotions through mimicry: A neurocognitive model of emotional contagion. *Neuroscience & Biobehavioral Reviews.* https://doi.org/10.1016/j.neubiorev.2017.05.013

PSYBLOG. (2016, July 23). The best way of empathizing might surprise you. https://www.spring.org.uk/2016/07/best-way-empathising-might-surprise.php

PsychCentral. (n.d.). https://psychcentral.com/
     lib/15-common-cognitive-distortions/

Psychology Tools. (n.d.). Information handout. https://www.psychologytools.
     com/resource/fight-or-flight-response/

Pyatt, E. (2010, October 20). *New media seminar week 6: "The medium is the
     message."* Elizabeth Pyatt's educational technology blog. Sites at Penn
     State. https://sites.psu.edu/ejp10tech/2010/10/20/new_media_semi-
     nar_week_6_the_m/ /

Rajmohan, V., & Mohandas, E. (2007, January–March). Mirror neuron sys-
     tem. *Indian J. Psychiatry, 49* (1)

Rayasam , R., & Reddy, S. (2020, March 9). *America held hos-
     tage by coronavirus.* Politico. https://www.politico.com/newslet-
     ters/politico-nightly-coronavirus-special-edition/2020/03/09/
     america-held-hostage-by-coronavirus-488525

Reinstein, J. (2021, May). *The unique pain (and anger) of grieving someone
     who refused a covid vaccine.* BuzzFeed News. https://www.buzzfeednews.
     com/article/juliareinstein/grief-for-people-who-refused-covid-vaccine

Reiss, H., & Neporent, L. (2018). *The empathy effect.* Sounds True Publishing

Rempala, D. (2013). Cognitive strategies for controlling emotional contagion.
     Journal of Applied Social Psychology, 43, 1528–1537

Resnick, B. (2017, May 25). *The dark allure of conspir-
     acy theories, explained by a psychologist.* Vox https://www.
     vox.com/science-and-health/2017/4/25/15408610/
     conspiracy-theories-psychologist-explained

Ronson, J. (2015a). *So you've been publicly shamed.* Penguin

Ronson, J. (2015b, February 12). How one stupid tweet blew up Justine
     Sacco's life. *New York Times.* https://www.nytimes.com/2015/02/15/maga-
     zine/how-one-stupid-tweet-ruined-justine-saccos-life.html

Rosenbusch, H., Evans, A., & Zeelenberg, M. (2019, November). Multilevel
     emotion transfer on YouTube: Disentangling the effects of emotional
     contagion and homophily on video audiences. *Social Psychological and
     Personality Science, 10* (8), 1028–1035. Article first published online: Janu-
     ary 25, 2019

Ruiz-Grossman, Sarah. (2020, May 27). White woman fired from job after
     calling cops on black man in Central Park. *Huffington Post.* https://www.
     huffpost.com/entry/white-woman-cooper-fired-called-police-black-man-
     central-park_n_5ecd7199c5b670f88ad499c4

Rutherford, A. (2015, March). Why racism is not backed by science, *The Guardian*. https://www.theguardian.com/science/2015/mar/01/racism-science-human-genomes-darwin.

Schoenewolf, G. (1990). Emotional contagion: Behavioral induction in individuals and groups. *Modern Psychoanalysis, 15*: 49–61

Segal, J., Smith, M., Robinson, L., et al. (2020, October). *Nonverbal communication and body language.* HelpGuide. https://www.helpguide.org/articles/relationships-communication/nonverbal-communication.htm

Stavrova, O., & Ehlebracht, D. (2016, January). Quoted in *Scientific American Mind.* https://www.scientificamerican.com/article/cynicism-may-cost-you/

Seligman, M. (2006). *Learned optimism: How to change your mind and your life.* Vintage

Shafer, J. (2019, January 9). *Why horse-race political journalism is awesome.* Politico

Shortell, D., Carrega, C., & Campbell, J. (2020, August 30). *Vigilante group activity on the rise, worrying law enforcement and watchdog groups.* CNN. https://www.cnn.com/2020/08/30/politics/vigilante-group-activity-kenosha/index.html

Solomon, E. (2020, November 23). *Emotional self-control: The EI competency that affects everything.* Linked-In. https://www.linkedin.com/pulse/emotional-self-control-ei-competency-affects-elizabeth-solomon/?trackingId=G%2BveW1kIQ8eYdCf5P%2B8uBQ%3D%3D

Statista. (n.d.). https://www.statista.com/statistics/1093256/novel-coronavirus-2019ncov-deaths-worldwide-by-country/

Stat. CDC (2018, September 26). 80,000 people died of flu last winter in U.S., highest death toll in 40 years. *Associated Press.* https://www.statnews.com/2018/09/26/cdc-us-flu-deaths-winter/

Stedman, S. (2019). *Real news: An investigative reporter uncovers the foundations of the Trump-Russia conspiracy.* Skyhorse Publishing.

Stevens, M., & Haag, M. (2019, February 22). Jeffrey Skilling, former Enron chief, released after 12 years in prison. *New York Times.* https://www.nytimes.com/2019/02/22/business/enron-ceo-skilling-scandal.html

Stevenson, S. (2013, August 12). We're no. 2! We're no. 2! *Slate.* https://slate.com/business/2013/08/hertz-vs-avis-advertising-wars-how-an-ad-firm-made-a-virtue-out-of-second-place.html

Stromberg, J. (2015, March 20). *The science of why we love to root for underdogs*. Vox. https://www.vox.com/2015/3/20/8260445/underdogs-psychology

Surowiecki, J. (2004). *The wisdom of crowds. Why the many are smarter than the few and how collective wisdom shapes business, economies, societies, and nations*. Doubleday

Thibodeaux, W. (n.d.). Want to know if someone is trustworthy? Look for these 15 signs. Inc. https://www.inc.com/wanda-thibodeaux/want-to-know-if-someone-is-trustworthy-look-for-these-15-signs.html

Thomas, C. (2013). *Emotional empathy and cognitive empathy*. Teleos Leadership Institute. http://blog.teleosleaders.com/2013/07/19/emotional-empathy-and-cognitive-empathy/

Tindle, H. et al. (2009, August). *Optimism, cynical hostility, and incident coronary heart disease and mortality in the women's health initiative*. Circulation. . 10.1161/CIRCULATIONAHA.108.827642

Tomasulo, D. (2020). *Learned hopefulness: The power of positivity to overcome depression*. New Harbinger

Treisman, R. (2021, April). *Darnella Frazier, teen who filmed Floyd's murder, praised for making verdict possible*. NPR. https://www.npr.org/sections/trial-over-killing-of-george-floyd/2021/04/21/989480867/darnella-frazier-teen-who-filmed-floyds-murder-praised-for-making-verdict-possib

Tucker, J. A (2016, October 11). Presidential candidate can't threaten to imprison his opponent if he wants to live in a democracy. *Washington Post*. https://www.washingtonpost.com/news/monkey-cage/wp/2016/10/11/a-presidential-candidate-cant-threaten-to-imprison-his-opponent-if-he-wants-to-live-in-a-democracy/

University of Massachusetts Amherst. (n.d.). *Motivational interviewing. Definition, principles and approach*. http://www.umass.edu/studentlife/sites/default/files/documents/pdf/Motivational_Interviewing_Definition_Principles_Approach.pdf

Urban Dictionary. https://www.urbandictionary.com/define.php?term=Cancel%20Culture

van Prooijen, J-W., & Krouwel, A. (2019). Psychological features of extreme political ideologies. *Current Directions in Psychological Science*

Vigdor, N. (2020, July 26). The Houston Astros' cheating scandal: Sign-stealing, buzzer intrigue and tainted pennants. *New York Times*. https://www.nytimes.com/article/astros-cheating.html

Vittori, J. (2020, March 20). *Corruption vulnerabilities in the U.S. response to the coronavirus*. Carnegie Endowment for

International Peace. https://carnegieendowment.org/2020/03/20/corruption-vulnerabilities-in-u.s.-response-to-coronavirus-pub-81336

Wallace-Wells, B. (2020, March 11). Cancel culture is not a movement. *New Yorker*. https://www.newyorker.com/news/annals-of-populism/who-is-in-charge-of-cancel-culture

Weir, K. (2019). Politics is personal. *Monitor on Psychology*. American Psychological Association

Weir, K. (2020). Why we fall for fake news: Hijacked thinking or laziness? American Psychological Association. https://www.apa.org/news/apa/2020/02/fake-news

Westby, J. (2019, July 24). *The great hack: Cambridge Analytica is just the tip of the iceberg*. Amnesty International. https://www.amnesty.org/en/latest/news/2019/07/the-great-hack-facebook-cambridge-analytica/

Willis, J. (n.d.). *Understanding how the brain thinks*. Edutopia. https://www.edutopia.org/blog/understanding-how-the-brain-thinks-judy-willis-md

Wirz, D. (2018, February). Persuasion through emotion? An experimental test of the emotion-eliciting nature of populist communication. *International Journal of Communication 12*, 1114–1138, p. 25. ISSN 1932–8036/20180005 https://ijoc.org/index.php/ijoc/article/view/7846

Wu, C. (2020, December 17). No, there are no microchips in coronavirus vaccines. *New York Times*. https://www.nytimes.com/2020/12/17/technology/no-there-are-no-microchips-in-coronavirus-vaccines.html

Wyver, R., Clore, G., & Isbell, L. (1999). Affect and information processing. In *Advances in Experimental Social Psychology*

Your Dictionary. (n.d.). Samples of figurative language. https://examples.yourdictionary.com/examples-of-figurative-language.html.

About the Author

Bruce Hutchison, Ph.D. writes the kind of book that is needed in the times of emotional turmoil that we live in. A retired clinical psychologist with over 50 years of experience performing psychotherapy, counselling, consultation, and assessment, Dr. Hutchison has experienced and identified emotional contagion in many of his sessions with his clients, when emotions move and flow from client to therapist. He has appeared on TV, radio, and has travelled giving many speeches and talks about various topics in bettering oneself. An award-winning psychologist, he is known throughout Canada, and has been an avid follower of Canadian and American news. As a Canadian, he has been close enough and yet far enough away from the U.S. to get a subjective-objective view, one where he has "no skin in the game." He can be a little more objective, and less infected by the emotional infection he says flows in the U.S. media and society. But he is close enough to read the situation and be affected by American politics. He shares his insights with us in this ground-breaking book. He lives in Ottawa with his wife Catherine and their cat.

Printed in Great Britain
by Amazon